Urban Growth Dynamics

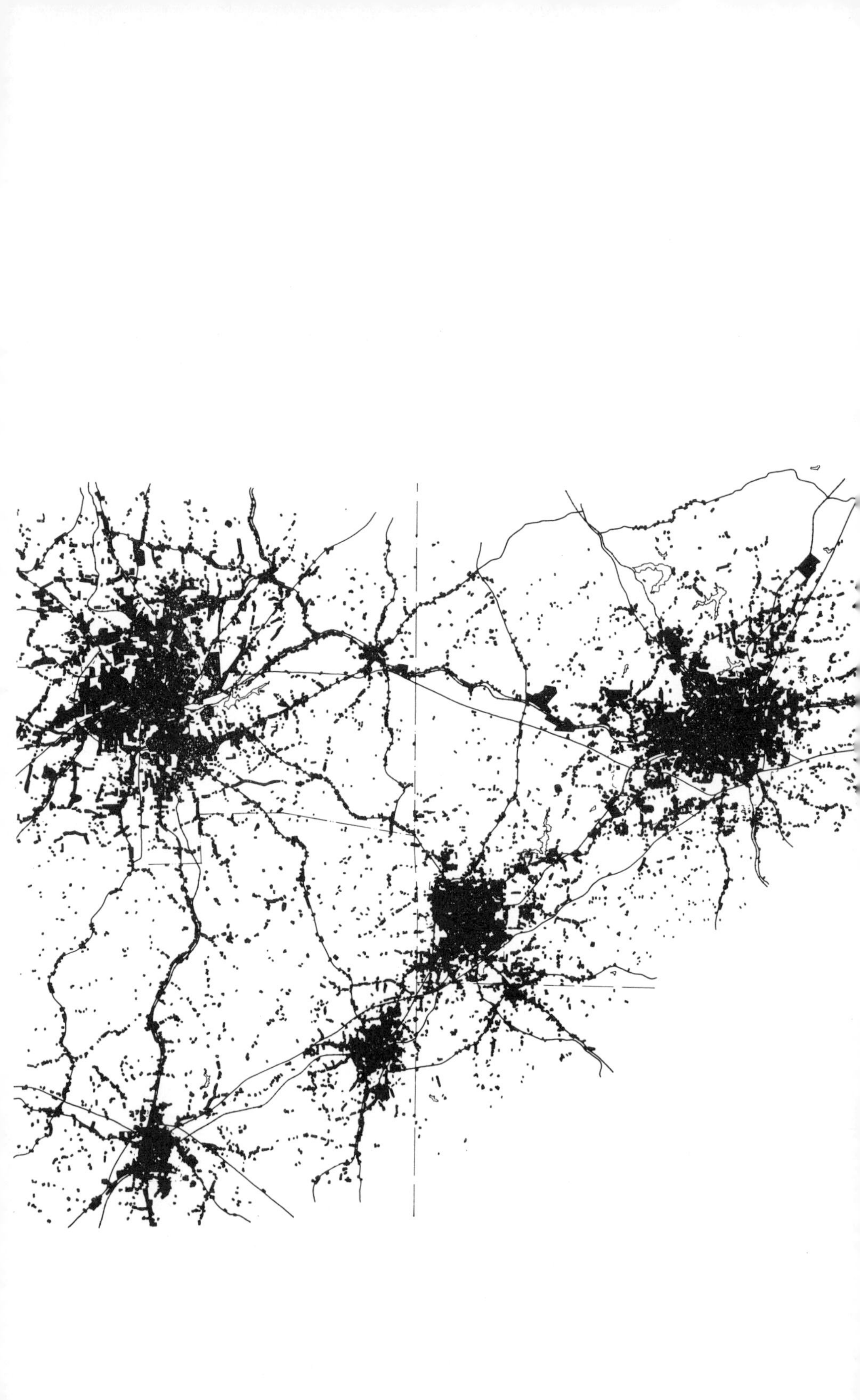

Urban Growth Dynamics

In a Regional Cluster of Cities

F. Stuart Chapin, Jr., and Shirley F. Weiss, Editors

Institute for Research in Social Science, University of North Carolina

John Wiley and Sons, Inc. New York · London · Sydney

THIRD PRINTING, FEBRUARY, 1966

Library of Congress Catalog Card Number: 62-19867

Printed in the United States of America

Preface

In the decade since the midcentury, there has been a build-up in the momentum of popular interest in urbanization and a flurry of speculation on its meaning for the average American family. "Cities in flood," "megalopolis," "urban sprawl," and other similar terms have become familiar expressions for characterizing the growth, and such terms as "suburbia" and "cities in ferment" are indicative of the speculative mood as to the implications of this growth for living patterns. The fifties did not produce the "urban explosion," as writers like to call it. The seeds of the growth had been sown long before, and the war years which in some ways retarded growth also served to launch it.

First, we might note the "normal" upward trend in the growth of urban population. Urban population increased 146.8 per cent from 1900 to 1940. From 1940 to 1950, the war decade, it increased another 29.6 per cent, and in the last decade it has increased by 29.3 per cent. A second noteworthy factor is the new productive capacity of the nation which was developed during the war years to a point that the national economy could accommodate and promote urban population growth. Finally, coupled with the economic capacity to accommodate a larger population was the subtle social psychology of "a new day"—the impact of the change from an atmosphere of self-denial and postponement that characterized the depression years and war era to a whole new era of optimism, prosperity, and revitalization. The urbanization we are witnessing today, then, is in part a result of a general long-standing growth trend, in part a result of a war-stimulated economy, and in part the effect of a frame of mind, all three of which combined to produce unprecedented internal migration and a step-up in the rate of household formation. Cumulatively, these factors have had a powerful impact on cities here and around the world.

This book does not dwell on these trends. It accepts them as background premises and turns directly to the phenomenon of urbanization and its implications for changed patterns of living. While the book uses one study locale—the Piedmont Industrial Crescent of North and South Carolina—much of what is reported here has import for other regions of similar characteristics and in a similar stage of development. At the outset it should be emphasized that the cities in this region are not like traditional metropolitan centers. Indeed, with few exceptions they cannot properly be considered metropolitan in any usual sense of the word. Yet they have qualities which have led us to believe that this region possesses metropolitan characteristics.

Of special interest in connection with the urbanization of this region is its apparent transformation into a metropolitan classification without passing through the stages of development associated with the older, established metropolitan areas of the North. It will be remembered that in the older urbanized areas there was first a period of centralized urban development following the Industrial Revolution. This was succeeded by a period of decentralized urban development accompanying the expansion of mass transit and electric power. More recently, these areas have been experiencing a scatterized form of urban development associated with the widespread use of the automobile. The Crescent, therefore, provides an opportunity for the study of urbanization produced by a totally new technological era. In a very fundamental sense, it offers opportunities to investigate the implications for human values and social change of a form of urbanization which is devoid of these earlier preconditioning stages of urbanism, each of which in various ways has left a deep and lasting imprint on cities in the older sections of the country. More particularly, since there is present in incipient form in the Crescent a wide range of urban-growth problems, there is an unusual opportunity to observe patterns of political and social action in response to these problems, and to identify choices open to the region for influencing the forms that urbanization take—forms that might minimize problems and maximize the living qualities.

Thus, in some respects, this book is a sketch of a segment of American society in transition from a rural to an urban environment. Even as we are seeking to explore the dynamics of a transformation of such far-reaching significance, we are aware that this is but one episode, but a momentary glimpse of a society being propelled into profoundly more far-reaching transformation. With transcontinental distances shrinking to a matter of minutes and intercontinental commuting in sight, the community of the future may well have hemispheric dimensions. This is not to minimize the importance of studying urban-growth dynamics in communities as we know them today, but more to dramatize the need for a well-documented, base-line view of a region of this kind as a basis for comparative studies and the observation of social change as it unfolds in the future.

The research summarized in this book was made possible by a Ford Foundation grant to the University of North Carolina at Chapel Hill. It is the product of a group effort involving specialists in anthropology, city and regional planning, economics, political science, social psychology, and sociology. Some twenty faculty members and senior staff together with twenty-seven research assistants from these fields constituted the staff of the Urban Studies Program of the Institute for Research in Social Science during the period that research was in progress from 1957–1961. It builds on a group approach to the study of urban phenomena that developed out of shared teaching and research interests and a study seminar of a small group of the faculty dating back four years prior to the time this research was initiated. At the same time, it sets the stage and provides an overview for a continuing series of core studies which have been projected at the University of North Carolina for the decade ahead.

This book is a symposium summary of a program of studies focused on the Crescent. It does not address itself to the so-called "metropolitan problem"—the governmental and fiscal aspects of urbanization—on which many other studies have focused. These aspects of urbanization are being dealt with by the University's Institute of Government. While recognizing these considerations as a vital part of solving problems of urban growth and development, this book dwells more on economic, political, and social dimensions of urban growth, and on the environment within which it is taking place, that is, the physical patterns of urban change.

Finally, it may be observed that we have chosen to look at a relatively few key facets of urban change in some depth. In the early stages of the research we considered another option, an approach predicated on one integrated research design. This choice was rejected. While holding out the possibility of a result more extensive in scope, we concluded that this breadth would be gained at the sacrifice of depth and that the final effect might be more "inhibited homogenization" than "integration with imagination." The research reported herein should be examined from this viewpoint. Whether the creativity stimulated by the chosen approach will have a more lasting effect in generating further probing and understanding of the nature of urban change remains to be determined in the years ahead.

F. STUART CHAPIN, JR.
SHIRLEY F. WEISS

Chapel Hill, North Carolina
September 1962

Contents

Urban Growth Dynamics

Chapter 1

Introduction

*by F. Stuart Chapin, Jr.**

IT SEEMS abundantly clear that for some time to come social scientists will be drawn to investigating the all-pervading cultural change stemming from the urbanization we are caught up in today. Without arguing the complexities of the mix of forces at work or the ramifications of their origins, we can now easily accept the fact of the great and continuing drift toward an urban society. While the signs of urbanization are unmistakably clear, the implications to human thoughtways and behavior are not so well understood. Moreover, since the full force of growth is still to be felt, it will be some time before the environmental factors which are conditioning attitudes and behavior in urban society can be fully explored and evaluated.

Nevertheless, there is an urgent need to lay the groundwork for research which inevitably will absorb social scientists for the next generation. This has been an underlying premise of the group of researchers who are reporting in the chapters to follow. While in the pursuit of the Piedmont Industrial Crescent studies there has been no expectation of introducing any new theory explaining urban-growth dynamics—considering both the relatively underdeveloped state of knowledge about urban processes and the far-reaching changes

* Acknowledgment is made for the contributions to this chapter by Shirley F. Weiss. The sections on economic and population patterns and urban-growth problems are based on her research and were drafted by her. Acknowledgment is also made to Frederic N. Cleaveland for his considerable contribution in spelling out the urban-studies schema outlined in this chapter.

still in progress—even so it has been constantly in the thinking of the group that this region offered a good laboratory area to test out approaches which might later be put to work in more definitive studies. Thus, the research undertaken sought not only to collect cross-section views of thoughtways and behavior as these may be detected and studied here in relation to existing general theory in the social sciences, but also to make an initial series of base-line observations for a longer term undertaking. But along with the long-range interest, the group has also been cognizant of certain immediate applications of these studies—the implications of present-day attitudes and behaviors for public policy and private decisions in the context of an urbanizing society as it exists today.

Each of the chapters that follow, therefore, reports on a specific area of inquiry which has been given special attention by the investigator in a basic research framework from his own field and which at the same time contributes to the common objective of supplying information and insights into the changes occurring in this area that would be useful to policy makers.

The Broad Perspective of the Studies

There are two bases of group activity which, though not evident on the surface of things, supply linkage to the individual investigations. One stems from a rationale, an admittedly primitive one, which the group hammered out some years before the studies reported here were actually initiated. The other stems from a shared realization that, while results of the studies necessarily would be fragmentary in relation to what must ultimately be undertaken, certain findings, as previously noted, would have policy implications. Further, these findings would be useful for decisions of public officials and the business community in adapting to the changes that are engulfing the urban centers in this region and in other areas similarly situated.

A Rationale for the Studies

The elements of a rationale that give these studies as a group an underlying relationship were developed over a two-year period in the course of a series of seminars which were instituted to gain some insight into what came to be loosely referred to as "urban processes." The entire group of social scientists recognized that whatever discipline from which they approached the dynamics of urban growth, there was an essentially common concern with *process*, defined simply as a *sequence of change*. In the course of studying process, a way of thinking has emerged which constitutes the basis of a common framework for these studies.

In one sense the framework is a classification system in that it provides a basis for participant researchers to tie into specific elements of one framework and orient their research in relation to the work of others. But at the same time and in a more fundamental sense, it points toward an essentially behavioral-science approach to the study of urban growth dynamics. It also provides a basis for relating, in an urban-studies context, the widely ranging individual interests of such a group of researchers, yet allowing each the latitude to work in his own discipline.

There are four elements to the framework. First, there is a central concern for human actions described in terms of *behavior patterns*. Two other components are *urban development* as an end result of actions and the *value systems* of urban society as the primary source of impulse for actions. The behavior patterns that originate from a value stimulus and culminate in a particular impact on the urban scene are thus the connective link. In the broad view of urban processes, these action sequences are important "carriers" of urban change, that is, they constitute a process that alters the environment, which change in turn often produces a feedback to the process. Although different studies in the subsequent chapters are concerned with various urban processes, there has been a general interest in *control processes*, a fourth element in the framework, that is, an interest in studying how directed influences can alter behavior patterns, and thereby modify urban development toward certain predetermined goals. This interest has to do with providing policy makers with approaches to solving the kinds of questions taken up in the next section of this chapter.

This rationale for urban studies can be spelled out further as follows. The term *urban-living patterns* is conceived as encompassing various forms of individual-, group-, and community-behavior characteristics of day-to-day city life. Illustrative of these urban-living patterns are the journey to work of the head of the household; neighboring, shopping, schooling, family visiting, church going, and outing patterns; civic-club-service activities, community-relations programs of firms;

and so on. These patterns of urban living in aggregate account for urban development. They are of course influenced to a significant degree by the *value systems* of the individual, the group, and the community. However difficult it is to identify, measure, and interpret values, basic knowledge about value systems motivating behavior in the city is obviously essential to a full analysis of patterns of urban living. A wide variety of kinds of values and value systems held by individuals, groups, or even by a community as a whole have relevance to urban studies. Of particular interest are economic, political, and other institutional values of both organized groups (for example, public agencies and special interest groups), and a variety of unorganized groups or aggregates in the community such as ethnic groups, immigrants from rural areas, various economic classes, and the citizenry in general. Chapters 9, 10, 11, and 12 are in some measure germane to both value- and behavior-pattern elements in the urban-studies framework.

Urban development is conceived broadly and simply as change in the city—whether it be the expansion of population and land area, shifts in land-use patterns or transportation systems of the city, changes in the pattern of industrial or commercial development, or alterations in the community's social, political, and economic institutions. It is noted that, whatever the degree of conscious control, urban development occurs as a consequence of various forms of deliberate, often planned, behaviors. In addition to the rather obvious examples of individuals influencing urban development such as a developer building a Levittown at the outskirts of an urban center, these behaviors may be seemingly random activities of a variety of individuals, as, for example, when workers in a factory seek to move their families out of crowded, "old" residential areas near the plant to less densely populated fringe areas of the city. Or they may be a complex of seemingly random economic activities of an aggregate of many business firms influencing the economic development of an urban center. Or these patterns of behavior may grow out of the policies and programs of public bodies like city councils and planning agencies, or the decisions and implementing actions of organized private groups such as the banking interests, corporations, labor unions, real estate boards, merchant associations, or neighborhood clubs. Chapters 4, 5, and 13 tend to tie into the urban development part of the schema, and Chapters 2, 3, and aspects of Chapters 6 to 12 deal with behavior patterns which in a general or specific sense have consequences for urban development.

When individual actions and group decisions, policies, programs, and activities seek to modify prevailing attitudes and behavior patterns or create new attitudes and behavior responses in the interests of achieving certain forms of urban development, they become "controls." While seeking to influence, feedback effects from controls may result in modifications of these controls. Among the research group there has been a special interest in studying the formal and informal *control processes* of organized public and private groups. Although all chapters deal with this element of the framework to varying degrees, Chapters 6, 7, 8, and 9 have given particular attention to this aspect of the rationale. Special interest has been shown in control systems of city-planning agencies and other local governmental agencies as involved, for example, in such activities as public housing, urban-renewal programs, or annexation. The control systems of formal business, industrial, and professional groups as involved in such activities as credit and mortgage regulations of banking institutions, restrictive covenants of real estate groups, industrial development schemes of civic promotional groups, land ownership and tax policies of business and industry, and so on, although not covered in this series of studies, are also an important part of the rationale. In work scheduled within this framework, the early seminars noted that careful analysis must be undertaken not only of control processes consciously planned to influence urban development but also those control processes designed for some other purpose which have "by-product" implications for urban development. In addition, consideration of the interaction of public and private control systems and how the informal leadership in a community influences the policies and implementing control systems of the more formally organized groups in the city have been emphasized.

The Policy Implications of These Studies

The other kind of organizational underpinning to these studies is built around questions of special interest to policy makers. While the studies summarized in this volume are not wholly occupied with policy questions nor always directly concerned with them, there are nevertheless cues that can be taken from the whole series of investigations which will be useful to those who must make decisions, both in the public and the private domain. To facilitate the use of the findings in this respect, each of the four parts of this book picks up and develops the themes appropriate to that part from the following questions, and the last chapter picks up the threads from the chapter conclusions, relates them, and indicates some of the applications of the research in achieving more rational adaptation to urbanization in this area and in others with similar characteristics.

Broadly, four leading questions were posed at the outset:

1. What is the growth potential of the urbanizing area—its outlook for economic development and population changes—and what are the economic variables?

2. What are the socio-political variables that impinge on urban development and affect the extent to which the potential can be realized?

3. What are the social correlates of growth of this kind and what are their implications for urban-living patterns?

4. What are the factors governing physical expansion of urban areas and in what ways may these findings assist in charting growth for the future?

Thus, to those interested in the policy implications of the research, these questions provide a key as to where, in the four parts of this volume, insights can be found relevant to these general themes.

Part One therefore has a predisposition to examine urban-growth dynamics in the vein of how much growth, how distributed, and what kinds of the economic factors tend to regulate this growth. Since, elsewhere in the country, effort has already been devoted to experimenting with techniques of economic analysis in the study of urban growth, a major effort in this study was directed toward investigating some of the characteristics and the variables of economic development as observed in the Piedmont Industrial Crescent. Thus, questions were asked about the industrial make-up and employment structure. What changes are occurring in relation to the South and the rest of the country, and what are the indications that these changes will figure importantly in the future? How do some of the characteristics of the area's labor components affect the economic outlook—for example, in terms of labor productivity, in terms of labor mobility? Is the regional system of cities in the Crescent and are its smaller cluster groups economically integrated? Is there an economic basis for identifying the entire belt of cities as one system or the clusters as subsystems? Besides questions of the dynamics of economic interaction in the larger region, there are other questions concerning interaction between the city and its agricultural hinterland. For example, has the growth of urban centers altered the pattern of agricultural output in the immediately surrounding hinterland area? All of these variables of economic growth have import for decision making in both the public and private sector of urban development.

Accepting the economic outlook that studies of the foregoing type provide, Part Two then examines factors of a socio-political character that are expected to have an influence on urban growth. For example, what are the patterns of community leadership and how do leaders reach decisions on problems and issues of urban development? Considering some key issues that develop around problems of urban growth, how does the governmental decision-making process resolve issues and solve problems? What role do urban planners play with respect to these decisions? What leadership is exercised by industrial executives and businessmen in urban affairs? To what extent does the grassroots citizenry participate in efforts to deal with urban problems and issues, and how important is Negro as compared to white participation in civic affairs? All of these questions hold the key to the vigor, imagination, and success of public and private action programs aimed at solving problems which in turn affect the extent to which an area realizes its full growth potential.

Another dimension, with which Part Three is largely concerned, relates to the implications this growth would have for living patterns. In urban centers where rural backgrounds are still in preponderance, what motives impede and impel participation? To what extent do newcomers become enculturated into the community and become active in community affairs? Do their attitudes differ from those of old-timers? What are the satisfactions and the irritations of residents with their physical surroundings? How important are the living qualities of the city as compared to opportunities to find employment and the opportunities for social participation? Does the area have a high career mobility and under what conditions are changes in intergenerational career patterns in particular evidence? These questions reflect upon value systems held by the area's residents, their behavior patterns and how emotionally prepared they are for growth problems ahead, and to what extent they will tend to identify themselves with action programs aimed at solving these problems.

Finally, Part Four raises questions concerning the implications of the forecast economic growth for physical patterns of urban expansion. What structures the land-development patterns of urban areas? What kinds of choices are open to clusters of cities and individual centers, and what kinds of public policies in the provision of urban services and facilities would minimize problems and maximize opportunities for achieving any chosen goals for the physical development of urban areas? All of the foregoing questions are of great importance to decisions of a public and a private nature.

The linked nature of the preceding questions indicates the complexity of urban-growth dynamics. While studies reported here do not provide answers on all matters referred to nor do they supply complete answers on any of the questions dealt with, they do shed light on a wide range of variables of urban growth which must be taken into account by policy makers in solving urban-growth problems.

The Locale of These Studies

While this volume is directed more toward selected aspects of the processes of urbanization than upon an area study as such, it is nevertheless useful at the outset to give a brief place description of this region. Accordingly, in the next few pages we seek to supply the reader with some brief reference points about the Piedmont Industrial Crescent —its urban character, its physical features, its historical setting, its economy and population, its governmental characteristics, its urbanization problems, and its "character" as a whole.

The Urban Character of the Crescent

With an urban-oriented population of about 1½ million, the Piedmont Industrial Crescent is a system of industrializing cities clustered along the transportation corridor connecting the Southeast with the Northeast. Rupert B. Vance gave this region its name thirty years ago (1932, pp. 32–33), and in focusing our studies on the heart area of his Crescent—a sixteen-county section of Piedmont North and South Carolina—we have borrowed the name and have used it, perhaps somewhat loosely, for this smaller more limited area.

For those who associate "urban" with traditional massive, sprawling metropolitan centers, this area would pass unnoticed. Yet if the basis for classifying a people and its environmental setting as "urban" derives from its economic, political, and social orientation, then the Crescent is distinctly urban as will become abundantly clear in later chapters. To go a step further, one of the early hypotheses of this series of studies posed the proposition that the Crescent could be viewed as a "polynucleated metropolitan region." It was reasoned that since the city-to-city patterns of interaction (living in one city and working in another, the regional organizations of wholesaling and retailing activities, the intercity family visiting patterns, and so forth) appeared to have similarities to those found within the traditional single-centered metropolitan area, this region possessed distinct qualities of metropolitan-ness. The findings reported in several parts of this book (notably Chapters 2 and 3) lend some support to this kind of proposition. While some of the studies in a somewhat loose sense do view the sixteen Crescent counties as a metropolitan-like region, most studies use the term "metropolitan" without reference to particular clusters of cities in close physical proximity to one another or to specific individual centers.

Physical Setting

In a spatial sense the physical form of urbanization in the Crescent is rapidly changing. Under impact of the modern highway, the original bead-like pattern of urban centers strung out along the railway routes that cross the Piedmont has been transformed into a series of city clusters. But with the new interstate system of superhighways tending to stretch development out along the system's main axes, the cluster pattern may well give way to belts of continuous urban development. Presently this system makes the individual centers an average of twenty minutes apart driving time along the principal 260-mile axis. (See Figure 1-1.)

The Crescent study locales used in succeeding chapters are both urban-centered and regional in extent. In the community studies some seven of the North Carolina centers received concentrated attention. Drawing almost exclusively on our own field investigations and sampling surveys, these studies focus primarily on Raleigh, Durham, Burlington, Greensboro, High Point, Winston-Salem, and Charlotte. Depending generally on secondary sources of data, the regional studies focus on the sixteen counties that form the core area of the Piedmont in North and South Carolina. This area extends from Wake County (containing Raleigh, N. C.) at the northeast extremity to Greenville County (containing Greenville, S. C.) at the southwestern end of the transportation corridor. Several of the regional studies examine the sixteen Crescent counties in relation to North and South Carolina and Georgia, and several of the community studies, for comparative purposes, look at cities outside the Crescent cluster.

The Piedmont Plateau is a fairly level region. While slopes between

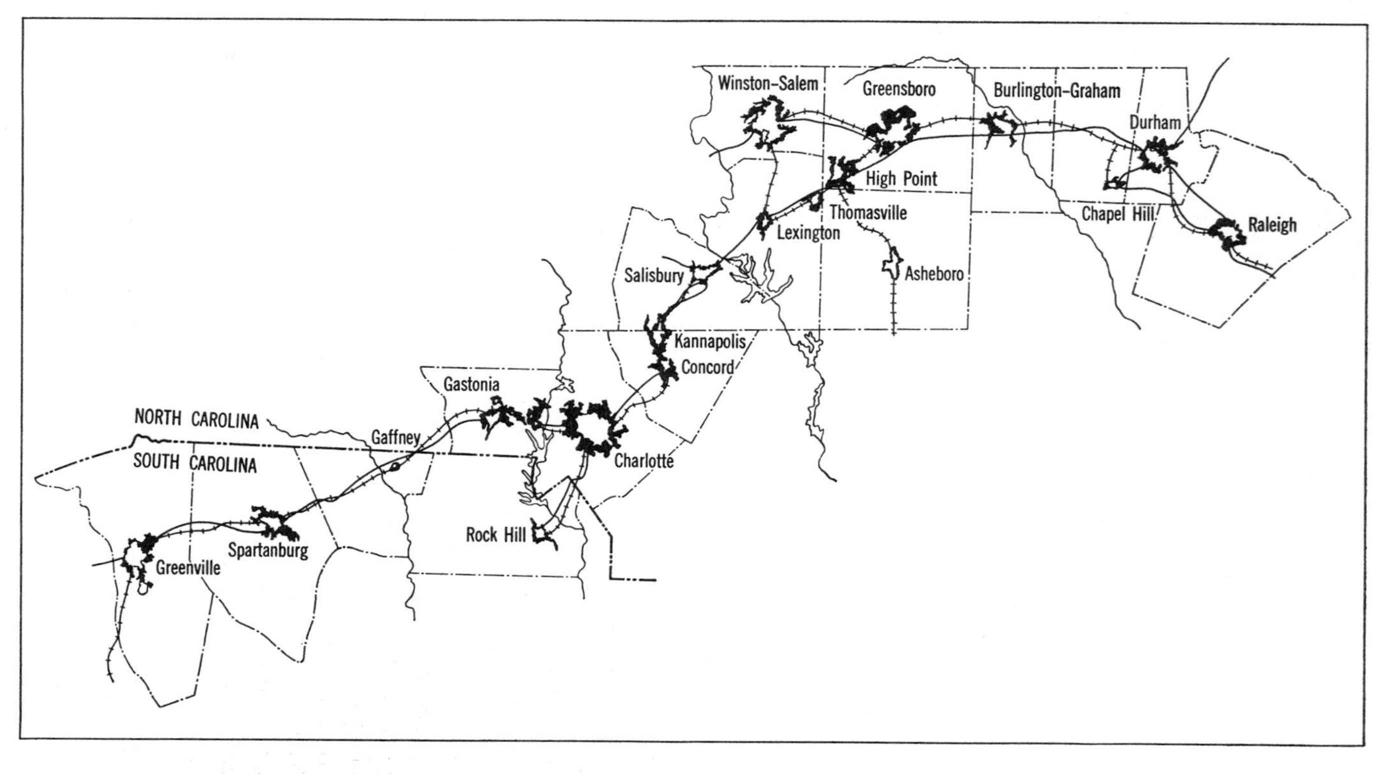

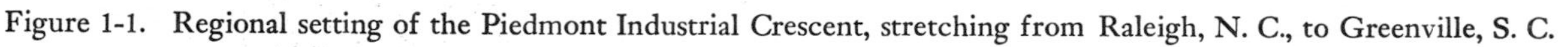
Figure 1-1. Regional setting of the Piedmont Industrial Crescent, stretching from Raleigh, N. C., to Greenville, S. C.

the principal river basins are for the most part gently undulating, there are scattered sections where the Piedmont joins the mountain counties with marked extremes of topography. The sixteen counties drain into five distinct river basins: Neuse, Cape Fear, Yadkin-Pee Dee, Roanoke-Chowan, and Catawba-Santee. As can be noted in a succeeding section, it is the random location of cities in relation to these river basins that is at the root of the water problem facing several cities in the Crescent.

Historical Threads of Development

While randomly placed in relation to watersheds, the locations of cities in this region are not without some reason and order. Being essentially landlocked, the Piedmont Crescent's early development was shaped to a very large extent by the railroads, especially the state-built sections (now leased) that were combined with privately built stretches to form the main line of the Southern Railway between Washington, Atlanta, and New Orleans. Just as the railroads opened up commerce between the Crescent communities and the markets of the Northeast, the later push for farm-to-market road systems, especially in North Carolina, served to develop the trade function and to further strengthen the position of these communities.

If transportation systems provided a key impetus to the growth of this region, the industrialization of the Piedmont provided a powerful complementing stimulus. Beginning in the early 1900's with the introduction of hydroelectric power, industrial development has been gradually gaining momentum. With the availability of electric power, manufacturing enterprise took root along the railroad system where access to markets was assured. Later the farm-to-market roads also served to extend the radius of labor pools for these developing industrial centers and provide easier access to local sources of raw materials. In recent years part-time farmers have become a significant source of labor, especially for manufacturing activity, working on a shift basis or possessing unusual seasonal requirements. And now the superhighway system ushers in an era of still further growth. With many of the centers now forming metropolitan-like clusters of cities, economic integration of the region becomes more pronounced. (See Chapter 2.)

All this growth has been superimposed on an agricultural economy of small farm operators and tenants characteristic of this region. The farm economy is closely linked with the local raw material-oriented industries which had their beginnings in the period that the Piedmont was settled by Virginians and in-migrants from more northerly points. These migrants were of diverse national and religious origins—Scotch-Irish, English, German, Pennsylvania Dutch, Moravian, and Welsh settlers. The traditions of the small farm persist to this day, although the trends indicate the small farms are disappearing to a considerable degree. (See Chapter 5.)

Thus the historical threads of the present-day Crescent date back to the years of colonial settlement beginning in the 1740's, the initial period of economic development preceding the Civil War, the later industrial revolution beginning in the 1870's, the introduction of electric power in the early 1900's, and continue down to the present era of new industrialization, new capital investment, and stepped-up urbanization.

Economic and Population Patterns

Through this period of more than two centuries of development, the Piedmont Crescent steadily moved ahead of other regions in the Carolinas. While seaports (Charleston), state capital functions (Columbia), and resort attractions (Asheville) have provided impetus for attracting industrial enterprise in selected other locations, nowhere in the two Carolinas has there been the concentrated form of urbanization as that which is in progress in the Piedmont Industrial Crescent. While comprising 11 per cent of the land area of the two Carolinas, the 16 Crescent counties have more than 29 per cent of the two-state population, 36 per cent of the retail sales, 49 per cent of the value added by manufacture, and 55 per cent of the wholesale sales. Compared with the South Atlantic region and the nation as a whole, these 16 counties have a considerably larger share of manufacturing and wholesaling activity than would be indicated by their share of the nation's population.

Of the 2 million people now resident in the 16 counties, more than 61 per cent of them are classified as urban under census definitions now in use. It is perhaps more meaningful to think of the population in Crescent counties in increments. First, there are the more than 1 million persons living inside the 20 larger urban places; second, there is another half million wholly urban-oriented, but forming the urban fringe and the new "scatterized urban" settlement pattern beyond the urban fringe; and third, there is a sizable proportion of the remaining half million classed as "partly urban" in the sense that they supplement family farm income with part-time employment in urban areas. In the 1950–1960 decade, the population increase in the 16-county Crescent region was 21 per cent, veritably a straight-line extension of the growth rate established during the 1940–1950 period. This compares with a population increase for the nation as a whole of some 18 per cent in the last decade. (See Table 1-1.)

While the region is experiencing a pronounced upward population growth which appears to be distributing itself in new spatial patterns around the old centers, the urban centers themselves continue to grow. (See Table 1-2.) Indeed three-quarters of the 1950–1960 growth occurred in urban places. This contrasts with the older mature areas of urbanization in the North where central cities are losing population. While a substantial amount of the growth in urban places has occurred by annexation, it is clear that urbanization in the Crescent is still in a youthful stage of evolution. There are six Standard Metropolitan Statistical Areas (SMSA's) in the Piedmont Crescent (Raleigh, Durham, Greensboro-High Point, Winston-Salem, and Charlotte in North Carolina, and Greenville in South Carolina). The number of SMSA's was the same in 1950 and 1960.

There is, however, another population change of significance. Not only are the urban centers increasing in size, but as a group, urban centers have experienced an escalator-like shift upward in population-size groups. While in 1950, there was but one city (Charlotte) in the over 100,000 category, in 1960 there were three (Charlotte, Greensboro, and Winston-Salem). Reaching down to the small-city category, the number of cities 25,000 and over increased from nine to twelve in the 1950–1960 decade.

Governmental Organization

Another measure of the urbanization in the Crescent is to be found in the numbers and kinds of local units of government. The characteristics common to areas in advance stages of urbanization—the proliferation of special units of government, overlapping jurisdictions, and generally the fragmentation of functions granted to the original governing bodies—are nowhere near the problem proportions that exist in the established metropolitan areas elsewhere. The Crescent region presents an extraordinarily simple picture in this respect. In the six SMSA's in the Crescent, the Census of Governments (1957) lists a total of sixty-three units of government. The region is comparatively

Table 1-1. Piedmont Industrial Crescent, Population Distribution by County: 1950 and 1960

COUNTY	LAND AREA SQ. MI.	POPULATION		POPULATION PER SQ. MI.		% URBAN [a]		POPULATION GROWTH % INCREASE 1950–1960	
	1960	1950	1960	1950	1960	1950	1960	Total	Urban
North Carolina									
Alamance	434	71,220	85,674	164	197	41.5	51.2	20.3	48.3
Cabarrus	360	63,783	68,137	177	189	66.0	67.7	6.8	9.6
Davidson	546	62,244	79,493	114	146	39.7	39.4	27.7	26.5
Durham	299	101,639	111,995	340	375	72.2	75.6	10.2	15.4
Forsyth	424	146,135	189,428	345	447	65.8	69.2	29.6	36.4
Gaston	358	110,836	127,074	310	355	55.2	61.8	14.7	28.3
Guilford	651	191,057	246,520	294	379	66.0	76.1	29.0	48.6
Mecklenburg	542	197,052	272,111	364	502	71.5	78.0	38.1	50.5
Orange	398	34,435	42,970	87	108	26.7	29.3	24.8	37.0
Randolph	801	50,804	61,497	63	77	15.2	25.3	21.0	102.3
Rowan	517	75,410	82,817	146	160	41.1	47.2	9.8	26.1
Wake	864	136,450	169,082	158	196	53.1	63.2	23.9	47.4
N. C.—12-County Subtotals	6,194	1,241,065	1,536,798	200	248	57.6	64.4	23.8	38.4

South Carolina									
Cherokee	394	34,992	35,205	89	89	35.5	43.2	0.6	22.6
Greenville	789	168,152	209,776	213	266	59.9	63.7	24.8	32.7
Spartanburg	830	150,349	156,830	181	189	34.6	36.1	4.3	8.9
York	685	71,596	78,760	105	115	49.1	52.0	10.0	16.5
S. C.—4-County Subtotals	2,698	425,089	480,571	158	178	47.1	51.3	13.1	23.1
16-County Totals	8,892	1,666,154	2,017,369	187	227	54.9	61.3	21.1	35.1

Source. U. S. Bureau of the Census.

[a] 1960 Census definition.

free of overlapping jurisdictions and, while there are indications that very soon the Crescent will begin experiencing some difficulties in this respect, as yet there are no serious problems occasioned by urbanized areas spilling over county or state lines.

Table 1-2. Population of Cities of over 5,000, Piedmont Industrial Crescent: 1950 and 1960 (without Adjustment for Interim Expansions of Corporate Limits)

	1950	1960	% INCREASE 1950–1960
North Carolina			
Asheboro (Randolph)	7,701	9,449	22.7
Burlington (Alamance)	24,560	33,199	35.2
Chapel Hill (Orange)	9,177	12,573	37.0
Charlotte (Mecklenburg)	134,042	201,564	50.4
Concord (Cabarrus)	16,486	17,799	8.0
Durham (Durham)	71,311	78,302	9.8
Gastonia (Gaston)	23,069	37,276	61.6
Graham (Alamance)	5,026	7,723	53.7
Greensboro (Guilford)	74,389	119,574	60.7
High Point (Guilford)	39,973	62,063	55.3
Kannapolis (uninc.) (Cabarrus-Rowan)	28,448	34,647	21.8
Lexington (Davidson)	13,571	16,093	18.6
Raleigh (Wake)	65,679	93,931	43.0
Salisbury (Rowan)	20,102	21,297	5.9
Thomasville (Davidson)	11,154	15,190	36.2
Winston-Salem (Forsyth)	87,811	111,135	26.6
16-City Subtotals	632,499	871,815	37.8
South Carolina			
Gaffney (Cherokee)	8,123	10,435	28.5
Greenville (Greenville)	58,161	66,188	13.8
Rock Hill (York)	24,502	29,404	20.0
Spartanburg (Spartanburg)	36,795	44,352	20.5
4-City Subtotals	127,581	150,379	17.9
20-City Totals	760,080	1,022,194	34.5

Source. U. S. Bureau of the Census.

There are some distinctive differences in the organization of local government in the two Carolinas, but in both states the structure continues to be relatively simple. In North Carolina, for example, the allocation of functions between city and county has been made largely on the basis of the incidence of need for services. Thus, the county assumes primary responsibility for health, welfare, education, and judicial services, and municipalities take responsibility for urban-type functions (Institute of Government, 1960). The county, the municipality, and the special district (e.g., sanitary districts and rural fire protection districts) are the significant units of local government characteristic of this region.

The picture of local governmental finance in the Crescent also is considerably less complex than in the older established metropolitan areas. In North Carolina, the patterns in the allocation of financial responsibility between local and state government are unusual. An outgrowth of depression conditions of the 1930's, the state assumes a major financial responsibility for local school and highway costs. Local school boards continue to have responsibility for capital and maintenance costs of schools, but base pay for teachers comes from the state. The State Highway Commission is responsible for all county roads, shares costs of major street construction inside municipalities, and contributes a half cent of the gas tax for the construction and maintenance of minor streets inside city limits. While these adjustments in financial responsibility fortuitously cushion for the time being the impact of steadily increasing costs of city services and facilities in this region, pressures on the property tax and other sources of revenue are expected to increase as more and more urban-type functions are demanded in urbanizing areas.

Urban-Growth Problems

Problems of the increasingly complex governmental structure and the steadily mounting governmental costs of providing for urban growth are symptomatic of still other problems of urbanization that are even now beginning to intrude on Crescent urban centers. In the course of acquiring what is the equivalent of three cities of the size of 1960 Winston-Salem over the past decade, the urban Crescent is chafing with a variety of urban-growth problems for the first time. Since the growth is not superimposed in efficient city units of the size of Winston-Salem but distributed rather widely—some of it dispersed into new subdivisions that cities have been scrambling to annex and some of it scattered over the countryside beyond like seeds in the wind —problems inevitably appear.

To determine the range of problems and assess their prevalence and incidence among urban centers in the Crescent, a special survey was undertaken. The vantage point chosen was that of the public official, including the mayor, city manager, city engineer, planning director, and city councilmen. In each of the 19 cities surveyed, more than 50 per cent of the public officials indicated that parking, traffic congestion, streets, and highways were major problems or likely to become major problems in the near future. Next highest on the list were downtown deterioration (13 cities) and sewage disposal (12 cities). Land use and regional planning were each perceived as major problems in 11 cities, and schools and recreation-parks, each in 10 cities. According to Table 1-3, some of the pressing problems of other metropolitan areas are still in the minority in the Crescent, such as air and water pollution, but others, such as juvenile delinquency, are apparently becoming more prevalent (6 cities).

Having examined the broad range of problems confronting the Piedmont Crescent, it may be well to recall Vance's early optimism on the fortunate development pattern of the area which might avoid the growing pains of urbanization:

> The diffused pattern of urbanization now taking shape in the Piedmont has much to commend it to the regionalist. . . . While the South develops the small city, the medium city, and a few large cities, it need not produce the metropolis. Thus it may avoid traffic congestion, the creation of slum areas, the loss of time going to and from work, and the corrupt and inefficient municipal housekeeping almost inevitably attached to overdeveloped population centers. If such a program is possible, the South may finally attain many of the advantages of contemporary industrialization without suffering its accompanying deficiencies and maladjustments. (Vance, 1932, p. 507.)

While in the intervening years many new deficiencies and maladjustments from the processes of growth have appeared, this opportunity for a happier solution to the Piedmont's problems of growth than has been achieved in other sections of the country still exists today.

Character of Crescent Cities

In many respects the visual character of Crescent cities is a reflection of the transition from the disappearing rural to the emerging in-

Table 1-3. Major Problems Now or Likely to Become Major Problems in Near Future, as Perceived by Public Officials in 19 Crescent Cities: Summer 1959

PROBLEMS AS LISTED IN SURVEY QUESTIONNAIRE [a]	NUMBER OF CITIES IN WHICH SPECIFIC PROBLEM WAS CITED IN MORE THAN 50% OF RESPONSES [b]
Parking, traffic congestion	19
Streets and highways	19
Downtown deterioration	13
Sewage disposal	12
Land use	11
Regional planning	11
Schools	10
Recreation-parks	10
Subdivision regulation	8
Drainage	7
Industrial development	6
Juvenile delinquency	6
Zoning regulation	5
Housing	5
Water supply	5
Crime rate	4
Civil defense	4
Public safety	3
Airports	2
Health control—hospitals	2
Railroads	2
Water pollution	1
Air pollution	1

[a] Excluding fiscal and governmental organization problems which were omitted from survey questionnaire owing to their general prevalence in one form or another.

[b] Out of 186 public officials included in the survey, 172 responses were received (92.5 per cent) and 169 were used for reporting purposes. All mayors, city engineers, and planning directors responded, with only 14 councilmen failing to complete the survey schedule.

dustrial atmosphere in this region. The open-order pattern of development provides a striking contrast to the image that has been built up in the literature about the big, sprawling, densely developed metropolitan areas of this country.

An airplane flight along the Crescent's transportation corridor gives visual evidence of the open character of development. There is a penetration of the countryside into the developed areas in the Crescent, and just where the lines between country and city begin are not always discernible. Yet the splatter of urban development intensifies at frequently spaced intervals. At dusk the build-up in the pattern of blinking lights provides the unmistakable benchmarks where development intensifies, with the splash of neon lights identifying the central business districts.

A tour through the typical Crescent city brings out the low density character of residential areas. Structures are predominantly single family (average of four dwelling units to the acre), with many of them built in developments that retain the wooded character of the forest areas to be found alternating with tobacco fields and pasture land in rural sections. FHA-style garden apartments are the common forms of higher density development, with only two or three centers having high-rise apartments. The Crescent city is not without its drab areas, and these are frequently either sections that were originally built as company housing, usually for textile workers, or areas of Negro occupancy. Urban blight occurs on a relatively small scale, and a slum usually consists of small pockets of dilapidated structures in obsolete or poorly laid out neighborhoods.

The one-stop large shopping center has become a commonplace form for business expansion, and with the appearance of this kind of development, the downtown businessmen in each of the larger cities have been pressing for programs to revitalize the old center. Some office functions are decentralizing. In one city a doctors' village has been established in an outlying area and insurance offices have been developed in a park setting. A decentralized pattern of industrial development has long been characteristic of the Piedmont. New industry continues to go into outlying areas, but it is seeking industrial park settings. The Research Triangle Park in the Raleigh-Durham-Chapel Hill area which is designed to accommodate industrial research laboratories is an example of the newer kinds of industrial areas that are being emphasized by Crescent cities in their industrial promotional efforts.

The automobile is the major form of local transportation, although all of the larger centers have bus systems in operation. Expressway systems are under construction or in advanced stages of planning in the larger centers. Along with the emphasis on the automobile, there is a tendency for highway frontages to go into strip development. Perhaps partly attributable to a heritage of an earlier era which placed a premium on self-reliance and the individual fending for himself and partly to the recent rural background of the residents of Crescent cities, there is an initial suspicion of and resistance to development controls that would minimize the adverse effects of this kind of development. While some aspects of subdivision control and zoning widely accepted elsewhere are not acceptable in Piedmont Crescent cities, the resistance to development controls is disappearing in the face of pressures of growth and the problems noted above.

With this thumbnail sketch of the Piedmont Industrial Crescent we have sought to provide enough background on the area so that chapter authors need not digress from the subject area of their research and the reader need not feel the vagueness with a place which unfamiliarity sometimes engenders. One final word relative to the organization of material in the sections should be inserted at this point. While Chapters 1 and 14 coupled with the introductions to the four parts of the volume will assist the browsing reader to get an idea of the scope of the book and some notion of the theoretical frame of reference and the policy implications of the research, the vital quality of this research is only to be found in the individual Chapters 2 through 13. Indeed, many readers may best satisfy their interest by selective reading in the individual chapters and only a cursory examination of other parts.

REFERENCES

Institute of Government (1960), "Memorandum on Special Features of North Carolina Government Which Are Pertinent to Discussion Topics in Seminar on 'State Government and the Metropolian Area' to Be Held at the Institute of Government, Chapel Hill, December 1–3, 1960." Chapel Hill, N. C.: University of North Carolina.

Vance, Rupert B. (1932), *Human Geography of the South.* Chapel Hill, N. C.: University of North Carolina Press.

Part One

Economic Orientations to Urbanization

by Lowell D. Ashby

REGIONS SUCH AS the Piedmont Industrial Crescent are sometimes approached as if they were analogs of the contemporary "underdeveloped nation." But how useful is such an analogy in the present case? An underdeveloped nation, in current usage among economists, is primarily concerned with attaining a position from which growth in income or other measures of individual well-being is possible, if not assured.[1]

The Crescent area stands in a distinctly different position. It is not a nation, nor is it primarily concerned with "development" in the special sense used above. In this old industrial area development has long since occurred. The economic status of the people has been on the rise since the middle of the nineteenth century. It could hardly have been otherwise since this area is merely a small geographic component embedded in an enormous and growing national economy which has long since traversed the developmental hump.

The Crescent's growth in the usual measures of economic well-being is assured merely by its place in a dynamic national economy. However, there is nothing determinate or assured about the relative rate or quality of this economic betterment. The participation of this small region in the self-sustaining national growth will depend upon the mix of economic and social processes and labor-force participation that it achieves. The initial mix may be a matter of historical and geological accident. At any time, of course, the mixture of processes and labor-force participation is a viable one. Its feasibility is attested by its mere existence as an operating regional segment of a larger economy.

In considering the possibilities for economic change, we are aware that tomorrow must resemble today, since the cumulation of past commitments must far outweigh the increment of change of the moment. Yet it is just these increments at the "growing edge" of a subregional economy that carry the seeds of eventual far-reaching change.

In economic as in other matters, values condition or control behavior or actions. These in turn effect change. The achievement of change inevitably constitutes a demonstration effect with powerful repercussions on objectives and underlying values. At any stage in this circle of events, however, certain issues lie implicit in the process. Some of these are examined here in relation to the Crescent.

Perhaps the most basic issue is the question of the self-consciousness or identity of this area. Are the cities of the Crescent area interdependent, or are they independent and aloof like strangers who chance to stand at the same bus stop? The basic issue concerns the strength of the interaction between these urban clusters. If a certain critical urban mass is essential prior to rapid and sustained economic growth, then it is of the utmost consequence whether the Crescent constitutes an urban area of two millions or merely a group of twenty small cities each of which is entirely self-centered and among which there is little or no social or economic specialization. If the cities are unrelated, then each is oriented mainly to its own small hinterland and to the national market beyond for an export outlet and a source of specialized imports. The question is whether each city is to perform every function in a small way or whether each may act in a specialized way for a larger urban area.[2]

Specifically, it is a matter of consequence as to whether the financial resources of the area are to be drawn from a group of scattered and parochially oriented banks or whether a large financial center in one or more cities operates with an area or region-wide horizon. It does make a difference whether small neighboring cities insist on separate sanitary and water supply solutions or on separate airports with duplicating inadequacies.

The growth potentials of the Crescent in terms of relevant economic variables very nearly depend upon a state of mind, for whatever the present condition, the current changes must have the utmost ultimate importance for the economic and social cohesiveness of the area. And just this qualitative outcome may be decisive as between a reluctant and a dynamic pattern of change for all.

Since the self-identity or state of mind of the area is crucial, the patterns of human mobility within and through the Crescent are of the greatest importance. Here the value systems and thought patterns of people have a remarkable dualistic role. The Crescent area, because it is essentially urban, operates as a migratory terminal point. But the individual migratory paths terminating here are not a random set. The area and its industrial and social activities exert a selective attraction. Individuals are attracted who find their own tastes and capacities in rapport with the area's opportunities. But their mere arrival may thus re-enforce a pre-existing composite value system. The system of selective attraction also works from the other end. The Crescent is not merely a terminus but also a point of migratory origin. Some of the area's youth leave; others stay. Here again values determine who stays, but the particular individuals who stay are likely to re-enforce a preset value bias.

There is definite recognition of the net out-migration experienced in a limited way by the Crescent and to a greater extent by the surrounding area. There is less recognition that the selective migration operates in at least two stages. The Crescent is shown in the present studies to be a net gainer from the South Atlantic states and a net loser to the rest of the nation. Thus the self-re-enforcing value system which gives any region its persistent character may be strongly at work. At the same time with the introduction of new industrial processes and other migrant-precipitating elements, the opportunity for large-scale change is evident.

The relative weakness of the Crescent area as a net migratory terminus stems from its heavy commitment to industries of slow or negative employment-expansion rates. The population growth of the Crescent undoubtedly turns upon whether or not rapidly expanding economic activities can be superimposed on the present structure. In the past there is much evidence to suggest that the industrial structure has been self-perpetuating as to character. This has made the pace of expansion self-perpetuating. Self-extending attitudes toward unionization (both on the part of employers and employees), minimum wage legislation, and fair employment practices have been in evidence. All of this constitutes a powerful demonstration of persistence of regional character. The character of a region such as the Crescent is essentially determined by its particular industrial mix and the labor force compatible with that mix. The particular mix in the Crescent currently demonstrates a high degree of stability of employment while it is less favorably situated in terms of productivity (capacity to generate income) and growth (capacity to absorb a rapidly expanding labor force).

The self-image of a region such as the cluster of cities making up the Piedmont Industrial Crescent may weigh heavily as to what it can do. A man may succeed because he works hard, but it is just as likely that he works hard to perpetuate the image of success. And so it is, in a more complex fashion, with regions. What it does affects its character, which then shapes what it can do. Small changes in industrial activities may act as the indispensable trace elements to vast eventual change. The work of half-a-dozen strategically placed entrepreneurs or civic leaders may be decisive for a region.

In the period ahead the indications are that the Crescent will serve as an urban migratory terminal point for much of the surrounding agricultural population. In addition, current investigations have indicated that the presence of this sprawling, mixed urban-rural area has encouraged many farm families to take part-time nonagricultural employment. Since this nonagricultural employment provides a cash income, it tends to displace that part of the agricultural enterprise that would otherwise provide the major cash income, namely tobacco cultivation.

While the urban areas of the Crescent appear to have altered the nature of nearby farm dweller's activities, there is no evidence to the effect that the mere presence of urban areas has altered the efficiency with which inputs are converted to outputs within agricultural activities. Thus the findings fail to confirm the well-known Schultz hypothesis that the source of income inequalities in American agriculture must largely lie in the difference in farm orientation to urban centers. An implicit issue presents itself. Does failure to confirm the Schultz hypothesis merely reflect the diluted nature of the urbanization in the Crescent, which is in return the result of a weak pattern of interaction among Crescent cities? Given a changed industrial mix involving a stronger pattern of interaction within the Crescent and compatible with a more rapid urban-population expansion, the impact on adjacent agricultural processes might be drastically different. Likewise, beyond a critical urban population threshold, the effect on adjacent agriculture might well change.

From a given configuration of industrial and labor-force commitments, it is obvious that the paths of potential economic change are multiple. The implicit question concerns the best or optimal course. But a decision between even two prescribed courses of economic and social change implies some hierarchy of underlying values. Since it stems from different interests with distinct and different value systems, it is difficult even for a city to set up sharply defined economic or social objectives. Owing to the lack of sharp identity already noted, this difficulty is multiplied for an area such as the Crescent. It is virtually certain that the loyalty of many leading citizens to a corporation or a profession or even a lodge is stronger and more persistent than dedication to civic enterprise, much less to the civic affairs of a whole regional cluster of cities. Nevertheless change can be evaluated only in terms of defined objectives and their underlying values. If these collective objectives and values do not exist they must nevertheless be invented or assumed.

If a Crescent objective is assumed, then it may or may not fall within a range feasible with existing industrial, governmental, and other processes, and given labor force and other resources. Assume that it is feasible. This does not imply that it is optimal. It may be that a given objective can be improved in all its dimensions, both quantitative and qualitative. It is likely that this is true since most areas, the Crescent being no exception, fail in complete resource utilization. There exist both unemployment and underemployment. In addition the same resources might be put into economic activities with higher net payoffs. This involves no more than a variation in the intensity with which established processes are used in order to achieve a better result. Finally, invention and/or innovation is always an avenue for the change of a given set of activities—either by the change of established processes or the introduction of new ones. None of the suggestions made here necessarily involves a change in values or qualitative objectives; yet changes are likely.

Still another course of action involves the introduction of a new industry or industries which already exist in established form elsewhere. For example, a large home-grown corporation with large accumulated financial reserves (depreciation or other) may decide to diversify by going into a compatible but quite different industry. This choice may be motivated by strictly economic considerations. It may also be motivated in part by considerations of employee welfare in terms of stability, productivity, and expansibility of employment. A change in industrial direction may well imply a change in value systems. Once the deed is done and a different industrial commitment is made, the labor force that is clustered by the new industry is likely to amplify the change in the value system which induced it. Parallel changes may of course occur because outside corporations decide to locate specified operations in the area. Such locations will come in response to certain values and opportunities in the area and in turn will amplify or extend certain elements of the local value system. A significant difference, of course, is that in addition to the indigenous corporate leadership, such changes may introduce the "corporate executive nomad" whose almost exclusive interest is in the corporate hierarchy.

The competitive posture between regions, where the gain of one area merely offsets the loss of another, can emerge at any stage. Of course, the physical shifting of industries rarely if ever occurs. Consequently the dead-weight loss of interregional migration in the sense of pointless moving costs will be slight or nonexistent. The commitment of depreciation and other financial reserves in one area rather than another does not usually imply heavy cost disparities. Moreover, until the point of interregional conflict is reached, the gain in any one area in the management of its own resources is a net national gain as well.

The Crescent area is fortunate in that its major industrial commitments are not to an exhausted or exhausting set of natural resources. Virtually anything on the nonresource-wasting menu is possible in terms of incremental change. The real issues here (as in numerous other regions) involve the revolutionary changes implicit in new modes of thought and action. It probably requires more courage to contemplate what might be than what is, and just such contemplation may be the most decisive trace element of all in the soil of economic and social improvement.[3]

FOOTNOTES

1. For an example of this usage see Ranis and Fei (1961).
2. In the terminology of interindustry analysis, the question is whether the cities constitute mere systems of separate and completely separable processes or industries, or whether, in contrast, they form a larger and indecomposable set of processes. If they are the latter, then in the aggregate they may comprise an urban mass exceeding that critical level at which new processes and activities are readily tested and assimilated.
3. See the reference to David Riesman in Meyerson (1961).

REFERENCES

Meyerson, Martin (1961), "Utopian Traditions and the Planning of Cities," in Lloyd Rodwin (Ed.), *The Future Metropolis.* New York: George Braziller.

Ranis, Gustav, and John C. H. Fei (1961), "A Theory of Economic Development," *The American Economic Review,* LI:4, 533–565.

Chapter 2

Patterns of Economic Interaction in the Crescent

by Ralph W. Pfouts *

THE PIEDMONT CRESCENT, which stretches from east of Raleigh to west of Charlotte, has attracted a great deal of attention both from within and from outside North Carolina. The attention from within the state is understandable because the Piedmont is the industrial and commercial heartland of North Carolina.

Any man of affairs in the state is likely to have dealings within this area. Politicians and public servants of the state (the two classes are not necessarily mutually exclusive) must reckon with the interests of this populous and prosperous area. Individuals who have studied North Carolina's social and economic features have found the Piedmont Crescent to be especially interesting as a mainspring area in the state's progress. But all of these different types of persons have found something else about the Crescent that challenges their interests, something that also draws interested scrutiny from outside the state.

Many people have observed that interrelationships between cities in the Piedmont Crescent appear to be unusually strong and diffuse. This is sometimes expressed by saying that people within the Crescent look to each other much more than they look outside the Crescent. The

* Acknowledgment is made of the valuable assistance provided by Mrs. Franklee G. Whartenby, Research Fellow, and Eugene A. Thomas and David G. Davies, Research Assistants.

intended implication is not that this is a provincial area, but rather that this is an area in which the residents find many common interests and many mutually advantageous transactions. The interrelationships are not only economic but social and political.

These strong relationships have raised the conjecture that the Piedmont Crescent may be the skeleton of an enormous metropolitan area of the future, a skeleton that will later be clothed with the flesh of population and commerce. The thought is that this area may some day become similar to the area from Norfolk northward to Boston, which is clearly emerging as a continuous urban region. From Norfolk going northward, one passes almost continuously through built-up areas until one passes Boston. Thus the hypothesis has been advanced that the Crescent is a similar, but smaller area in an earlier stage of development. This type of area is coming to be referred to as a "polynucleated" urban area.

This chapter reports research done to test the hypothesis that the Piedmont Crescent has the economic features of a polynucleated urban region. In other words, the purpose of the research was to determine the extent of economic integration among communities in the Crescent, that is, to test the extent to which trade and other economic intercourse takes place between Crescent cities. It may be taken as a working premise that if there is a high degree of economic interaction between the cities, this finding would lend support to the belief that the Crescent is a polynucleated urban area. A low degree of economic interaction would militate against the belief.

Three types of data have been used in attempting to measure the extent of economic interaction: charge-account data for major department stores in each of the Crescent cities; truck freight hauled between Crescent cities and between Crescent cities and the rest of the country; and telephone calls between Crescent cities. The department-store data represent retail trade; the trucking data represent industrial and wholesale flows; and the telephone data cover business calls and have a sociological component as well. It would have been extremely desirable to use additional types of data. Clearly, a complex region cannot be adequately analyzed in terms of three series of data. Specifically, some type of data on financial flows such as bank clearings between the cities would have added a great deal to the study, but this proved impossible to obtain.

The processing of the data has taken place at two levels. The first of these might be called the process of classification. In this procedure items of data are classified as to the cities connected by the datum. The end result of this is a table such as the table showing retail trade areas of the Crescent cities.

The second level of processing the data is more rigorously analytical. It makes use of the "gravity model" concepts that have found their way into spatial economic studies in recent years. The name comes about because the methods yield equations analogous to those in the theory of gravitation in physics. The advantage of the method is that it yields numerical values that might be called "coefficients of attraction" between the communities. These values can be compared with those found for other localities to determine whether economic integration in the Crescent is stronger than in other regions.

Finally, it should be noted that the tests of economic integration presented in this chapter are not conclusive; they are indicative or suggestive. Not enough different types of data have been studied to form ironbound conclusions. In addition, we lack sufficient similar data and tests on other regions that might be compared with the present data and tests. Some more or less comparable studies have been made elsewhere, but these are too few in number to allow much in generalization. Nevertheless, the results reported here are believed to be valid and to offer a good deal of new information on the Crescent; the chief need is additional data about the Crescent and, for purposes of comparison, other regions.

Retail Trade as a Measure of Economic Integration

One useful indication of the extent of economic integration which exists among communities is the amount of retail purchasing done in the communities by individuals living in the surrounding area. A survey of this sort of economic activity can point out not only the general directions of retail traffic but also the relative drawing power of the various cities. Obviously, distance is the prime factor in determining where people from small towns go to do most of their "city" retail purchasing, but it is a characteristic of the geography of the Piedmont Crescent that the five major cities—Durham, Raleigh, Greensboro, Winston-Salem, and Charlotte—are situated in such a way that there are large groups of smaller towns which are more or less equidistant from two or more of the larger cities. (This is particularly true of the Greensboro–Winston-Salem area and the Raleigh-Durham area.) Thus the shape and extent of a city's out-of-town retail influence cannot be explained entirely in terms of distance.

Even more basic, so far as the present study is concerned, is the question of how the areas between these cities are shared in regard to retail trade. That is, does a given city have its own satellite area which is economically loyal in this respect, or do the various cities encroach on others' domains, with a resultant interlocking pattern of retail purchasing? If the latter proves to be true, then we may surmise that, from the standpoint of retail buying, the Piedmont Crescent does appear to be a polynucleated area; that is, the area as a whole is an economic entity, marked by several nuclei—the five major cities. This is in opposition to an area in which each city dominates its own area, with little or no interrelationship between the various segments.

Fortunately, there were available for this study large bodies of data consisting of the charge-account records held by major stores in the various cities. (The use of these data and no other rules out, of course, the cash purchases made in the cities, but this is impossible to ascertain and would probably constitute a minor element in the cases of many types of merchandise.) In each of the major cities of the Crescent, the out-of-town charge accounts carried at each of three or four large department stores were tallied and totaled for the city as a whole. These raw numbers of accounts held by out-of-town customers were then converted to the number of accounts per 1,000 inhabitants of the given town.

These data were then adjusted in two ways. In one case, all towns with fewer than 500 inhabitants or fewer than 20 charge accounts per 1,000 inhabitants were ruled out of a given city's area; in the second case, only those towns with fewer than 100 inhabitants or fewer than 15 charge accounts per 1,000 were ruled out. Thus we have constructed two tests to determine the retail areas attached to the major cities, the first test being somewhat more stringent than the second. For example, the town of Boger City, with 15 accounts in Charlotte per 1,000 population, would be excluded from the Charlotte area in the first case but included in the second.

It is clear that both of these tests are based on arbitrary criteria. What particular significance can be attached to 20 charge accounts per 1,000 inhabitants or to 15 charge accounts per 1,000 persons? There is no strong objective reason for choosing either of these or any other particular number. Thus as in all choices of critical points in measurement, we are fundamentally making arbitrary decisions.

Such decisions can be defended only by an appeal to intuition; we contend that subjectively those values that we have chosen seem like reasonable values.

Geographic Patterns of Economic Interaction

The data are first examined for the geographic patterns of retail trade. Figures 2-1 and 2-2 were drawn to show the appearance of each city's area as delineated by the two methods. The patterns discernible in these maps, of course, are determined by the methods used, and the problem thus becomes largely that of where to draw the line in omitting or including a given town. The first test has an advantage in that the exclusion of extremely small towns helps rule out the greater distortions which would occur in the pattern to the distribution of accounts per 1,000 figures; on the other hand, the large number of small towns which dot the Piedmont area is a factor in favor of lowering the town population to 100 in an effort to get a more representative sample.

Figure 2-1 (including towns of over 500 and with 20 or more accounts per 1,000 people) presents a rather surprising appearance in that there is a comparatively small amount of overlap between any pair of cities. Each city seems to have its own particular out-of-town trading area. The largest overlap is that which occurred between Charlotte and Winston-Salem in a three-cornered area in the west central part of the state. A smaller overlap occurs between Charlotte and Greensboro in the Sand Hills area, and there is also a small amount of shared area between Greensboro and Winston-Salem.

Perhaps the most unexpected result, when the data are handled in the first method, is the complete cleavage that appeared between the Raleigh-Durham area and the Greensboro–Winston-Salem–Charlotte area, a fact that would militate against the polynuclear theory. Not only do Durham and Greensboro fail to share any area between them, but there appears a definite cleavage between the two in the shape of a small triangular area which had only a negligible amount of retail trade in both cities.

The visual impression given by this map is that each of these cities is hemmed in, so far as its retail expansion is concerned, by the next city. The Raleigh area is much more developed in the eastern direction than the western, where it is apparently stopped by Durham; Durham appears to be blocked on all four sides; the Winston-Salem

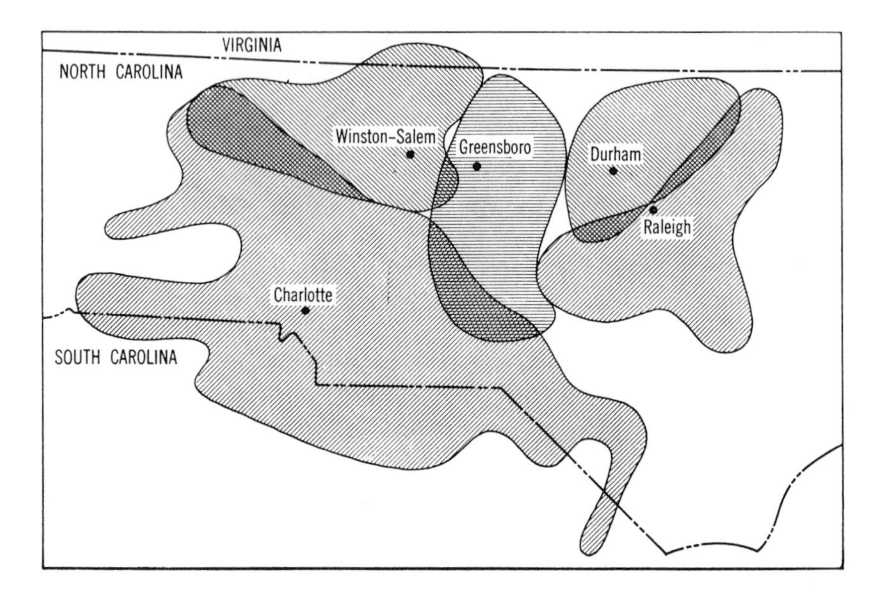

Figure 2-1. Out-of-town accounts for selected department stores in Raleigh, Durham, Greensboro, Winston-Salem, and Charlotte. Each shaded area represents the generalized shape of the charge-account area of the indicated city based on the locations of towns of 500 or more population with at least 20 charge accounts per 1,000 inhabitants.

area fans out toward the north and west but is very small on the east side of the city, where Greensboro cuts into the area; and there seems to be mutual blocking among Greensboro, Winston-Salem, and Charlotte in the west central part of the state. With nothing on the south or southeast to impede it to any great degree, Charlotte's trading area has spread out over the upper part of South Carolina to a marked degree. Charlotte's actual trading strength on this southern edge could be established by examining charge-account data of department stores in Greenville, Spartanburg, and Columbia in South Carolina.

The third finding disclosed by this map is that there are large parts of the eastern and southeastern part of the state that apparently are not integrated economically with any of the major cities, as measured by department-store trade. This is contrary to the popular idea that Raleigh dominates the eastern part of the state. As the first figure shows, the Raleigh area stops short of the tidewater area, leaving an area extending about 100 miles to the coast and about 70 miles to the southeast. It may be that the retail trade from the lower section of this area goes to Wilmington and the upper part to Richmond, and that investigation of these two cities would result in a fan-shaped area beginning at Durham and spreading to the northeast and southeast.

In any event, when the data are handled in this manner (omitting all towns with fewer than 500 people and fewer than 20 accounts per 1,000 inhabitants), the indications are that the Piedmont area, rather than being a polynucleated, crescent-shaped area, divides itself into two areas: one, the Greensboro–Winston-Salem–Charlotte area, which more nearly conforms to the concept of an economically integrated area; and second, the Raleigh-Durham area, which apparently operates within a limited sphere, untouched by the other major North Carolina cities, and is possibly linked to the northeast and southeast rather than to the west.

When the data are adjusted in the second manner—including all towns that have 100 or more inhabitants and 15 or more accounts per 1,000 inhabitants—the results are somewhat less surprising. First, there

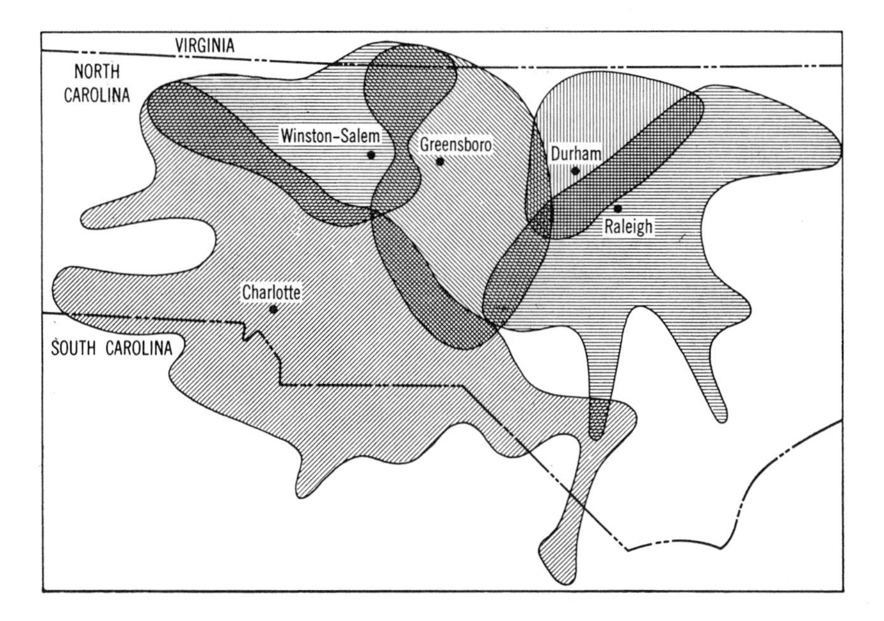

Figure 2-2. Out-of-town charge accounts for selected department stores in Raleigh, Durham, Greensboro, Winston-Salem, and Charlotte. Each shaded area represents the generalized shape of the charge-account area of the indicated city based on the locations of towns of 100 or more population with at least 15 charge accounts per 1,000 inhabitants.

appears a fair amount of overlap among all the cities and less indication that the cities are hemmed in by each other. Greensboro, in particular, at the approximate center of the Crescent, seems to project in all directions.

A second finding in Figure 2-2 is that the Raleigh area stretches out farther toward the coast and toward the southeast than it appeared to in Figure 2-1, and touches both the Greensboro and Charlotte areas. This expansion indicates, of course, that Raleigh reaches into some rural areas which were omitted from the first sample. However, apparently the same thing does not hold for Durham; as can be seen, the Durham area remains quite small despite the less rigorous test employed in constructing this map. For one reason or another, Durham appears to have been unable to extend its sphere of retail influence much farther than about 30 or 40 miles, as compared with Raleigh, for example, which draws customers from a distance of 60 miles or more.

The appearance of Figure 2-2 is considerably more favorable to a polynucleated theory for the Piedmont Crescent than Figure 2-1. Even apart from the fact that the results of the second test were more nearly the expected ones, it is probable that this test is the more appropriate of the two, in view of the large number of very small towns in the Piedmont Crescent. It may be, too, that the number of charge accounts per 1,000 population should be lowered to 10 rather than 15, which would no doubt extend most of the areas somewhat farther.

There are, of course, certain factors about the data used which might conceivably change both maps somewhat. First, current charge accounts were used, while the population figures were those for the 1950 census, except in the case of a few of the larger towns which conducted individual censuses in 1956. Secondly, resources available did not permit the canvassing of more than four stores in each city (in Greensboro, accounts in only three stores were analyzed). It was considered best to use only department stores; probably a more extensive sample including specialty stores would change the distribution somewhat. However, the stores that were checked in each town ranged in general from those drawing low-income groups to those tending to draw trade from the higher-income groups, so that the sample may be considered fairly representative.

A third less important factor is that in two or three instances the stores themselves supplied the data, being unable or unwilling to open their files to the researchers. While the furnished data are considered reasonably accurate, they may constitute percentage estimates rather than actual counts. Thus it is possible that some of the smaller towns were omitted in these tallies, or lumped into one group.

Statistical Tests of Economic Interaction

The previous section indicated the purely visual findings which appeared from the charge-account data of the five major North Carolina cities of the Crescent. The present section will present a somewhat more analytical approach in the nature of the gravity models mentioned in the introduction. These models employ certain statistical procedures in an effort to obtain a numerical measurement of the retail attraction exerted by these cities.

Two different models have been employed in analyzing these charge-account data, both based largely on the factor of distance. Distance is, of course, the basic factor in determining where people from rural and small town areas go to do their city buying, but it is not the only factor involved in this decision, nor are its effects always completely direct. The first analysis of the relationship of retail trade and distance uses a regression analysis to determine more exactly what influence distance has on out-of-town trade. Here again we have two tests: the first includes those towns with 500 or more inhabitants and 20 or more charge accounts per 1,000 population in the city in question; the second includes all towns with 100 or more population and 15 or more accounts. These are referred to as Test 1 and Test 2, respectively.

When the number of charge accounts per 1,000 population was plotted against distance on an arithmetic scale, it was obvious that a straight-line regression equation did not fit these data well. However, a straight-line regression equation fitted to the logs of both sets of numbers yielded a fairly good fit. Computations using logs yielded results shown in the table.

CITY	ESTIMATING EQUATION	r	s	LEVEL OF SIGNIFICANCE
Durham	$\log X_{12} = 3.6853 - 1.2686 \log X_2$	−.64	.36	.005
Raleigh	$\log X_{12} = 4.0355 - 1.5032 \log X_2$	−.83	.24	Below .001
Greensboro	$\log X_{12} = 3.5910 - 1.1406 \log X_2$	−.79	.22	Below .001
Winston-Salem	$\log X_{12} = 2.7490 - 0.5245 \log X_2$	−.43	.36	Between .02 and .01
Charlotte	$\log X_{12} = 2.7356 - 0.6420 \log X_2$	−.69	.22	Below .001

The term X_2 was used to denote distance (in miles), the independent variable, and X_1 to denote the number of accounts per 1,000 population in each town, the dependent variable. The first numerical value in each equation is log *a* or the starting point of each line of regression. The second value is *b*, representing the slope of the line, or the change occurring as the dependent variable changes. It is this *b* value with which we are concerned, since it represents the mathematical relationship of retail trade and distance. The *r* value is the correlation coefficient between charge accounts and distance; the *s* value is the standard error of estimate; both *r* and *s* are measures of goodness of fit or of how closely the fitted equation approximates the actual data values. Finally, the level of significance indicates the likelihood of getting such an *r* value as was obtained, by chance. All of the probabilities are small.

As the preceding tabulation shows, the correlation between retail trade and distance is quite high in four cases and fairly high in the fifth (Winston-Salem), and the levels of significance show that such values are quite unlikely to have occurred by chance. In spite of these statistical virtues, it may be seen that the correlation coefficient for Winston-Salem is appreciably below those of the other cities. This means that a substantial proportion of the variance in the charge-account data is not explained by distance in the case of Winston-Salem. In a practical sense this could mean that the sample for Winston-Salem was inadequate in some way or that additional variables beside distance should be used in the regression analysis. However, it is clear the distance is a significant determinant of charge-account location.

The *b* values for Durham, Raleigh, and Greensboro hover fairly closely around unity, indicating that, as distance from the city increases, the number of out-of-town charge accounts per 1,000 population decreases at a corresponding rate. For example, if distance from the city is doubled, the number of accounts is cut by slightly more than one-half for Durham and Greensboro and about two-thirds for Raleigh.

In the case of Charlotte we find a considerably smaller *b* value, indicating that distance has a smaller influence on out-of-town trading. This is to be expected, as Charlotte is of a size to offer products and services that are not available elsewhere. The *b* value for Winston-Salem is more puzzling, since it is even smaller than that for Charlotte. The only explanation that occurs readily is that the northwest corner of North Carolina really has no other large town to go to except Winston-Salem, and the people must perforce do their city trading there or not at all. This explanation seems to be in line with the appearance of the Winston-Salem area in Figure 2-1.

For the data adjusted in the second manner (including all towns larger than 100 and having more than 15 accounts), the results were as shown in the table.

CITY	ESTIMATING EQUATION	r	s	LEVEL OF SIGNIFICANCE
Durham	$\log X_{12} = 3.8472 - 1.4232 \log X_2$	−.65	.41	Below .001
Raleigh	$\log X_{12} = 2.8654 - 0.7628 \log X_2$	−.54	.40	Below .001
Greensboro	$\log X_{12} = 3.0834 - 0.8432 \log X_2$	−.57	.38	Below .001
Winston-Salem	$\log X_{12} = 3.5044 - 1.1116 \log X_2$	−.79	.26	Below .001
Charlotte	$\log X_{12} = 2.8291 - 0.7206 \log X_2$	−.66	.23	Below .001

In the cases of Durham and Charlotte, the b values obtained by this method are not appreciably different from those obtained by Test 1. The inclusion of the smaller towns was thus not sufficient to change these two samples to any great degree. For Raleigh and Greensboro, however, there are fairly sizable decreases in the b values which must be noted. These decreases indicate that Raleigh and Greensboro extend their trading areas somewhat, if the requirements of Test 2 are used. That is, if we include all villages of any size at all in the sample, it becomes apparent that Raleigh and Greensboro extend their trading area farther than was at first assumed, but extend it in an unspectacular manner into the more or less rural areas. Figure 2-2 verifies this finding. Why these two cities should have this particular drawing power among the smallest towns is probably the result of a complex of economic, social, and geographical reasons which would bear further investigation.

The Winston-Salem area becomes even more of a puzzle when the two b values are compared, for with Test 2, the b value doubles itself and distance is revealed as much more important for Winston-Salem than it appeared to be in Test 1. Probably the most likely explanation of this is that by using the standards of Test 2 the Winston-Salem sample was almost doubled in size, with a resultant effect on the values obtained in this way which is probably more representative of the true situation. One of the effects of the second test is to increase the geographical trading area of each city. The changes of the b value in the regression equation suggest that effect of distance is not uniform. In other words, as you get farther from the city, the effect of additional distance on department-store sales changes; moreover, the change in the present sample does not appear to be uniform. Between the two tests, the b value for Winston-Salem increases, showing an increasing effect of distance, while the b value for Raleigh falls, showing a decreasing effect. This points up the fact that interrelations between communities are very complex and require a careful study of the entire geographical area.

With the exception of Winston-Salem, all of the correlation coefficients are less in Test 2 as compared with Test 1. This supports our supposition that as distance increases, its power to explain or account for department-store sales diminishes. But we have the exception of Winston-Salem which presumably finds a relatively rich trade territory in the northwest portion of the state at quite a distance from the city itself.

The equations shown above could be used to obtain estimates of the overlap between cities. Assume, as an example, that there is a town exactly midway between Charlotte and Greensboro, that is, 45 miles from each of these cities. If we substitute 45 into the regression equations for Charlotte and for Greensboro, we find the expected number of charge accounts per 1,000 population.

If such a substitution is made in the appropriate equations of the second set, we find that we would expect the intermediate town to have 43 charge-account customers per 1,000 population in Charlotte and 49 in Greensboro. Thus it is feasible to use our equation in estimating overlap of retail areas of various cities. No attempt is made to present systematic evidence on overlap derived from the equations because this would simply involve choosing arbitrary values to substitute into the equations.

To summarize the previous findings, the numerical value of the correlation between distance and out-of-town retail trade depends on what requirements are set up to define the "out-of-town" area. Since North Carolina is predominantly a state of small communities, perhaps Test 2, including all towns of more than 100 people, is the more appropriate. If this is the case, then the coefficient of distance (the b value) appears to be between 0.7 and 1.4, or in the neighborhood of 1.0. This is confirmed by the fact that when the data for all five cities are combined (using the requirements of Test 2) the regression equation is $\log X_{12} = 3.0164 - 0.8238 \log X_2$ (X_2 being distance and X_1 the number of accounts), and the coefficient of distance is thus slightly over 0.8. This figure is in fairly close agreement with the exponent of distance of unity which was obtained by Zipf (1949). However, Reilly (1929) concluded that the exponent was 2, and Carroll (1955) found a coefficient of distance of about 2.8. (This last was the result from a sample of long-distance telephone calls.) Certainly, further study and a considerably more extensive sample are necessary before a definitive statement can be made as to the exact relationship of distance and trade in the Piedmont Crescent. On the basis of the present data, it would appear that the charge-account-distance relationship is not more than unity; at least, it does not approach 2 or 3.

A second type of model used in investigating economic interaction in the Crescent is also based on distance, although in a different manner. This model utilizes the commercial attraction concept based on the gravity methods employed by Zipf (1949) and Stewart (1950), with certain variations which were necessary to fit the charge-account data into this model.

For each major city, the towns that had 100 or more inhabitants and 15 or more accounts per 1,000 population in the city in question were grouped according to their distance from the city. That is, all towns from 0 to 19 miles from the city were put into Group 1; all those from 20 to 39 miles became Group 2; all those from 40 to 59 miles, Group 3; those from 60 to 79, Group 4; and all those 80 miles or more became Group 5. These intervals were arbitrarily set up on the assumption that the first group would involve about a half-hour's trip to the city; the second, about an hour; the third, an hour and a half, and so on.

The mean distance of each group was computed and also the total population of each group. These figures were designated, respectively, as D and P_b. The population of the city was designated as P_a, and this figure was paired with P_b and D for each group. A value obtained by multiplying P_a by P_b and dividing by D was computed and designated as X_2, or the independent variable, for each group. The dependent variable, X_1, was the total number of charge accounts carried by each group in the city. There were thus five pairs of items for each city. Correlation coefficients were computed for each city, with highly significant results.

CITY	CORRELATION COEFFICIENT
Durham	.78
Raleigh	.85
Greensboro	.90
Winston-Salem	.94
Charlotte	.68

These coefficients are all positive in sign, since when D increases, the X_2 value decreases in size, as X_1, the number of accounts, is also decreasing.

For each city, then, an estimate of the commerical attraction, which is a numerical expression of the relative drawing power of the cities, was computed, using the formula

$$CA = r^2 \sum \frac{P_a P_b}{D_{ab}}$$

where r^2 is the correlation coefficient squared, P_a is the population of the city, P_b the population of all the towns included in the group, and D_{ab} is the average distance of that group of towns from the city.

We assume that there is a certain quantum of commercial attraction interacting between the cities at any one time. The total figure or the figures for each city are not very helpful when the absolute amount is considered, because we have little data on similar values for other groups of cities to use as a basis for comparison and judgment. If the figures are expressed as percentages of the total (as they are in the table), they indicate the relative strengths of the cities.

CITY	PER CENT OF TOTAL
Durham	7.25
Raleigh	9.75
Greensboro	29.27
Winston-Salem	20.17
Charlotte	33.56

With respect to out-of-town retail-drawing power, these percentages are much as we might expect, with the possible exception that Raleigh's share is smaller than we would have been led to believe on the basis of the figures. This is no doubt partially explained by the fact that while the Raleigh area does have several long off-shoots of retail trade, none of these reaches into a heavily populated area, and none of them involves a large number of buyers.

The general impression obtained from the commercial attraction model bears out those indicated by Test 2 of the first model. As the preceding percentages show, there are two powerful retail centers (Greensboro and Charlotte) and another quite strong one (Winston-Salem) in fairly close proximity to each other, indicating the probability of considerable overlap among these cities. The Raleigh-Durham area, as before, appears to be the weak link in the chain. The commercial attraction figures are so much smaller for these two cities that one must speculate on whether these cities are sufficiently similar to the other three to be considered a part of the same economic area.

As pointed out in the preceding section, any conclusions drawn about the Piedmont Crescent as to the economic basis of the polynucleation hypothesis must at present be tentative and indicative only of tendencies rather than absolute conclusions. However, on the basis of the charge-account data collected for this study, it appears that the polynucleation hypothesis has considerable merit, particularly with regard to the Greensboro–Winston-Salem–Charlotte area, which shows a fairly large amount of interarea trade. Whether the Durham-Raleigh area is linked strongly enough with the western area to be included in the same economic entity is difficult to say on the basis of the present data; but in view of the changes that occurred in the overall picture when the sample was enlarged, it is likely that with an even more extensive sample we would find that this eastern section, too, is in some degree tied into the Crescent economically and socially. Certainly, there is enough evidence of polynucleation to make further study and comparison with similar areas worthwhile.

Wholesale and Industrial Activity and Economic Integration

We continue the discussion of economic integration in the Piedmont Crescent employing tools of analysis similar to those used above and extending their application to other areas of activity. Where previously we dealt with retail trade, here we will be concerned with wholesale and industrial trade as reflected by intercity commodity flows.

At the outset it should be noted that the scope of study becomes more narrowly defined. Where previously the investigation dealt with the major Crescent cities and their geographical area of influence, here we deal solely with the five major cities, their influence and importance as compared one with the other. The cities involved are North Carolina's most important members of the Piedmont Crescent, namely, Charlotte, Winston-Salem, Greensboro, Durham, and Raleigh. This restriction to the major cities permits a somewhat more elaborate analysis than was possible for the retail trade area.

The data which are considered indicative of intercity commodity flows are truck haulings between the Crescent cities, which were collected at strategic weighing stations along the main traffic arteries of the Crescent. During the same season and for like periods of time, bills of lading of carriers passing these points were photographed; later these were classified according to city of origin and destination and the weights connected with each tabulated. This process yielded a number of tables which provide the basic data for the following analysis.

The methodology used here employs various statistical techniques and adopts a rigorous definition of gravitational attraction. The major portion of the analysis is devoted to applying this gravity model to the Piedmont Crescent and then interpreting its results. One of the chief benefits gained from such a method is that it yields a "coefficient of attraction" for each city involved and for each area of activity investigated. These coefficients invite comparisons with each other and with those of similar studies made in other localities. The analysis finally leads to a single statistic which indicates the degree of integration between the cities involved; this statistic, too, is most illuminating when used comparatively.

Lying at the core of the following analysis is the definition of gravitational attraction; it is defined formally by the equation

$$G = k \sum_{j=1}^{n} \frac{P_i P_j}{D_{ij}}$$

where k is a constant coefficient of determination, P_i is the population of city i; P_j is the population of city j where j goes from 1 to n; and D_{ij} is the distance between cities i and j.

Distance may be considered as the friction to be overcome before interaction can take place in any given sphere of activity. It is intuitively obvious that it bears an inverse relationship to interaction, but this fact is rigorously borne out in the succeeding regression analysis. Another bit of information pertinent to the gravity model may also be gleaned from the regression. The distance factor has for some time been a source of much debate among theoreticians who suggest that impact of distance is not uniform from region to region, and therefore its relationship to the basic equation is not a simple inverse one but rather one in which distance is raised to some power. Indeed, the equation is frequently written in the form

$$G = k \sum_{j=1}^{n} \frac{P_i P_j}{D_{ij}^{\alpha}}$$

where $\alpha = f(1/P_j)$, $g(1/D_{ij})$ or some constant whose proposed value

Table 2-1. Commodity Flows between Principal Crescent Cities in North Carolina, 1958

FROM	FREIGHT IN THOUSANDS OF POUNDS SHIPPED TO				
	GREENSBORO	RALEIGH	CHARLOTTE	WINSTON-SALEM	DURHAM
Greensboro	. . .	125.8	230.0	623.8	22.5 [a]
Raleigh	191.9	. . .	96.5	58.3	8.5 [a]
Charlotte	138.4	130.5	. . .	285.3	125.6
Winston-Salem	579.6	100.3	307.4	. . .	28.4 [a]
Durham	255.8	10.1 [a]	76.3	8.5 [a]	. . .

[a] Outside 2 standard deviations from regression line; omitted from calculations.

has varied from less than unity to more than 3. The value of this exponent is often determined by the b_{12} value of a regression line such as the one to be presented. Since the calculations yield a b_{12} value of 1.0694, we shall proceed using unity as the exponent of distance in the gravity equation.

Table 2-1 contains a portion of the data derived from the sample; column one designates the city of origin, and columns two through six the cities of destination and the quantity shipped. For example 125.8 thousand pounds of freight were shipped from Greensboro to Raleigh, and 230.0 thousand pounds were shipped from Greensboro to Charlotte, etc. Unfortunately, with respect to Durham the sample has proved inadequate on a few items; items falling outside a locus two standard deviations from the calculated regression line were omitted from the calculations.

Figure 2-3 identifies that part of the Crescent being investigated and indicates highway distances between cities. We observe that as distance increases freight shipped decreases rapidly; however, as distance continues to increase the decrease in tonnage becomes less rapid, virtually leveling off. If this locus were represented geometrically, it would resemble a second-degree curve which approaches the X-axis asymptotically. Variables so related may be translated into logarithms and the computations made simpler by virtue of the fact that the locus is transformed into a straight line (see Figure 2-4).

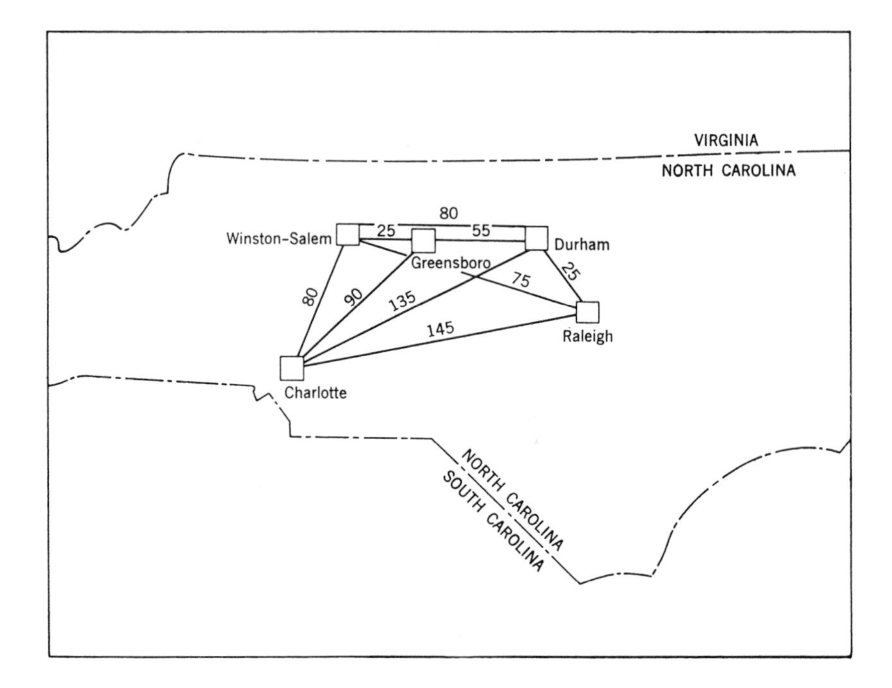

Figure 2-3. Highway distances between major Crescent cities in North Carolina.

A regression computation showing weight of goods shipped as a function of distance was undertaken. The computations produced a number of interesting results. We have already mentioned the b_{12} value and its relation to the gravity model. The estimating equation whose locus (a straight line) is plotted in Figure 2-4 has the property that the sum of the computed values is equal to the sum of the observed values and, within the limits of computational accuracy, the sum of the deviations about the line is zero. The equation, which is $\log X_{12} = 4.2838 - 1.0694 \log X_2$, proves useful in estimating values of the dependent variable (i.e., amount of freight) for given values of the independent variable (i.e., distance).

Continuing, we may also note the relatively strong correlation coefficient ($r_{12} = -.85$), the negative sign indicating the inverse relationship between distance and weight. The coefficient of determination ($r_{12}^2 = .72$) permits the following statement: approximately 72 per cent of the variation in weight can be accounted for by the variation in distance.

The existence of a correlation coefficient gives no assurance of the existence of a causal relationship between the variables; indeed, the relationship may be due purely to chance. This is the null hypothesis considered and subsequently rejected by the significance test. With regard to the foregoing analysis, this allows us to state that the correlation coefficient is too great to be believed to have come by chance from a population in which there is no relationship between the variables.

The regression analysis yields a b_{12} value of 1.0694, which we round to 1 and use as the distance exponent in a further application of the gravity model to the Crescent cities.

The next task is to determine the value of the constant k. As previously noted, this is the coefficient of determination, or literally stated, the proportion of variation in interaction which can be accounted for by variations in population and distance. Specifically it is the r_{12}^2 value of a regression of X_1 on X_2, where X_1 is the freight shipped and X_2 is the ratio P_iP_j/D_{ij}. From the information given in

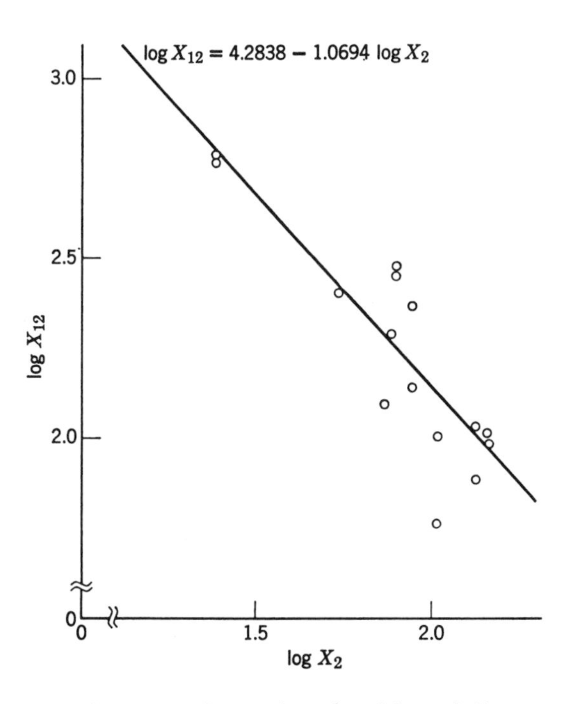

Figure 2-4. Regression of weight and distance shipped for freight in the Piedmont Crescent.

Table 2-2. Population-Distance Ratios

	GREENSBORO	RALEIGH	CHARLOTTE	WINSTON-SALEM	DURHAM
Greensboro	. . .	71.4	124.0	276.8	106.9
Raleigh	71.4	. . .	74.5	63.8	227.5
Charlotte	124.0	74.5	. . .	174.4	87.8
Winston-Salem	276.8	63.8	174.4	. . .	91.8
Durham	106.9	227.5	87.8	91.8	. . .

Figure 2-3, these ratios are computed and recorded in Table 2-2. These ratios are used as the independent variables in a regression equation in which weight of goods shipped is the dependent variable. This will lead to a value for *k*.

The results here are subject to the same type of interpretation as given before. The scatter points and the estimating equation, which is $X_{12} = -30.8 + 2.04X_2$, are plotted in Figure 2-5. Note that the correlation, although of a different geometric nature, has been in-

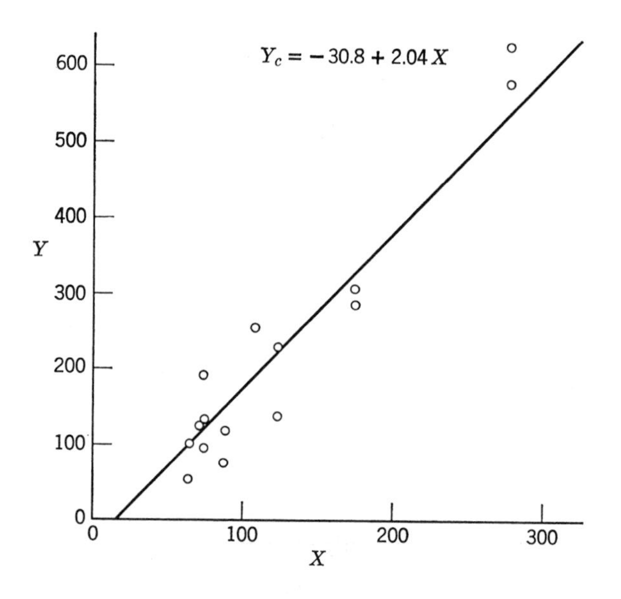

Figure 2-5. Regression of weight of goods shipped between Piedmont cities on population-distance ratios.

creased by adding the population factor. Thus the correlation coefficient is .90, and approximately 81 per cent of the variation in freight shipped can be accounted for by variations in the population-distance ratio. This is precisely the statistic we set out to find, and it will appear later as the constant k used in determining the coefficient of gravitational attraction for each individual city; ascertaining these coefficients is the final step in completing the model application in the wholesale-industrial sphere.

The gravity equation presented earlier may be written in another form

$$CA_i = k\left(\frac{P_iP_1}{D_{i1}} + \frac{P_iP_2}{D_{i2}} + \cdots \frac{P_iP_{i-1}}{D_{i,i-1}} + \frac{P_iP_{i+1}}{D_{i,i+1}} + \cdots \frac{P_iP_n}{D_{in}}\right)$$

where the coefficient of gravitational attraction for any city i is the product of k and the sum of the appropriate population-distance ratios. The results of applying this equation are given in the table.

CITIES	CA_i	PER CENT OF TOTAL
Winston-Salem	497.6	23.4
Greensboro	474.9	22.3
Durham	421.5	19.8
Charlotte	377.8	17.7
Raleigh	358.5	16.8
Total	2,130.3	100.0

Although the coefficients are the most illuminating when contrasted with comparable statistics of studies of other localities, they permit a variety of inferences to be made regarding integration and other economic characteristics. Notice, for example, that Winston-Salem occupies the dominant position with respect to commercial attraction among the cities whereas Raleigh has the least power to attract of the five. It may also be observed that per cent values in the preceding tabulation are all of the same order of magnitude. This suggests that no one city dominates the area. Hence the relation is not that of planet and satellite but that of coordinate entities. This adds support to the hypothesis that this is a polynucleated area.

Other characteristics emerge when the coefficients are used in conjunction with additional truck data afforded by the sample. The data are arranged according to two geographical areas: (1) the North Carolina Piedmont area in which the named cities are located, and (2) the rest of the country outside this area. The "in-out" column of the tabulation below shows the amount of freight in thousands of pounds originating at each city and terminating somewhere outside the Crescent; the "out-in" column shows the freight originating outside the Crescent and terminating in each of the given cities.

	IN-OUT	OUT-IN
Charlotte	1,579.7	1,674.4
Greensboro	1,144.9	1,167.0
Winston-Salem	517.5	572.0
Raleigh	147.6	513.4
Durham	98.9	431.2

By using the data on both internal and external freight shipped in combination, we can infer, for example, that Charlotte has a strong external orientation since its gravity coefficient is the second lowest with respect to attraction among the Piedmont cities, yet it exchanges the largest quantity of goods with outside areas. Greensboro, it would seem, has both a strong internal and external orientation, while Winston-Salem is strongly oriented internally. Raleigh and Durham, while fairly strong within the Piedmont, are less so externally.

Thus Charlotte emerges as the city with the strongest external orientation, but it does not emerge as the city that overwhelmingly dominates the Crescent. Winston-Salem, Greensboro, and Durham show stronger internal commercial attraction, and Raleigh is not far behind Charlotte. Greensboro emerges as a balanced city strong both within and without the Crescent. Winston-Salem is very strong within the Crescent but not so strong outside.

The final step to be undertaken in this portion of the study refers back to the regression analysis and the locus of the estimating equation, $Y_c = -30.8 + 2.04X$, plotted in Figure 2-5. The coefficient of elasticity along this line gives us, in one useful statistic, the degree of integration among the cities. It is equal to the product of the derivative with respect to X and the ratio of the means, formally:

$$\eta_{yx} = \left(\frac{dY}{dX}\right)\left(\frac{\overline{X}}{\overline{Y}}\right)$$

$$= 2.04\left(\frac{123.5}{221.7}\right)$$

$$= 1.14$$

Traditionally, the possible values that an elasticity coefficient may take are subdivided into three broad categories each revealing the general relationship existing between the variables under scrutiny. For values greater than unity ($\eta_{yx} > 1$) the coefficient is said to be elastic; this signifies that for a given percentage change in the independent variable there is an accompanying but greater percentage change in the dependent variable. For values equal to unity ($\eta_{yx} = 1$) the coefficient is said to be unitary, in which case the variables change *pari passu.* For values less than unity ($\eta_{yx} < 1$) the coefficient is said to be inelastic; here a percentage change in the independent variable is accompanied by a lesser percentage change in the dependent variable.

Hence the coefficient arrived at above ($\eta_{yx} = 1.14$) is elastic and may be interpreted as follows: a 1 per cent change in the population-distance ratio is accompanied by a 1.14 per cent change in the quantity of freight shipped. Obviously, the more highly integrated an area is, the greater would be the change occurring in the quantity of freight shipped; likewise, the less integrated an area is, the less would be the change occurring in the quantity of freight shipped. Thus, the indicator η_{yx} varies directly with the degree of integration indigenous to an area in a particular activity. In the following section this statistic will be used to compare the degree of integration associated with the spheres of activity investigated in this study.

The fact that the elasticity coefficient is greater than unity gives no grounds for asserting that there is, in a loose sense, more than "normal" industrial and wholesale integration within the Piedmont Crescent. In other words, the economic integration in the industrial and wholesale spheres more than overcomes the retarding force of distance.

Telephone Calls as a Measure of Interaction

In the foregoing analysis we have gone through a step-by-step application of the gravity model to the five major Crescent cities. It dealt with one particular segment of the economy, namely, the wholesale-industrial segment. In this section we shift our emphasis to a more broadly defined area, that of over-all socio-economic integration. This, we have assumed, is reflected in the number of toll calls placed between individuals and organizations of the various cities.

The sample was prepared by the traffic department of the Southern Bell Telephone Company. It represents the average toll messages be-

Table 2-3. Toll Calls between Crescent Cities

FROM	CALLS MADE TO: GREENSBORO	RALEIGH	CHARLOTTE	WINSTON-SALEM	DURHAM
Greensboro	. . .	207	455	446	113
Raleigh	230	. . .	348	95	437
Charlotte	504	330	. . .	334	104
Winston-Salem	601	113	402	. . .	61
Durham	158	534	151	61	. . .

tween Crescent cities for a two-day period in August 1958. Table 2-3, containing the sample data, indicates both the cities of origin and destination and the number of calls involved.

The analysis of the telephone data that follows will be undertaken by the same methods used in the analysis of the truck data. Figure 2-6 shows a scatter diagram and a fitted regression line for the telephone data.

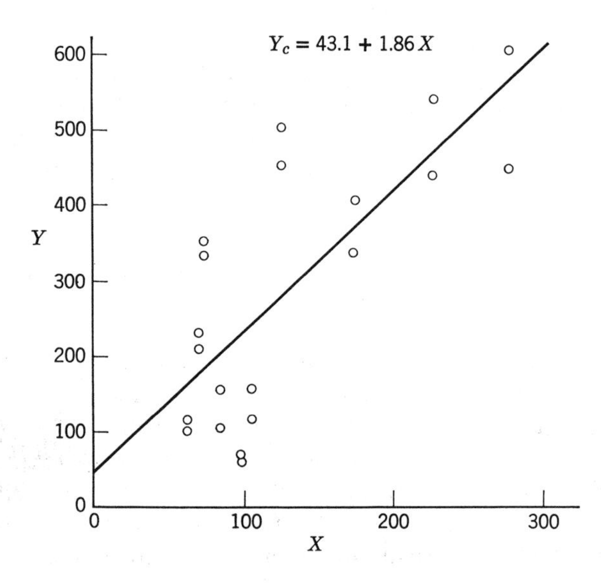

Figure 2-6. Regression of telephone calls on population-distance ratios.

First, in a regression analysis of toll calls on P_iP_j/D_{ij}, we ascertain the coefficient of determination (i.e., r_{12}^2) which is to be used as the constant k in the model. The correlation shows that variations in population-distance ratios account for approximately 56 per cent of the variation in the number of toll calls made between the Piedmont cities, while the positive sign of the correlation coefficient signifies that the variables are directly related.

The locus of the estimating equation $Y_c = 43.1 + 1.86X$ is plotted in Figure 2-6, and while at first glance it may appear that a second-degree curve would more closely fit the data, this is not actually the case. For we find that in fitting a second-degree curve, the data yield the following estimating equation: $Y_c = 41.5 + 1.88X - 0.000068X^2$. Comparing the two equations we see that in the second the Y-intercept (41.5) is only slightly less, the slope at the origin (1.88) only slightly more, and the rate of change of the slope at the origin (0.000068) so small that its influence is negligible except for very large values of X. Since simplicity is desired and no violence is done to the analysis, we accept the straight-line regression as a satisfactory fit of the data.

Again the significance test allows us to reject a null hypothesis that the correlation may have been a chance eventuality from a population in which the two variables are unrelated.

We proceed next to find the coefficients of gravitational attraction using .56, the coefficient of determination, as the value of k in the gravity equation. The results of these computations are given in the table. Comparing these coefficients with those obtained earlier, we

CITIES	CA_i
Winston-Salem	339.8
Greensboro	324.3
Durham	287.8
Charlotte	258.0
Raleigh	244.8

note first that the relative positions of the cities remain unchanged; Winston-Salem exerts the greatest attractive force, followed closely by Greensboro, then Durham, Charlotte, and Raleigh in that order. More importantly, we see that in each case over-all socio-economic attraction among the cities does not reach as great an intensity as their attraction for one another in the wholesale-industrial sphere.

The statement is further substantiated when we examine the degree of socio-economic integration and compare it with that of the wholesale-industrial sphere. The statistic used for this purpose is the coefficient of elasticity along the regression line $Y_c = 43.1 + 1.86X$. When this is calculated in the same way as before we find its value to be 0.85; thus a 1 per cent change in the value of the independent variable is accompanied by an 0.85 per cent change in the value of the dependent variable. This is 29 percentage points less than in the previous case where the η_{yx} value was found to be 1.14. The over-all socio-economic integration appears to be substantially less than the wholesale-industrial integration. Thus the two concepts, attraction and integration, tend mutually to fortify one another and to corroborate the above statement.

However, the question as to whether or not the elasticity coefficient measuring the degree of industrial-wholesale integration is significantly greater than that measuring the degree of over-all socio-economic integration, as indicated by the telephone calls, should be investigated. This is a problem emanating from the use of sampling and statistical techniques. Literally, the difference between the two coefficients may be due simply to chance rather than to any real difference between the areas that they represent. The solution to this problem rests on somewhat complex statistical principles involving transformations, various distributions, and ratio tests, but we will consider only the hypothesis and conclusion.

The hypothesis is that both the elasticity coefficient for the industrial-wholesale data and the elasticity coefficient for the socio-economic data are equal to each other. The test, when it is carried through, shows that we must reject this hypothesis at the 5 per cent significance level. Thus we cannot agree that the difference between the two coefficients is due to chance.

The consequence of this test is that we conclude that the data show that wholesale-industrial interaction in the Piedmont Crescent is stronger than socio-economic interaction. In evaluating this result, it must be recalled that the conclusion is based on only two types of data, each represented by a sample. Thus there are two questions that remain: Would other types of data representing wholesale-industrial interaction and socio-economic interaction show different results? To what extent is each sample representative? It is pointless to conjecture about the first of these questions. With regard to the second question, it may be observed that the freight-data sample was larger than the telephone-call sample.

Conclusions

Is the Crescent a polynucleated urban area? Unfortunately, as was pointed out in the beginning, this question cannot be answered conclusively, but the evidence reported above will support some tentative conclusions. It is to be emphasized that our results do not suggest that the Crescent is an enormous urban region of the future, nor do they show that it is not taking that form. The results do suggest that a marked degree of economic interaction exists between the Crescent cities.

In retail trade the overlapping of trading areas suggests appreciable economic integration. Thus in Figure 2-2, Charlotte overlaps the trading areas of Winston-Salem, Greensboro, and Raleigh. Durham is the only city not competing directly with Charlotte; however, it overlaps Raleigh and Greensboro. Both the figures and the coefficients of attraction suggest however that the Crescent divides into two trading areas, the one made up of Charlotte, Greensboro, and Winston-Salem, and the other including Raleigh and Durham. The coefficients of attraction also suggest that the interaction in the Charlotte–Greensboro–Winston-Salem area is stronger than in the Raleigh-Durham area.

Wholesale and industrial buyers usually range farther afield than the consumers. Consequently, we would expect evidence of more interaction at pre-retail level than at the retail level, and this is decidedly the case in the Crescent.

The coefficients of attraction for the trucking data suggest a substantial amount of interaction. In addition the fact that these coefficients do not vary greatly from city to city suggests that the area is relatively homogeneous with respect to economic interaction and consequently can be thought of as an integrated area. No one city dominates the area as Charlotte does in the retail trade data. Indeed Charlotte's coefficient of attraction is smaller than those of Winston-Salem, Greensboro, and Durham for the trucking data. Finally, we recall that the elasticity coefficient for these freight data is larger than unity and thus indicates a substantial amount of economic integration. All of this evidence suggests strongly an unusual degree of economic integration at the pre-retail level in the Crescent.

The telephone-call data are taken to represent both sociological and economic interaction. Generally speaking, they show less interaction than the other two sets of data. There are many possible explanations for this difference, and it is pointless to conjecture about the apparently weak relationship without further facts. The coefficients of attraction for the telephone data are generally smaller than for the trucking data, although, as in the case of the trucking data, the cities on the ends of our study area, Raleigh and Charlotte, show smaller coefficients than the more central cities. Presumably this is because Charlotte does a good deal of trading with South Carolina and Raleigh with eastern North Carolina, both outside the study area. The elasticity coefficient for the telephone-call data is less than 1 (0.85), an indication of no strong interaction.

Thus, in summary, the economic interactions are strongest in wholesale and industrial trade, rather surprisingly strong in retail trade, but not strong at all for the socio-economic area presented by the telephone-call data.

The great lack of the foregoing analysis is the absence of data from other similar regions that could be compared to the Crescent data. If such data were available we could say that the Crescent is more or less integrated in a specific field of activity than another region. As it stands, we must rely on abstract measures such as the elasticity coefficient.

REFERENCES

Carroll, J. Douglas, Jr. (1955), "Spatial Interaction and the Urban-Metropolitan Description," *Papers and Proceedings of the Regional Science Association*, Vol. 1.

Reilly, William J. (1929), "Methods for the Study of Retail Relationships," *Research Monogram*, No. 4, *University of Texas Bulletin*, No. 2994. Austin, Tex.: University of Texas Bureau of Business Research.

Stewart, John Q. (1950), "Potential of Population and Its Relationship to Marketing," in Reavis Cox and Wroe Alderson (Eds.), *Theory in Marketing*. Homewood, Ill.: Richard D. Irwin.

Zipf, George K. (1949), *Human Behavior and the Principle of Least Effort*. Reading, Mass.: Addison-Wesley Press.

Chapter 3

Labor Mobility in the Crescent

by Robert L. Bunting *

THE MOVEMENT of a worker from one job to another often has widespread effects. Some of these effects, primarily personal to the individual making the change, include changed interpersonal relationships, changed responsibilities, and changed occupational status. Other effects of a job change may be those felt by the members of the worker's family, who often find various aspects of their lives altered—sometimes drastically, as when the move involves geographic change of residence or sharp change in income. Finally, of course, such changes have diverse effects upon the society as a whole, effects that may be reflected in the stability of the community, its values, its standard of living, and so on. Labor mobility, in a word, is a phenomenon of such broad impact as to be of interest to virtually all social scientists.

This chapter is concerned with the impact of mobility upon a region's economizing efforts, that is, upon the region's confrontation with the central economic fact of life: scarcity. It examines the impact of mobility on the sixteen counties in the Piedmont Industrial Crescent, drawing comparisons with characteristics in the three-state area of North Carolina, South Carolina, and Georgia.

The importance of labor mobility to the economizing process has long been appreciated by economists. They have expressed this appreciation by many theoretical and empirical attempts to understand more clearly the causes and effects of worker relocation. These re-

*Acknowledgment is made of the valuable assistance provided to this study by Peter A. Prosper, Jr., Research Assistant.

search efforts have utilized a variety of definitions of the term "labor mobility." The operational definition employed in this chapter is a restricted one: movement of workers from one employer to another.

The economist's interest in labor mobility, however broadly or narrowly defined, is primarily a manifestation of his concern with a broad range of problems commonly referred to as resource-allocation problems. Collectively, they are the central problem of economic theory: how can the community use its limited resources most effectively? This is the problem of economic efficiency which the history of the world suggests is ever present.

It would be out of place here to attempt a detailed description of the means by which the free market mechanism puts resources where they ought to be, according to efficiency criteria. The essence of the process may be seen, however, by brief reference to the structures of prices in the two markets of the economist's competitive model. The first—the "market for final products"—consists of a set of interrelated prices on the economic goods desired by the community; this price structure constitutes a form of social consensus on the way resources should be used. The second—the "market for factors of production" —consists of a structure of prices of the instruments of production, such as the services of "land" or "labor"; this is the market that, in effect, carries out the instructions of the community, as those instructions are revealed by the final-products price structure. For any particular set of basic conditions—the quantity and quality of resources available, the productive and organizational techniques known, and the system of priorities held by the members of the society—the interplay of market forces will result in equilibrium price structures in these two markets which provide optimum rates of production and consumption. Any change in those basic conditions will bring about changes in the two structures of prices which will guide the system to a new equilibrium position, involving new rates of production and consumption.

Students of resource use focus their attention primarily upon the reallocative effectiveness of the market for factors of production. The importance of this area of study becomes apparent with only a brief survey of the magnitude of the task in the United States today. For many aspects of the given conditions—resources, technology, and tastes —are in a constant state of change. The population is growing; the labor force is changing in size and composition; techniques of production literally change from day to day with discoveries that bring about as much alteration in the economic landscape within a few years as, not so long ago, took place in a century or two; and so on. The point is obvious: with such powerful forces of change constantly pressing upon it, the economy's ability to adapt is a matter of tremendous importance.

The role of this labor-mobility study is immediately apparent. It is to provide new increments of knowledge about actual movement of the most important resource of all, labor, in a particular sector of the economy. In so doing it will provide a firmer basis for judgments concerning the allocative effectiveness of the regional economy. It is to be hoped that it will thereby contribute to the improvement of those public-policy decisions, at both state and local levels in North and South Carolina, resting upon such judgments.

The present chapter has three parts. The first gets directly at the effectiveness of the labor market in this region by comparing its mobility rates with those of other areas. The second part attempts to use the same basic data to test indirectly the validity of referring to the Crescent as a metropolitan unit. The third part is an effort to measure the influence of labor mobility into and out of the Crescent upon the size and composition of its labor force.

The data to be explored here were obtained from the Bureau of Old-Age and Survivors Insurance (BOASI). The particular workers investigated in this study are those who (*a*) were in the Bureau's continuous work history sample and (*b*) worked at some time during 1953 in covered employment in North Carolina, South Carolina, or Georgia. The number of workers was 30,614. Since the continuous work-history sample contains 1 per cent of the workers covered by Old-Age and Survivors Insurance, the total population represented was more than 3 million. The form of these data makes it possible to follow roughly a worker from job to job.

These BOASI data are increasingly being recognized as a major source of information about worker mobility. Mention should be made, however, of certain restrictions upon their usefulness which derive from inherent limitations or from decisions regarding research procedures.

1. Approximately 21 per cent of civilian employment was not covered by the Old-Age and Survivors Insurance program in 1953.

2. The data provide no direct information about the occupation of covered workers.

3. A mobile worker is defined here as one who had two or more

employers during the year. Thus intrafirm job changes are not recorded. On the other hand, dual jobholders—workers holding two jobs simultaneously—are counted as mobile workers.

4. The location of some workers was unknown. For certain parts of the investigation it was necessary to exclude these workers, who are referred to as "state-wide" workers. Another group, the self-employed, was excluded entirely.

It seems probable that the net effect of these factors is to cause the data presented here to understate the extent of job change.[1]

Extent and Characteristics of Labor Mobility

To trace how much labor movement actually takes place and the degree to which labor mobility is more characteristic of certain types of workers than others, flows are examined in the sixteen Crescent counties—twelve in North Carolina (Wake, Durham, Orange, Alamance, Guilford, Forsyth, Randolph, Davidson, Rowan, Cabarrus, Mecklenburg, and Gaston) and four in South Carolina (York, Cherokee, Spartanburg, and Greenville). In order to increase the meaningfulness of the information about mobility in the Crescent, comparative data are provided for five other groupings of counties in North Carolina, South Carolina, and Georgia. The six comparative areas are the following:

Area Group One: Atlanta metropolitan area.

Area Group Two: All metropolitan areas in the three states, except Atlanta and those included in the Crescent.

Area Group Three: Piedmont Industrial Crescent.

Area Group Four: All nonmetropolitan, non-Crescent counties in North Carolina.

Area Group Five: All nonmetropolitan, non-Crescent counties in South Carolina.

Area Group Six: All nonmetropolitan counties in Georgia.

The metropolitan areas are defined, with minor modifications, according to 1950 Census definitions of standard metropolitan areas.

At the outset, it may be noted that the total number of workers in the Crescent sample was 6,984. Of these, 1,836 or 26.3 per cent were mobile as that term is used here; and 883 of the mobile workers (12.6

Table 3-1. Mobility among Workers of Six Area Groups Which Constitute the Three States of North Carolina, South Carolina, and Georgia, 1953

MOBILITY STATUS	AREA GROUPS						
	ONE	TWO	THREE [a]	FOUR	FIVE	SIX	ALL
Number of workers	3,108	3,901	6,984	5,457	2,728	4,520	26,698
Percentage nonmobile	69.9	71.5	73.7	73.4	77.4	73.2	73.2
Percentage mobile	30.1	28.5	26.3	26.6	22.6	26.8	26.8
Migrants	16.0	14.9	12.6	14.5	12.3	15.8	14.2
Nonmigrants	14.1	13.6	13.6	12.2	10.3	10.9	12.6

[a] The Piedmont Industrial Crescent.

Note. For similar percentages based on highly comparable data, see Bogue (1952), Table VI-4. The Bogue percentages show a higher range, from 24 to 35, with an over-all average of 30.

per cent of all workers) were migrants, that is, workers who crossed county lines. Table 3-1 makes possible a comparison of these results with those of the other five area groupings and with the total of all six groups together.

The last column of the table shows that slightly more than one of every four covered workers in the three-state area had more than one employer during the year. The percentage of mobile workers whose moves carry them across county lines is generally larger than that of workers who are mobile within the counties. This is so for all area groupings combined and for each of the groupings individually, except for the Crescent, where non-migrants exceed migrants by one percentage point.

Thus far the mobility of labor has been discussed as if labor were homogeneous. In fact, many studies have indicated that mobility patterns vary among different groups of workers. Among the most completely documented of these variations are those associated with sex, race, and age. More specifically, previous studies have generally shown that mobility decreases as age increases, that males are more mobile than females, and that Negroes are more mobile than non-

Negroes. (See Aaronson and Keller, 1946; Bakke, Hauser, Palmer, Yoder, and Kerr, 1954; Palmer, 1954; and Reynolds, 1951.)

The sample of workers drawn from the Crescent was investigated in a preliminary fashion to see if it appeared that these same mobility patterns would occur. The results presented in Table 3-2 bear out the findings of these earlier studies. They show that the percentage of males who change jobs is greater than that of females, and migrants are more numerous relative to nonmigrants among males than among females. Similarly, Negroes are more mobile and migratory than non-Negroes, and workers less than 30 years old are more mobile and migratory than those over 30.

When cross-tabulations of sex, race, and age are introduced, additional insights into labor mobility patterns are possible.[2] Sex differences in mobility are both pronounced and pervasive. For non-Negroes, Negroes, the two combined, and for both age classes in each of these race categories, the male mobility rate is greater than that for females. For all classes combined, the male rate exceeds the female rate by slightly more than 60 per cent, but the range of variation in the percentage amount by which the male rate exceeds the female rate is wide, from 23.4 per cent (younger non-Negroes) to 185.4 per cent (older Negroes). For both races the sex differential grows as age increases, since the female mobility rates fall off more rapidly than do those of the males. As implied above, there were no negative differentials, that is, no classes in which the female rate was greater than the male rate.

Table 3-2. Mobility Percentages of Crescent Workers by Sex, Age, and Race

		SEX		AGE		RACE	
MOBILITY STATUS	TOTAL	MALE	FEMALE	LESS THAN 30	30 AND OVER [a]	NON-NEGRO	NEGRO
Nonmobile	73.7	69.0	80.8	66.1	78.2	75.9	65.3
Mobile	26.3	31.0	19.2	33.9	21.8	24.1	34.7
Migrants	12.6	16.4	6.9	17.0	10.1	11.4	17.5
Nonmigrants	13.6	14.6	12.3	16.9	11.7	12.7	17.2

[a] Includes age unknown.

The direction of age differences in mobility is constant also. For all classes, the younger workers are more mobile than the older ones. For both races and sexes combined, the younger worker mobility rate is 55.5 per cent greater than that of older workers; and the age differential is least (39.7 per cent) among non-Negro males and greatest (136.2 per cent) among Negro females.

The differential between the mobility rates by race is a substantial 44.0 per cent, the Negro rate being the greater. In contrast with the sex and age patterns described above, however, this differential is not consistent. It is large among male workers but nonexistent among female workers. More exactly, the Negro mobility rates exceed the non-Negro rates for both age classes of males by more than 50 per cent. Among females, however, the Negro rate is 12.0 per cent greater than the non-Negro rate among younger workers, whereas it is 3.0 per cent smaller among older workers. Combining these two female-age classes provides rates that are almost equal.

The foregoing investigation has shown that the aggregate mobility rates for Crescent workers as a group are resultants of corresponding rates for various subgroups among which there is a substantial amount of diversity. It has shown, moreover, that this diversity obtains for sex, race, and age classes independently, that is, each of these worker characteristics seems to exert a separate influence on mobility. A further question is whether the Crescent mobility patterns are typical in these respects. A check of the other areas examined in the three states indicates that the patterns found in the Crescent are indeed typical of those for the other area groups and for the three-state region as a whole. Sex and age differentials hold for each race class for all areas considered individually and combined. Also confirmed is the fact of a sizable race differential among males, Negroes being more mobile. At the same time comparison reinforces the earlier observation that, among females, the race differential tends in the other direction, with non-Negroes being more mobile.[3]

Thus it is seen that the general level of mobility and the age, sex, and race characteristics of mobile workers in the Crescent are highly similar to those throughout the three-state area. The important question which has not been investigated thus far is the significance of the mobility levels encountered. The South has often been referred to as the region in which the problem of labor immobility is most acute. Bald figures such as those presented here cannot prove or disprove the contention that labor movement is inadequate for purposes of proper resource allocation. There are, however, two other studies which have used BOASI data to produce mobility percentages which are highly comparable with those of this study. Such a comparison may be helpful in indicating the extent to which there are mobility problems peculiar to the region of which the Crescent is a part.

The first of these two studies was done by Aaronson and Keller (1946); it includes data for six separate years, 1938 through 1943. Roughly 1 per cent of all workers covered by Old-Age and Survivors Insurance who worked during these years were included in these nation-wide samples; sample size varied from 277,000 to 465,000 workers. The other study is the investigation by Bogue (1952) of mobility in Michigan and Ohio during the year 1947, which also used a 1 per cent sample of workers drawn from the BOASI files. The total number of workers involved was 54,737. Data from these two studies will be compared with the data of this study, which, as has already been pointed out, are also a BOASI 1 per cent sample, consisting of 30,614 workers who were employed at some time during 1953 in the three-state area of North Carolina, South Carolina, and Georgia.

Mobility percentages computed from the data of these three studies are presented in Table 3-3. Of the six years investigated by Aaronson and Keller (1946), it seems reasonable to look to 1941 as the most satisfactory for purposes of comparison. The extraordinary depression effects are not as strong as in the preceding three years and the equally abnormal effects of the war are not nearly as pronounced as in the following two years. Fortunately, the form of these 1941 data was such as to make it possible to compare mobility rates within sex and race classes with those of the Bogue study (1952) and of the present study.

The general picture presented by the data in Table 3-3 is simple to characterize. The mobility rates of this study are smaller than those of the other two. This is true in the aggregate, within sex classes, race classes, and sex-race classes, almost without exception. The largest differences in mobility rates are found among the female workers. Thus it appears that mobility is generally lower among Southern workers, especially among Southern female workers, than among workers in Michigan and Ohio and in the United States as a whole. However, there are many factors other than geographic location which could explain the observed differences. Several of the more obvious of these deserve mention.

First of all, over the years the coverage of the Old-Age and Survivors Insurance Program has increased. The 1953 sample covered a larger proportion of the total labor force than did those of the earlier years.

Table 3-3. Mobility Percentages of Three Studies Using Old-Age and Survivors Insurance Data, by Sex and Race

SEX AND RACE	MOBILITY PERCENTAGES BY AUTHORS OF THE THREE STUDIES: AARONSON AND KELLER (1946, p. 70) [a]	BOGUE (1952, p. 26)	BUNTING
Year of data	1941	1947	1953
All workers	32.9	33	29.3
males	35.6	35	34.3
females	25.8	28	20.8
Non-Negroes	32.2	33	27.6
males	34.8	34	31.6
females	26.1	28	21.3
Negroes	40.2	40	34.6
males	44.3	44	41.7
females	18.7	25	18.9

[a] Aaronson and Keller (1946, p. 13) provide mobility percentages for six years, as follows:

1938—22.9 1939—25.2 1940—26.9
1941—32.9 1942—38.1 1943—36.6

The percentages of the labor force covered in the years 1941, 1947, and 1953, respectively, were approximately 60, 60, and 79 (Aaronson and Keller, 1946; U. S. Department of Commerce, 1948; U. S. Department of Commerce and U. S. Department of Health, Education, and Welfare, 1955). What sort of effect would this have? The program was put into operation on a partial coverage basis, with most of manufacturing industry being covered from the beginning. Domestic service and agricultural labor were brought under the program much later. It is probably accurate to say that generally the additions to coverage which have taken place since the outset of the program have brought in workers with fewer skills, less secure attachments to the labor force, and less secure attachments to particular jobs. Such workers tend to be more mobile. Thus, increased coverage would probably tend to make the 1953 rates greater than those for 1941 and 1947.

Another factor is the level of unemployment. In general, mobility is thought to be inversely related to the level of unemployment, workers being less liable to quit in search of better jobs if the number of alternative job opportunities is small. Conditions in 1953 were apparently conducive to relatively high mobility, the unemployment percentages being 2.5 for 1953, 3.6 for 1947, and 9.9 for 1941. (See U. S. Bureau of the Budget, 1955, p. 23.)

A third factor is the stage of the business cycle. This affects mobility, independently of its effect upon the level of employment per se, through its effect upon expectations concerning changes in the level of employment opportunities. Periods of boom and full employment represent periods of optimism, and periods of decline and depression represent periods of pessimism—in labor markets as elsewhere. All three of these years were associated primarily with the upswing or the top of the cycle, periods of optimism. It would be hazardous, on the basis of present knowledge, to try to distinguish among them in this connection.

A fourth factor which might underlie the observed mobility differences is some sort of abnormal stress or strain involving special economic adjustment. For these three years, of course, the primary such factor was war. The very great mobility rate shown in Table 3-3 for 1942, over and above the level of say, 1947, is surely explained primarily by the tremendous dislocation associated with reorienting our economy toward the creation and support of a mammoth war machine. But it would again be risky to attempt to specify one of these years as having its mobility rates most affected. For none of the three study years compared in Table 3-3 stands out as one of extraordinary mobility associated with moving into or moving out of a war economy.

Since age has been shown to be a factor in labor mobility, the fact that the data of Table 3-3 were not standardized for age might explain the observed mobility differences. In 1950 the median age of the United States population as a whole was 30.2 years, that of the East North Central States was 31.2, and that of the South Atlantic States was 27.3. (U. S. Bureau of the Census, 1953, Table 1.) The lower median age in the South would probably tend to push in the direction of making mobility rates of this study greater than those of the other two earlier studies.

Another determinant of mobility is occupation. Certain occupational categories, such as professional, technical, and kindred workers, tend to be characterized by low mobility, whereas others, such as farmers and farm managers, tend to be characterized by high mobility. (U. S. Bureau of the Census, 1957, Table 2.) Thus areas could differ in the aggregate mobility rates of their work forces if the occupational composition of those work forces varied. Examination of the distribution of occupational groups by region shows that the South Atlantic States tend to contain relatively fewer of the low mobility workers and relatively more of the high mobility workers. (U. S. Bureau of the Census, 1952, Table 79.)

Similarly, the extent of unionism is often referred to as an important influence on mobility. Parnes (1954, p. 125) has observed that "Although the empirical evidence concerning the relative mobility of union and nonunion workers is inconclusive, there seems to be a consensus among students of the labor market that the net effect of trade unionism has been to diminish labor mobility." But it is common knowledge that union membership is relatively low and union power relatively less in the South. Again, on the basis of this factor alone, mobility rates in the South should be higher than those in other parts of the country.

A final factor affecting mobility will be called the secular influence. It is defined to include a rather loose grouping of aspects of the economy which have changed over the years from 1941 to 1953. Included in this group are, first, changes in the framework of formal (legal) and informal (customary) rules and regulations within which buyers and sellers in labor markets operate. On the basis of present knowledge very little can be said about the aggregate impact of these changes. Second, changes occur in institutional arrangements which obviously tend to inhibit worker mobility, such as the growth of union and nonunion seniority programs, pension plans, and other welfare benefits. Third, there is a group of related factors which tend to make for wider knowledge of and easier access to alternative job opportunities. Among these are the increase in job density associated both with growth of the economy and with urbanization, and the vast expansion of transportation facilities in terms of highway construction. A fourth factor is a change in attitude of workers. There appears to be an increasingly widespread disposition to view change in residence and geographic area as something not especially extraordinary, and even as something desirable in its own right. Omitting (as unknown) the first of these secular factors, the best judgment of the net impact of the factors would appear to be in the direction of a secular increase in mobility.

The preceding brief analysis probably recognizes the major forces which could cause the 1953 rates to differ from the earlier ones, but it is impossible, on the basis of present knowledge, to combine these forces into an adjustment index which would properly reflect their relative influences. Nevertheless, it does seem reasonable to express the judgment that they do not explain the differential, for they clearly tend in the other direction. That is, in combination their effect would be to make the 1953 rates exceed those of earlier years. Thus the evidence tends to support those labor-market observers who have suggested that mobility in the South is less than in other sections of the country. The difference in rates is not great among male workers. However, it does appear to be appreciable among females. There is an obvious need for further study of the causes and significance of this phenomenon. It may indeed be true that worker attitudes or the industrial structure within which Southern workers operate tend to make mobility less than in other parts of the country, thereby posing the possibility of a resource-use problem. If so, it may well be that action designed to increase labor mobility, such as further development of job informational services, could profitably be undertaken by Southern states.

"Metropolitan-ness" of the Urban Crescent

With this picture of the mobility characteristics in the Crescent and other areas, we might ask: What can labor mobility tell us about the meaningfulness of referring to the Crescent as a metropolitan region? As brought out in the last chapter, the patterns of economic interaction in some of the Crescent city clusters possess characteristics that bear a resemblance to the conventional single-centered metropolitan area. Labor mobility characteristics offer still another opportunity to test an underlying hypothesis of the Crescent studies, namely, that the Crescent is a metropolitan-like region, possibly an embryo belt of urbanization that will become continuously developed in the years ahead.

This region contains several important standard metropolitan areas, and therefore it is to be expected that the area as a whole will show metropolitan traits. For example, it is probably safe to predict that the percentage of highly trained professional people is greater in the Crescent than in, say, the nonmetropolitan sections of Georgia. Here the aim is to use mobility data to test for a degree of "metropolitan-ness" greater than that to be expected from observation of the relative size of the metropolitan and nonmetropolitan components. If the test produces positive results, the mobility data will tend to support the notion that the Crescent has a metropolitan unity which is, in some sense, greater than the sum of its parts. If, on the other hand, the data lean in the other direction, this will suggest that the Crescent may not be usefully treated as a metropolitan region for purposes of economic analysis.

The notion that a study of the mobility characteristics of the Crescent might be revealing as regards its metropolitan-ness is implicit in a finding from the Bogue study. One of the most persistent characteristics of the data which he explored was the tendency for a larger portion of the movement of workers in nonmetropolitan areas to involve crossing county lines than that of workers in metropolitan areas. (Bogue, 1952, p. 88.)

Preliminary calculations made it appear that this condition prevailed in the three-state area in 1953. Thus total migrants (workers with two or more employers in different counties) as a percentage of total mobile workers (all workers with two or more employers) were found to be 54.8 per cent for all nonmetropolitan workers throughout the area and 51.1 per cent for the metropolitan workers. Comparable differences existed when the percentages were recomputed within sex categories, the female difference being 6.5 percentage points and the male difference being 2.6 percentage points.

Using this characteristic of the data, the test of Crescent metropolitan-ness consists of two parts. First, the result obtained in the preliminary calculations just described must be verified by comparing migration rates for specific groupings of metropolitan areas and nonmetropolitan areas within these three states. The second step consists of computing migration rates for the Crescent and comparing them with those of these same groupings of metropolitan and nonmetropolitan areas.

The question under examination in the first operation may be stated in this fashion: After age, sex, and race factors have been removed from the data by cross-classification, is the metropolitan-nonmetropolitan difference still evident? This check consists of a series of "yes" or "no" answers to the question: Does a comparison of the migration percentages of two groupings of metropolitan counties with those of the nonmetropolitan counties in the three states support the hypothesis that migration occurs relatively more frequently in nonmetropolitan than in metropolitan areas? In order to dampen the variation

Table 3-4. Two Sets of Tests of the Hypothesis That Migration Is a Relatively More Common Mobility Response among Nonmetropolitan Workers Than among Metropolitan Workers

RACE, SEX, AND AGE CLASSES	MIGRANTS AS A PERCENTAGE OF MOBILE WORKERS [a]: ALL NONMETRO-POLITAN AREAS (GROUPS 4, 5, AND 6)	ATLANTA (GROUP 1)	ALL OTHER METROPOLITAN AREAS (GROUP 2)	IS THE COLUMN (2) PERCENTAGE GREATER THAN THE COLUMN (3) PERCENTAGE?	IS THE COLUMN (2) PERCENTAGE GREATER THAN THE COLUMN (4) PERCENTAGE?
(1)	(2)	(3)	(4)	(5)	(6)
Non-Negro males					
less than 30	60.6	62.2	56.8	No	Yes
30 and over [b]	55.3	59.1	59.1	No	No
Non-Negro females					
less than 30	52.2	43.5	51.2	Yes	Yes
30 and over [b]	44.1	39.8	37.2	Yes	Yes
Negro males					
less than 30	67.1	48.2	60.8	Yes	Yes
30 and over [b]	57.0	57.9	49.2	No	Yes
Negro females					
less than 30	50.7	37.1	15.2	Yes	Yes
30 and over [b]	35.0	29.7	22.6	Yes	Yes

[a] A migrant is a mobile worker at least two of whose employers are located in different counties.
[b] Includes age unknown.

in the migration percentages, the nonmetropolitan area data (Area Groups 4, 5, and 6) were combined. The individual tests of the hypothesis consist of a comparison of the Atlanta and "All Other Metropolitan Areas" percentages with this nonmetropolitan combined percentage. Since there are eight age, sex, and race subclassifications, this procedure provides eight separate tests, as shown in Table 3-4.

The tests which compare the Atlanta metropolitan area with the nonmetropolitan area groupings show results supporting the hypothesis five out of a possible eight times. Comparison of "All Other Metropolitan Areas" with the nonmetropolitan area groups provides supporting evidence seven out of a possible eight times. Together, these two sets of tests indicate that the tendency for nonmetropolitan migration percentages to exceed metropolitan percentages, observed by Bogue (1952) in the Ohio and Michigan data, exists in the three-state mobility data also.[4] Thus it is appropriate to pass to the examination of the Crescent percentages in the light of these findings.

As already pointed out, the Crescent contains within itself both metropolitan and nonmetropolitan counties, so the problem to be analyzed here may be stated as: Using migration percentages as indicators of metropolitan-ness, what is the relationship between the migration percentages that we would expect to exist, given the composition of the area as between metropolitan and nonmetropolitan counties, and those that do actually exist?

Within age, sex, and race classes, a migration percentage has been computed for all metropolitan areas in the three states except those in the Crescent, and another migration percentage for all nonmetropolitan areas in the three states except those in the Crescent. Since 60.5 per cent of the Crescent workers in this sample were in metropolitan areas, the expected migration percentage may be assumed to be 60.5 per cent of the distance between these two aggregate migration percentages, measured from the latter to the former. To illustrate, if the migration percentage for the nonmetropolitan areas were

Table 3-5. Tests of the Hypothesis That the Piedmont Industrial Crescent Has Mobility Characteristics More in Common with Metropolitan Areas Than with Nonmetropolitan Areas

RACE, SEX, AND AGE CLASSES	MIGRANTS AS A PERCENTAGE OF MOBILE WORKERS: ALL NONMETROPOLITAN AREAS (GROUPS 4, 5, AND 6)	ALL METROPOLITAN AREAS (GROUPS 1 AND 2)	EXPECTED CRESCENT [a]	ACTUAL CRESCENT (GROUP 3)	TESTS OF METROPOLITAN-NESS: IS THE EXPECTED RATE GREATER THAN THE ACTUAL RATE?
(1)	(2)	(3)	(4)	(5)	(6)
Non-Negro males					
less than 30	60.6	59.5	59.9	53.1	Yes
30 and over	55.3	59.1	57.6	51.1	Yes
Non-Negro females					
less than 30	52.2	47.6	49.4	40.8	Yes
30 and over	44.1	38.5	40.7	32.6	Yes
Negro males					
less than 30	67.1	56.3	60.6	59.5	Yes
30 and over	57.0	52.7	54.4	51.4	Yes
Negro females					
less than 30	50.7	26.5	36.1	40.0	No
30 and over	35.0	26.5	29.9	18.2	Yes

[a] Computed as follows: Col. 2 − .605 (Col. 2 − Col. 3).

60 per cent and that of the metropolitan areas were 50 per cent, the expected migration percentage for the Crescent would be approximately 54 per cent.

If the actual migration percentages are, on balance, smaller than the expected percentages, this evidence suggests that the Crescent has certain economic characteristics in common with more clearly defined metropolitan areas. In seven out of a possible eight tests, as shown in Table 3-5, the results support the hypothesis that the Crescent does in fact have labor-mobility characteristics resembling those of other metropolitan areas in the three states.

In view of the fact that the underlying causes of this migration phenomenon are yet to be studied, and in view of the fact that there is variation in the results obtained from the several area groups, it would be premature to draw more than two cautious conclusions from this investigation. First, migration does appear to be relatively more common among mobile workers of nonmetropolitan areas, as previously observed by Bogue (1952). Second, the data strengthen the hypothesis that the sixteen-county Piedmont Industrial Crescent may meaningfully be studied as a metropolitan community.

Impact of Mobility upon the Crescent Labor Force

Labor flows into and out of the Crescent are of interest because of their effect upon the size and composition of the Crescent labor force. The purpose here is to report briefly on that effect and on the directions and magnitudes of the flows which brought it about, as shown by the 1953 BOASI data.

Table 3-6 presents three percentage distributions of the workers flowing through the Crescent, according to geographic area of origin (for in-migrants) or destination (for out-migrants). Several aspects of the data deserve comment. They show that the Crescent has migration contact with all nine Census Divisions of the United States, and that there are three clearly defined levels of interaction. As would be expected most of the in-migrants come from, and most of the out-migrants go to, the South Atlantic Division of which the Crescent is a part. Three-fourths of total migration involves this division. Almost 16 per cent of total migration is attributable to the Middle Atlantic and East North Central Divisions, with the remaining six divisions accounting for less than 9 per cent of the total.

Table 3-6. Percentage Distributions of Crescent In-Migrants, Out-Migrants, and Total Migrants, among Nine Census Divisions

CENSUS DIVISIONS (U. S. BUREAU OF THE CENSUS, 1953, p. *viii*)	MIGRATION FLOWS [a]		
	IN	OUT	TOTAL
New England	0.9	0.9	0.9
Middle Atlantic	5.3	10.5	8.0
East North Central	5.8	9.6	7.7
West North Central	1.4	0.7	1.0
South Atlantic	81.7	69.9	75.7
East South Central	2.3	3.8	3.1
West South Central	1.6	2.0	1.8
Mountain	0.0	0.4	0.2
Pacific	0.9	2.2	1.6
Total	100.0	100.0	100.0

[a] An in-migrant is a sample worker whose last employer of 1953 was in the Crescent but whose first employer of 1953 was outside the Crescent; an out-migrant is one whose first employer was located in the Crescent and whose last employer was located outside the Crescent. Total migration is the (absolute) sum of the two.

While the migration relationships just cited refer to total flow, these relationships may be clearly seen in both components of the total in Table 3-6. There is a difference between these components, however, which is noteworthy. The South Atlantic Division is considerably more dominant among in-migrants than among out-migrants. The significance of this will become more obvious as the data are examined further.

Turning to an examination of the net impact of these flows on the Crescent's labor force, it is necessary to look more closely at the figures underlying these percentages. With the total number of out-migrants in the 1 per cent sample exceeding the total number of in-migrants by sixteen workers, the Crescent's net loss was approximately one-fourth of 1 per cent of all workers in the Crescent sample. While the loss was small, the data tend to support the commonly held idea that the Crescent is part of a labor-exporting region.

But a good deal of interesting information underlies the preceding summary statement. Detailed examination reveals that the net loss of workers resulted from a net inflow among non-Negroes and a larger net outflow among Negroes. But when age is considered the picture is less clear-cut. For Negroes, all age-race-sex-classes show net out-migration except females over 49 years of age. But for non-Negroes, the male and female patterns seem to be reversed. Males show relatively large inflows among young workers and comparable outflows among workers in the middle-age class, while females show inflows among the middle-age class and outflows among the young. Thus the net effects of migration upon the Crescent's labor force, in absolute terms, might be summarized as follows. There are strong outflows of Negroes under 49 years of age. Among non-Negroes, strong inflows among young male workers and outflows among males in the 30–49 age class dominate counter flows in each class among females.

By expressing net migration figures as percentages of the total number of workers in the appropriate age-sex-race class for the Crescent as a whole (Table 3-7), it is possible to examine the relative impact of migration upon these classes. As far as age is concerned, they show that the greater impact is upon the younger groups. Race differences are also shown to be very large, with the Negro percentages tending to be almost ten times as large as the non-Negro percentages, in addition to having opposite flow directions.

Table 3-7. Net Migration Percentages for the Piedmont Industrial Crescent, by Age and Race within Sex Classes [a]

AGE CLASS	BOTH RACES AND SEXES	NON-NEGROES			NEGROES		
		BOTH SEXES	MALES	FEMALES	BOTH SEXES	MALES	FEMALES
Less than 30	−0.12	0.69	1.55	−0.32	−3.09	−2.15	−5.02
30–49	−0.42	−0.11	−0.89	1.06	−1.63	−1.42	−1.97
49 and over [b]	0.09	0.12	0.35	−0.35	0.00	−1.25	2.38
Algebraic sum	−0.23	0.22	0.15	0.31	−1.90	−1.68	−2.32

[a] Net migration percentages were computed by dividing the number of net migrant workers by the total number of workers in the corresponding age-race-sex class whose first covered employers of 1953 were in the Crescent.
[b] Includes age unknown.

When the personal characteristics of mobile workers and the *regional* aspects of their job changes are viewed simultaneously, it may be seen that the Crescent is a net exporter of workers of both races to three of the four Census Regions into which the nation is divided. (U. S. Bureau of the Census, 1953, p. viii.) It is a net receiver of workers, predominantly non-Negroes, only from the South. The net outflow to the North Central Region consists of both races in about equal numbers, but the net outflow to the Northeast Region consists mostly of Negroes whereas that to the West is primarily non-Negro. Two aspects of the sex composition of these flows also deserve mention. The outflow to the West is predominantly female whereas that to the North Central Region is the result of a very strong outflow of males which is slightly countered by a small inflow of females. (See Bunting and Prosper, 1960, pp. 61–62.)

Moving from a *regional* to a *divisional* geographic viewpoint makes it possible to sharpen these results, and at the same time to see more clearly the significance of an earlier comment: "The South Atlantic Division is considerably more dominant among in-migrants than among out-migrants." Comparison of flows between the Crescent and South Atlantic Division with flows between the Crescent and all other census divisions shows that the Crescent gains workers, especially young, white ones, from the South Atlantic Division. It loses workers to the rest of the nation in numbers exceeding its gains from the South Atlantic Division. These losses are pervasive, dominating both sexes within both race groupings and all age classifications. In brief, these data support the hypothesis that the Crescent tends to serve as a way-station. Young (predominantly white) workers move in from the immediately surrounding areas. Negroes in their twenties and thirties and non-Negroes in their forties and fifties move out to other parts of the nation—primarily to the North. (See Bunting and Prosper, 1960, Table XX, p. 64.)

It should be noted that no extensive analysis comparing labor flows through the Crescent and the Atlanta metropolitan area was included in the study. However, the data made it possible to obtain comparative flow statistics which give indication that these two areas play quite different roles in the economy of the South. Whereas it appears to be appropriate to refer to the Crescent as a way-station, this description does not at all apply to Atlanta. The Crescent is a net loser of labor, its heavy inflows from the South Atlantic States being more than offset by losses to most of the other geographic divisions.

Atlanta, on the other hand, is a net gainer of labor and these gains are made at the expense of all other geographic divisions except the West South Central one.

Summary and Conclusions

In this chapter a sizable body of data has been explored for the purpose of casting light on three separate aspects of the Crescent and its economy: the level of mobility and the characteristics of mobile workers, the metropolitan-ness of the Crescent, and the flow of workers through the Crescent. The data were obtained from the one per cent work history sample of the Bureau of Old-Age and Survivors Insurance. A total of 30,614 workers who worked at some time during 1953 in North Carolina, South Carolina, and Georgia were included in the study sample.

Mobile workers were defined as those who had more than one employer during the year. The data showed that 26 per cent of the employees in the sample were mobile according to this definition; slightly less than one-half of these were migrants, that is, mobile workers whose moves carried them across county lines. Comparing these percentages with those for five other groupings of counties, which represented the non-Crescent portions of the three states from which the data were drawn, showed the mobility percentage to be typical of the three-state area and the migration percentage to be slightly less, in comparison with mobile nonmigrants, than those of the five area groupings.

Earlier studies using BOASI data have shown that mobility rates vary with sex, age, and race. The Crescent data clearly supported these earlier findings. Within race and age classes, clear-cut and strong differences in mobility occurred between sexes (males being more mobile than females), and within race and sex classes there were the same sort of age differentials (workers less than 30 years old being more mobile than those over 30). The race differential (within sex and age classes) was interesting in that it persisted strongly among males (with Negroes being more mobile than non-Negroes), but among females it was not large and it tended in the other direction.

Considering the problem of labor mobility in relation to effective utilization of the area's labor resources, comparisons of mobility percentages within sex and race classes were made with similar percentages from two other studies, both of which used BOASI data. One of these studies used a nation-wide sample (Aaronson and Keller, 1946) and the other used a sample drawn from Michigan and Ohio (Bogue, 1952).

The data comparisons showed that male mobility percentages of the three-state Southern area were slightly lower (about 2 percentage points) than those of the other two studies, and that female percentages were substantially lower (5 to 7 percentage points). Since the study years varied, several possible sources of the differential (changed OASI coverage, business cycle factors, the extent of unionism, etc.) were briefly examined but they did not seem to account for the lower Southern mobility rates. The appropriate conclusion appears to be that there is empirical justification for the belief that mobility is less in the South than in other parts of the nation. This conclusion, in turn, suggests a direction of further study directed toward a deeper understanding of this characteristic. Improvement of the economic efficiency and growth potential of the study area may require action aimed at increasing the willingness and ability of workers to change jobs.

The second purpose for which the mobility data were used was to test the Crescent for its "metropolitan-ness." The idea of using mobility data for this purpose was suggested by a finding in the Michigan and Ohio study: Bogue's data showed that there was a stronger tendency for labor mobility to carry across county lines in nonmetropolitan than in metropolitan areas.

The test for metropolitan-ness consisted of computing expected migrant percentages for each of eight age, race, and sex classes and comparing these with the actual migrant percentages for the Crescent. In seven out of eight comparisons the Crescent percentages were lower than the expected percentages. This meant that the Crescent migration percentages were more like those of a metropolitan area than would have been predicted on the basis of the Crescent's metropolitan-nonmetropolitan labor-force composition. Thus these tests support the view that the Crescent may meaningfully be thought of as a metropolitan unit for purposes of certain types of economic analysis.

Finally, the flows of labor into and out of the Crescent were examined with a view toward understanding their geographic aspects and their influence on the size and composition of the Crescent labor force. Three-fourths of the movement into and out of the Crescent occurred within the South Atlantic states. Another 16 per cent was accounted for by the Middle Atlantic and East North Central states.

Focusing on the age, race, and sex characteristics of these flows, the data showed net inflows of non-Negro males and females and net outflows of Negro males and females. These flows exerted larger percentage effects upon the young component of the Crescent labor force than upon the old, and substantially larger percentage effects upon the Negro component than upon the non-Negro component.

A simultaneous look at geographic aspects and personal characteristics of worker flows was enlightening. It showed the Crescent to be a net gainer of workers from the South Atlantic Division. These gains were concentrated primarily among young and old non-Negroes. The Crescent was a net loser of workers to the rest of the nation in almost all age, race, and sex classes, losses among younger Negro males being especially severe.

Thus the data provide a fairly clear picture of the multiple impact of labor mobility upon the labor force of the Crescent. It tends to decrease labor-force size, to change labor-force composition away from workers in the age range between 20 and 60, and to alter labor-force composition in the direction of non-Negroes.

FOOTNOTES

1. For more detail concerning the basic data, a description of machine procedures, and elaboration upon the shortcomings listed in the text above, see Bunting and Prosper (1960, pp. 10–16, Appendix A and Appendix Tables C-I and C-II).
2. For detailed breakdowns, see Bunting and Prosper (1960).
3. All of these results are supported by a quite different technique of analyzing these same data for the sex, age, and race characteristics of mobile workers. (See Bunting, 1960.) It should be noted also that both the Bogue (1952) and the Aaronson and Keller (1946) studies showed an inversion of race differentials as between males and females.
4. These results are not unequivocal. The three sex-age-race classes for which the answer was "No" in Column 5 of Table 3-4 contained 61.1 per cent of the combined mobile workers in Area Groups 1, 4, 5, and 6. The one class for which the answer was "No" in Column 6 contained only 12.5 per cent of the combined mobile workers in Area Groups 2, 4, 5, and 6.

REFERENCES

Aaronson, Franklin M., and Ruth A. Keller (1946), "Mobility of Workers in Employment Covered by Old-Age and Survivors Insurance," Bureau of Research and Statistics Report 14, mimeographed. Washington: U. S. Social Security Administration.

Bakke, E. Wight, Philip M. Hauser, Gladys L. Palmer, Charles A. Myers, Dale Yoder, and Clark Kerr (1954), *Labor Mobility and Economic Opportunity.* Technology Press of Massachusetts Institute of Technology, Cambridge, and John Wiley and Sons, New York.

Bogue, Donald J. (1952), *A Methodological Study of Migration and Labor Mobility in Michigan and Ohio in 1947*, Scripps Foundation Studies in Population Distribution, No. 4. Oxford, Ohio: Scripps Foundation.

Bunting, Robert L. (1960), "Labor Mobility: Sex, Race, and Age," *Review of Economics and Statistics*, **42**:2, 229–231.

Bunting, Robert L., and Peter A. Prosper, Jr. (1960), *Labor Mobility Patterns in the Piedmont Industrial Crescent*, Urban Studies Program, Institute for Research in Social Science. Chapel Hill, N. C.: University of North Carolina.

Palmer, Gladys L. (1954), *Labor Mobility in Six Cities.* New York: Social Science Research Council.

Parnes, Herbert S. (1954), *Research on Labor Mobility.* New York: Social Science Research Council.

Reynolds, Lloyd G. (1951), *The Structure of Labor Markets.* New York: Harper & Brothers.

U. S. Bureau of the Budget (1955), *1955 Historical and Descriptive Supplement to Economic Indicators.* Washington: Government Printing Office.

U. S. Bureau of the Census (1952), *Census of Population: 1950, General Characteristics, U. S. Summary*, Report PB-1, Preprint of Vol. II, Part I, Chap. B. Washington: Government Printing Office.

U. S. Bureau of the Census (1953), *County and City Data Book: 1952.* Washington: Government Printing Office.

U. S. Bureau of the Census (1957), *Current Population Reports*, Series P-50, No. 70. Washington: Government Printing Office.

U. S. Department of Commerce (1948), *Business Establishments, Employment and Taxable Payrolls, First Quarter 1947.* Washington: Government Printing Office.

U. S. Department of Commerce and U. S. Department of Health, Education, and Welfare (1955), *County Business Patterns, First Quarter 1953.* Washington: Government Printing Office.

Chapter 4

Industrial Development Trends and Economic Potential

by Lowell D. Ashby *

THE TWO CAROLINAS form a geographical, economic, and cultural matrix enclosing their urbanized industrial core. Today this urbanized corridor comprises a population in excess of two millions.

As industrial areas are measured in the American time scale, this is an old area. It has been settled by the white man for more than two hundred years. Aboriginal trading paths appear to have channeled the first North-South migrations to the west of the geological fall line which separates the Piedmont from the Coastal Plain. These movements of the European immigrants led to chance settlements. It was not, however, until political considerations in the middle of the nine-

* In the preparation of this chapter the author acknowledges the very great assistance of Donald J. Schilling during the academic year 1959–1960. During this year Mr. Schilling prepared the basic nonagricultural employment estimates of 146 counties of the two Carolinas. This involved both direct computation and, when facilities became available, computer programming.

Also the author wishes to acknowledge the very considerable aid of the University of North Carolina Computation Center both in basic data preparation and in data analysis. In the course of using Computation Center facilities the author acknowledges the indispensable programming aid and advice given by Fern E. Ashby.

Finally the author acknowledges the research orientation of the Department of Economics and the School of Business Administration which has made participation in this program possible.

teenth century dictated the location of the first major East-West railroad that the nucleus of the present urban corridor was firmly laid.[1] In the present day, intercity links grow firmer with rapid intercity and interstate highway and airline transit and the other forms of communication and economic interaction which they help to generate.[2]

The present chapter reviews the broad economic characteristics of the two-state urbanized corridor hereafter referred to as "the Crescent." This sixteen-county area is examined in the context of larger regions. From population, labor force, and employment characteristics, attention is shifted to growth rates in income and population. This is followed by an examination of the industrial structure of employment. Attention is given both to percentage changes and to absolute changes in the period after World War II. Conditions of employment stability, productivity, and growth are summarized for the several regions in terms of national industry characteristics. Finally, industry-shift patterns are considered and a plausible shift pattern is considered for the decade ending in 1967.

Labor-Force Participation and Underemployment

In 1950 the Crescent population participated in the civilian labor force to the extent of 42.4 per cent while the non-Crescent population participation rate was 35.2 per cent. This greater Crescent participation rate is due to several factors. First, a larger portion of the Crescent population falls in the age bracket (14 years old and over) within which labor-force participation is counted. Second, in the industrialized areas more married women take part-time work. This action moves them into the labor-force category.[3]

The civilian labor force includes two major subcomponents, the employed and the unemployed. The employed group deserves broad characterization at this point because it gives much of the color and tone to the Crescent area.

As of April 1, 1950, the Crescent area had an employment composition moderately weighted with private wage and salary workers as to class, heavily weighted with operatives as to occupation, and heavily weighted with manufacturing as to industry. However, it is well to recall that these are the broad strokes. Underneath these generalities, the variability among the Crescent's sixteen component counties was very great in many respects. Also, although there has been considerable growth and change in the last ten years, the broad characterizations and the particular county exceptions remain largely applicable as of 1960.

Despite the greater urbanization of the Crescent area, it shares some of the industrial characteristics of the non-Crescent area. Thus in both areas there were many people with both small-scale farming and industrial labor-force (particularly manufacturing) attachments. Thus it is the relatively rare individual who had *no* employment available. However, textile-mill products, while highly prosperous during and immediately after World War II, have evidenced some degree of price and output instability in the latter part of the period under review. In general it is difficult for soft consumer goods, such as textiles, to maintain their relative importance in the nation's consumption budget. Moreover, it is increasingly difficult to keep domestic mills competitive with the growing foreign capacities in this industry. Examination of insured unemployment rates suggests that while unemployment in the Crescent area was generally less severe than that in the nation from 1947 through 1950, the reverse has been generally true in subsequent years. (Ashby and Park, 1961, Table 20, p. 63.)

Accurate measurement of total unemployment rates is difficult in states and regions except at the infrequent decennial enumeration points. However, some types of information are not obtainable even on these infrequent occasions. For example, it is not possible to ask an individual on a census enumeration whether or in what degree he is "underemployed." As the term is generally understood, underemployment is a condition wherein personal capacities are less than fully utilized or utilized in a nonoptimal fashion. Thus the mere status of employment by no means precludes the dual simultaneous status of underemployment. Underemployment is often associated with industries and/or regions where investment per worker is low or where, due to a decline in the industry itself, the workers are not effectively used even at the given level of capital intensity. In the Southeast as a whole capital intensity has been in the past rather low per worker in some industries, notably agriculture. While on the decline as to employed numbers, agriculture has also fallen short of absorbing the entering male labor-force participants in most rural areas. The consequence has often been that the marginal product per worker has been extremely low and in some areas possibly negative during the interval when able workers were making the migratory industrial adjustment.[4] Such low marginal productivity is but the obverse side of what is called underemployment. Both are evidence of an extended lag in employment adaptation.

Though underemployment exists, it is most certainly less serious in the more urbanized areas. In the vicinity of the more rapidly growing industrial sectors (compared to agriculture which is on the decline), errors in placement or adjustment are both more quickly detected and when detected more quickly rectified. It is therefore a basic hypothesis that employment maladjustment or underemployment is somewhat less serious in the Crescent than in the non-Crescent portions of the two-state area.[5]

Growth in Income, Population, and Per Capita Income

The incomes of any region are largely explainable in terms of industrial and occupational composition. This is true despite the fact that within occupational or industrial categories there remain variations

Table 4-1. Personal Income, Total Population, and Per Capita Income, Crescent Compared with Larger Regions, 1950 and 1958

	PERSONAL INCOME		POPULATION		PER CAPITA INCOME	
	1950	1958	1950	1958	1950	1958
Crescent [a]	$ 2,215,267,000	$ 3,470,089,000	1,669,764	1,969,233	$1,327	$1,762
North Carolina and South Carolina less Crescent	3,761,733,000	5,771,911,000	4,511,236	4,890,767	834	1,180
North Carolina and South Carolina	5,977,000,000	9,242,000,000	6,181,000	6,860,000	967	1,347
United States less North Carolina and South Carolina	219,496,000,000	348,300,000,000	145,053,000	166,372,000	1,513	2,094
United States	225,473,000,000	357,542,000,000	151,234,000	173,232,000	1,491	2,064

[a] Twelve counties in North Carolina and four counties in South Carolina.

Sources. Personal income data: National and state estimates are from U. S. Department of Commerce (1956 and 1960). County income estimates are based on Jones (1957), Paterson and Wilcox (1959), and N. C. Department of Tax Research (1960).

Population data: National and state estimates as of July 1 for each year are from the Bureau of the Census. County population estimates as of July 1 are distributions of the state control totals by way of allocation vectors synthesized from basic census enumerations in 1940, 1950, and 1960. All estimates are of total population. Total population includes persons in the armed forces stationed in each state and excludes members of the armed forces abroad.

in income depending on race, sex, age, experience, and other factors.[6] No attempt is made here to explain the income level of the two Carolinas or the Crescent area in a quantitative fashion. Rather the present emphasis is on the level of income as measured.

In 1950, the personal income of the two Carolinas amounted to $5,977,000,000. Of this total, $2,215,267,000 was received by residents of the Crescent area. With about 37 per cent of the personal income and about 27 per cent of the population in the two-state area, the per capita income of the Crescent stood considerably higher than that of the surrounding counties in 1950. The Crescent area per capita income has been measured at $1,327, whereas that of the non-Crescent area has been measured at $834 for 1950. The respective per capita personal incomes for 1958 have been measured at $1,762 and $1,180. Basic data on personal income, population, and per capita personal income for the several areas are presented in Table 4-1.

From the data on income and population it is possible to estimate per capita income for the Crescent and other areas of interest. More-

Table 4-2. Growth Rates in Personal Income, Total Population, and Per Capita Income, Crescent Compared with Larger Regions, 1950 to 1958

	PERSONAL INCOME	POPULATION	PER CAPITA INCOME
Crescent	0.05770	0.02083	0.03610
North Carolina and South Carolina less Crescent	0.05497	0.01015	0.04437
North Carolina and South Carolina	0.05599	0.01311	0.04232
United States less North Carolina and South Carolina	0.05941	0.01729	0.04141
United States	0.05932	0.01712	0.04149

Source. Computed from basic data presented in Table 4-1. The growth rates are implicit in the beginning and terminal values of income and population. See Ashby and Spivey (1957). In the present case the analytical method has been applied to current dollar rather than to constant dollar ("real") income. Where r_z, r_p, and r_y represent growth rates respectively in personal income, total population and per capita personal income, it may be noted that $r_y = [(r_z + 1)/(r_p + 1)] - 1$. Thus per capita income growth is a function of the growth rates in personal income and in total population.

over, it is possible to measure the compound annual growth rates in income, population, and per capita income implicit in data of the basic type presented in the first table. Relevant compound annual growth rates in these three variables are presented in Table 4-2.

As the growth rates are measured, it turns out that the growth rate in per capita income can be fully expressed in terms of the growth rates of income and population. This relationship is shown in Figure 4-1. In this figure a given regional point measures the population growth rate horizontally and the income growth rate vertically from the origin. The growth rate in per capita income is then proportional to the perpendicular distance of the given point from the 45-degree line. The 45-degree line would represent the locus of regional points having zero growth in per capita income. Also shown are the loci of points for the individual counties of the Crescent area.

While all the points plotted in Figure 4-1 fall into the upper half of the northeast quadrant, considerable variation in county patterns is evident. For example, the greatest population growth rate occurred in Mecklenburg (Charlotte) while the greatest total personal income growth occurred in Forsyth (Winston-Salem). The growth rate in per capita income was greater in Forsyth as would be evident from relative lengths of lines drawn from county points perpendicular to the 45-degree line.

Changes in Employment Structure, 1947 to 1957

In this section the primary emphasis is upon an examination of Crescent employment structure against a background of three other non-overlapping regions.

It was observed in Figure 4-1 that the rate of population growth in the sixteen-county area was more than double that of the remainder of the two Carolinas in the period 1950 to 1958. The aggregate performance of the area is also to be distinguished from that of the remainder of the two-state area when total employment is examined as in Table 4-3. It is apparent that whereas agricultural employment declined in all four regions, as in the entire nation, nonagricultural employment increased in all four regions.

The agricultural employment decline in the Crescent area was slightly less than that in the non-Crescent area of the two Carolinas (28.3 per cent versus 28.5 per cent). However, the decline in the

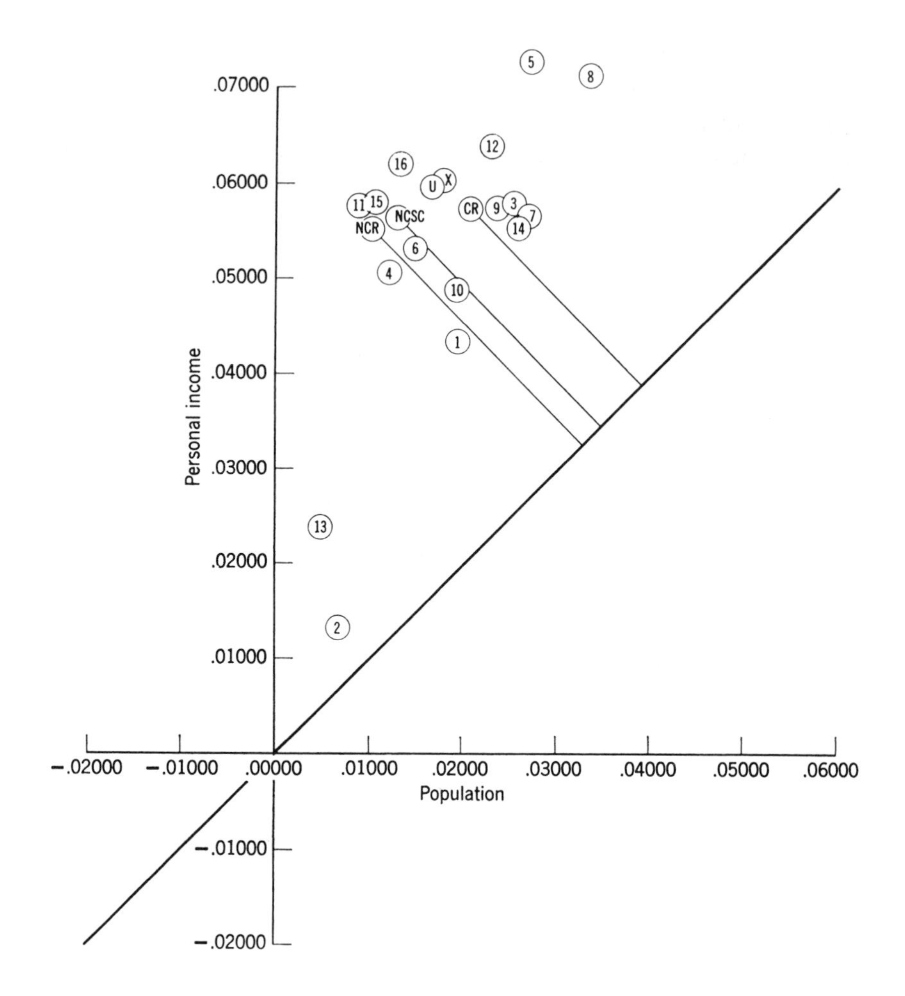

Figure 4-1. Compound annual growth rates, personal income, population, and per capita income, 1950 to 1958. (1) Alamance, N. C.; (2) Cabarrus, N. C.; (3) Davidson, N. C.; (4) Durham, N. C.; (5) Forsyth, N. C.; (6) Gaston, N. C.; (7) Guilford, N. C.; (8) Mecklenburg, N. C.; (9) Orange, N. C.; (10) Randolph, N. C.; (11) Rowan, N. C.; (12) Wake, N. C.; (13) Cherokee, S. C.; (14) Greenville, S. C.; (15) Spartanburg, S. C.; (16) York, S. C. CR = Crescent; NCR = N. C. and S. C. less Crescent; NCSC = N. C. and S. C.; X = U. S. less N. C. and S. C.; U = United States. *Note:* The plotted points (circles) have three interpretations. The horizontal distance from the origin measures compound annual growth rate in population. The vertical distance from the origin measures compound annual growth rate in personal income. The perpendicular distance from the 45-degree line measures relative compound annual growth rate in per capita income. *Source:* Table 4-2 and subsidiary materials.

Table 4-3. Total Employment by Agricultural and Nonagricultural Workers, Crescent Compared with Larger Regions, Annual Averages for 1947 and 1957 [a] *(Thousands of Persons)*

	1947	1957
Crescent [b]		
Agricultural	113.0	81.0
Nonagricultural	531.7	655.1
Total	644.7	736.1
N. C. and S. C. less Crescent		
Agricultural	820.0	586.0
Nonagricultural	758.0	971.9
Total	1,578.0	1,557.9
Non-Carolina South [c]		
Agricultural	3,809.0	2,494.0
Nonagricultural	7,268.9	9,857.9
Total	11,077.9	12,351.9
Non-South		
Agricultural	5,640.0	4,416.0
Nonagricultural	34,554.5	40,542.9
Total	40,194.5	44,958.9
United States [d]		
Agricultural	10,382.0	7,577.0
Nonagricultural	43,113.1	52,027.8
Total	53,495.1	59,604.8

[a] The sum of 12 monthly values divided by 12.

[b] Twelve counties in North Carolina and four counties in South Carolina.

[c] Eleven states: Alabama, Arkansas, Florida, Georgia, Kentucky, Louisiana, Mississippi, Oklahoma, Tennessee, Texas, and Virginia.

[d] Forty-eight states and the District of Columbia.

Sources. Agricultural:

United States—U. S. Department of Agriculture (1958, Table 3).

Other regions—1957 is from U. S. Department of Agriculture (1958, Tables 30, 31, and 32). 1947 was estimated on the basis of a projection to earlier years of a straight line regression. In this regression time is the independent variable and the per cent which each region or state constitutes of the national total for each employment category in the years 1950 through 1957 is the dependent variable. Per cents in each category so derived for the earlier year were then applied to the national total of the category (family or hired) to derive employment estimates for regions and states. Allocations of state control totals to counties in North Carolina were synthesized by a computer program which relied on the Census of Agriculture, as of April 1, 1940 and April 1, 1950, as bases.

Nonagricultural: As in Table 4-5.

non-Carolina South was much stronger (34.5 per cent) while that for the non-South was much weaker (21.7 per cent). These percentage changes show the important fact that the two Carolinas did not keep pace in "de-agriculturalization" with the remainder of the South. They also yield the somewhat surprising indication that the loss of agricultural employment in the Crescent counties advanced at about the same rate as in the more rural portions of the two-state area.

The percentage increase in nonagricultural employment in the Crescent area was smaller than that in the non-Crescent (23.1 per cent versus 28.2 per cent). However, the increase in the non-Carolina South was much stronger (35.6 per cent) and that in the non-South was distinctly weaker (20.7 per cent). These contrasts in general illustrate the fact that the relatively nonindustrialized areas (with a relatively small growth base) can often make a stronger showing than can the highly developed areas.

Figure 4-2 gives a visual impression of the nonagricultural changes within the two-state area. The relatively large nonagricultural employment gains in Wake, Guilford, Forsyth, Mecklenburg, and Greenville counties are evident. The figure, however, shows only absolute changes and gives no impression of rates of change relative to the original attainments at the start of the period.

In Table 4-4 it is possible to find indication of the effect of the changes just noted in terms of percentage composition, per cent of national total in the industrial categories in each region, and a measure called "relative importance." The changes of the period shifted the Crescent percentage composition away from agricultural and toward nonagricultural employment. The percentage of the nation's workers in each industrial category accounted for by the region was not perceptibly changed. Finally, the relative importance of the region in agricultural, nonagricultural, and total employment declined. A different outcome on this latter item could have been attained as a result of either a more rapid employment expansion or a less rapid population growth than was experienced in the period. Similar comparisons are available for other regions.

Agricultural employment is divided into two groups, the family workers (farm operators and members of their families) and hired workers. While the Crescent area lost family workers, it has made a slight gain in hired workers. The same patterns prevail in the non-Crescent area. In contrast, in the remainder of the nation declines were registered both in the family and hired-worker categories. It is probable that the decline in hired agricultural workers in the remainder

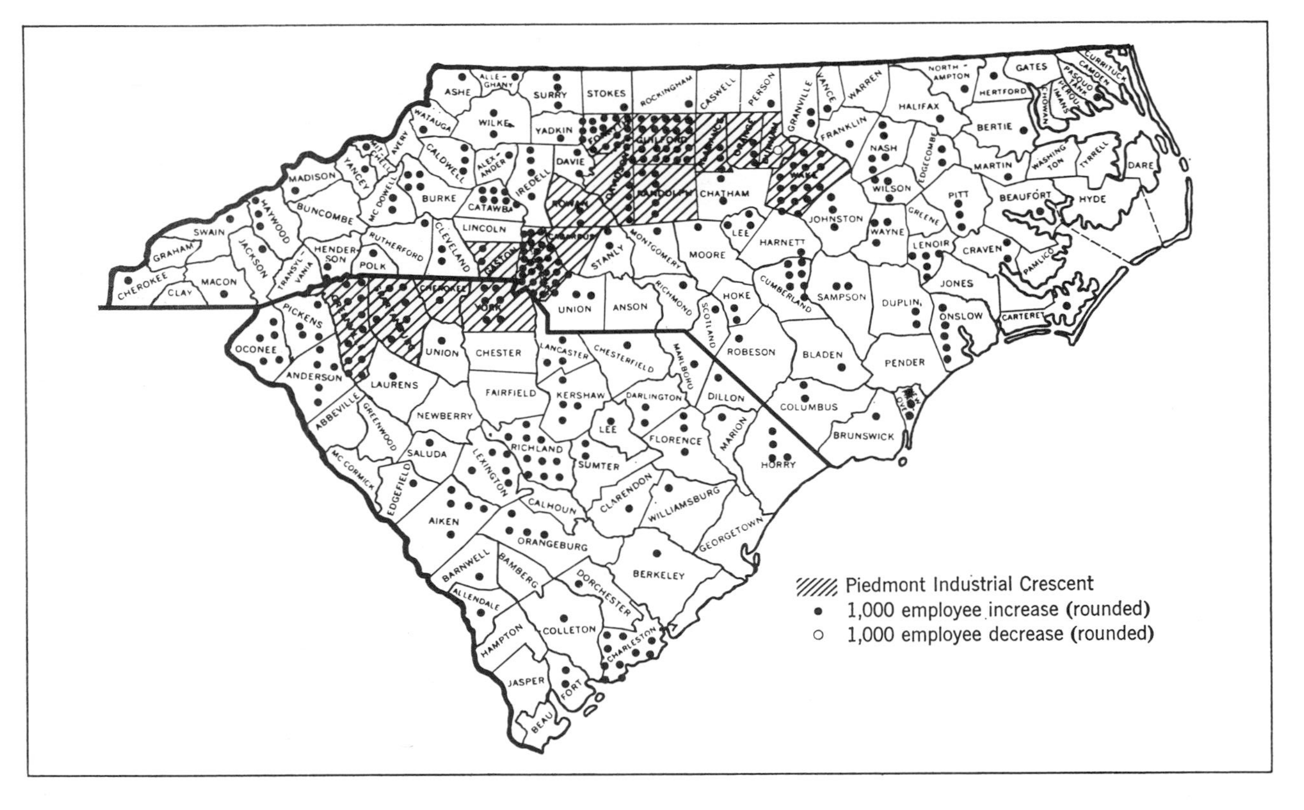

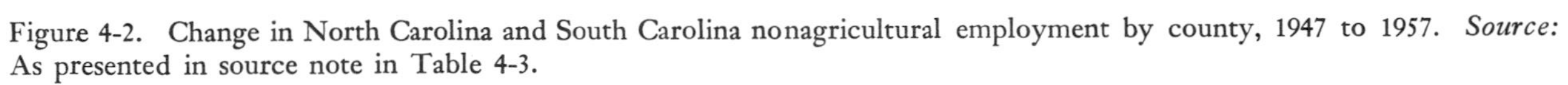

Figure 4-2. Change in North Carolina and South Carolina nonagricultural employment by county, 1947 to 1957. *Source:* As presented in source note in Table 4-3.

Table 4-4. Total Employment by Agricultural and Nonagricultural Workers, Crescent Compared with Larger Regions, Selected Measures for 1947 and 1957

	PERCENTAGE COMPOSITION		PER CENT OF NATIONAL TOTAL IN EACH CATEGORY		RELATIVE IMPORTANCE [a]	
	1947	1957	1947	1957	1947	1957
Crescent						
Agricultural	17.5	11.0	1.1	1.1	1.03	0.93
Nonagricultural	82.5	89.0	1.2	1.2	1.16	1.10
Total	100.0	100.0	1.2	1.2	1.13	1.08
N. C. and S. C. less Crescent						
Agricultural	52.0	37.6	7.9	7.7	2.67	2.69
Nonagricultural	48.0	62.4	1.8	1.9	0.59	0.65
Total	100.0	100.0	2.9	2.6	1.00	0.91
Non-Carolina South						
Agricultural	34.4	20.2	36.7	32.9	1.55	1.41
Nonagricultural	65.6	79.8	16.9	19.0	0.71	0.81
Total	100.0	100.0	20.7	20.8	0.88	0.88
Non-South						
Agricultural	14.0	9.8	54.3	58.3	0.75	0.80
Nonagricultural	86.0	90.2	80.1	77.9	1.11	1.07
Total	100.0	100.0	75.1	75.4	1.04	1.04
United States						
Agricultural	19.4	12.7	100.0	100.0	1.00	1.00
Nonagricultural	80.6	87.3	100.0	100.0	1.00	1.00
Total	100.0	100.0	100.0	100.0	1.00	1.00

[a] Relative importance is computed as follows. Let E_s/E_n be the decimal ratio of state or regional employment in a given category (such as agricultural workers) to national employment in that category. Let P_s/P_n be the decimal ratio of state or regional total population to national (48 states and the District of Columbia) total population (including armed forces stationed in each area but excluding armed forces stationed overseas as of July 1 for each year). Then the relative importance of a given category for a given year for a given area is (E_s/E_n) divided by (P_s/P_n). This can also be expressed as (E_s/E_n) multiplied by (P_n/P_s). If a region had the amount of employment expected in a given category solely on the basis of total population, its relative importance index would be 1.00. This is the index value in all cases for the nation. The theoretic limits for the index are zero on the low side and infinity on the high side; thus it does not constitute an ideal index. Nevertheless, as a simply computed indicator of major trends in broad categories, this or a similar measure is useful.

Source. Basic population data are from the Bureau of the Census estimates as of July 1 for each year. A computer program synthesized county population estimates as of July 1. Basic employment data are from Table 4-3.

of the nation merely reflected rising productivity and improved technology. While these factors also undoubtedly operated in the Carolinas, they appear to have been combined with an employment pattern for which family workers were less adequate than formerly. Part-time work off the farm may have been replaced by hired work on the farm. Also, with the small farms characteristic of the two Carolinas, it was quite feasible for farm operators to work for each other in special seasons on an "exchange" basis. Such operators and/or their families might then appear in the hired- as well as in the family-worker category. Finally, some expansion of the truck- and fruit-crop acreage in the two states undoubtedly increased use of migrant hired workers.

The composition of the agricultural employment in both the Crescent and the non-Crescent areas of the two Carolinas shifted strongly away from family workers and toward hired workers. A similar change in composition occurred in the other two regions, though it was much less strong in the non-Carolina South and virtually of no consequence in the non-South. While its share of the nation's family workers declined, the Crescent's share of the nation's hired workers showed an increase and, as already noted in Table 4-4, its share of total agricultural workers remained about the same. The Crescent's relative importance in the family-worker group decreased, but its relative importance in the hired group increased. While the same statements were true of the non-Crescent area of the two Carolinas and the non-Carolina South, the non-South essentially reversed this pattern.

Table 4-5 is a presentation of the major industry divisions within the total of nonagricultural employment. Evident are the Crescent's very small commitment to mining at one extreme and its extremely heavy commitment to manufacturing at the other. The largest percentage gains in employment in the Crescent, non-Crescent, and non-Carolina South regions occurred in the division of employment comprising finance, insurance, and real estate. However, in these same regions the absolute increases in this division were relatively modest. In all three regions the largest absolute gains occurred in the wholesale and retail trade division. Numerous other comparisons are implicit in the data.

In Table 4-6 may be found compositional changes for the Crescent as regards nonagricultural divisions. For example, the Crescent experienced a slight de-emphasis of manufacturing and some increased emphasis in the wholesale and retail trade division. On the other hand,

Table 4-5. Nonagricultural Employment by Major Industry Divisions, Crescent Compared with Larger Regions, Annual Averages for 1947 and 1957 [a] *(Thousands of Persons)*

	1947	1957
Crescent		
Mining	0.9	1.4
Contract construction	29.1	35.2
Manufacturing	273.0	303.3
Transportation and public utilities	34.3	41.9
Wholesale and retail trade	91.6	128.3
Finance, insurance, and real estate	14.3	26.1
Service and miscellaneous	50.4	58.3
Government	38.1	60.6
Total	531.7	655.1
N. C. and S. C. less Crescent		
Mining	3.1	3.7
Contract construction	33.6	46.8
Manufacturing	340.9	392.2
Transportation and public utilities	43.6	46.9
Wholesale and retail trade	139.6	205.5
Finance, insurance, and real estate	10.7	24.2
Service and miscellaneous	68.6	85.4
Government	117.9	167.2
Total	758.0	971.9
Non-Carolina South		
Mining	304.6	337.5
Contract construction	433.6	654.1
Manufacturing	1,920.0	2,361.7
Transportation and public utilities	782.7	844.8
Wholesale and retail trade	1,682.5	2,465.6
Finance, insurance, and real estate	221.9	409.6
Service and miscellaneous	809.8	1,149.6
Government	1,113.8	1,635.0
Total	7,268.9	9,857.9
Non-South		
Mining	631.6	468.2
Contract construction	1,501.7	2,126.9
Manufacturing	12,710.5	13,663.4
Transportation and public utilities	3,230.1	3,256.2
Wholesale and retail trade	7,178.3	8,731.4
Finance, insurance, and real estate	1,396.4	1,921.8
Service and miscellaneous	3,730.4	4,847.3
Government	4,175.4	5,527.7
Total	34,554.5	40,542.9

Table 4-5 (Continued)

	1947	1957
United States		
Mining	940.2	810.8
Contract construction	1,998.0	2,863.0
Manufacturing	15,244.4	16,720.6
Transportation and public utilities	4,090.7	4,189.8
Wholesale and retail trade	9,092.0	11,530.8
Finance, insurance, and real estate	1,643.3	2,381.7
Service and miscellaneous	4,659.2	6,140.6
Government	5,445.3	7,390.5
Total	43,113.1	52,027.8

[a] See Table 4-3, footnotes *a–d*.

Sources. United States, Non-South, and Non-Carolina South: U. S. Department of Labor (1958).

Other regions: Allocations of state control totals to counties in North Carolina and South Carolina relied principally upon covered employment under the state Unemployment Insurance programs for the larger firms (7 employees or more) and upon covered employment under the Old-Age and Survivors Insurance programs for the smaller firms. Additional sources were used in the allocation of railroad employment within the transportation and public utilities division and in the allocation of the government division.

no very significant changes occurred in the per cent of national industry division totals to be found in the Crescent region. The relative importance indices indicate a gain for mining, transport-utilities, trade, finance, and government. But losses are registered for contract construction, manufacturing, and services. As for all nonagricultural employment, the table shows that the Crescent registered a decline (as did the preceding Table 4-4). This decline reflects the high degree of nonagricultural commitment which the Crescent had in common with the non-South at the opening of the period. The non-South also lost in relative importance in nonagricultural employment. During the same period the non-Crescent and the non-Carolina South regions were going through an earlier phase of the industrialization process and were making gains in relative importance regarding total nonagricultural employment.

Because of the Crescent's extremely heavy commitment in manufacturing employment, this alone of the major industry divisions is

Table 4-6. Nonagricultural Employment by Major Industry Divisions, Crescent Compared with Larger Regions, Selected Measures for 1947 and 1957

	PERCENTAGE COMPOSITION		PER CENT OF NATIONAL TOTAL IN EACH CATEGORY		RELATIVE IMPORTANCE [a]	
	1947	1957	1947	1957	1947	1957
Crescent						
Mining	0.2	0.2	0.1	0.2	0.09	0.15
Contract construction	5.5	5.4	1.4	1.3	1.37	1.07
Manufacturing	51.3	46.3	1.8	1.8	1.69	1.58
Transportation and public utilities	6.4	6.4	0.8	1.0	0.79	0.87
Wholesale and retail trade	17.2	19.6	1.0	1.1	0.95	0.97
Finance, insurance, and real estate	2.7	4.0	0.9	1.1	0.82	0.96
Service and miscellaneous	9.5	8.9	1.1	0.9	1.02	0.83
Government	7.2	9.2	0.7	0.8	0.66	0.72
Total	100.0	100.0	1.2	1.2	1.16	1.10
N. C. and S. C. less Crescent						
Mining	0.4	0.4	0.3	0.4	0.11	0.16
Contract construction	4.4	4.8	1.7	1.6	0.57	0.57
Manufacturing	45.0	40.4	2.2	2.4	0.76	0.82
Transportation and public utilities	5.8	4.8	1.1	1.1	0.36	0.39
Wholesale and retail trade	18.4	21.1	1.5	1.8	0.52	0.62
Finance, insurance, and real estate	1.4	2.5	0.6	1.0	0.22	0.35
Service and miscellaneous	9.0	8.8	1.5	1.4	0.50	0.48
Government	15.6	17.2	2.2	2.3	0.73	0.79
Total	100.0	100.0	1.8	1.9	0.59	0.65
Non-Carolina South						
Mining	4.2	3.4	32.4	41.6	1.37	1.78
Contract construction	6.0	6.6	21.7	22.8	0.91	0.98
Manufacturing	26.4	24.0	12.6	14.1	0.53	0.60
Transportation and public utilities	10.8	8.6	19.1	20.2	0.81	0.86
Wholesale and retail trade	23.1	25.0	18.5	21.4	0.78	0.91
Finance, insurance, and real estate	3.1	4.1	13.5	17.2	0.57	0.73
Service and miscellaneous	11.1	11.7	17.4	18.7	0.73	0.80
Government	15.3	16.6	20.4	22.1	0.86	0.94
Total	100.0	100.0	16.9	19.0	0.71	0.81
Non-South						
Mining	1.8	1.2	67.2	57.8	0.93	0.80
Contract construction	4.4	5.2	75.2	74.3	1.04	1.02
Manufacturing	36.8	33.7	83.4	81.7	1.15	1.13
Transportation and public utilities	9.3	8.0	79.0	77.7	1.09	1.07
Wholesale and retail trade	20.8	21.5	79.0	75.7	1.09	1.04

Table 4-6 (Continued)

	PERCENTAGE COMPOSITION		PER CENT OF NATIONAL TOTAL IN EACH CATEGORY		RELATIVE IMPORTANCE [a]	
	1947	1957	1947	1957	1947	1957
Finance, insurance, and real estate	4.0	4.8	85.0	80.7	1.18	1.11
Service and miscellaneous	10.8	12.0	80.0	79.0	1.11	1.09
Government	12.1	13.6	76.7	74.8	1.06	1.03
Total	100.0	100.0	80.1	77.9	1.11	1.07
United States						
Mining	2.2	1.6	100.0	100.0	1.00	1.00
Contract construction	4.6	5.5	100.0	100.0	1.00	1.00
Manufacturing	35.4	32.1	100.0	100.0	1.00	1.00
Transportation and public utilities	9.5	8.1	100.0	100.0	1.00	1.00
Wholesale and retail trade	21.1	22.1	100.0	100.0	1.00	1.00
Finance, insurance, and real estate	3.8	4.6	100.0	100.0	1.00	1.00
Service and miscellaneous	10.8	11.8	100.0	100.0	1.00	1.00
Government	12.6	14.2	100.0	100.0	1.00	1.00
Total	100.0	100.0	100.0	100.0	1.00	1.00

[a] Relative importance is computed as explained in note *a* of Table 4-4.

Sources. Basic population data are from the source cited in Table 4-4. Basic employment data are from Table 4-5.

examined in greater detail—at the two-digit Standard Industrial Classification (S.I.C.) level. These results are too voluminous for detailed presentation but they can be broadly summarized.

Both in the Crescent and the non-Crescent areas of the two Carolinas the overwhelmingly dominant manufacturing industry group in 1947 was textile-mill products (respectively 68.0 per cent and 50.5 per cent). By 1957 this concentration had ameliorated slightly to 58.5 per cent and to 46.4 per cent respectively. During the period there had been an 8.4 thousand loss in the 16-county area and a 9.9 thousand gain in the other 130 counties of the two-state area.

More striking is the fact that both areas contained a larger per cent of the national total at the end than at the beginning of the period. Thus the two states contained 26.9 per cent of the national total in 1947 and 35.9 per cent of the total in 1957. The heavy textile concentration persisted in the two-state area even while the industry nationally suffered a 24.8 per cent decline amounting to a national employment loss of 330,000.

Parallel to the textiles group there were increases in the per cent of national employment in tobacco manufactures, furniture and fixtures, and numerous other manufacturing industry groups in the Crescent and non-Crescent areas. However, as noted below, the highly successful competitive performance in the separate manufacturing industry groups did not result in any gain in relative importance in the total national manufacturing picture.

Limiting a general summary to absolute employment changes, it may be said that the Crescent has (1) continued the "balancing out" of agricultural in favor of nonagricultural employment commitments, (2) made the agricultural decline almost entirely in terms of family workers, actual slight gains having been registered in hired workers, (3) made impressive portions of the nonagricultural gains in the manufacturing, trade, and government divisions, and (4) made gains in apparel, furniture, chemicals, machinery, and electrical machinery, and losses in textile-mill products in the manufacturing industry division.

Going beyond the absolute changes, it should be noted that the Crescent area lost in relative importance in agricultural employment, in nonagricultural employment, and in total employment. The decline in relative importance in agriculture is not surprising since the Crescent is an urbanizing region. The decline in position in total nonagricultural employment occurred despite gains in position in over half the industry divisions. And the decline in total manufacturing status occurred despite status gains in 18 out of 21 industry groups within manufacturing!

As will be emphasized later, within manufacturing as within nonagricultural employment generally, the competitive gains of the region tended to be canceled by penalties inherent in specialization in industries with slow growth or declining national characteristics.

Capital Intensity, Productivity, Growth, and Stability

The two Carolinas experienced expenditures for manufacturing plant and equipment averaging in excess of 220 million dollars per year during the period 1947 through 1956. This expenditure volume represented about 3.1 per cent of the national total during the ten years.[7]

Whereas the two Carolinas had in excess of 4 per cent of the nation's manufacturing employment in the years 1954, 1955, and 1956, they had a little more than 3 per cent of the nation's manufacturing plant and equipment in place.[8] This makes a point concerning the manufacturing industry structure of the two Carolinas. It is generally "light" industry in the sense that the dollar volume of plant and equipment in place is proportionately of less weight in the national structure than is its corresponding employment volume. This observation is not true, however, for the non-Carolina South. Here the manufac-

Table 4-7. Mean Income Originating Per Person Engaged in Production, Increase Factors, and Relative Standard Error of Estimate, Industry Divisions and Selected Manufacturing Groups, United States, 1947 through 1957

	INCOME ORIGINATING PER PERSON (DOLLARS)	INCREASE FACTORS	RELATIVE STANDARD ERROR OF ESTIMATE
Agriculture, forestry, and fisheries	2,928	0.9732	1.0171
Mining	5,782	0.9817	1.0351
Contract construction	3,884	1.0332	1.0334
Manufacturing	5,334	1.0145	1.0364
Transportation and public utilities	5,526	1.0035	1.0202
Wholesale and retail trade	4,006	1.0163	1.0103
Finance, insurance, and real estate	11,084	1.0415	1.0144
Services and miscellaneous	6,396	1.0187	1.0175
Government [a]	3,691	1.0329	1.0194
All industries [b]	4,700	1.0137	1.0152
Food and kindred products	4,836	0.9999	1.0091
Tobacco manufactures	5,884	0.9955	1.0340
Textile mill products	3,764	0.9713	1.0302
Apparel and other finished products	3,150	1.0053	1.0167
Lumber and furniture products	3,693	0.9912	1.0450
Paper and allied products	5,998	1.0233	1.0200

[a] Federal military wages and salaries and federal military personnel are excluded from the basic computations for the government division.

[b] Federal military wages, federal military personnel, rest of the world national income, and rest of the world personnel are excluded from the basic computations for the line representing all industries.

Table 4-7 (Continued)

	INCOME ORIGINATING PER PERSON (DOLLARS)	INCREASE FACTORS	RELATIVE STANDARD ERROR OF ESTIMATE
Printing, publishing, and allied industries	5,219	1.0215	1.0051
Chemicals and allied products	7,703	1.0237	1.0387
Products of petroleum and coal	14,260	1.0060	1.0244
Rubber products	5,541	1.0085	1.0484
Leather and leather products	3,332	0.9918	1.0149
Stone, clay, and glass products	5,432	1.0104	1.0286
Metals, metal products, and miscellaneous	5,573	1.0216	1.0498
Machinery, except electrical	5,759	1.0175	1.0719
Electrical machinery, equipment, and supplies	5,351	1.0419	1.0820
Transportation equipment, except automobiles	5,148	1.1059	1.1643
Automobiles and automobile equipment	7,885	1.0099	1.0609

Source. Basic data are from the U. S. Department of Commerce (1958). Income originating per person is the mean of the income originating per person engaged in production for each of the years 1947 through 1957. Increase factors are the antilogs of the "*b*" values obtained when a straight line is fitted to the logs of the employment data by least squares. An increase factor of 1.0137 for all industry means that the compound annual growth rate in the number of persons engaged in production in all industries was about 1.37 per cent per year. The increase factor for agriculture, forestry, and fisheries indicates a negative compound annual growth rate. This compound rate of decline was $(0.9732 - 1.000) \times 100$ or about 2.68 per cent per year.

The relative standard error of estimate is the antilog of the value obtained by the expression $\sqrt{\frac{(\log Y - \log Yx)^2}{N}}$. In the case of all industries this antilog is 1.0152. In theory this value could be as low as 1.000 provided that there were absolutely no deviation between the original data and the fitted trend points. Consequently, the higher the value of the relative standard error of estimate, the less closely the original employment data conform to the fitted trend. The less close this fit, that is the more pronounced the departures of actual employment from the constant growth trend, the greater the indicated instability of the industry.

turing commitment includes, for example, petroleum, a high capital-intensity industry group.

In Table 4-7 are presented key indices relating to the productivity, growth, and stability of selected national industry groups. Since these are *national* measures, they cannot be considered precisely representative of conditions in the selected regions considered above. A generalization can be made, of course, to the effect that the larger the proportion of a particular national industry encompassed by a particular region, the greater the relevance of the national industry's indices to that particular region. In some degree, however, national characteristics of industries serve to characterize such an industry wherever it is found.

When all industry's characteristics are taken as the unit measure, the relative position of the various industry groupings can be determined in terms of that standard. Thus the standardized indices in terms of all industry units are presented in Table 4-8.

For example, the productivity entries indicate how income originating in an industry (all factor incomes, including wages, salaries, rents, interest, and profits) per person engaged in production compares with a similar measure for all industry. Thus agriculture rates low on productivity while the finance, insurance, and real-estate division rates high.

Growth is measured in terms of the relationship between a fitted constant growth rate for an industry's employment compared with a similar constant for all industry. Here it may be noted that mining is a declining industry division and contract construction is a growing industry division. Among the manufacturing industry groups included in Table 4-8, textile-mill products shows up as a declining group and electrical machinery appears as a rapid growth group.

Finally, stability is measured in terms of how closely the annual average employment conforms to a constant rate of expansion (or decline) in the series. In the basic index form the "highest value" an industry can have in this respect is the lowest index, namely 1.0000. When these indices are transformed as in Table 4-8 the larger indices represent a relatively high degree of time series conformity to constant growth rates, and vice versa. In this respect the trade division rates high while the manufacturing division rates low on stability. Similar comparisons may be made among the manufacturing industry groups shown.

Each industry division and each industry group will be found to have its own constellation of values among the standardized indices of pro-

Table 4-8. Productivity, Growth, and Stability in All Industry Units, Industry Divisions, and Selected Manufacturing Groups, United States, 1947 through 1957

	PRODUCTIVITY [a]	GROWTH [b]	STABILITY [c]
Agriculture, forestry, and fisheries	0.6229	1.9570–	0.8926
Mining	1.2302	1.3396–	0.4337
Contract construction	0.8265	2.4218	0.4562
Manufacturing	1.1348	1.0616	0.4183
Transportation and public utilities	1.1758	0.2554	0.7519
Wholesale and retail trade	0.8524	1.1920	1.4775
Finance, insurance, and real estate	2.3583	3.0338	1.0557
Services and miscellaneous	1.3609	1.3662	0.8709
Government	0.7854	2.4056	0.7846
All industries	1.0000	1.0000	1.0000
Food and kindred products	1.0289	0.0086–	1.6742
Tobacco manufactures	1.2518	0.3275–	0.4481
Textile mill products	0.8009	2.0989–	0.5039
Apparel and other finished products	0.6703	0.3903	0.9137
Lumber and furniture products	0.7857	0.6432–	0.3383
Paper and allied products	1.2761	1.7053	0.7603
Printing, publishing, and allied industries	1.1104	1.5721	2.9727
Chemicals and allied products	1.6390	1.7320	0.3933
Products of petroleum and coal	3.0341	0.4394	0.6241
Rubber products	1.1789	0.6198	0.3144
Leather and leather products	0.7090	0.5977–	1.0217
Stone, clay, and glass products	1.1557	0.7605	0.5329
Metals, metal products, and miscellaneous	1.1858	1.5795	0.3057
Machinery, except electrical	1.2252	1.2776	0.2118
Electrical machinery, equipment, and supplies	1.1385	3.0622	0.1856
Transportation equipment, except automobiles	1.0953	7.7348	0.0926
Automobiles and automobile equipment	1.6776	0.7217	0.2498

[a] Productivity is the average annual income originating per person engaged in production in each of the industry divisions and manufacturing industry groups during 1947–1957 (Table 4-7) as a multiple of the same measure for all industries. Example for agriculture, forestry, and fisheries: 2,928/4,700 = 0.6229.

[b] Growth is the increase factor in each industry division and manufacturing industry group during 1947–1957 less 1.000 taken as a multiple of the same measure for all industries. Example (from Table 4-7) for agriculture, forestry, and fisheries:

$$(0.9732 - 1.0000)/(1.0137 - 1.0000) = (-0.0268)/(0.0137) = -1.9570.$$

[c] Stability is the reciprocal of the relative standard error of estimate in each industry division and manufacturing industry group during 1947–1957 (Table 4-7) less 1.0000 taken as a multiple of the same measure for all industries. Example for agriculture, forestry, and fisheries:

$$\frac{1}{(1.0171 - 1.0000)/(1.0152 - 1.0000)} = 0.8926.$$

Source. Basic data are the unrounded version of data included in Table 4-7.

ductivity, growth, and stability. Were the data available, individual industries such as cigarettes (S.I.C. 211) or tobacco stemming and re-drying (S.I.C. 214) could be similarly analyzed. However, whether or not the analysis is carried to finer industrial detail, a problem is faced in relating these particular industry characteristics to the regions of interest.

It would appear to be a reasonable hypothesis that the characteristics of a region with respect to its employment productivity, growth, and stability will be determined by its particular employment structure, since the national characteristics for each component element of the

Table 4-9. Total Industry Productivity, Stability, and Growth, Crescent Compared with Larger Regions, 1947 to 1957

	CONVEX COMBINATIONS OF INDUSTRY DIVISION INDICES [a]		
	PRODUCTIVITY	GROWTH	STABILITY
Crescent	1.04990	0.97342	0.76442
N. C. and S. C. less Crescent	0.89098	0.14515	0.82170
Non-Carolina South	0.97952	0.70105	0.86249
Non-South	1.05277	1.05378	0.81779
United States	1.03332	0.95593	0.82649
	NATIONAL STANDARD CONVEX COMBINATIONS OF INDUSTRY DIVISION INDICES [b]		
	PRODUCTIVITY	GROWTH	STABILITY
Crescent	1.016	1.018	0.925
N. C. and S. C. less Crescent	0.862	0.152	0.994
Non-Carolina South	0.948	0.733	1.044
Non-South	1.019	1.102	0.989
United States	1.000	1.000	1.000

[a] These are weighted averages where the weights on the respective industry indices (Table 4-8) are applied in accordance with the amount of employment in these industries in 1957 as shown in Table 4-5.

[b] These are the convex combinations above where every entry is divided by the national entry.

Source. Basic data are from Tables 4-8 and 4-5.

structure can be specified. Proceeding on this basis each region's characteristics are specified as a convex combination (weighted average) of the national characteristics of the component industry divisions.

In Table 4-9 it would appear that the Crescent region closely resembles the non-South in respect to productivity, growth, and stability. This conclusion, however, results from the use of broad industry divisions as building blocks. The smaller and more specialized the region, such as the Crescent, the less appropriate the use of these broad overall industry division characteristics. The obvious remedy is to examine not merely the characteristics of the broad divisions but in addition the characteristics of the particular regional industrial commitments within these broad divisions. Unfortunately data limitations prevent such as examination, except for manufacturing which alone represented over 41 per cent of the Crescent's employment in 1957. Such an examination is highly relevant.

Nationally, manufacturing rates slightly higher than "all industry" on productivity and growth, and rates considerably lower on stability. It is a fact, however, as shown in Table 4-8, that almost the reverse is true of those parts of the manufacturing industry division in which the Crescent has a large stake, such as textile-mill products and the lumber-furniture groups.

The result of the combination of the national characteristics of the manufacturing industry divisions is shown in Table 4-10. Here it is evident that the Crescent region resembles the non-Crescent region of the two Carolinas much more than it resembles the non-South.

The ideal comparison cannot be made because data do not permit direct comparisons of income origination, growth rates, and stability in all industries as they are actually to be found in the several regions. The examination of regions through the national characteristics of their component industries at best does not permit sharp focus on regional characteristics. Here even this has not been possible in any detail except in manufacturing—the other employment commitments being represented only as major industry divisions. Within manufacturing alone, however, the Crescent in the period 1947 to 1957 was very low in terms of productivity, drastically low in terms of growth, and slightly low in terms of stability. Characterization with respect to analysis of *all* two-digit industry groups has not been possible.

Since slow growth is suggested as the most acute problem of the Crescent, the analysis is narrowed at this point to consideration of growth, past and prospective. At the same time the analysis is intensified by relating growth to migration and industrial shift patterns.

Table 4-10. Manufacturing Productivity, Stability, and Growth, Crescent Compared with Larger Regions, 1947 to 1957

	CONVEX COMBINATIONS OF MANUFACTURING INDUSTRY GROUP INDICES [a]		
	PRODUCTIVITY	GROWTH	STABILITY
Crescent	0.90553	0.94104−	0.59216
N. C. and S. C. less Crescent	0.90874	0.76262−	0.58757
Non-Carolina South	1.14333	0.77532	0.71428
Non-South	1.15301	1.52261	0.64927
United States	1.14082	1.30941	0.65619
	NATIONAL STANDARD CONVEX COMBINATIONS OF MANUFACTURING INDUSTRY GROUP INDICES [b]		
	PRODUCTIVITY	GROWTH	STABILITY
Crescent	0.794	0.719−	0.902
N. C. and S. C. less Crescent	0.797	0.582−	0.895
Non-Carolina South	1.002	0.592	1.089
Non-South	1.011	1.163	0.989
United States	1.000	1.000	1.000

[a] These are weighted averages where the weights on the respective industry group indices (lower section of Table 4-8) are applied in accordance with the amount of employment in 1957.

[b] These are the convex combinations above where every entry is divided by the national entry.

Source. Basic data are from Table 4-8 above and from 1957 manufacturing industry group employment (not shown).

Growth, Migration, and Industrial Shift

In the preceding section slow growth in the Crescent and surrounding areas was indicated in the postwar years. It is well to recognize, however, that industrial growth is guided and directed by broad economic forces. The continuing rise in incomes of the nation's consumers has tended to place a premium on consumer appliances and luxuries heretofore unknown. At the same time such income rises have done little to stimulate the demand for basic agricultural products where consumer satiation is reached at a lower level of income. The result is the well-known "cost-price" squeeze which occurs in agriculture when the prices that farmers receive for agricultural outputs rise at a pace slower than the prices these same farmers pay for agricultural machinery, fertilizer, and other inputs.

This cost-price squeeze makes nonfarm employment opportunities more attractive than those on the farm. It sets up an industrial migration which has reduced the farm population of the United States by more than 4 million persons between 1950 and 1960 (U. S. Department of Commerce and U. S. Department of Agriculture, 1959). This process is at the base of the mainstream of industrial migration. Agriculturally committed areas continue to generate labor-force participants at a faster pace than they generate employment opportunities. The nonagriculturally committed areas stand in a complementary position —generating fewer labor-force participants than job opportunities.

Net migration for the period 1950 to 1960 was generally outward for states of heavy agricultural commitment and generally inward for states of a highly urbanized character. Even after the urbanizing process of the 1950's, the two Carolinas remain dominantly rural. In this respect they differ from the non-Carolina South and the non-South.

Owing to the nature of its agricultural technology, North Carolina in 1950 had retained its small farms and heavy farm population to a greater degree than most agricultural states and even more than most agricultural states in the South. As a consequence, North Carolina's out-migration rate was stronger in the 1950's than it had been in the 1940's. In contrast, in South Carolina and other southern states the out-migration process diminished in the 1950's from the 1940–1950 level. With North Carolina's rate increasing and South Carolina's decreasing in the 1950's, the two-state *rate* remained at the level of the 1940's. In absolute numbers, on the other hand, the two states had net out-migration of 488,000 in the 1940's and 549,000 in the 1950's (U. S. Department of Commerce, 1961).

In addition to the strong out-migration which the two Carolinas continue to generate, it has been shown that they are in some measure way-stations in the path of the out-migratory currents originating in other southern states (Bunting and Prosper, 1960). All of this adds up to a tremendous urbanization potential in the Crescent. The Crescent is the nucleus of a two-state agricultural area with a net out-migrant flow of over 50,000 per year. In addition it is a natural first stop for many thousands of industrial migrants from other southern states on their way northward and eastward.

Obviously, however, the Crescent does not and will not realize its urbanization potential without an industrial structure with growth characteristics capable of absorbing a larger part of this migratory flow. The general nature of the problem is well known and fairly well understood. What may be less clear is the heavy role of inertia. The two Carolinas have a built-in imbalance between generation of labor-force participants and generation of employment opportunities. Such an imbalance cannot be quickly changed since it is deeply rooted in a long-standing age distribution on the one hand and an almost equally long-standing industrial composition on the other.

In the period 1947 to 1957 the Crescent as the urban core of the two-state area made some contribution toward the righting of the migratory imbalance. However, the contribution was slight in comparison with the magnitude of the migratory currents. In particular, if the Crescent area's employment had grown at the national rate in the 1947 to 1957 period, its total employment would have been 718,000 in 1957. In fact it had achieved a total employment of 735,000. Thus by over-all national employment growth standards there was a net total employment in-movement amounting to 17,000. This, however, is the over-all picture.

The net in-shift of employment to the Crescent is made up of two parts, a competitive component and a compositional component.[9] Of the nine major industry divisions, shown earlier in Table 4-5, the Crescent made competitive gains in six. That is, six of the nine industry divisions showed more employment in 1957 in the Crescent than they would have been expected to show at national rates of increase on the 1947 base. These six included: mining; manufacturing (a manufacturing competitive gain of 4,000); transportation and public utilities; wholesale and retail trade; finance, insurance, and real estate; and government. There were competitive losses on the other hand in agriculture, contract construction, and services. These competitive losses, however, were smaller than the competitive gains so that on the whole the Crescent registered net competitive gains amounting to 21,000 employees. This is to say that, considering the industrial commitments it had, the Crescent gained 21,000 more employees than might have been expected solely in terms of national industrial expansion rates between 1947 and 1957.

The next question concerns how a competitive employment gain of

21,000 can be reconciled with a net over-all gain of 17,000. The answer is that the competitive gain was partially canceled by a compositional loss, so that the complete postwar picture of the Crescent's shift pattern is:

Competitive	(gain)	21,000
Compositional	(loss)	4,000
Net total	(gain)	17,000

The compositional losses are induced by having industries whose combined (weighted average) growth rate falls short of the national combined (weighted average) growth rate for all national industries. There are some regions, for example the entire non-South, which have compositional gains rather than compositional losses.

This is an illustration of how past commitments may act as a brake, rather than as a stimulus to employment expansion. If a region starts a period with heavy commitments to industries of slow-growth characteristics, it is not likely to achieve over-all rapid growth simply by doing well in those industries that it has.

A summary of gains and losses for four component regions of the national economy is:

	COMPETITIVE	COMPOSITIONAL	NET TOTAL
Crescent	21,000	−4,000	17,000
N. C. and S. C. less Crescent	48,000	−248,000	−200,000
Non-Carolina South	746,000	−737,000	9,000
Non-South	−815,000	989,000	174,000
United States	0	0	0

In summary, the Crescent's performance looks superficially good. What should be remembered, however, is that the Crescent is the only urban region shown and that it must be judged by a harsher standard than is applied to entire states or regions. The sum of the Crescent and the non-Crescent areas of the two Carolinas represents the totality of the two Carolinas. This result may be compared with that for the non-Carolina South:

	COMPETITIVE	COMPOSITIONAL	NET TOTAL
N. C. and S. C.	68,000	−251,000	−183,000
Non-Carolina South	746,000	−737,000	9,000

Here it is evident that whereas the large urban areas of the Carolinas were completely overwhelmed by their agricultural hinterland, the large urban industrial centers in the remainder of the South were able to achieve a slight regional in-shift.

This disparate outcome has been explained largely in terms of industrial structure. It must be remembered, however, that this is merely the reflection of the more rapid urbanization of the non-Carolina South as indicated in the censuses of 1950 and 1960.

Figure 4-3 graphically summarizes the competitive-compositional shift patterns of the two Carolinas, the non-Carolina South, and the non-South. The positions of the arrows (vectors) indicate both the size and the relative importance of the competitive and compositional

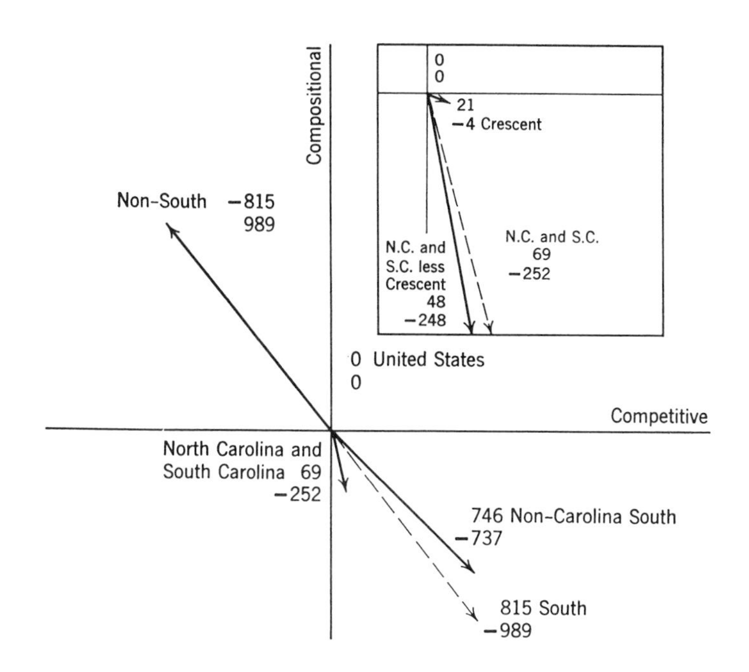

Figure 4-3. Competitive and compositional employment shifts, the Carolinas and selected regions, 1947 to 1957. *Note:* The end point of each arrow (vector) measures two things. Its horizontal distance from the origin measures competitive employment shifts. Its vertical distance from the origin measures compositional employment shifts. Thus upper figures represent thousands of competitive employment shifts; lower figures represent thousands of compositional employment shifts. The algebraic sum of the two figures represents net total employment shift. Two vectors may be added by summing their respective competitive and compositional shifts. *Source:* Basic data are estimates of average regional employment in the major industry divisions for the years 1947 and 1957. The data are given in Tables 4-3 and 4-5.

employment shifts over the period. Note that the combined Carolinas and the non-Carolina South experienced competitive gains and compositional losses. However, the relatively greater importance of the compositional losses in the two Carolinas is indicated by the steeper down-slope of their vector.

The sum of the vectors for the two Carolinas and the non-Carolina South yields the dashed vector which represents the position of the entire South. Directly opposed to the vector for the South is the vector for the non-South. The sum of these latter two vector points is the zero vector which represents the position of the continental United States (48 states and the District of Columbia). With the national industry increase factors taken as the standard of measurement, the national shift position is represented at the origin, by definition.

In order to show the position of the Crescent and non-Crescent areas within the two Carolinas, the vector for the two-state area is presented on a larger scale in Figure 4-3 (inset) as a dashed vector. Also presented are the component non-Crescent and Crescent vectors. The very steep slope of the non-Crescent stands in sharp contrast to the shallow slope of the Crescent-area vector. It is clear that the Crescent counties in the aggregate have made strong competitive gains relative to their compositional losses. It is equally clear that the area of the Carolinas outside the Crescent has had its employment shift pattern dominated by compositional losses due largely to the heavy agricultural commitment. Finally, it is apparent that had the Crescent area been able to perform in a more decisive manner—either by a change in the slope or the length of its shift vector—the effect on the two-state region would have been profound. This fact underlines the strategic importance of the Crescent as the urban core of the region, since it offers the only major migratory terminal point.

It is necessary to emphasize that the Crescent is not now, nor has it been a monolithic homogeneous area. Instead, as already indicated in such matters as total income and population growth, the several constituent counties behave in the most diverse ways. In Figure 4-4 the scale of Figure 4-3 (inset) is considerably enlarged. It is amplified to show not merely the shift pattern of the entire Crescent, but also the shift pattern of the separate sixteen Crescent counties. In this figure, instead of starting each county's vector at the origin, these vectors are entered alphabetically with each vector attached to the terminal point of the preceding chain of vectors. Of course, no matter what the order of entry, the terminal point of the final county vector must coincide with the terminal point for the entire Crescent vector. This is true because the shift pattern for the entire Crescent is but the sum of the shift patterns for the constituent counties.

Figure 4-4 makes it clear that almost every conceivable vector length and direction is to be found in the performance of the sixteen Crescent counties. Some counties performed rather strongly in making both competitive and compositional gains, notably Forsyth, Guilford, and Mecklenburg. The performance of some other counties appears to have been indifferent or downright perverse. Though measurement errors may indeed account for some of the apparently erratic behavior, there appears to be little doubt that at the least the performance was highly variable as among counties over the eleven-year period.

The manufacturing competitive gain of 4,000 for the Crescent contained in the analysis summarized above is labeled as net total gain in manufacturing in a subsidiary analysis of manufacturing.[10] The sub-

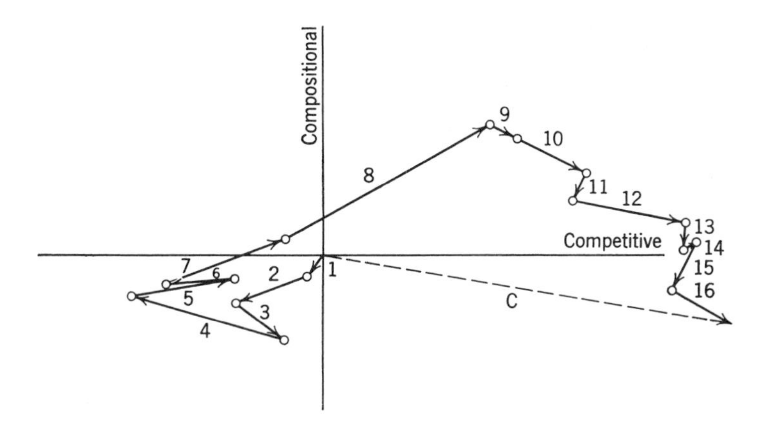

Figure 4-4. Industrial employment shifts, directional vectors, sixteen Crescent counties, 1947 to 1957. (1) Alamance (−964, −1,205); (2) Cabarrus (−3,650, −1,169); (3) Davidson (2,698, −2,073); (4) Durham (−8,258, 2,172); (5) Forsyth (6,114, 1,005); (6) Gaston (−4,191, −689); (7) Guilford (6,300, 2,745); (8) Mecklenburg (10,834, 6,045); (9) Orange (1,383, −766); (10) Randolph (3,855, −1,980); (11) Rowan (−984, −1,611); (12) Wake (5,924, −516); (13) Cherokee (−20, −1,486); (14) Greenville (579, 225); (15) Spartanburg (−1,352, −2,528); (16) York (2,949, −1,937). C = Crescent Total (21,217, −3,768). *Note:* The first figure represents competitive employment shifts; the second figure represents compositional employment shifts. Sixteen county vectors are here assembled to show their equivalence to the total Crescent vector. See also the note on Figure 4-3. *Source:* Basic data are estimates of average county employment in the major industry divisions for the years 1947 and 1957. The industry divisions are those identified in Table 4-5.

sidiary analysis concerns itself with the twenty-one two-digit manufacturing industry groups. It breaks the Crescent's net total gain into two familiar subcomponents, the competitive and the compositional. The results are:

Competitive	(gain)	76,000
Compositional	(loss)	72,000
Net total	(gain)	4,000

Again, the performance might have been stronger if either (1) the given component industry groups had grown at an unusually rapid pace or (2) the region had been endowed with a different set of component groups having faster growth characteristics performing at their normal growth rates. Since the Crescent's initial endowment of manufacturing was only 273,000 and its terminal amount was only 303,000, it would have been unreasonable to expect larger competitive gains than the 72,000 actually realized. On the other hand, to have significantly reduced the compositional losses would have implied a radically different industrial structure.

In the subsidiary analysis of manufacturing performance, the several regions are summarized as follows:

	COMPETITIVE	COMPOSITIONAL	NET TOTAL
Crescent	76,000	−72,000	4,000
N. C. and S. C. less Crescent	100,000	−82,000	18,000
Non-Carolina South	434,000	−178,000	256,000
Non-South	−610,000	332,000	−278,000
United States	0	0	0

The graphic presentation of these data proceeds from major regions through to the Crescent counties in Figures 4-5 and 4-6. Generally the manufacturing performance vectors show a shallower slope away from the horizontal than do the total industry vectors. This indicates that for most regions the compositional shifts are relatively less important within manufacturing than they were within total employment across all industry divisions. The opportunity for regional compositional variability is much less within the relatively homogeneous manufacturing industry division than is the case within the diverse and unlike major industry divisions.[11] Figure 4-5 (inset) shows the Crescent and non-Crescent areas with nearly identical competitive and compositional orientations. Figure 4-6 reveals a considerable similarity in orientation among the sixteen Crescent counties.

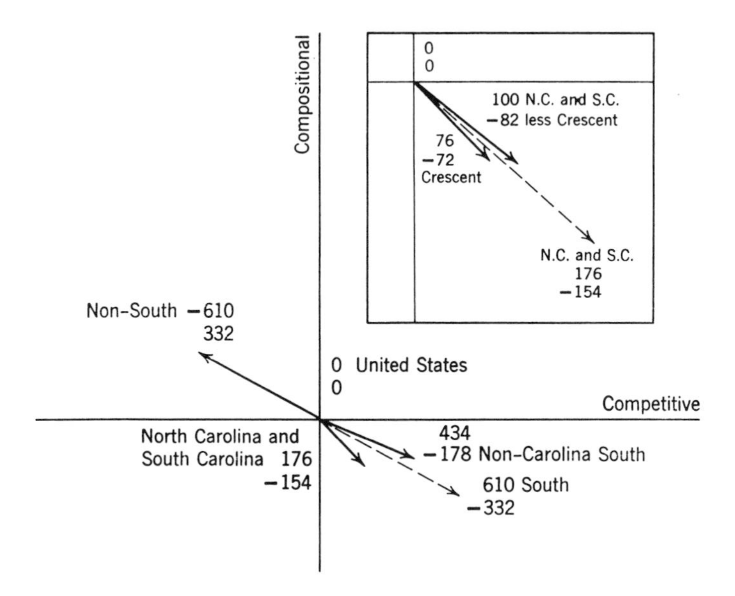

Figure 4-5. Competitive and compositional manufacturing employment shifts, the Carolinas and selected regions, 1947 to 1957. *Note:* Upper figures represent thousands of competitive employment shifts; lower figures represent thousands of compositional employment shifts. See also the note on Figure 4-3. *Source:* Basic data are estimates of average regional manufacturing employment in the 21 two-digit industry groups of manufacturing for the years 1947 and 1957. These data are not presented.

A Future Pattern

The population-growth pace of the urban Crescent in the years ahead will depend largely upon the extent to which adequately stable and remunerative job opportunities are made available to heads of households in the area.

The rate at which such opportunities become available will depend in considerable measure upon the industrial structure which exists today and upon the changes in that structure which are brought about in the future.

Since unique events are unpredictable, projections are useful for presenting plausible developments rather than predicted developments. With this qualification in mind, a projection is offered relevant to the pace of industrial growth.

The fundamental basis for this projection is the pattern of growth

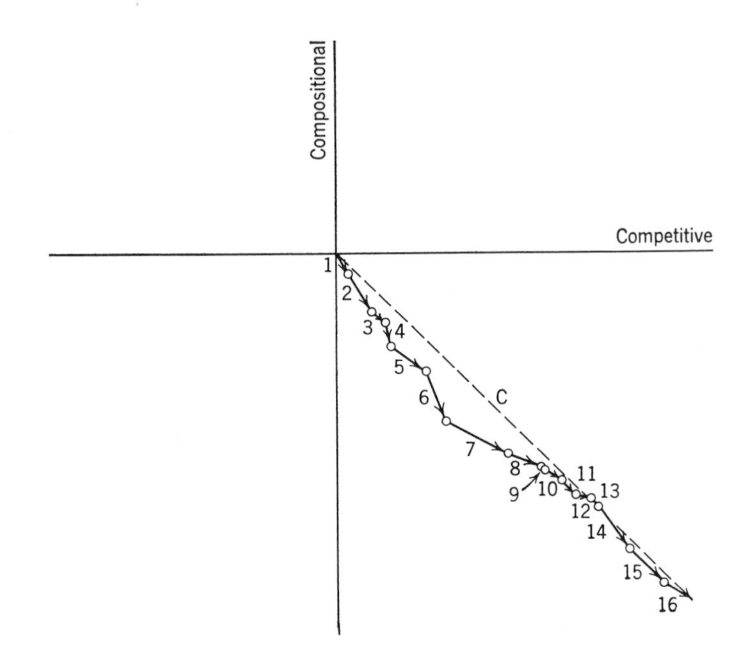

Figure 4-6. Manufacturing employment shifts, directional vectors, sixteen Crescent counties, 1947 to 1957. (1) Alamance (3,183, −4,550); (2) Cabarrus (4,501, −8,116); (3) Davidson (3,114, −2,305); (4) Durham (117, −4,241); (5) Forsyth (8,818, −5,973); (6) Gaston (3,580, −10,187); (7) Guilford (13,884, −6,806); (8) Mecklenburg (7,830, −3,154); (9) Orange (469, −493); (10) Randolph (4,454, −2,406); (11) Rowan (1,170, −2,342); (12) Wake (3,498, −1,069); (13) Cherokee (1,156, −1,176); (14) Greenville (7,349, −9,467); (15) Spartanburg (7,418, −7,233); (16) York (5,419, −3,634). C = Crescent Total (75,960, −72,152). *Note:* The first figure represents competitive employment shifts; the second figure represents compositional employment shifts. Sixteen county vectors are here assembled as a sequence to show their equivalence to the total Crescent vector. See also the note on Figure 4-3. *Source:* Basic data are estimates of average county manufacturing employment in the 21 two-digit industry groups of manufacturing for the years 1947 and 1957. These data are not presented.

rates for major industrial divisions anticipated for the United States by the United States Department of Labor (1960). While specific expansion rates have not been suggested by the United States Department of Labor, rates have been used here which are consistent with the range of rates anticipated by that agency.[12] When applied to the 1957 national employment levels in the several major industry divisions, these rates afford a plausible national level of employment in 1967, at the termination of another decade of growth. These projected changes involve continued decline in agriculture but expansion in all the other eight major industry divisions. The over-all industry expansion rate is 20 per cent.

The national projections having been made, projections are then made within the national control totals for the major regions of interest here.[13] The application of the industrial shift analysis to the projected major industry division employments yields the following results.

	COMPETITIVE	COMPOSITIONAL	NET TOTAL
Crescent	37,000	1,000	38,000
N. C. and S. C. less Crescent	104,000	−177,000	−73,000
Non-Carolina South	996,000	−382,000	614,000
Non-South	−1,137,000	558,000	−579,000
United States	0	0	0

It should be noted immediately that this projection indicates a "better" performance for the Crescent in the coming decade than in the one previously analyzed. The net total gain in the preceding decade was 17,000 workers, representing the combination of a competitive gain of 21,000 and a compositional loss of 4,000. In the present projection the net total gain is 38,000, composed of a competitive gain of 37,000 and a compositional gain of 1,000.

Thus in accordance with this projection the shift-pattern vector of the Crescent changes from a short length of a slightly negative slope to a longer length of a slightly positive slope.

An inspection of the projection will reveal, however, the better performance of the Crescent is set in the context of a better performance for the non-Crescent area of the two Carolinas and for the entire non-Carolina South.

It would appear that the entire South is "over the hump" as regards the entire shift pattern. The net total loss of 174,000 in the 1947–1957 period for the entire South contrasts with the net total gain of 579,000 (sum of Crescent, non-Crescent, and non-Carolina South) in the projected period. In one sense, however, the South's position has not yet matured. Even in the projected period the compositional loss for the South amounts to 558,000. This is largely attributable to the still large southern agricultural commitment as of 1957. Such compositional losses, however, are not likely to persist in those areas of the South (such as the Crescent) where the process of de-agriculturalization is well advanced.

It is well to emphasize that no matter what employment-growth pattern is projected for the several regions, their position as regards compositional gain or loss cannot be affected. Such gain or loss, under the particular analytical method used here, depends solely upon the pattern of national industrial growth rates and the initial industrial employment commitments of the several regions.[14]

There can be no doubt that the position of the South as a whole in regard to net total employment shifts will be much stronger in the 1957 to 1967 than in the 1947 to 1957 period. This change in position will undoubtedly accompany a continuing diminution of the rate of net out-migration from the entire South.

As the entire South becomes less agricultural and more urban, it becomes more "self-contained" as regards labor-force generation and the creation of employment opportunities. But while the non-Carolina South may be experiencing net total gains, it remains virtually certain that the non-Crescent area of the Carolinas will be experiencing diminished but continuing net total losses.

Thus the broad picture is of the Crescent enjoying net total gains but set in a matrix of some 130 counties which in the aggregate will be experiencing net total losses. Finally, the surrounding non-Crescent area will itself be contained in a non-Carolina South which is making net total gains.

It is quite plausible, with the stage thus set, that the "newcomers" to the Crescent will continue to be in large part the former residents of the non-Crescent area of the two Carolinas. It is also evident, however, that such Carolinians will find ample employment opportunity in the surrounding South.

The question as to what this means for the growth potential of the Crescent in relation to other urban centers of the nation and the South deserves consideration. On the comparative behavior of similarly situated small regions, it is not safe to make predictions, since such regions can be significantly affected by unique events. For example, a series of events consisting in imaginative industrial promotion has been in process even since the major terminal point (1957) for the employment estimates of this study. Another series of events has culminated in the establishment of a research park, an internationally significant research institute, and several nationally important research centers in the extreme eastern tip of the Crescent. The entire enterprise known as the Research Triangle offers the possibility of spearheading an entirely new era of industrial expansion in the region.

Recent events of the type just indicated have probably not been fully accounted for in the "mechanical" projection made above. But by their nature, such events cannot be fully considered. No large-scale comprehensive deterministic model lays down the industrial or urban-growth patterns which regions or cities must follow. In large measure the rates and kinds of growth in a particular urban area will depend on the screening process which that urban area *in itself* constitutes. Ours is a mobile population, especially at the growing edge. The Crescent and its constituent urban areas can shape their own characteristics as regards the productivity, growth, and stability of their employment opportunities. They can do this by giving special attention to the nature of the industrial change now in process. To get certain kinds of desired industrial expansion, the right growing conditions must be present. The Crescent is a region which today as never before is examining the trace elements in hand and the industrial expansions they are likely to induce. Superimposed on these research foundations are the day-to-day policy decisions which will confine or accommodate the growth potential of the coming decades.

FOOTNOTES

1. The author is indebted to Charles F. Floyd for the preparation of a historical survey on the location of North Carolina cities in the urban corridor.
2. See Chapter 2.
3. Women are excluded from the labor force by definition when their only work is housework. Of course, by census definition, they are counted as employed if it is indicated that they worked without pay for fifteen hours or longer on a family farm or in a family business.
4. See Chapter 3.
5. See Chapter 5.
6. A more complete treatment of the explanation of income differentials in terms of occupational composition will be found in Frank A. Hanna (1957).
7. Basic data from Huntley (1960, Table IIIA-1, p. 264).
8. Employment data are from U. S. Department of Labor (1958). Manufacturers' plant and equipment in place is an estimate resulting from application of straight-line depreciation to current dollar (historical cost) expenditures and are taken from Huntley (1960, Table VA-1, p. 282).
9. The method of derivation of the total net shift, competitive shift, and residual compositional shift is equivalent to that explained in Perloff, Dunn, Lampard, and Muth (1960, Chap. 5). These authors in turn credit earlier

work by Daniel Creamer, Wilbur Zelinsky, and Victor R. Fuchs. The particular method used by Perloff et al. places more emphasis on the additive nature of differential and proportionality shifts (here referred to following Dunn's usage in other papers as competitive and compositional). The results given can be obtained either through a simple arithmetical operation or as the inner products of properly defined vectors. Either method is amenable to the time-saving procedures of computer programming.

10. The subsidiary analysis is available as the output of a computer program which deals with nineteen component regions of the United States, sixteen of them being Crescent counties.
11. Though data were not available to make it possible, similar analysis of the competitive and compositional shifts within major industrial divisions other than manufacturing could have been made. Likewise, three-digit employment data could have been used to analyze the component parts of the two-digit competitive shifts. Conceptually, the method can be indefinitely extended to finer and finer industrial breakdowns.
12. The specific growth rates used (as decimal fractions) are:

Agriculture	−0.20	Wholesale and retail trade	0.30
Mining	0.10	Finance, insurance, and real estate	0.35
Contract construction	0.35	Service and miscellaneous	0.30
Manufacturing	0.20	Government	0.30
Transportation and public utilities	0.10	All industries	0.20

13. These projections rest on a simple assumption to the effect that the trends in the per cents which the several regions constituted of the national control totals in the years 1947 through 1957 will persist for the period 1957 through 1967. Thus for the Crescent, a straight line is fitted by least squares to the percentage points which the Crescent's agricultural employment constituted of the nation. The same is done for the three other regions of the nation. By statistical necessity, since the regression lines were fitted to percentages which added to 100 per cent, the projection or extension of these regression lines yielded percentages adding to 100 per cent in the projected years. These projected regional percentages of the national total necessarily precisely exhaust the national total for any given future year, such as 1967.
14. For example a "judgment" projection made independently of and prior to the "mechanical" projection described above turned out less favorable to the Crescent and to the entire South as follows:

	COMPETITIVE	COMPOSITIONAL	NET TOTAL
Crescent	11,000	1,000	12,000
N. C. and S. C. less Crescent	−19,000	−177,000	−196,000
Non-Carolina South	819,000	−382,000	437,000
Non-South	−811,000	558,000	−253,000
United States	0	0	0

Note that the compositional shift pattern is identical to that described in the "mechanical" projection for the reason cited. The compositional shift depends solely upon national growth rates and the industrial employment endowment of the several regions at the start of the period being analyzed.

REFERENCES

Ashby, Lowell D., and Sang O. Park (1961), *Financing Unemployment Compensation in North Carolina, 1936–1965.* Chapel Hill, N. C.: School of Business Administration, University of North Carolina.

Ashby, Lowell D., and W. Allen Spivey (1957), "Gains in Real Per Capita Income: A Method of Analysis," *The Southern Economic Journal,* XXIV:2, 148–157.

Bunting, Robert L., and Peter A. Prosper (1960), *Labor Mobility Patterns in the Piedmont Industrial Crescent,* Urban Studies Program, Institute for Research in Social Science. Chapel Hill, N. C.: University of North Carolina.

Hanna, Frank A. (1957), "Analysis of Interstate Income Differentials: Theory and Practice," *Regional Income Studies in Income and Wealth,* Vol. XXI, Conference on Research in Income and Wealth. Princeton, N. J.: Princeton University Press.

Huntley, Patrick Ross (1960), "State Distribution of Manufacturers' Plant and Equipment in Place, 1954–1956," unpublished Ph.D. dissertation, Department of Economics, University of North Carolina, Chapel Hill.

Jones, Barclay Gibbs (1957), *County Income Estimates for North Carolina Counties.* Chapel Hill, N. C.: School of Business Administration, University of North Carolina. North Carolina Department of Tax Research (1960), Press Release July 5, 1960, Raleigh.

Paterson, Robert W., and Pat. L. Wilcox (1959), "County Income Estimates for South Carolina," *Business and Economic Review.* Columbia, S. C.: University of South Carolina.

Perloff, Harvey S., Edgar S. Dunn, Jr., Eric E. Lampard, and Richard F. Muth (1960), *Region, Resources, and Economic Growth.* Baltimore, Md.: The Johns Hopkins Press.

U. S. Department of Agriculture, Agricultural Marketing Service (1958), *Farm Employment,* Statistical Bulletin No. 236. Washington: Government Printing Office.

U. S. Department of Commerce (1958), *Personal Income by States Since 1929.* Washington: Government Printing Office.

U. S. Department of Commerce (1958). *U. S. Income and Output, A Supplement to the Survey of Current Business.* Washington: Government Printing Office.

U. S. Department of Commerce (1960), *Survey of Current Business,* 40:8, Tables 1 and 2, p. 17. Washington: Government Printing Office.

U. S. Department of Commerce (1961), *Current Population Reports,* Series P-25, No. 227. Washington: Government Printing Office.

U. S. Department of Commerce and U. S. Department of Agriculture (1959), *Farm Population,* Series Census-AMS (P-27), No. 26. Washington: Government Printing Office.

U. S. Department of Labor, Bureau of Labor Statistics (1958), *State Employment.* Washington: Government Printing Office.

U. S. Department of Labor (1960), "Guide to Manpower Challenge of the 1960's" (for staff), Washington.

Chapter 5

The Agricultural Adjustment to Urban Growth

by William N. Parker and David G. Davies

RECENT EMPIRICAL STUDIES of the effects of urban growth on farm incomes in southern regions have been designed to test an hypothesis put forward by Schultz (1950 and 1951). The source of income inequalities within American agriculture, Schultz suggested, should not be sought in original differences in soil or quality of population. Difference in quality of population could not account for the depressed state of whole areas, and income differences from most other sources could be eliminated by factor movements on perfect markets. The source must lie rather in market imperfections related in some way to geographical position. Remoteness from the centers of urban industrial development, Schultz suggested, was the major cause of such imperfections. We might infer then that the poverty of some depressed areas relative to others might be remedied by placing such centers in the middle of depressed regions, or by improving the communication of economic opportunities from the existing centers to them.

To test this insight, some notable studies have been produced by Nicholls (1952, 1956a, 1956b, 1957a, 1957b, and 1960), Tang (1957 and 1958), Bachmura (1956), and Ruttan (1953 and 1955), employing data—mostly from the federal censuses—for a large number of counties in the Southern Piedmont, the Tennessee Valley, and the Mississippi Delta. In the present study, we have added to their evidence some calculations based on thirty-eight counties in the North Carolina Piedmont. Our study area includes all the counties of the Industrial Crescent and overlapping farming areas (as defined in the census).[1] In addition to producing a set of results roughly comparable to those of Nicholls and Ruttan for 1950, and generally reinforcing their conclusions, our study has also led us to examine more closely the hypothesis at the basis of this empirical work. Among the counties of the North Carolina Piedmont, the evidence of a relation between urbanization and the perfectness of factor and product markets is not strong, and the character of the underlying demand for cash income and rural living must be taken into account as a source of rural "immobility."

Urbanization Indicators and Median Farm Family Income

Urban-industrial centers have two features which must operate together in order to produce higher incomes for farm families in their neighborhood. First, there must be a general urban-rural, or industrial-agricultural differential in prices on factor and product markets. Second, knowledge of this differential must be better diffused nearer the city or industrial plant. If both these conditions exist, the differential may be expected to narrow near cities, and the returns to factors furnished by farm families to approach those to similar factors in other occupations. The communication which produces perfectness of factor markets depends, perhaps, more closely on the extent and size of the urban population, while the level of urban incomes indicates the potential differential which communication has to overcome. As indicators of urbanization therefore, it would seem best to use both variables, as Ruttan does in his study of 201 counties in the Tennessee Valley (1955). The indicators used by Nicholls for 20 counties in the Upper East Tennessee Valley (1956a, 1956b, and 1960)—per capita value added by manufacture and per capita nonagricultural payrolls—compound both these elements to a degree, and are perhaps the best indicators. In our region, several indicators of urban development, manufacturing employment, and urban incomes were used.

The association between the urbanization indicators and county median family income of farm families from all sources is significant in both the Tennessee Valley and the North Carolina Piedmont. Table

Table 5-1. Correlation between Urbanization Indicators and Median Income of Farm Families (All Sources)

INDICATOR	CORRELATION COEFFICIENT	
	r	*rho* [a]
Tennessee Valley (201 counties) [1]		
Median income of nonfarm families (1949)	.697 **	
Per cent of population nonfarm (1950)	.683 **	
Upper East Tennessee Valley (20 counties)		
Per capita value added by manufacture (1947) [2]		.783
Per capita nonagricultural payrolls (1949) [3]		.824
North Carolina Piedmont (38 counties) [4]		
Per cent of population nonfarm (1950)	.568 ***	
Per cent of population urban (1950)	.539 ***	
Per cent of population rural nonfarm (1950)	.125	
Per cent of employment nonagricultural (1950)	.555 ***	
Per cent of employment in manufacturing (1950)	.440 **	
Median income, urban families (1949)	.423 **	

[a] Spearman's coefficient of rank correlation.

* Significant at .05 level.
** Significant at .01 level.
*** Significant at .001 level.

Sources.
1. Ruttan (1955, p. 41).
2. Nicholls (1956a, pp. 277–302; 1956b, pp. 400–415).
3. Nicholls (1960, p. 148).
4. Calculated from 1950 Census and from Spivey (n.d.) employment data.

5-1 shows Ruttan's correlations, Nicholls' rank correlation coefficients, and the correlations for our own area. In the North Carolina counties, the simple correlation is highest between income and the per cent of population that is nonfarm (.568), and this is due almost entirely to the correlation with per cent of population that is urban. Correlation with per cent of population that is rural nonfarm is not significant. There is significant correlation with per cent of employment in nonagricultural industries, which is, of course, highly intercorrelated (.865) with the per cent of population in urban areas. Some influence of the urban-rural income differential may be indicated by the significant correlation (.423) of median incomes of farm families with median urban incomes. However, the intercorrelation between median urban income and the other indicators of urbanization is so high [2] that the inclusion of it in a multiple regression equation does not appreciably improve the result. For this reason, we employ singly in our discussion these simple indicators of urbanization of the population.

Urbanization and Average Incomes from Farming

The next question to be examined is whether the influence of urbanization is felt on incomes earned from farming itself, or through nonfarm earnings of the members of farm families. On this question, Ruttan's (1955) and our own studies have used measures of county income from farming, estimated for the Tennessee Valley area by T.V.A. and for the North Carolina Piedmont by Spivey (n.d.). Nicholls (1960) has estimated net farm income for his area from Census data, and adjusted the Census figures on farm workers to indicate man-year equivalents. He did not find a significant rank correlation (.132) of his urbanization indicator (per capita nonagricultural payrolls in 1949) with per farm net income from farming, but found a significant one (.595) with per worker net income from farming. As Table 5-2 shows, in neither Ruttan's area nor our own is the high correlation between urbanization and median incomes of farm families from all sources matched by a high correlation with incomes from farming. Ruttan's estimate eliminates nonfarm work from the calculation while our own is based on income per farm. The negative correlation is presumably due to the correlation of part-time farming with urbanization, discussed below. Table 5-2 also shows the high correlation of off-farm employment with urbanization and in the Tennessee Valley area with median farm income from all sources. In the North Carolina Piedmont, the correlation with median income from all sources is much lower, presumably because we used stricter measures of the drawing power of industrial employment: the per cent of farm operators working off the farm 100 days or more and the per cent of farm families with incomes from other sources in excess of income from farming. But the substitution of nonfarm for farm income appears to be so strong in

Table 5-2. Correlation of Farm Income with Urbanization and Nonfarm Employment Indicators[a]

	FARM INCOME INDICATOR			NONFARM EMPLOYMENT INDICATOR		
	ALL SOURCES	FARMING 1	FARMING 2	1	2	3
Urbanization indicator						
Tennessee Valley	.683	.069		.709		
North Carolina Piedmont	.568 ***		−.446 **		.666 ***	.623 ***
Nonfarm employment indicator						
Tennessee Valley 1	.726	.069				
North Carolina Piedmont 2	.340 *		−.849 ***			
3	.279		−.830 ***			

[a] Urbanization indicator: per cent of population nonfarm.
Farm income indicator: *all sources*—median family income; *farming:* 1, average income per farm worker from farming, and 2, average income per farm from farming.
Nonfarm employment indicator:
1—Per cent of farm population employed in nonfarm work.
2—Per cent of farm operators working off farm 100 days or more in the year.
3—Per cent of farm operators with family incomes from nonfarm sources exceeding incomes from farming.

*, **, *** Refer to Table 5-1 for levels of significance.

Sources. Tennessee Valley: Ruttan (1955, p. 41).
North Carolina Piedmont: Computed from data in 1950 Census of Agriculture. Income from farming as estimated by W. A. Spivey (n.d.).

Column 3 of Table 5-2, that it seems possible that the degree of rural underemployment was less on the whole in our area than in the Tennessee Valley.

Urbanization and Product Mix

In the urbanized counties, incomes of families living on farms are favorably affected by the opportunities of nonfarm employment. We would expect from this some readjustment in farm operations, in product mix, factor proportions, and scale of enterprise to permit this combination of farming with off-farm employment. For uncovering such delicate economic effects, the county data of the federal census are

Table 5-3. Correlation between Indicators of Specialization and Indicators of Nonfarm Employment, and Part-Time Farming [a]

Panel 1: NORTH CAROLINA PIEDMONT (38 counties)

INDICATOR OF SPECIALIZATION	INDICATORS OF URBANIZATION			INDICATORS OF PART-TIME FARMING		
	1	2	3	1	2	3
Share of farm sales [b] represented by:						
Livestock products	.28	.49 **	.61 ***	.91 ***	.92 ***	−.90 ***
Dairy	.37 *	.52 ***	.59 ***			
Poultry	−.05	.26	.41 *			
Meat	.36 *	.49 **	.50 **			
All crops	−.36 *	−.56 ***	−.60 ***			
Tobacco	−.27	−.41 *	−.50 **	−.84 **	−.84 ***	.86 **
Other crops	.15	.24	.31			

[a] Indicators of urbanization:
1—Per cent of population urban.
2—Per cent of employment nonfarm.
3—Median urban income.

Indicators of part-time farming:
1—Per cent of farm operators working off farm 100 days or more in the year.
2—Per cent of farm operators with family incomes from nonfarm sources exceeding incomes from farming.
3—Per cent of farms classified as "commercial."

*, **, *** Refer to Table 5-1 for levels of significance.

[b] Sales data from 1950 Census of Agriculture and Federal-State Crop Reporting Service (1951) combined.

Panel 2: UPPER EAST TENNESSEE VALLEY (20 counties)

INDICATOR OF SPECIALIZATION	COEFFICIENT OF RANK CORRELATION WITH VALUE ADDED PER CAPITA BY MANUFACTURE, 1947
Per 1,000 acres of improved farm land	
Production	
Corn	−.250
Tobacco	−.477 [a]
Numbers	
Swine	.459 [a]
Cattle	.317

[a] Significant at the .05 level.

Source. Nicholls (1956b, p. 1638).

exceedingly crude; ideally, we should have some sample of the adjustment on representative full-time and part-time enterprises. Nevertheless, one indication of the rough lines of the adjustment appears to come through in the data. In Table 5-3, Panel 1, a significant correlation appears between specialization in livestock and urbanization and a negative correlation between specialization in tobacco and urbanization. A similar phenomenon appears in Nicholls' study of the Upper East Tennessee Valley (1956b) (Table 5-3, Panel 2).

In Table 5-4, Column 2, we have correlated income from farming per

Table 5-4. Correlation between Indicators of Specialization and Various Measures of Farm Income, North Carolina Piedmont [a]

INDICATOR OF SPECIALIZATION	INDICATORS OF FARM INCOME: PER FARM FAMILY: FROM ALL SOURCES (MEDIAN) 1	INDICATORS OF FARM INCOME: PER FARM FAMILY: FROM FARMING (AVERAGE) 2	INDICATORS OF FARM INCOME: PER FARM WORKER: FROM FARMING (AVERAGE) 3
Share of farm sales represented by:			
Livestock products	.22	−.61 ***	−.43 **
Dairy	.32 *	−.55 ***	−.48 **
Poultry	.02	−.41 **	−.19
Meat	.23	−.68 ***	−.55 ***
All crops	−.32 *	.51 **	.34 *
Tobacco	.05	.74 ***	.44 **
Other crops	−.28	.69 ***	−.38 *

[a] Income indicators:
1—All sources, 1950 Census of Agriculture.
2—From farming per family, Spivey (n.d.) county allocations of proprietary income divided by Census count of farm families.
3—From farming per farm worker, computed as described in text.

*, **, *** Refer to Table 5-1 for levels of significance.

Sources. 1950 Census of Agriculture and Federal-State Crop Reporting Service (1951) combined.

farm family, with indicators of specialization; a significant negative correlation appears with the concentration on livestock products, and a high positive correlation with concentration on tobacco. Tobacco, it appears, remains the significant money earner of farm families, and it is its cash income rather than the income from other farm enterprises that is replaced on livestock and part-time farms.

The negative correlation between livestock farming and income from farming does not of course mean that livestock farming is unproductive, but indicates that livestock farms tend to locate in the counties where part-time farming is important. The very high correlation between livestock specialization and the part-time farming indicators (.91) bears this out. Tobacco is both labor-intensive and productive of cash income high enough to remove tobacco farms from the census part-time farm definition. The availability of nonfarm employment thus appears to produce a substitution of other enterprises, including livestock, for tobacco, on commercial and part-time farms alike.

Urbanization and Productive Farming

We come now to the central question raised by the Schultz hypothesis and the studies stimulated by it. Does urbanization produce conditions favorable to higher family incomes in farming itself? This question breaks down into two parts: (*a*) Is the value productivity of the factors employed in agriculture higher in the urbanized counties? (*b*) Is the capital market easier in the urbanized counties, so that farm families may own or control more productive factors outside their own labor and so share more fully in the property incomes from farming?

On the first question, the census data are, in our opinion, too crude to give very meaningful results. In our own study area we found that farm prices—one element in value-productivity differences—were not correlated with urbanization indicators. In Ruttan's study area (Table 5-2) incomes per farm worker from farming were not significantly correlated with urbanization. Nicholls' 1949–50 correlations (.595) between net farm income per farm worker and per capita nonagricultural payrolls fell to .375 in 1954. To produce a similar estimate for our own area, we set an estimate of farm employment by county [8] against the Spivey estimate of county net proprietary and hired labor incomes from farming. Correlating the resulting incomes per farm worker with indicators of urbanization, we found these results:

URBANIZATION INDICATOR	r
Per cent of population urban	−.21
Median urban income	−.15
Per cent of employment nonfarm	−.21

The allocation of the labor force on which this was based does not allow for county variations in number of workers per farm, which may be considerable. But the census labor-force estimate by county is based on the week preceding enumeration; its use as an allocator ignores county differences in seasonal labor.

But apart from the crudeness of the county allocators, the objections to all such indicators of single-factor productivity differences are enormous; they compound differences in productivity, differences in product mix, and differences in factor proportions in the production of given products. Estimates of capital-output ratios, and combinations of labor and capital to form an index of total inputs to measure intercounty differences in productivity have not been attempted.[4] Here a serious conceptual problem is posed by the direct effects of urbanization on land values in nearby agriculture.

Whatever the intercounty factor productivity differences, there are some indications of easier capital supply to farm families in the urbanized counties. In the Tennessee Valley studies, indicators of capital-land or capital-labor ratios were related to urbanization indicators. The results, as shown in Table 5-5, on the whole indicated correlations with the value of farm land and buildings per farm. For an area in the South Carolina and Georgia Piedmont, an index of capital per farm compiled for commercial and part-time farms separately by Tang (1957) showed rather low rank correlation (.467) for commercial farms and no correlation (.097) for part-time farms. However, in our study area, a similar index, compiled by summing the ranks of the counties with respect to a number of indicators of capital intensity, showed a high rank correlation (w = .810) with per cent of population that is nonfarm, and also with per cent working off farm 100 days or more (w = .739).[5] The average size of farm shows a low positive correlation with the indicators of part-time farming and no correlation with urbanization indicators. Tenancy shows a strong negative correlation with the urbanization indicators and a strong concentration in the tobacco counties (Table 5-6). The indications thus appear that cap-

Table 5-5. Correlation of Capital Intensity with Urbanization Indicators: Tennessee Valley [a]

Panel 1: TENNESSEE VALLEY (20 counties)

	RANK CORRELATION COEFFICIENT (*rho*)	
	1	2
Per farm worker		
All farm capital	.725 **	.805 **
Farm land and buildings (value)	.704 **	.841 **
Livestock (value)	.344	.535 **
Machinery and implements (value)	.245	.171
Per 1,000 acres improved farm land		
Tractors (number)	.475 *	
Horses and mules (number)	−.441 *	
Farm land and buildings (value)	.540 **	
All livestock (number)	.241	
Machinery and implements (value)	.107	

Panel 2: TENNESSEE VALLEY (107 tobacco and livestock counties)

	SIMPLE CORRELATION COEFFICIENT (*r*)
	3
Per farm worker	
Crop land	.099
Land and buildings (value)	.572 *
Tractors (number)	.309 *
Livestock (value)	.266

[a] Urbanization indicators:

1—Value added by manufacture per capita in 1947.
2—Value of nonagricultural payroll per capita in 1949.
3—Per cent of population in nonfarm employment in 1950.

* Significant at .05 level.
** Significant at .025 level.

Sources. Panel 1, Column 1—Nicholls (1956b, p. 1683).
Panel 1, Column 2—Nicholls (1960, p. 139).
Panel 2—Ruttan (1955, p. 53).

Table 5-6. Correlation among Indicators of Urbanization, Tenancy, Part-Time Farming, and Farm Size in the North Carolina Piedmont (38 Counties), 1950

	PER CENT OF POP-ULATION URBAN 1	PER CENT OF EM-PLOY-MENT NON-FARM 2	MEDIAN URBAN INCOME 3	PER CENT OF OPERATORS WORKING OFF FARMS 100 DAYS OR MORE 4	AVER-AGE SIZE OF FARM 5	PER CENT OF FARMS OPERATED BY TENANTS 6	PER CENT OF TOTAL SALES ACCOUNTED FOR BY LIVESTOCK 7	PER CENT OF TOTAL SALES ACCOUNTED FOR BY TOBACCO 8
1	1	.86 ***	.46 **	.53 ***	−.08	−.29	.28	−.27
2		1	.65 ***	.66 ***	−.07	−.47 **	.49 **	−.41 **
3			1	.67 ***	.26	−.55 ***	.61 ***	−.50 **
4				1	.34 *	−.82 ***	.91 ***	−.84 ***
5					1	−.46 **	.52 ***	−.46 **
6						1	−.80 ***	.71 ***
7							1	−.88 ***
8								1

* Significant at .05 level.
** Significant at .01 level.
*** Significant at .001 level.

Sources. Columns 1–6, 1950 Census of Population and Census of Agriculture. Columns 7–8, computed from 1950 Census of Agriculture and Federal-State Crop Reporting Service (1951).

ital markets permit the holding of relatively higher value land in farms in urbanized counties in some areas and are perfect enough to permit more extensive ownership by farm operators.

Conclusions and Implications

This chapter cannot claim to summarize all the work of the Vanderbilt economists directed toward testing the Schultz hypothesis, nor does it exhaust the research possibilities of the North Carolina Piedmont, even within the limits of the census data. In particular, separation of part-time and full-time farms, as done recently by Nicholls for his East Tennessee Valley counties (1960), should yield useful results. Studies based on the 1960 census are now in order to show the direction and rate of adjustment.

The strongest single conclusion evident particularly in our own area is the major influence of local industry and off-farm employment in raising incomes of families remaining on farms. If farm families can exchange idleness or low-productivity crops for cash incomes from nonfarm employment, without abandoning farm residence, they will clearly do so. This does not imply that nearby industry raises the rate of migration off the farms, distributes capital more liberally to them, or improves the market for farm products. Evidence on these points exists, especially with respect to capital availability, but, without sampling surveys of actual farms, either directly or from the census rolls, the evidence is indirect. Measures of capital in particular are obscured by the independent effects of urbanization on land values.

In the agriculture of the North Carolina Piedmont, at least, it seems likely that national product and labor markets have been long at work. Tobacco has a national market and Negro farm labor may be as mobile to points outside the region as within it. Here the hard core of rural poverty lies in the small tobacco farm cut off both by its location and by its production function from much off-farm employment. Urban growth at points within such an area takes advantage of many families' attachment to farm living. It offers them a means, alternative to tobacco, by which cash income can be combined with farm residence. Its superiority to tobacco farming for these purposes is sufficiently great to affect the choice of crops in the locality, but its effects are checked presumably by employment uncertainties and by the competition for land in the urbanized counties—before they produce any wholesale disruption of tobacco farming in the whole area.

Drastic change in the demand for cash income might empty out low-income farms. The age, quality, and general social mobility of the labor confined to these farms, however, must be taken into account in assessing the occupational choices displayed. Change would surely proceed faster with some push from the supply side—with, for example, consolidated tobacco allotments and mechanized techniques. Without such a push, tobacco appears even more habit forming to its growers than to its consumers. Whether inertia of this sort—on either side of the market—is called imperfect knowledge or a harmful preference depends upon one's tastes in preferences and in the choice of words.

Underlying demand patterns may, of course, as Schultz suggests (1950, pp. 13–14), be changed by the social influences stemming from nearby cities. For social change of this sort, a single great metropolis with intense and distinct urban culture traits might be more effective in the region than a string of smaller nuclei. But in this matter, the choice between the gradual drift and the sharp break is set by the character of the urban complex to which the countryside of the Piedmont Crescent is joined.

FOOTNOTES

1. These 38 counties comprise the four types of farming areas which contain the Piedmont Industrial Crescent of North Carolina. See North Carolina Agricultural Extension Service (1957, p. 1) for a description of the delimitation of North Carolina farming areas.
2. $r = .464$ for median urban income with per cent of population urban, and is higher with the other indicators.
3. To do this, we allocated the 1950 farm-employment figure of the Agricultural Marketing Service among the counties on the basis of the number of full-time and part-time farms, giving the former a weight of three and the latter a weight of one. Class VI commercial farms were included among part-time farms for this purpose. These weights were chosen because an estimate of farm employment in the state based on them matched the AMS figure almost exactly.
4. Nicholls (1960, p. 139) has attempted an index of total inputs to correlate with his urbanization indicator, based on adding together for each county its rank in number of workers per farm and in value of capital (including land) per farm and ranking the sum of ranks.
5. w = Spearman's coefficient of concordance. Fisher's variance ratio (F) in the two cases was 4.273 and 2.828, respectively. The index is based on the following items: value of land and buildings per farm, tractors per farm, cattle and calves per farm, per cent of farms with ponds, reservoirs or earth tanks, trucks per farm, amount spent on fertilizer per farm, acres of cover crops turned under per farm, per cent of farms with piped running water. Data are from 1950 Census of Agriculture.

   The index is the rank order of the sum of each county's rank in terms of each of the above capital components, with one exception—the ranks of counties were combined into a single index with respect to cattle and calves per farm and hogs per farm. This index supposedly approximates the "first principal component" of a number of measures of capital (in this case). See Kendall (1954). See also Tang's use of this statistic (1957, p. 668).

REFERENCES

Bachmura, Frank T. (1956), "Migration and Factor Adjustment in Lower Mississippi Agriculture, 1940–50," *Journal of Farm Economics* **XXXVIII:4**, 1024–42.

Bureau of the Census (1956), *1950 Census of Agriculture,* Vol. 1, Part 16. Washington, D. C.: U. S. Department of Commerce.

Federal-State Crop Reporting Service (1951), *North Carolina Agricultural Statistics; 1949 Issue,* Raleigh.

Kendall, M. G. (1954), "Notes on Multivariate Analysis." Blacksburg, Va.: Virginia Polytechnic Institute.

Nicholls, William H. (1952), "A Research Project on Southern Economic Development, with Particular Reference to Agriculture," *Economic Development and Cultural Change,* **I**:1, 190–195.

Nicholls, William H. (1956a), "Some Foundations of Economic Development in the Upper East Tennessee Valley, 1900–1950," *Quarterly Journal of Economics,* **LXIV**:4, 277–302; **LXIV**:5, 400–415.

Nicholls, William H. (1956b), "The Effects of Industrial Development on Tennessee Valley Agriculture, 1900–1950," *Journal of Farm Economics,* **XXXVIII**:5, 1636–49.

Nicholls, William H. (1957a), "Human Resources and Industrial Development in the Upper East Tennessee Valley, 1900–1950," *Quarterly Journal of Economics,* **LXXI**:2, 289–316.

Nicholls, William H. (1957b), "Relative Economic Development of the Upper East Tennessee Valley, 1850–1950," *Economic Development and Cultural Change,* **V**:4, 308–24.

Nicholls, William H. (1960), "Industrial-Urban Development and Agricultural Adjustments, Tennessee Valley and Piedmont, 1939–1954," *Journal of Political Economy,* **LXVIII**:2, 135–149.

North Carolina Agricultural Extension Service (1957), "Farming Opportunities in North Carolina," Extension Circular No. 355, Raleigh.

Ruttan, Vernon W. (1953), "Differentials in Farm Income and Employment in the Tennessee Valley Region Counties," TVA, Project on Research in Agricultural Development in the Tennessee Valley Region.

Ruttan, Vernon W. (1955), "The Impact of Urban-Industrial Development on Agriculture in the Tennessee Valley and the Southeast," *Journal of Farm Economics,* **XXXVII**:1, 38–56.

Schultz, Theodore W. (1950), "Reflections on Poverty within Agriculture," *Journal of Political Economy,* **LVIII**:1, 1–15.

Schultz, Theodore W. (1951), "A Framework for Land Economics–The Long View," *Journal of Farm Economics,* **XXXIII**:2, 204–215.

Schultz, Theodore W. (1953), *The Economic Organization of Agriculture.* New York: McGraw-Hill.

Spivey, W. A. (n.d.), "Employment and Income Data for N. C. Counties" (unpublished), Department of Economics, University of North Carolina, Chapel Hill.

Tang, Anthony M. (1957), "Industrial-Urban Development and Agricultural Adjustments in the Southern Piedmont, 1940–50," *Journal of Farm Economics,* **XXXIX**:3, 657–675.

Tang, Anthony M. (1958), *Economic Development in the Southern Piedmont; Its Impact on Agriculture.* Chapel Hill, N. C.: University of North Carolina Press.

Part Two

Leadership, Decision Making, and Urban Growth*

by Frederic N. Cleaveland

URBAN DEVELOPMENT in the Piedmont Industrial Crescent has not "just happened," rather, it has occurred as the outcome of a whole series of control processes or systems of control, both conscious and unconscious, formal and informal, public and private in character. Thus,

* The series of studies on leadership and community decision making carried on within the Urban Studies Program has been considerably more extensive than the work reported on in Part Two. In particular, note should be taken of two studies: (1) The research conducted by Paul W. Wager on county commissioners and city councilmen in selected areas of the Piedmont Crescent and their participation in solving problems of urban growth. Plans call for publishing

urban development has been guided, directed, stimulated at some points, redirected or perhaps blocked at other points, through a complex and never-ending stream of decisions, some of them public and many of them private, in which large numbers of individuals and groups have participated. The second major theme of this volume on the Piedmont Crescent is concerned with the exploration and analysis of these decision-making processes, and the detailed study of some of the strategically important individuals and groups participating in them. The purpose is to discover more about the way urban development and objectives are set and public choices are made—or to explore the nature of control processes at work, how and by whom they are set in motion, and with what consequences.

To open up this whole field of community leadership and decision making, a number of studies have been conducted in cities of the Piedmont Crescent following three distinct, although somewhat related, emphases: (1) studies exploring the nature of the decision-making process itself in urban communities, and the patterns of interaction and communication among participants in the process; (2) studies concentrating on particular types or classes of active participants (or leaders) in order to learn about their particular interests, their attitudes, their roles and activities in decision making related to urban development; and (3) studies concerned with mass citizen participation in the urban political process, including an exploration of attitudes toward growth problems, the range and forms of participation, and the significance or meaning of participation to the individual "actor." These emphases are not mutually exclusive, and the studies reported in Part Two tend to reflect some combination of them.

In examining the decision process special attention has been given in Chapter 6 to the crucial role of communication by organizing one research study principally around observations of the actual flow of communications among leaders and organized groups over a fairly extended period of time. This intensive case study of a series of decisions in one city highlights the interactions among government officials and concerned individuals and groups in the community, and suggests

the results of this research in the Urban Studies Research Paper series. (2) A comparative study of community political systems in two cities of the Piedmont Crescent was undertaken by Robert E. Agger during the first two years of the Urban Studies Program. It is expected that this research will be published by Professor Agger as part of a larger work. In addition, there were a number of student theses prepared on selected aspects of leadership and decision making in the Crescent.

a useful model for viewing and relating the behaviors of actors in a decision-making process. The studies of leaders and certain leadership roles reported in Chapters 7 and 8 also contribute insights into decision making by throwing light on when, how, and under what circumstances certain important "actors" become involved in the decision process.

Exploration of leader participation has been largely concentrated in two intensive studies: one concerns the role of the business executive in community affairs, and the other the complex roles of the urban planner. Both these studies included investigations in a number of cities in the Crescent, employing intensive interviewing as the principal device for gathering data. The objectives of the two studies are somewhat different however. In exploring the participation of business executives in urban-development affairs, particular attention has been given to the kinds of factors which encourage and discourage such participation. In studying the urban planner the principal concern has been to define and delineate the nature of his roles in urban development through a series of detailed case studies. Of particular interest are the influences bearing upon the planner which help to determine the particular "mix" of roles that tends to guide his behavior.

Chapter 9 reports on a significant study reflecting the third emphasis —mass participation. This is an investigation of the Negro communities in Durham and Winston-Salem, North Carolina, organized around a comparative analysis of differences in attitudes toward community-growth problems; differences in levels of participation in community affairs; and differences in degrees of political organization. This research was part of a larger endeavor incorporating identification and study of the acknowledged civic leaders in white and Negro communities of these two cities and surveys of random samples of white and Negro citizens in both cities. Only the analysis concerning the two Negro communities and Negro participation in the process of decision making affecting urban development is reported in this book.

This study affords ample support for the proposition that the processes of urban development are opening up a progressively more active role in civic affairs for Negroes and the Negro community in Southern cities. As politics in these cities become more competitive, more fraught with controversy and conflict among dominant interests—an inevitable by-product of growth and change—political leaders tend to seek the support of Negro voters, quietly, to be sure, in order to avoid alienation of other support, but nonetheless actively. At the same time these cities experiencing rapid growth are more likely to afford greater economic opportunities to Negroes, attracting increased migration from small towns and rural areas. Similarly, responding to the very process of urban development, the social systems of these cities tend to become less rigid and less repressive regarding social minorities. In such a setting the participation of Negro leaders and Negro voters takes on new significance as a force influencing public decisions regarding urban development.

The studies reported in these four chapters are in no sense designed to present a comprehensive account of the nature of decision making in the cities of the Piedmont Industrial Crescent. Nevertheless, certain generalized impressions do emerge, partly from these studies and partly from others conducted as part of the total research program but not reported here. A summary view of the characteristics of leadership and decision making that emerges from these studies would include at least the following impressions:

> The decision-making processes in these cities of the Crescent present complex and confusing pictures involving many participants, public officials, civic leaders, and organized groups both inside and outside formal government. In none of the communities studied does there appear to be a small group of "top leaders" completely dominating public decisions on a wide range of problems associated with urban development. At the same time the decision-making structures appear to be larger and more open in some communities than in others, with greater mobility among participants. Within any one community, leadership patterns tend to vary from one area of concern to another. Thus in the field of industrial development, for example, the decision-making structure may be large and relatively open with influence generally diffused; yet in school affairs the decision-making group may be relatively small with influence concentrated and only limited opportunity for new sources of leadership to emerge. In a number of cities studied, there is considerable evidence of increasing participation of Negro leaders in selected aspects of the decision-making process with regard to urban development.
>
> The technical expert, or professional, in some situations tends to become a decisive participant in urban-development decisions. At times his influence comes through his ability and initiative in having items placed on the informal agenda for community action. In other situations his virtual monopoly of technical information enables

him to influence and guide actions of formal decision makers to work toward desired ends.

There is clearly no "Crescent-wide" machinery, formal or informal, to bring leaders together; nor is there any evidence of a sense of identity of interest among decision-makers from city to city, county to county, which might provide the base for emergence of such a regional decision-making process. Nevertheless there are evidences of consultation among leaders across lines of local political jurisdictions. Some of these are formal arrangements, like the Research Triangle Regional Planning Commission area bringing together representatives of three county governments and three city councils. Others are informal arrangements involving decision makers of neighboring cities or of a city and its county, joining forces to seek a joint solution to a common problem.

What guidelines or suggestions for policy makers emerge from these discussions of the socio-political variables associated with urban development? They may take heart from the increasingly important roles that trained professionals—city manager, urban planner, community recreation specialist, and so on—are taking in community decisions concerning matters within their expert competence. Perhaps the contribution of these specialists to the subtle processes of political innovation can be enhanced by positive efforts to bring into closer association the policy makers and the trained specialists in urban development. For example, community leaders, both in and out of government, can encourage the earlier involvement of the city planner in discussions of approaches to industrial development. The planner holds a key position near the center of a communications network involving most if not all local governmental officials with a stake in urban development. By bringing him early into discussions of objectives, policy alternatives, and approaches to development, there is every reason to expect more rational decision outcomes and better coordination of both public and private activities related to development.

Chapter 6

Political Decision Making in Arcadia *

by Benjamin Walter †

THIS CHAPTER deals with three public decisions made in Arcadia, a North Carolina Piedmont Crescent city. All are concerned with urban development, but each has purposely been selected to vary in other respects. One, a decision to construct a new city hall, simmered for nearly a decade before resolution; another, to build a public housing project with federal funds, erupted precipitously and was settled in a few hectic months. The first decision may be faced in roughly similar form in towns and cities of any size, from a drowsy rural village in Iowa to a frantic industrial metropolis. Small towns and great cities alike have had to decide between refurbishing the old or constructing the new; such choices are no respecters of community size. Most

* "Arcadia," like all proper names mentioned in this chapter, is a pseudonym. Although most of the events recorded are matters of public record, some are not. Anonymity shields all participants from possible embarrassment.

† This research could not have been completed without assistance from others. Public thanks should be given to Michael Wise and Allan Williams for categorizing Arcadia's voting precincts according to color and class; to David L. Mundy who "shadowed" some of Arcadia's administrators while choices were being made; and to a political scientist who must remain anonymous but whose dissertation study supplied certain data which would not otherwise have been unearthed. A special measure of gratitude is due one other person, formerly a graduate student in the Department of City and Regional Planning at the University of North Carolina, who must also remain anonymous to shield the identity of Arcadia. His master's thesis, written independently, provided assurance that the data are correct. Many have unknowingly assisted; text references and bibliography record the author's debt.

smaller cities, however, have thus far been spared the local political conflicts which follow in the wake of public housing and urban renewal, the other two issues we shall explore in Arcadia. The money required to remedy sprawling blight quickly outpaces the limited financial resources of even the largest municipalities, and the private sector of the economy has generally perceived bigger payoffs from alternative investments. If federal housing and urban renewal programs have greatly diminished nettlesome problems of economic cost and financial incentive, cities must still agree to participate. This is more than a simple matter of having a solemn city council pass a stirring resolution, or of having it designate a new squadron of bureaucrats to "coordinate" the decisions of local and federal governments. On the contrary, participation in such programs is at root *political* rather than administrative. It entails higgling and haggling, a laborious process of stimulating and piecing together the support of interested citizens and political-interest groups, and fending off, placating, or overriding opposition.

Taken by themselves, these case studies are simply academic *curiosa*, vignettes of political history in a Southern city of some 100,000 souls. Deliberately viewed in more ambitious focus, however, they bear upon the most persistent and beguiling questions of all political theory: Who really rules? The political order of the local community is rather more complicated than many imagine. Compared with the immense, sprawling network of influence and intrigue found at state and national capitols, it appears almost mischievously simple. Yet, for all its attractive economies of scale, political life in the local community was barely touched until the publication of Floyd Hunter's *Community Power Structure* (1953) less than a decade ago. In the concluding sections, we shall first recapitulate the major elements of an extraordinarily influential theory explaining the distribution of power in local communities. Then we shall project the three Arcadia case studies against this theory, and offer some suggestions for alternative explanations. If the discussion seems to bear more than a coincidental relationship to state and national politics, this is all to the good; for progress in social science often is simply a process of conveying explanations from where they can be conveniently found to where they are urgently needed.

We have many options to explain the distribution of power in local communities. In some textbook theories, the council shapes policy and the city manager appears only as its shy and docile servant (Herson, 1957). No sophisticated reader needs to be told that the actual skeins of influence weave a strikingly different pattern from those which formal charters and professional norms prescribe. As Wood (1959, pp. 183–185) has shown, the iron necessities of building and maintaining a favorable ratio of political support over political opposition have enticed the most fastidious city managers into the rough and tumble of political life, a change in function somewhat belatedly noted and ambiguously certified by the Code of Ethics of the International City Managers' Association. And nowhere is the line between advice and direction so tenuous as on those occasions when a full-time professional administrator confers with a group of part-time amateur councilmen. The city manager, Wood suggested, may have developed two operational codes, one for public declamation and the other for private use. Still another line of speculation might hold that the actual networks of political influence cut rudely athwart the formal authority of legal governments. In particular the high socio-economic status of the councilmen might lead a cynical observer to conclude that they are the agents who safeguard and promote the alternatives preferred by a hidden local economic elite.[1] There is literally no limit to speculation about the distribution of power in modern political systems, and, taken at face value, few explanations are so bizarre as to warrant dismissal out of hand.

In discussing power, we will follow customary usage and define it as the initiation of decision alternatives finally adopted over opposition, or as the successful veto of alternatives others propose (Simon, 1953; Lasswell and Kaplan, 1950). To identify the powerful in Arcadia (or any other place) requires the careful dissection of a sample of important decisions. It is to this task that we now turn.

Arcadia Acquires a New Municipal Building

Origins

To many interested citizens, the old municipal building at the corner of Lee and Bragg seemed an anachronistic anomaly in midcentury Arcadia. Its bluff and dingy gray façade looked unmistakably fusty among the sleek windows of the department stores and banks that lined Lee Avenue, Arcadia's main street. When Everett Beardsley, Arcadia's first city manager, took office in 1947, he remarked that the building had not kept pace with an expanding and dynamic city. Its limited space had forced administrative departments to reconnoiter and find room elsewhere. One had to set up shop in the basement of the Arcadia Sports Arena a few blocks away; another had found crowded shelter in a fire station. Portions of other departments had migrated to the municipal building "annex," actually a decrepit concrete shed once used to store spare parts. Partitions had been thrown up within the main building from time to time, but the addition of each new official rendered the change obsolete almost as soon as it was made. Beardsley assigned a new building a highly preferred position on his list of priorities.

For three years nothing was done. A new building was bound to be expensive, and both manager and Council were constrained by promises made during the 1947 campaign not to hike the tax rate "without due cause." Late in 1949 Beardsley began to seek the means for erecting a new building. The downtown merchants were pinched by the tight parking situation, and Beardsley approached Theodore Pomeroy, the executive secretary of the Merchants' League, with the first viable alternative to finance the construction of a new building.

This alternative was a model of simplicity. The Merchants' League would buy the building, raze it, and erect a pigeon hole parking establishment upon the cleared site. The city would then use the proceeds of the sale to construct a new municipal building. To stimulate "general citizen interest," the *Morning Clarion* championed the proposal in its editorial columns.

The initiators had failed to reckon with costs. Estimates prepared by Sidney Langston, Arcadia's city planner, showed that the Merchants' League could construct similar facilities elsewhere downtown for about a third of the cost per car. The availability of a cheaper option made the costs of participation excessive for the merchants, and the idea was quietly but effectively scuttled.

The First Bond Issue: 1953–1954

Beardsley had turned in his resignation in 1950 as an indirect result of a number of petty scandals, one of which involved a lurid alienation of affections lawsuit. He was succeeded by Emery Saunders who was as appalled by the cramped working conditions and the enforced exile of many of his workers as his predecessor had been. Early in 1953 Saunders asked Langston to develop a number of options which might relieve the congestion. Shortly afterwards Langston presented two proposals. One would have moved an entire department and the Recorder's Court over to the warehouse on Beauregard Street, thus creating more space in the old municipal building. The other plan, which both Langston and Saunders favored, provided for the construction of a new building, but no site was specified.

Council reaction was mixed. Edward Hulme, claiming special expertise because of his experience as a successful contractor, argued that Saunders' cost estimates were hopelessly optimistic and opted for the first of Langston's two plans. Mayor Ferrabee, a professor at the local university, opposed Langston's first option on the grounds that it was at best a stop-gap solution, good for a year or so until the same dreary process of jerry-built partitions and departmental exiles would have to begin anew. By the time the Council had concluded its preliminary search for a viable alternative two months later, five separate alternatives were on the agenda.

The new Council that convened in the fall was no less discordant than its predecessor. Some wanted to build on the Sports Arena site; others wanted to move to the heart of the business district; and Hulme heroically announced he would hold out to the last for his Beauregard Street plan. Already somewhat befuddled by the profusion of available alternatives, the Council was soon bombarded by a legion of ambiguous clues when it solicited and attempted to measure the reaction of important publics. The Sports Arena had been dedicated as a war memorial, and the American Legion testily deplored the sacrilege of erecting a secular building on consecrated ground. Someone had suggested that the city build either on Chestnut or Villipigue squares, two small parks near Lee Avenue. Chestnut Square received the enthusiastic support of Peter Jameson, a hardware dealer who had twice sat on the Council and had been mayor from 1951 to 1953; and Councilman Butcher, a news commentator for a local radio station, strode off to gauge public opinion. The first four groups encountered, the Garden Club, the Rose Society, the Arcadia Women's Club, and the Council of Architects, all disapproved for esthetic reasons. They did not want the last bit of green space downtown to disappear under the steam shovel. Unsure whether the proposal could pass a bond referendum—or whether there would have to be a bond referendum at all—the four councilmen reluctantly dismissed Chestnut Square.

Meanwhile William Mosby, vice president of Guaranteed Insurance and currently president of the Arcadia Chamber of Commerce, declared he wanted the site farther downtown. Merchant League Director Theodore Pomeroy still opted for the Sports Arena, as did Jack

Levy, a downtown jeweler and a perennial but unsuccessful Council candidate; Mrs. P. F. Roswell, the wife of a former lieutenant governor, executive secretary of the state Automobile Dealers' Association, and chairlady of the Arcadia Women's Club; and F. Rennie Hargroves, a furniture dealer. The manager of a Lee Avenue department store and a prosperous realtor both wanted to renovate the current building. In a rather casual newspaper poll some businessmen declared they wanted the building to remain where it was; an equal number desired a new one on Chestnut Square. Others wanted the building placed closer to the center of the business district in order to encourage growth; some thought putting it downtown would stifle growth. The Council had even taken to the airwaves in an effort to ascertain *vox populi;* all they heard was the confused jangle of discordant voices. To an astounding degree the businessmen seemed unable to agree on any deliberate strategy, any order of priorities, any set of criteria to be used in choosing a specific alternative. The leaders of the two local "peak" associations, the Merchants' League and the Chamber of Commerce, disagreed, and the cacophony could be heard up and down Lee Avenue. No stable coalition of business leaders could be built upon the shards. Babel reigned triumphant in Arcadia.

The Council decided to postpone choice until after the revenue had been raised. Early in May, Councilman Eric Lowndes, the district manager for a chain of movies, moved adoption of an $855,000 bond issue to be approved in July by public referendum. Later he revised the figure to $750,000, but failed to specify a site.[2] The ordinance squeaked by the Council four votes to three. Mayor Ferrabee and Lowndes wanted a new building at any site whatsoever and persuaded two other councilmen to side with them even though no agreement was reached as to where the building would be placed. Hulme adamantly refused to consider any other plan. Now that the Sports Arena [3] was no longer available, Councilman Strowd, a prosperous retail merchant, joined Hulme since his alternative was the second least costly plan. Edward Lipton voted against the bond ordinance since it would have permitted a new building on the old site, an alternative entirely repugnant to him. Lowndes tried to assure him the Council would vote against building at the old site once the issue had been approved, but the recalcitrant Lipton could not be budged.

Upon hearing of the Council's decision, the Planning Commission urged selection of a site on Mosby Avenue which both Saunders and Langston had favored as a device to arrest stagnation in a declining business area. The majority on the Council adamantly refused to stipulate any site, feeling that the fragile coalition in favor of the bond issue would be wrenched apart if the Council were forced to make a specific choice. The Merchants' League was also perturbed at the Council's failure to select a site. In a letter sent to the Council three days before the referendum, Pomeroy said the executive board of the League had always favored a new building but did not want it erected at the present site, a possibility the bond ordinance did not foreclose. In the letter was an implicit threat that the Merchants' League would find it very difficult to rally its members in favor of an indefinite alternative. The Chamber of Commerce tepidly endorsed the bond issue. Lowndes pleaded with the Council to heal its schism and go before the people united in favor of the bond issue, but Lipton and Hulme could not be swayed and Strowd was absent.

In such situations the rational political gamesman would want to expand the size and mobilize the intensity of his coalition by offering side payments of various sorts to refractory parties: the elimination of a provision particularly abhorrent to the faction he wanted to attract, a promise of future influence, or some other concession. The marginal cost to the legislator of such side payments is typically quite small, sometimes only the time it takes to make one more speech. But Lowndes was torn between the horns of a particularly bleak and unremitting dilemma. The Council had to select a new site or forego the enthusiastic efforts of the Chamber of Commerce and the Merchants' League. Yet if Lowndes had tried to push for a definite selection he certainly would have lost his tender majority on the Council. The risks were great and the costs were intolerable. Lowndes did not press the matter.

Two days before the election Pomeroy asked for the endorsement of the Merchants' League at a meeting of its board of directors. The gathering had been hastily summoned, and only eight of the fifteen members were present. Five voted in favor of Pomeroy's motion. Peter Jameson, who was one of the three dissentients, angrily withdrew his firm from the League and sharply took Pomeroy to task for his insolence in presuming to speak for the organization without consulting its membership or the rest of the executive board. The day before the election the morning paper printed an advertisement in favor of the bond issue endorsed by some of the brightest luminaries in Arcadia's social and economic firmament. Signing, among others, were Avery Holmes and William Mosby, two wealthy insurance executives; Henry Perkins and John Smathers, chairmen of Arcadia's two largest corporations and directors on the board of one of its major banks; Gerald Sauvinet, the university's president; Reginald Bostwick, the proprietor of a prosperous sporting goods store; Mrs. Joan Simmons, the dean of a fashionable woman's college; and ex-Councilmen Carol Rolfe and Onslow Wilson.

But their benediction, though additionally sanctified by a fervent editorial in Henry Marlowe's *Morning Clarion,* failed to mobilize the one resource that counts in elections: numbers. The bond issue failed by a vote of 1,138–1,120. As in previous bond elections, few bothered to vote; less than 10 per cent of the registered electorate went to the polls that muggy day in July.

The Second Bond Issue: 1955–1956

Several new faces were on the scene when the new Council assumed office in 1955. Lowndes, Ferrabee, and Strowd had been returned to their green leather armchairs. Butcher had been elected but had immediately resigned. The councilmen appointed Bostwick as his successor, and Bostwick's vacated position as chairman of the Planning Commission was filled by Joseph Llewellyn, a former city clerk and acting city manager after Beardsley had resigned. The tyros on the Council were George Alton, a realtor, and Fred Bearden, a wealthy jeweler. Sidney Langston meanwhile had left Arcadia for an attractive job elsewhere, and Everett P. Rosemond, the son of an Halcyon County employee and a local boy whom many thought could be easily intimidated, had replaced him as city planner.

Rosemond surprised everybody. He first persuaded the Planning Commission to reject both the present location and the Sports Arena as possible sites. He also convinced the commissioners to consider sites located in the expanding business area south of Lee and north of Bragg, a choice that differed from Saunders' who still preferred the Mosby Avenue lot.[4] Langston had persuaded the commissioners that location south of Lee would strangle business growth; Rosemond convinced them that nothing could possibly do it more good. At Rosemond's instigation, the commission presented a slate of three sites to the Council: the first, a property on Pickett; the second, a much larger lot on Forrest and Bragg; the third, a lot just around the corner from the second. About one crucial matter all were agreed: a site had to be chosen before submitting the bond issue to the people.

Anticipating the fight soon to take place in Council, Rosemond began enlisting support for his preferred site and sought tactfully to show why Saunders' first choice was less attractive. One important piece of information Rosemond knew: Saunders would try to sell the Mosby site as a reclamation project to politically active businessmen. Rosemond tried to appeal to the predispositions of businessmen in another way:

> The reason for a possible location on the north side of Lee Avenue is to aid in the rehabilitation or at least in the stemming of the encroaching blight from that direction. This action of course has its merits. However, the Planning Commission believes that other means would accomplish this move effectively, such as large parking areas. . . . One public building would have little effect.

Thus Rosemond sought to influence businessmen through changing their expectations as to the payoffs that could be expected from the Mosby Avenue site. In politics each seeks the maximum benefit for himself and tries to slough the costs off to others. The prospects of having the taxpayers foot the bill to resuscitate a flagging sector of the business district might gain many adherents, but it was too early to tell. Utilizing both his own expertise and the prestige that a planning commission composed predominantly of respected businessmen would command, Rosemond transmitted the information that might block the flow of the politically active to Saunders' side—a threat that their rewards would not be significantly increased by choosing the Mosby Avenue lot.

The battle meanwhile was being waged on another front. At its April meeting the Council, at Saunders' suggestion, cut the number of alternatives to four: (1) the Pickett Avenue site, (2) the Mosby Avenue property, (3) the Hulme plan, and (4) the Kenney freehold, a large estate that had in the meantime been offered for sale to the city. Strowd, Hulme, and Bearden, all of whom wanted the Sports Arena as either their first or second choice, did not want it scratched from the list of options and voted against the motion; the others voted for it. The councilmen had neatly snuffed out the commission's second and third choices. The Kenney property, located near the governmental buildings on Lee Avenue, was kept in the running as a last resort if the Mosby and Pickett Avenue locations were priced too high. Rumor had it that the Pickett Avenue location would cost anywhere from $400,000 to a flat million and the Mosby Avenue site only about $350,000. The Council had been quoted a price of $175,000 for a portion of the Kenney property.

All councilmen at this time apparently had perfect information about the preference orderings of their colleagues. These were:

	STROWD AND HULME	BEARDEN	LOWNDES	ALTON	BOSTWICK AND FERRABEE
1.	Hulme's Plan	Sports Arena	Pickett	Pickett	Mosby
2.	Sports Arena	. . .	Kenney	Mosby	Kenney

Rosemond had in addition two more important items of political intelligence: Bearden, Bostwick, and Ferrabee all objected to the high cost of the Pickett Avenue lot, and Bearden wanted a new building somewhere, preferably at moderate cost. Rosemond attempted to alter their preferences by forecasting a low purchase price for his preferred location. If persuasively communicated, this information would lessen the costs of agreeing on his terms. In an attempt to diminish or obliterate the one crucial constraint, he claimed the Pickett Avenue site could probably be bought for $400,000. True, Bostwick and Ferrabee had stated no preference at all for the lot on Pickett Avenue, but Rosemond thought they could be persuaded. Both had said they would choose any "reasonable" site rather than indefinitely perpetuate the stalemate. Since Lowndes and Alton could be expected to stand firm on Pickett, a switch would yield the needed majority. Such matters are not resolved in an instant, and the Council adjourned.

A few weeks later the Council asked the Arcadia Board of Realtors to sell the old building for no less than $400,000. In early July, as the carillons atop the bank appropriately tolled "Shall We Gather at the River?," the auctioneer received a single bid of exactly $400,000 for the old building. A week later the Council met. Lowndes, fearing the electorate would think the bid too low, wanted to reject it but was voted down. Alton proposed acceptance of the Pickett Avenue property but, predictably, was joined only by Lowndes. As Rosemond had feared, Bostwick and Ferrabee had been discouraged by the auction and did not want to pay the high price ($625,000–$719,500) the appraisers had set on the Pickett Avenue property. Lowndes immediately suggested his second priority. Bostwick, Ferrabee, and Bearden joined him in voting to buy a portion of the Kenney estate costing $339,000. The Council had in effect ignored the recommendations of both the city manager and the Planning Commission.

Before the necessary bond ordinance could be prepared, the state announced its intention to buy the Kenney property. Acting with unaccustomed alacrity, the councilmen decided to have the commission's original second choice on Bragg and Forrest appraised. Support for the Hulme Plan meanwhile had picked up momentum. Although there is no evidence they ever coordinated their efforts, the Halcyon County Bar Association and three former councilmen (including Peter Jameson) declared their intention to have the municipal building stay at the present location. The councilmen considered Jameson's opposition particularly discommoding since he had led the ticket each time he had run for office and was considered enormously influential among his fellow businessmen.

Late in August the Council reconvened and proposed bond issues of $1,325,000 if the lot on Forrest and Bragg were chosen and $1,625,000 for the Pickett Avenue lot. Saunders, aware that the Council was tacitly discarding his preferred choice, pleaded eloquently for its reconsideration. He offered it as a prime opportunity to rescue the north side of the business district from impending decay. Rosemond had done his work well. The Council told Rosemond to take the Planning Commission into the Council antechamber and come up with a site. Opinions on the commission were divided. Some, fearing the higher bond issue would lose in the election, wanted the Forrest Street lot in preference to the site on Pickett Avenue. Rosemond effectively stemmed the incipient backrush, and the commission, now determined to settle for nothing less than the best, recommended Council acceptance of the Pickett Avenue location.

Fearing the expensive lot would fail in the referendum, only Alton, Lowndes, and Bearden voted for the Forrest Street lot and the motion was lost. Hulme and Strowd were determined to stick with Hulme's plan until the bitter end. Ferrabee and Bostwick had hopes the price quoted for the Pickett Avenue lot was too high and did not want to pay for land on Bragg and Forrest which the city could not use.

With the defeat of the Forrest Street location, only Pickett remained. It passed by a vote of four to three. Lowndes, who still hoped to reopen debate on the less expensive Mosby Avenue location, joined the perennially adamant pair of Hulme and Strowd. Lowndes knew Alton would vote for the Mosby Avenue site and felt confident Ferrabee and Bostwick would prefer it to Hulme's plan. The vote was taken quickly and Lowndes had no chance to communicate his choice of strategies to the other Council members. The referendum was scheduled for December.

Early in November the battle lines were drawn. Ex-mayor Peter Jameson and Hudson Stryker, the owner of an automobile dealer's franchise, formed a businessman's committee to fight the bond issue. The committee (which seems to have consisted solely of Stryker and

Jameson) ran a series of newspaper advertisements drawing attention to the higher tax rate which would be needed to pay for the new building. Opposing them was the Arcadian League for a New Municipal Building (ALNMB), on whose letterhead appeared an impressive array of civic stalking horses. Among others who formed the League were Henry Perkins, Jr., vice president of Arcadia Lumber, a board member of the Arcadia National Bank and son of the Henry Perkins who had been a leader on the 1954 committee; the ubiquitous Miss Carol Rolfe; P. Baldwin Chambers, sexagenerian president of Southern Coachlines and a director of fifteen separate corporations; Benjamin Richardson, whose position as head of the Excelsior Dairies earned him an income of about $30,000 a year and a seat on the board of directors of the Arcadia National Bank; Henry Marlowe; ex-Councilman Corey Pycroft; and Dr. and Mrs. Roger Anderson, the former a fashionable physician and his wife, president of the Arcadia Women's Club. The charter members of the ALNMB, in turn, created a larger organization which they called the Bond Issue Boosters United (BIBU). This organization coopted so many representatives of various ethnic and religious groupings that it looked like Arcadia viewed through the large end of a telescope. Dr. Daniel Rosenbaum lent his name to the BIBU, as did F. P. "Tiny" Smith, a Negro mortician and once an unsuccessful candidate for the City Council, and C. J. Williams, a Negro lawyer and representative on the Arcadia School Board. Dr. James Maloney, an osteopath, appeared on the same letterhead with Dr. Roger Anderson and Mrs. Hall Smythe, wife of an insurance executive and member of the Arcadia Housing Authority. Osie Montaigne, pastor of the Second Baptist Church (colored) took his place in the lists alongside a state senator and two sons of former governors known for their segregationist sentiments.

The tactics of the BIBU were indistinguishable from those ritually used by busy participants in Hospital Linen Drives, the Downtown Club, and other restless devotees of Civic Progress. They proclaimed progress to the various women's clubs, church socials, literary society, and the Chamber of Commerce luncheon and, no doubt, in the locker-rooms of the Arcadia Country Club. They peppered airwave and television screen with blurbs and pleas imploring citizens to help erect a new monument dedicated to civic pride and municipal virtue. Henry Marlowe favored it in the editorial columns of the *Morning Clarion.* By comparison, Peter Jameson's efforts seemed moribund and the Halcyon County Bar Association had evidently lost its taste for combat.

In December Arcadia's voters made their second trip to the polls

Table 6-1. Color, Social Class, and the Vote in 1954 and 1956

	1954 MUNICIPAL BUILDING			1956 MUNICIPAL BUILDING			1956 FLUORIDATION		
TYPE OF PRECINCT	% YES	NUMBER OF VOTES (= 100%)	% VOTING	% YES	NUMBER OF VOTES (= 100%)	% VOTING	% YES	NUMBER OF VOTES (= 100%)	% VOTING
Negro	46.8	77	2.5	24.0	288	8.2	27.3	286	8.2
Lower class	46.4	388	9.9	25.5	882	21.0	32.9	878	20.9
Negro and lower class (combined)	46.5	465	6.6	25.1	1,170	15.2	31.5	1,164	15.2
Middle class	47.7	1,084	9 2	36.0	3,789	23.3	53.5	3,794	23.3
Upper class	50.1	809	15.7	45.3	2,281	36.3	70.3	2,295	36.5
City Totals	48.3	2,358	9.8	37.3	7,240	24.0	55.3	7,253	24.0

in two and a half years. That day they decided to fluoridate Arcadia's water. They decided against the bond issue.

To compare the results of the 1954 and 1956 elections is particularly rewarding (Table 6-1). First, the turnout in precincts of all social types increased markedly from the rather desultory levels of 1954. Compared with the first election, over three times as many enrolled Negroes, and over twice as many voters in the other social categories, went to the polls. Despite the vigorous efforts of the BIBU, the percentage voting *against* the bond issue also increased in each category. Even in the wealthy precincts where the BIBU might be expected to have the most influence, almost 55 per cent voted against the bond issue, contrasted to the very slight 1954 majority in its favor. In the middle-class precincts 64 per cent voted in the negative; in 1954 slightly more than 52 per cent cast ballots against issuing bonds. The BIBU, composed of Arcadia's leading social and economic notables, may have had some effect in getting the voters to go to the polls; it evidently could not influence the distribution of votes in its favor. The BIBU had access to, and thoroughly exploited, its resources of time, money, talent, and prestige. Through Henry Marlowe and Corey Pycroft it enlisted the power of the press and obtained a favored position on the air. But the BIBU, like the smaller battalions of the social and economic elite in 1954, had no access to the one resource that counted: sheer numbers of people.

It is sometimes suggested that citizens have a natural tendency to vote against referenda and bond elections out of perennial pettiness and invincible perversity. The figures for the 1956 fluoridation referendum should swiftly dispel that notion. Although both issues brought approximately the same number of voters to the ballot booth, the affirmative vote for fluoridation in all social categories was higher than that for the municipal building bond issue. Indeed, of all bond issues submitted for popular approval in city-manager Arcadia, only the municipal building referenda have ever failed.

The Third Bond Issue: 1957

The second referendum had meant what? The voting returns had provided the councilmen with information they could use to appraise the chances of future alternatives, but what was that information? How was it to be interpreted? Hulme and Strowd claimed the resounding defeat meant that the electorate was unwilling to finance a new municipal building through issuing bonds. With the significant exception of the 1954 referendum, they argued, no bond issue had ever failed, and the drubbing the electorate had administered left no doubt as to its preferences. The other councilmen thought citizen misunderstanding and the size of the bond issue had conspired to bring about its defeat. Few people had realized that the greater part of the revenue would be borrowed in short term notes, leaving only a small portion for debt service. High finance, one said, is after all a very intricate matter and one would therefore have to excuse the citizen who was frightened by the sheer immensity of the ballot. Next time the electorate would have to be better informed.

As the first step, the Council scheduled a public meeting. At the appointed hour, the Council, the Planning Commission, and six citizens filed into the Council chamber. Saunders and Lowndes had in the meantime persuaded Peter Jameson that the Mosby Avenue location would cost only about $6,000 more than Hulme's plan and provide three times as much space. Jameson announced that he and Hudson Stryker, another ex-councilman, were fully prepared to devote their time and energy on behalf of a new municipal building on Mosby Avenue.

After a rather frivolous session in which some councilmen said they favored a site either at the Arcadia Airport or the City Cemetery and others a location near the railroad tracks and a huge drop forge, the Council once more agreed to ask the Planning Commission to suggest a location. Rosemond, now aware the Saunders-Lowndes-Jameson-Stryker coalition was sponsoring Mosby Avenue, rallied the commission in support of his preference. Rosemond asked the commission to recommend the purchase of a half block, bounded by Johnston, Forrest, and Bragg. This site, it might be noted, was just two blocks south of the Pickett Avenue site and was catty-corner from the commission's third choice a year before. Rosemond argued that his preferred location was accessible, situated on a hilltop (a boon to "civic pride"), had the necessary space, and could be purchased for a reasonable price. But the truly telling argument, the one that appealed most to the commission, was that blighted property would be removed. The commission could recommend the Mosby Avenue location as only a distant second best.

Again the councilmen had disclosed their preferences to one another. From their many conversations each councilman knew, or thought he knew (which is quite the same thing in analyses of this sort), what the others desired. When the Council met on January 22, the members had ranked their preferences in the following manner:

	FERRABEE	HULME	STROWD	LOWNDES	BOSTWICK AND ALTON	BEARDEN
1.	Against Hulme's Plan	Hulme's Plan	Hulme's Plan	Mosby	Bragg	Sports Arena
2.	...	...	Mosby	...	...	...

Alton immediately proposed adoption of the Bragg Street lot and was quickly seconded by Bearden.[5] The motion was quickly replaced by a substitute, a substitute to the substitute, and a substitute to the substitute to the substitute. Lowndes, Bostwick, and Ferrabee were determined no vote would be taken that night. Hopelessly ensnarled, the councilmen passed on to more congenial matters.

At the next meeting, George Averill, top executive of a large Arcadia business firm and a bellwether in the Chamber of Commerce, presented a petition signed by many Chamber of Commerce members asking the Council to approve the Bragg Avenue site which the Planning Commission had endorsed. Mayor Ferrabee testily responded that the results were tragic the last time the Council had yielded to the commission's recommendation. Tempers were running high. Saunders called the Planning Commission to his chambers and pleaded for the Mosby Avenue site as a means of rehabilitating the decrepit portion of the business district. Rosemond, again seconded by the commission, said the present building had been at the east end of Lee

Avenue since the beginning of the century and had not done very much to attract business there. Council elections were now a few weeks off and nothing more happened.

Strowd, Alton, and Bearden decided to abstain from the 1957 elections. Hulme and Bostwick were defeated. Joining Lowndes and Ferrabee, the two holdovers on the Council, were Jason Edwards, a builder; Kenneth Blair, administrative assistant for one United States Senator and campaign manager for another, and, at the time he ran for council, executive secretary of the state bankers' association; Joseph Vall, a suburban stationer; former councilmen Harold Brisbane and Hudson Stryker. The Council elected Lowndes mayor, even though he ran sixth in total votes. (This was a departure from the usual convention of automatically designating the top vote getter as mayor.) In his inaugural speech, the new mayor reaffirmed his intention to complete a new building, and he toured the usual round of civic clubs speaking in its behalf. Just two months after the May election, the Council unanimously chose Mosby Avenue, by now the only site open, and set a date in October for a public referendum on a bond issue of $988,500.

The Board of Directors of the Arcadia Merchants' League enthusiastically recommended the site, as it had the Pickett Avenue location the year before. This time, however, the press was not solidly behind the bond issue. Henry Marlowe could see no particular virtue in transforming a civic temple into a rehabilitation project, and the editor of the *Afternoon Herald* objected vehemently to its "great distance" from the center of downtown growth. Lowndes replied savagely. In a public letter, he reminded the *Herald's* editor that he had a year ago supported the Pickett Avenue location, a site no farther from the heart of the business district than Mosby was. Jameson, long a supporter of the Mosby Avenue location, capriciously defected from its supporters and entered a coalition against the bond issue together with Alton and Hulme.

As usual, a Booster's Club was formed to promote the bond issue. Corey Pycroft, by now doubly battle scarred, became chairman, and Carol Rolfe was appointed vice chairman. George Averill, now a high officer in the Chamber of Commerce, appeared on the committee, as did Theodore Pomeroy of the Merchants' League. Also enlisted were Councilmen Blair, Brisbane, Stryker, Edwards, and Lowndes, two directors of insurance firms, and the daughter-in-law of a former governor. Though smaller and less polyglot in composition than the

Table 6-2. Color, Social Class, and the Vote in the 1957 Bond Election

TYPE OF PRECINCT	% YES	NUMBER OF VOTES (= 100%)	% VOTING
Negro	45.3	287	8.0
Lower class	44.1	653	15.9
Negro and lower class (combined)	44.5	940	13.8
Middle class	42.0	2,773	17.9
Upper class	43.2	1,701	26.7
City Totals	42.8	5,414	18.3

BIBU, the Booster's Club employed many of the same tactics. The committee brimmed over with prestige and status.

The bond issue, however, went down to defeat for the third time. A somewhat different pattern of voting prevailed, as Table 6-2 shows. Although the turnout resembled previous elections, lower-class and Negro precincts turned in much higher minorities for the bond issue than ever before. Over 60 per cent of the voters in one of the lower-class precincts (where the building would have been constructed) voted *for* the issue, as compared with the 86.2 per cent who had voted *against* the Pickett Avenue site the year before. In the Negro precinct immediately adjoining, 54.6 per cent voted for the 1957 issue compared with 23.7 per cent that had been for the issue the year before. These were the largest net shifts, although the changes in the other lower-class and Negro precincts were much higher than the average shift in the city as a whole.

In all three elections the size of the affirmative vote was positively related to the face value of the proposed bond issue. Hulme and Strowd may have been correct after all.

Building without a Bond Issue

Once more the councilmen had to sit down and analyze the election returns, but this time they agreed on what had happened and what had to be done. If the building were ever to go up, some set of techniques would have to be found to by-pass a public referendum, now seen as far too risky and embarrassing. Lowndes had been quietly at work forming a new citizens' committee—this time not to help pass a bond issue but to discover means of averting one. The organization was headed by Owen Mott, vice president of a local bank and member of the Planning Commission. The other members were Corey Pycroft; Avery Holmes, manager of a loan company; Mrs. Daisy Bolling, wife of an elderly attorney who had once served on the Planning Commission; Harmon Busbee, publishing executive and an officer of the Merchants' League; Joan Brent, the wife of a prominent attorney; James Kerr, a labor union leader; John Faircloth, president of the Arcadia Council of Civic Associations; C. J. Williams and "Tiny" Smith. The committee was later expanded by the addition of more prestigious names: among them a Negro who had once run for the Council; George Averill; a Jewish lawyer; a bank vice president; the president of a fuel company and contracting supply firm; and the wives of a number of professionals. In composition it was a miniature slice of the junta of one hundred that had failed to put the bond drive over the year before. With the obvious exception of any delegates from white lower-class precincts, the committee was Arcadia in miniature. Lowndes hoped it would have dual legitimacy, both of prestige and of a "democratic grass roots" representation. Through joint membership on both the City Planning Commission and the citizen committee, Owen Mott provided vicarious access for Everett Rosemond; and the presence of Harmon Busbee and George Averill assured the receptivity of both the Chamber of Commerce and the Merchants' League. In March the committee announced its approval of two options: the Hakluyt freehold on a block bounded by Forrest, Brady, Johnston, and Clay streets and, as a last resort, the Sports Arena. Rosemond, who had been in continuous contact with the committee through its chairman, announced that he was pleased with the site. It is perhaps not entirely accidental that the location was on the same block that Rosemond had favored and Saunders had opposed in 1956.

Someone on the committee had discovered that cities could, with the approval of a state agency, issue without a referendum up to 67 per cent of the face value of bonds retired the previous year.[6] This was an important discovery, for it meant the city could go ahead with the building without calling a bond election. Toward the end of April the Council met to vote on the site. Councilman Jason Edwards had reached the executors of the Hakluyt estate and had arranged a price of $395,000 for the property. Councilmen Stryker and Brisbane, however, announced they still preferred the Mosby Avenue lot.

The same financial arrangements, they argued, could be used to purchase the site that had been the Council's initial preference the year before. Blair, for his part, held out for the Sports Arena. Edwards argued that Mosby Avenue had since been rezoned to neighborhood business and would therefore be far more expensive than the Hakluyt property. Lowndes, Vall, Edwards, and John Cram (a pharmacist the Council had appointed to fill the seat vacated by Ferrabee's death) voted for the Hakluyt property; Blair, Brisbane, and Stryker cast their ballots in the negative. Saunders announced he would have bonds of $333,000 issued and sold. This sum, Saunders calculated, when added to deposited funds and the money expected from the sale of municipal property, would furnish all necessary revenues.

In the resulting jubilation and despair nobody knew whether the Council had passed both the bond issue and the site, or the site alone. The city clerk ruled that only the site had been approved. Blair, in a last ditch attempt to eliminate the Hakluyt property, decided to ask that it be approved in public referendum. By the same vote that had chosen the Hakluyt freehold in April, the Council passed the bond ordinance in May. Lowndes and Vall had asked George Averill to "bring along a crowd," and this time the Council chambers overflowed with citizens, many of whom had come in response to telegrams he had sent out in behalf of the Chamber of Commerce. Stryker was genuinely surprised: "If I had known this had been turned into a public hearing, I would have brought an equal number of opponents." Jameson, Stryker, Blair, and Brisbane, joined by Amos Weeks, Jr., son of a former United States Senator and leader of the anti-city manager forces in 1947, tried to form a coalition of the disaffected. Few could be persuaded to join; those who did quickly recognized they had no legal resources or political strength to marshal, and the incipient movement shriveled.

The Council moved swiftly. It auctioned off some miscellaneous parcels of municipal property and received a bid of $350,000 for the old building that had once been optimistically valued at $600,000. The Council at first unanimously voted to reject the bid; but, when no better offers were received, voted to accept it over the objections of Stryker and Brisbane. Blair, recognizing the fight was lost, dispiritedly voted "present." The Council soon let out contracts and, in September of 1960, held a housewarming party in its new quarters, a victory celebration for a protracted campaign that had begun a full decade before.

Selection and Acceptance of Harley Court

Ideologues of the left extol "planning"; those of the right abhor it. It is extraordinary but true that what both mean by "planning"—circumventing the normal market constraints for allocating goods and resources—is not planning at all, but usually a series of pragmatic responses to unanticipated crises. Such a case is public housing. After the Second World War the leaders of the American Legion, faced by the threat posed by the rival American Veteran's Committee and the unmistakable demand of returning veterans for roofs over their heads, were forced to cast aside their ritual opposition to "socialism" and reluctantly join advocates of public housing. Because of the articulate and widespread demand, it became politically imperative for Congress to enact some sort of housing legislation. Title III of the Taft-Elender-Wagner Act passed in 1949 authorized subsidies and credit for local housing authorities to build living units on either slum or vacant land.

Public Housing for Arcadia

By late 1955 the Arcadia Housing Authority had built two projects: one for whites and the other for Negroes. In November the regional office at Atlanta announced it had reserved 3 million dollars for the construction of 300 additional units in Arcadia. Although local housing authorities are legally autonomous of local councils, they are not so in fact. A council, if piqued, can mine the paths local housing authorities have to travel: by withholding the appropriations needed to pave streets and install water lines; by forcing discomfiting changes in zoning ordinances; and, perhaps most important of all, by mobilizing any latent public opinion against public housing.

Shortly after word of the reservation had been received, William Robinson, chairman of the Arcadia Housing Authority and a professor of hydraulics, and Jeffrey Pitt, an attorney and vice chairman of the Authority, asked the Council to reaffirm Arcadia's desire for public housing. Rex Cravier, a local realtor whom Pitt had persuaded to attend, said he favored public housing because poor families could not afford the housing private enterprise could build. Unsympathetic realtors and developers howled "socialism," claiming that many supposedly impoverished public housing tenants drove expensive cars of recent make. The motion passed by a vote of four to two with Councilmen George Alton and Edward Hulme casting the negative votes. In seeming contradiction, Alton said that vigorous enforcement of local housing ordinances could alleviate blight without any taint of governmental intervention. Hulme's negative vote was not entirely unanticipated; he had also dissented in 1949. Strowd, who had been expected to join Hulme, this time cast his lot with the Council majority. He explained his vote by saying: "It has not been easy for me to resolve my position . . . but I have seen it in its true light as a charitable proposition."

The Selection of a Site

At this time the Arcadia Housing Authority consisted of Robinson, Pitt, David Upchurch, president of the Thrift and Security Bank, Mrs. Hall Smythe, and Nathan Bolt, a very prosperous builder. Together, they had all the resources commonly associated with power: wealth, status, prestige. They were all highly intelligent people. For "selling" public housing to various clienteles these were unquestionably potent attributes, but the Housing Authority first had to select a site. And Housing Authority members soon recognized they had neither the training, information, nor knowledge to choose one of the many alternatives open to them.

They sought the city planner's counsel. Rosemond had been studying housing conditions in Arcadia whenever he could steal some time from routine obligations. When the federal reservation was first announced Rosemond suggested an area of some 25 acres east of the Sports Arena as a prime candidate for rehabilitation. Inhabited totally by Negroes, the site was a shambles of squalid shacks haphazardly strewn along nearly impassable streets. There were other blighted areas in Arcadia, but Harley Court had adequate utility service (which would decrease the city's financial contribution to the project) and was located within walking distance of a large school with empty classrooms. Persuaded by Rosemond's impressive show of professional expertise, the Housing Authority, the City Planning Commission, and Emery Saunders all in quick order deferred to his choice of alternatives.

Opposition

On January 18, the *Morning Clarion* triumphantly announced that Council ratification of the Harley Court project was by now a foregone conclusion. Its members had been invited to an informal meeting of both the Housing Authority and Planning Commission late in January, and, but for Hulme and Alton, no opposition had been raised to the site Rosemond had selected. The outcome seemed sure.

The *Morning Clarion* was wrong. No one had reckoned with the Reverend Lawrence Appleton, pastor of the United Holiness Church. With Appleton as their spokesman, 40 Negro homeowners appeared at the Council's first meeting in February to protest the Housing Authority's choice. Appleton, who rented five homes in the area and lived in another, said the Harley Court project would evict 150 families without their consent. "It would mean death to put some of them out," he implored. "They are old; some are bedridden . . . would it profit anyone to put out 150 families so you could move in 300?" Others said the project would liquidate their life savings:

> It is not a matter of money. I have worked all my life to get a home here. I go to sleep thinking I've got one and I wake up the next morning and find it is going to be taken away from me.

The Negroes owning rental housing in Harley Court, Appleton implored, were not idle landlords passively making fortunes by charging high fees for dismal hovels. Rather, they were hard-working men hoping to eke out meager incomes through renting respectable dwelling units for reasonable rents.

Bostwick, who as head of the Law and Finance Committee had originally introduced the proposal to the Council, said he had been quite unaware of any objection and was now prepared to reverse himself. The Council, while not officially disapproving the site, suggested the Authority find a less populous area. Eric Lowndes quickly entered a motion to adjourn before further harm was done, and Mayor Ferrabee accepted it with alacrity and evident relief.

Rosemond and Robinson met after the conclusion of the Council meeting and agreed not to eliminate the Harley Court site without a fight. In a special meeting called the following Saturday, Robinson argued it would be impossible to secure competent appraisals and search titles on alternative locations before the July 31 deadline. Unless the Authority met the deadline, Robinson threatened, the funds reserved for Arcadia would be paid forfeit to other communities. Unmoved, the Council told Rosemond and Robinson to search for other sites.[7]

Early the following week the Housing Authority began to forage for alternative locations. They discovered three, all in Negro areas.

Robinson, still opposing any change in plan, again asked for Rosemond's opinion. The city planner said the first site, located on a hillside with huge outcroppings of rock, would be costly to construct and was too far from existing schools. The second, he claimed, would require the provision of municipal water lines and sewer mains; and the third, which would also need additional sewerage and water facilities, could be entered only through a junkyard. Accepting his appraisal, the Housing Authority relinquished any thought of canvassing other options and resolved either to press for Council acceptance of Harley Court, or to find some way of getting along without it. Indeed, as Rosemond took pains to underscore, the situation in Council was far from hopeless. Lowndes, Bearden, and Ferrabee would certainly vote for the site; Alton and Hulme were in unalterable opposition. Strowd, he said, would probably defect from his earlier stand and join Hulme and Alton. If a tie resulted, Bostwick, then vacationing in Florida, could be summoned to cast the deciding ballot.

If, by some unforeseen circumstance, the Council disapproved, the Housing Authority could still go ahead with the project. The attorney at the Atlanta regional office had assured Robinson that Council acceptance was not mandatory, only desirable. In any case the new Council to be elected in May might rescind the decision. As a last resort, the Housing Authority could make side payments to the refractory Negroes. The Housing Authority could buy up homes and sell them back at a great loss, on condition they be removed from the area. In short, Rosemond had tried to alter any disposition to accept alternate sites by supplying Authority members with three important bits of information: (1) Council acceptance of Harley Court could not be completely discounted; (2) the Council might not invest money to provide the necessary public utilities for the other sites, making them much less attractive than Harley Court; and (3) if all else failed, the Authority could draw upon some of its own resources to placate Negro opposition. The Housing Authority decided not to budge.

At the Council meeting held on February 15, Mrs. Helena Jackson, a registered nurse, and Louis Fifield, an office machine salesman who had once run in the Democratic gubernatorial primaries, took time out from their fight against fluoridated water to protest public housing and call for a return to the ancestral virtues of untrammeled free private enterprise. Lowndes entreated the Council not to turn its back upon the Housing Authority and force the federal government to spend its money somewhere else. But the result of the vote was never in doubt. With Bostwick absent, the Council divided evenly and the the motion was lost. Both newspapers had been among the Housing Authority's most vociferous supporters and excoriated the Council for its reversal. The editor of the *Afternoon Herald* wrote:

> Bernard Strowd voted for the project in November because "private industry had failed to do the job." . . . Yesterday it was the old Strowd again, the Strowd who told this paper not long ago that everybody has the right to have a hole in his roof.

For its part, the Housing Authority announced it would go ahead with its plan to build Harley Court, willy-nilly.

The conflict, at first confined to the Council, Fifield and Jackson, the Arcadia Housing Authority, and the delegation of Negro home-owners, now began to expand in size and deepen in intensity. Bostwick, although expected to return for the next Council meeting, had already said he might reverse his earlier stand in favor of the project. Negro tenants had begun to speak timidly for public housing, and Appleton countered by forming a Home Owners' League. Intimidating letters, crudely scrawled and anonymous, were sent tenants who had visibly sided with the Housing Authority. One even threatened to find a Negro tenant a home in Mount Pleasant (the local Negro cemetery) if he persisted in his support of public housing. Rosemond, Mrs. Smythe, and Professor Robinson met this move with one of their own; they persuaded the League of Women Voters and other civic associations to pass resolutions in favor of the Harley Court project and to have representatives on hand for the next Council meeting. At its last meeting in March the Council approved the site by a vote of four to three. As Rosemond had predicted, Bostwick voted to sustain the Housing Authority's decision. Bostwick explained he would have preferred another site but would vote for Harley Court rather than sacrifice public housing. The strategy Rosemond and Robinson had so carefully devised had finally paid off. By refusing to allow their allies on the Housing Authority and City Council to decide among additional sites, they had left them only the choice between Harley Court and no public housing at all.

Urban Redevelopment in Arcadia: Dewy Bottom

In 1908, the year the old municipal building was erected, the Arcadia Women's Club hired an architect to prepare a master city plan.

Predictably, nothing happened. Although some of his notions were startling and imaginative, no techniques had been provided to ensure their acceptance by politicians, and all such comprehensive plans require the coercive resources of government for their execution. In 1922 Mayor Harvey Andrews established the City Planning Commission to remedy the problems presented by:

> Lee Avenue . . . a street to inspire us with pride, till it strikes an obstruction, shoots off at an angle, greatly restricted by width, and then by sundry crooks and turns finds its way into the open country. Had a city planning board been operating in Arcadia a century ago the railroads would not have been allowed to cut across street extensions without providing bridges or underpasses. . . . There is no way to get across (the railroads) without flying. . . . Even today within a bowshot of the heart of the city, streets are being laid out and graded very much as though the owners of the property regarded the making of streets as nobody's business but their own. . . . (Arcadia has) streets that start somewhere, traverse a few blocks, and get nowhere; streets that were laid out with no earthly purpose but to sell building lots; streets that start again, go on farther and then give up in despair of making a worthwhile connection. . . .

The Planning Commission completed some admirable reports and studies but could find no political support. Arcadia's politicians were not being peevish or perverse; their reluctance was based on an astute estimate of the opportunities open to them. No one questioned the costliness of the plans and subplans; the tax base was constricted and any attempt to have raised it would certainly have irritated the very citizens whose votes were needed to keep the politicians in office. As if by some Gresham's Law, the Planning Commission abandoned its more ambitious aspirations, forgot innovation completely, and buckled down to the routine and comparatively noncontroversial work of allocating rewards and deprivations through making and relaxing zoning regulations.

Title I of the 1949 Taft-Ellender-Wagner Act provided the means for surmounting the financial obstacles that had thus far impeded any substantial progress. Congress authorized municipalities to borrow money and receive outright cash subsidies for the acquisition and razing of blighted property; to plan for its redevelopment and then resell the cleared land to private redevelopers at a substantial loss. Many feel that the act in effect allowed cities to grant covert bounties to private realtors and contractors for undertaking urban redevelopment. Not only did Title I exhibit startling financial ingenuity; it was also politically adroit. To some large realtors and developers it presaged the end of public housing and assured local contractors economies of scale. Although it tended to nullify or diminish the opposition of influential producer groups that had previously obstructed governmental intervention, it did not provide techniques for securing the cooperation of local political officials and political elites. This the act left to local initiative.

First Steps

By 1955 not a single dollar had been returned to North Carolina cities for urban redevelopment. In October the Planning Department drafted a Minimum Housing Standards Ordinance and submitted it to the Council. Rosemond knew that federal regulations required such ordinances before cities could be eligible for urban-renewal grants. The potential payoffs appeared great, and Rosemond deployed his resources of time and energy to assure adoption of the ordinance. He conferred with the local realtors, the architects, the plumbers, and the electricians and allowed them to veto provisions he thought insignificant. Finally all the producer groups were more or less satisfied and agreed not to oppose the ordinance before the City Council.

Mayor Ferrabee, Lowndes, and Bostwick promised Rosemond they would vote for the ordinance when it was introduced in December. The conservative faction, consisting of Alton, Hulme, and Strowd, was determined to fight it on ideological grounds:

> The Council does not have the wisdom to decide what the minimum standards should be . . . slum clearance can best be solved by free enterprise, with limited government interference, in an open market.

By February Rosemond's efforts were beginning to pay dividends. The Council passed his plumbing code over the opposition of a solitary plumber who claimed the ordinance forced the use of cast iron pipe and discriminated against contractors who employed less expensive clay and composition pipe. The Arcadia Council of Architects let the Council know its members favored the ordinance as a deterrent to disease, juvenile delinquency, crime, and slums. The League of Women Voters, egged on by Rosemond, Robinson, and Mrs. Hall Smythe, sent a barrage of telegrams to the councilmen asking them to back the housing ordinance. In addition, the League's officers regularly dispatched representatives to the Council so as to know what was "going on."

By comparison the opposition was spotty and disorganized. One of the dedicated dissidents, Kenneth Blair, proclaimed he was "in favor of retaining the rights of the individual to live in housing he could afford." Louis Fifield, Cato-like, protested the intrusion of government into private affairs, and Mrs. Barbara Waldston, superintendent of the Halcyon County Welfare Department, complained that 1,500 Arcadia families then receiving aid would be "forced to cut down on food and other budget items" as they spent money to bring their properties up to standard. One realtor confirmed Strowd's prediction that improvements would result in a rent increase, but the Board of Realtors, evidently won over by Rosemond's earlier concessions, did not object.

On the fourth day of April the ordinance passed the Council. According to the *Clarion's* reporter, the initial measure had been so extensively revised, patched up, and watered down that no member knew what was in the bill the Council finally passed. In a futile last minute attempt to dampen the Council's enthusiasm for the bill, Hulme said it would cost $100,000 a year to enforce, but Saunders said only one additional inspector would be required. Only Hulme and Strowd voted to kill the ordinance; all others voted affirmatively.

Rosemond and Lowndes had pieced together a coalition to pass the Minimum Standards Housing Ordinance. Rosemond, together with Mrs. Smythe and Professor Robinson, had given point to the vague humanitarianism of the League of Women Voters. By making expedient and marginal concessions Rosemond had enlisted the support of the realtors, the plumbers, the architects, and the electricians, and Lowndes had been instrumental in rallying his fellow councilmen. Lowndes and Rosemond had played the game with their cards held close to their chests; few had been told the passage of the ordinance would be the prelude to urban redevelopment. By not tipping their hands, Lowndes and Rosemond had avoided transforming an insignificant skirmish over minimum housing regulations into a gigantic battle over urban renewal.

Building Support

The first obstacle successfully hurdled, Rosemond set foot upon the road that would eventually lead to agreement on the desirability of urban renewal for Arcadia. There were many strings to Rosemond's bow and he exploited his available resources to the maximum. He persuaded John Evers to give him space in the *Afternoon Herald* (more likely than the *Clarion* to be read at home in the evenings) for a series of articles on urban redevelopment. He alternately stressed the horrid living conditions in portions of Arcadia and the progress that cities like Norfolk in the neighboring state of Virginia had made in alleviating noisome squalor with federal funds. He contrasted the disproportionate share of fire and police protection which Arcadia slums drew with the slender portion of taxes its inhabitants contributed. To the denizens of the Lions' Club, the Merchants' League, and the Chamber of Commerce, he pointed out how the investment of federal funds in blighted areas would, in a decade's time, increase property values, which, in turn, could be taxed to liquidate Arcadia's original contributions. He in no way attempted to expunge the conservative business creed by a fatuous (and probably unsuccessful) appeal to humanitarian motives. He simply appealed to the avaricious postulates underlying the creed. Taxpayers, he emphasized, were being forced by federal policies to buy urban renewal whether they liked it or not. Since 1949 North Carolina had been obliged to buy some 8 million dollars' worth of redevelopment and had not received a penny in return. The tax dollars its citizens had contributed were being used to finance urban renewal in other cities throughout the land but were not being used in Arcadia at all. It seemed eminently sensible to Arcadia's businessmen to reap some benefits from outlays they were being forced to surrender to the federal government.

By Sptember 1957 Rosemond's arduous campaign had struck many responsive chords and he was prepared to present urban redevelopment to the Council. He knew he could count on Mayor Lowndes, who had once lobbied for urban renewal before a congressional committee, to press for Council adoption. When they broached the matter to the Council, Hudson Stryker, who was regarded as one of the three arch-conservatives on the Council, said, "In principle I'm opposed to it. In practice, I'm for it. . . . I'm for working out a project that will benefit Arcadia. I say let's get in with both feet as soon as we can." Brisbane meekly said he "was for part of it." Only Blair was adamant. He viewed urban redevelopment as merely one more devious "extension of government to get hands on private property." Joseph Vall said he would bend every effort to get the Chamber of Commerce behind it.

Early in 1958 urban renewal was discussed before a joint meeting of the Planning Commission and the City Council. Approval was unanimous. Blair, recognizing that nothing could now stem the tide, was absent. At the next Council meeting, Vall, Stryker, Edwards, and Lowndes called for "immediate steps" toward establishing a program for Arcadia. John Cram voted "present." Only Blair registered his opposition. After the Council had passed its statement of intention, he said, "I was in Washington when the darn thing was born. A man named (Senator) Hugh Peacock (his boss while he was an administrative assistant) fought it. The federal government ain't my daddy rabbit."

With Blair in solitary opposition, the Council agreed to hold a public hearing the first week in April. His fight now futile, Blair rang down the curtain in one last clap of oratory as accurate in its charges as it was fervent in its rhetoric:

> The newspapers in Arcadia have supported Mr. Rosemond's views and have quoted various statistics which I suppose Mr. Rosemond compiled and released . . . (they) characteristically have not given the other side of the story.

He could not have been more correct.

Recognizing the struggle was over, Blair did not attend the public hearing. Lowndes had invited a number of prestigious citizens to register their approval and certify urban renewal in Arcadia. Peter Jameson and Paul Amery, president of the Arcadia Chamber of Commerce, acclaimed the proposed program as a marvelous opportunity. Mrs. Evelyn Badgett, an architect's wife and president of the League of Women Voters, said urban redevelopment would keep blight from spreading into adjacent areas. Professor Joseph Robinson was present to express his assent and brought along a university colleague for good measure. The Fellowship of Southern Churches had sent a congratulatory telegram, and the pastor of the biggest and wealthiest Baptist church in Arcadia bestowed his blessings in person. With Blair absent, Council approval was unanimous.

There is, all politicians realize, many a potential slip between pledge and performance. An urban redevelopment commission still had to be named and approved, money had to be appropriated, a site had to be chosen for Arcadia's first project, and plans had to be prepared for federal approval. The coalition of civic notables which Lowndes and Rosemond had created to proclaim the legitimacy and acceptability of urban redevelopment was inherently unstable and dissolved soon after its members had made known their positions. The League of Women Voters left to study and debate the problems of inadequate schools and polluted water; the church leaders could hardly be expected to have the talent or the interest for stubborn detail; and the merchants and businessmen struck camp in order to tend the concerns that provided them with their livelihood.

The five men appointed to the Urban Redevelopment Commission had all indicated their support of the program at one time or another; indeed, this was one of the criteria Lowndes, Rosemond, and Edwards used in evaluating potential candidates. Emery Rockwell, director of development for the Piedmont Electric Power Corporation, had boosted urban renewal in the Chamber of Commerce. Perkins Swanton, president of the local Negro bank, strongly approved of the project as a means of ameliorating Negro housing conditions. George Downs, a prominent realtor; John McMullan, an architect; and John Bullock, a bank vice president who eventually became chairman, had all been avid supporters. Their elevated statuses could be used, if the occasion so demanded, to blunt any charge that urban renewal was the sly but odious brainchild of some latter-day New Deal socialists.

Though all eminent and respected people, they had neither the time nor the expertise personally to take charge of the work that had to be done before the July 1 deadline for application. The first and most important item was the selection of a site. Rosemond, who had been canvassing alternatives for some time, decided to submit Dewy Bottom as his choice. It was just a few blocks away from the central business district and businessmen, Rosemond calculated, would be in favor of removing a noxious eyesore so close to their places of business. Dewy Bottom also had the highest proportion of substandard housing in Arcadia, making it a sure bet to appeal to the League of Women Voters. Since the racial composition of Dewy Bottom was mixed, Perkins Swanton would eagerly fight for it if any opposition happened to develop. Early in May Rosemond recommended adoption of the location to the City Planning Commission. As usual, its members deferred to Rosemond. He next met with the newly formed Urban Redevelopment Commission to announce that the Planning Commission had certified Dewy Bottom. The commissioners consented to his choice without a quibble.

No one who has lived through the middle of April needs be told how grotesquely complicated federal forms can be, and the members of the Redevelopment Commission once again lacked the time, knowledge, and perseverance to wade through the bundle of application forms that had to be submitted by the first of July. Rosemond and his staff in the City Planning Department consented to prepare applications for planning and survey forms. Federal authorities, apparently taking account of the lack of time, had told Rosemond he needed to prepare only "skeletal" plans and estimates. Then, in one of the irritating reversals that have furnished such rich fodder for lampoons of bureaucratic procedure, federal officials informed Rosemond he would have to submit complete working plans. The message was received three days before the applications were due. In a furious rush, Rosemond and his meager staff stayed up most of the two remaining nights in June to finish on time.

Events now moved rapidly. In September the Housing and Home Finance Agency certified the housing plans Rosemond had laid out for Dewy Bottom. In December officials approved a capital grant reservation of some $960,000 for the program and advanced the $45,000 Rosemond had asked for preliminary surveys and the salary to be paid the Commission's executive secretary. On the last day of January the following year the FHA approved Arcadia's application for mortgage insurance for 380 units of low cost housing for displaced residents. In March the Council appointed Joseph Llewellyn as executive secretary of the Commission. Llewellyn, who had been within Rosemond's orbit of influence as a member of the Planning Commission, was responsive to him thereafter. Rosemond, who had said his involvement with the Commission would terminate with Llewellyn's appointment, helped Llewellyn prepare various reports and survey the area slated for relocation. After the Council had approved Arcadia's application for a federal loan to finance its share of the costs, the project finally moved through its initial stages.

Power Elites: Theory and Confrontation

Sociological Theory: The Political Rewards of Status

The most important feature of the theory that many sociologists have evolved about politics in the local community is the summary premise that political power is simply socio-economic status perfectly refracted. Nowhere has the thrust of this dominant assumption been more sharply underscored than in a series of three books spanning nearly a quarter of a century: *Middletown* (Lynd and Lynd, 1929), *Middletown in Transition* (Lynd and Lynd, 1937), and *Community Power Structure* (Hunter, 1953).

The Lynds summarized the allocation of political power in a passage so compact and striking that it deserves quotation:

> Middletown has, therefore, at present what amounts to a reigning royal family. If . . . one views the Middletown pattern as simply concentrating

and personalizing the type of control which control of capital gives to the business group in our culture, the Middletown culture may be viewed as epitomizing the American business-class control system. . . . The business class runs the city. The nucleus of business-class control is the X family. (Lynd and Lynd, 1937, p. 77.)

Larger in size and economically more diversified than Middletown, Hunter's Regional City was too unwieldy to be monitored and minutely coordinated by any single family. But wealth and status were still the crucial resources that lay behind the exercise of power. Regional City was governed by an interlocking directorate of 40 men: 23 drawn from the top echelons of business, commercial, and manufacturing organizations; 4 from government; 2 from labor organizations; 6 from professional occupations (5 of these, significantly, were corporation attorneys); while the remaining 5 were idle rentiers. These leaders were clotted into an intricate web of informal cliques, guided by a tiny nucleus of "top leaders" who adjusted their strategies and goals. A notch beneath were the perennial hustlers: middle-level organization men, nouveaux riches, clerics, teachers, politicians, and the formal leaders of a ragtag assemblage of civic groups and other voluntary associations. These second stringers busily conducted distracting and noisy games that earned them reputations as "community leaders"; actually, they did little more than enact the demands of their superiors. Far from counterpoising elite power, politicians supplied legitimacy to the decisions of business leaders; public officials and other visible "civic leaders" were custodians for their interests.

Both the Lynds and Hunter argued that the power to make governmental decisions and shape political attitudes rests on access to wealth, high social status, and dominant economic position, scarce resources always found sharply concentrated in a tiny fraction of the adult population. When shrewdly utilized, these resources allow their possessors to amass and organize political power. Not only can the wealthy and status elite rival the structure of legal authority, they can exploit their resources to stabilize it, dominate it, and even warp it to serve their own ends. The Lynds and Hunter assumed throughout that economic power is primary and political control derivative. In both Middletown and Regional City, businessmen held the hero's share of real property and capitalized investment. Not only did this earn them esteem and recognition, it also enabled them to buy and sell the personal services of politicians, educators, and clerics on favorable terms. Members of the ruling business elites sustained only the most trivial costs in their efforts to influence the outcomes of governmental choices. Typically, the sole alternatives forgone in exerting political influence were the time and money consumed in making an appearance at a civic luncheon to endorse a pet "project"; in asking the editor of a trade publication to sack a "radical" columnist; or in hiring docile ministers and educators who would compose raucous anthems hymning the virtues of "free private enterprise." Compared to the huge volume of resources that could be poured into efforts to influence political decisions, these expenditures were generally quite small. What made them so prepossessing was that they served as credible surrogates for the massive sanctions that potentially supported elite demands; in war and politics the sheathed sword intimidates the armless. These resources could have been called up and pitched into the fray, but the threat of their use was sufficient to snuff out incipient opposition.

According to both the Lynds and Hunter, the general equation for determining the distribution of power in local communities becomes almost mischievously simple. Those who attain high socio-economic status will also control the decisions of public governments, and those deprived of wealth and social pre-eminence will be politically impotent. Since wealth and status are bound to be sharply concentrated, it therefore follows that political power will be also. The wealthy few will employ their resources to monopolize political power and enjoy all the benefits political control can secure—including, of course, continued access to the economic resources that alone can guarantee future political influence.

Furthermore, knowing the way wealth and social position are allocated enables one to explain observable differences in levels of political participation. Decades of public opinion research have many times over confirmed the proposition that political activity is an increasing function of socio-economic status. The breadth and intensity of political activity declines drastically as one descends the ladders of wealth and preferred social station; with each rung, apathy measurably increases. Stratification analysis poses a ready and entirely plausible explanation for this phenomenon. Since the political expenditures of the rich are typically paltry and their store of resources great, engaging in political activity does not place an especially heavy drain upon their supply of resources. Because costs are low, activity is high. The deference their status confers and their wealth commands also permits them to maneuver decorously and adroitly behind the scenes whenever a gaudy display of power would be thought vulgar. In short, the rich suffer no depreciation in prestige and rectitude for their participation in interelection "politics," an activity many Americans seem to find wicked and odious when practiced openly.

The political resources of the poor are, *ex hypothesi*, meager; they have neither the wealth nor the status to convert at low discount into political power. Empty pockets cannot purchase the favor of mercenary politicians, and the depressed status of the lower socio-economic strata cannot be used to wedge open official doors and unlock governmental cash boxes. They cannot even stimulate an alliance with the chronically energetic middle classes, for they are far too busy currying favor with their social betters to make trustworthy partners. On even the most optimistic estimate, the costs of utilizing their resources to secure a favorable political response are so gross as to make political action inherently irrational. Thus is the observable political apathy of the poor and underprivileged explained.

What of political conflict? What cleavages and alignments will develop as opposing forces take sides? Since people strive incessantly to add to their supplies of scarce resources, elite members will choose any alternative (including governmental inaction) that promises to produce some concrete benefit greater in value than the resources that must be sacrificed to achieve it.

> [In Regional City] the leaders are interested in maintaining their own positions which give them such things as wealth, power, and prestige. They are fearful that any swaying of the balance of power may destroy the positions they now hold. . . . (Hunter, 1953, p. 233.)

In the pathetic calculus that the Lynds and Hunter applied to political decisions in order to weigh their benefits and estimate their costs, the total volume of community resources is so scanty that the winners, intentionally or not, are unable to sustain or improve their position without inflicting severe hardships upon the losers. In political conflict, evidently, the winner's prize must simultaneously be a measure of the loser's sacrifice; one can satisfy his aspirations for the goods and services allocated through public governments only by denying the goals of others. On this analysis, politics emerges as a zero-sum game par excellence; when someone wins, someone else must lose. For someone to add to his stock of scarce resources, another's must shrink to a corresponding degree. Since the oligarchical few with access to the crucial resources of wealth and status must always win, it follows that the many tragically subsidize their own defeat. There is no way to elude this bleak conclusion.

A corollary of this argument is that everybody has some appreciable stake riding on the outcome of every political decision. Empirically, it is true, losers sometimes act as if they did not. On some occasions, the entire community seems united. On others, the losers seem quite benumbed to the fact that they are being plundered by an avaricious oligarchy. The Lynds, in particular, used two ingenious devices to explain away apparent inconsistencies between hypothesis and recorded data. If the lower social strata seem to hold elite preferences, or if they appear indifferent to controversies where they stand to lose, it is for one of two reasons. Either they so dread the victor's retribution that they are afraid to express their "real" preferences, or they have been so thoroughly hectored by shrill elite propaganda that they disavow their "objective" preferences and foolishly support alternatives framed to benefit elite groups at their expense. The first explanation is, of course, a logical extension of the argument previously advanced to account for lower-class apathy. The second can be valid if and only if the elite faction generates the alternatives to which the nonelite later comply in a sort of socially conditioned reflex, a point we shall question in the concluding section.

Elite preferences must be unified; the theory *logically* requires it. We cannot have oligarchical rule without assuming a basic community of interest among the rulers. For, if elite members are divided in their political preferences, then decision outcomes would necessarily favor one faction at the expense of the other. If this were so, and people with prestige and money sometimes lost, then wealth and status would no longer be the sole resources leading to domination over the decisions of public governments. The primary postulate of stratification theory would be fallacious, and this, obviously, would not do.

Over-all, the political theory implicit in the *Middletown* series and in *Community Power Structure* boasts one great and sweeping virtue: complete simplicity. It is, in fact, very nearly a comprehensive theory of politics, a simple formula that can be invoked to dissolve the complex riddle of actual events. To know everything about the politics of the local community, all that is really needed is a statistical table describing the distribution of money and allocation of esteem. From this all else confidently follows. Variations can be inferred in the style and frequency of political participation, the alignments political conflict will produce, and a map charting the distribution of political power—in short, answers to most of the enduring problems of political theory. Does sociological theory provide a good approximation for describing the political system of Arcadia? It is to this concluding question we now turn.

Cynics might claim that the formal constitutional structure of Arcadia government has been ingeniously contrived to simplify control by the well-to-do. Its rules severely limit the opportunities lower-class people have to gain seats on the Council; they also restrain them from turning their votes into power over specific governmental decisions. Much has been written extolling the virtues of competitive political parties as the ultimate guarantors of political equality; most of it is sheer romance. Although it is true that the votes of beggar and millionaire are weighted equally in a perfectly competitive struggle for public office, electoral arithmetic alone does not produce an egalitarian distribution of power on each specific interelection choice made by public officials. Who claims this claims far too much. On the other hand, so long as small numbers of candidates have to vie with each other for the greater part of the public vote, there is always the possibility for various groups to barter their votes as prepayment for the favors contestants for elective office promise to bestow. In this way, competitive elections help insure the responsiveness of politicians to groups that make their policy preferences known as they march off to the ballot box.

In nonpartisan Arcadia, however, competition for elected office is sharply attenuated, for it does not penetrate deeply into low-income precincts. The explanation is simple. Because the lower-class white and Negro precincts ordinarily contribute only about 20 per cent of the actual vote, candidates can afford to offer their wares in markets attended primarily by middle- and upper-class people: the League of Women Voters, the Rotarians, the Lions' Club, the Merchants' League, the Arcadia Chamber of Commerce. It is true that the neighborhood and Negro candidates who are not flustered by status differences amiably and gravely discuss "community issues" at the open meetings of the League of Women Voters. But this is the only social link they can forge with political activists. They have no way to crack the luncheon clubs, the business meetings of the Merchants' League or the Chamber of Commerce, and, of course, the inevitable cocktail party. Since the candidate from the affluent southwest precincts knows he can ride into office on the votes polled in his part of the city, no profit is to be gained by hiring and sustaining a corps of functionaries to solicit votes in low-income wards. Successful candidates do not need to be informed of the preferences of low-income wards because they can gain Council seats without their support.

Constitutional rules and procedures have been eloquently defended on many grounds, but perhaps none commands such wide and fervent assent as the argument that they hold potential tyrannies firmly at bay. Yet, in Arcadia, the constitutional formulas governing the acquisition and retention of public office appear to operate in favor of the status elite. In fact, it is tempting to invert the usual justifications for constitutional restraints and argue that nothing is so likely to insure oligarchical rule as the procedures which gull the people into believing their representatives govern responsibly. Spelled out, the argument might run something like this. Representatives of the ruling oligarchy are solemnly chosen according to "democratic" procedures, and this helps legitimate their rule. But the constitutional procedures themselves are trumped up; they are lotteries cunningly and elaborately rigged to perpetuate the rule of the status elite by guaranteeing wealthy notables or their deputies indefinite title to public office. The representatives so chosen, of course, claim the legitimacy of popular majorities earned by competing for the votes of an inclusive and free electorate. While in office, they cynically pretend to promote the interests of the people even though they are actually engaged in satisfying their own lust for political power. No matter how offensive their rule, they are virtually irreplaceable. If they are too incautious, they can bow out gracefully and designate their own successors. Because the system has a democratic façade and is swaddled in venerated procedures and ceremonials, the masses are fooled into thinking their rulers govern responsibly. Nothing could be further from the truth.

The Resources of Political Power: Variety and Efficacy

As we have seen, the linchpin of the stratification theory of politics is the plausible axiom that superior socio-economic status is the sole resource that can be translated into effective power over governmental decisions. By dissecting the three issues we have previously chronicled from agitation to resolution, we can determine whether the explanatory hypotheses correspond to politics in Arcadia.

VOTES. In Arcadia, as in most other American communities, one vote is possessed by every adult who is not a felon or a lunatic. Thus the right to cast a ballot is not correlated with socio-economic status. Each adult may use his vote; the only scarce resources the act consumes are the few minutes it takes to mark a ballot or trip a lever on a voting machine. When a citizen votes directly on acts of legislation, his expression of preference directly decides the outcome. In majority elections, the tabulated preference of each citizen is given equal weight in the act of choosing alternatives. If the cardinal postulate of stratification theory is correct, no alternative preferred by members of the social mobility should be rejected by popular vote. Yet on three separate occasions in Arcadia, the citizenry turned down options preferred by the elite faction. In fact, only once did a municipal building bond issue pass even in the upper-class precincts, and then only by the most slender of all possible majorities. (See 1954 election, Table 6-1.)

The massed status and wealth of Arcadia's putative "ruling elite" could not be directly transformed into influence over the voting behavior of Arcadia's citizens. This much is clear from the voting statistics; the task is to explain why. Money can purchase many things: services, commodities, even affection of a sort. But buying and selling votes is both prohibited by law and proscribed by widely shared normative codes. Suppose this were not so. Suppose further the dubious proposition that the construction of a new municipal building was a matter of such pressing concern to elite members that they were prepared to bribe the very large number of middle- and lower-class people who did not vote at all. Successful bribery would have achieved their ends, for casual inspection of Tables 6-1 and 6-2 will show that the abstainers in each bond election could have passed the bond issues if they had voted for them. Because each voter has only a tiny impact on the result of any election, the true reservation price for his vote is low. It is even less for the person who is so indifferent between the alternatives scheduled for public referendum that he decides to abstain. All he requests is enough money to overcome his reluctance to go to the polls. Given such a distribution of preferences and money, the rich could bribe the indifferent to pass measures the status elite prefers. But the anonymity and secrecy of the ballot prohibits the bribe taker from certifying that he has kept his end of the bargain; it also deters the bribe giver from offering money since he cannot be certain he will receive a favorable vote in return. A thoroughly unscrupulous bribe taker might even welsh on his promise and vote for the other side after having pocketed the inducement. True, these illustrations are drawn from a never-never land of the imagination. In the real world, however, the same considerations keep any member of the status elite from intimidating voters by threatening the loss of their incomes and livelihoods. It is, therefore, not entirely clear why Hunter concluded that members of the power elite are able to "enforce their decisions by persuasion, intimidation, coercion, and, if necessary, force" (Hunter, 1953).

Unable to convert their preferred position in the distribution of income into influence over votes, the businessmen of Arcadia had to exploit their status as "community leaders," the glamorous local celebrities of a business civilization. They did invest in newspaper space and radio time, and, on their own testimony, many members of the three successive Booster's Clubs tried to sway their friends and business associates into supporting the bond issues. But the social contacts of businessmen were confined largely to other businessmen and their mates. The mercantile nobility did try to extend and diversify their orbits of effective social communication by having their wives "talk it up" before the audiences gathered at bridge and country club. The size of the constituency so assembled, however, was inherently limited to a very small fraction of Arcadia's adult population. There is a double irony here. The very exclusiveness that gave the active businessmen their elevated status also sharply restricted the domain of their effective interpersonal influence. And, in cleansing Arcadia of an unsavory political machine, the businessmen guaranteed that the City Council would be dominated by men drawn from their ranks; but at the same time they liquidated the one organization that could mediate between elite decision makers and the reserve army of the politically apathetic.

KNOWLEDGE, TIME, AND MOTIVATION. Very few governmental decisions, however, are made by referendum election. In the vast majority of cases, representatives elected by the voters (who are themselves only a minor fraction of the adult population) enact or reject different items of legislation. If the "power elite" can be overcome by greater numbers in public referendum, neither logically nor empirically does it follow that the elite group will fail to rule on the many decisions not subject to electoral choice.

Stratification theory asserts that administrators and politicians are simply the pliant agents of the "power elite." They are stripped of any real autonomy and independence; the wielders of social and economic power are the Unmoved Movers in the political realm. They compel without being compelled and control without being controlled; what happens in local politics is all a matter of their free choice.

As plausible and psychologically compelling as this theory seems to be, it founders unhappily on the facts of Arcadia politics. In every case, innovation took place as the instigation of one or another of Arcadia's administrative politicians. It was not any executive committee of the socio-economic elect who first spotted the "need" for a new municipal building; it was Everett Beardsley, the city manager. Although the Arcadia Housing Authority was composed of civic notables, it was Everett Rosemond, the city planner and son of a county employee, who prompted the selection of Harley Court. And, as the case study clearly shows, the city planner seized the initiative on urban renewal and formulated the strategy to guide it past a number of possible veto groups. Elite members did not prod him; he prodded them.

In these cases, the politician did more than register externally imposed pressures for innovation. Rosemond not only publicized urban renewal and accumulated the support of various prestigious organizations; in so doing, he sheared his opposition of any sort of respectable ideological camouflage. Urban renewal could not be attacked as "visionary" and "socialistic" without identifying the prestigious Chamber of Commerce as the vanguard of the radical left. Divine license for uncompromised free enterprise could not be claimed without tacitly excommunicating the Fellowship of Southern Churches and the pastor of the most fashionable church in town. The organizations paraded in support of urban renewal, it must be recalled, did not just show up one fine day before the Council to be counted. Their participation was not spontaneous; it was painstakingly induced by the city planner and Mayor Lowndes, his chief ally on the Council. So far from laying down policy dictates to be implemented by subordinate politicians, the "power elite" in Arcadia seems rather to have cloaked the choices of administrative politicians with the legitimacy of social respectability, certainly an unexpected inversion of sociological theory.

A small number of cases is obviously not enough to validate a network of explanatory hypotheses, but even a very few instances can suggest a sketch that may be tested in other settings. The critical resources involved in both Harley Court and Dewy Bottom were time, knowledge, and the motivation to expend both. Rosemond had generous supplies of all three, at least by comparison with the community notables whose support he mobilized to accomplish his purposes. Public housing and urban renewal placed heavy drains on his time and energy, and both issues required specialized knowledge that is not necessarily linked with income and social status. Appraising alternative locations for siting public-housing and urban-renewal projects demands intimate knowledge of many decisional variables: availability of service roads, utility lines, and drainage facilities; capacity and convenience of schools and playgrounds; where and how to obtain complementary federal resources; prices for real estate, and all the rest. Laymen, even very prestigious laymen, are notoriously inclined to infer the ability of experts from the most superficial clues: professional status, college degrees, reputation, and fees charged. Rosemond's choices, it will be remembered, were accepted without modification by the civic notables who manned the Urban Redevelopment Commission, the Arcadia Housing Authority, and the City Planning Commission. To understand the grounds on which his recommendations were based, the commissioners would have needed at least the equivalent of graduate training in city planning and a thorough immersion in city, state, and federal regulations circumscribing the fiscal and physical planning of housing and urban-renewal projects. This technical and contextual knowledge the commissioners conspicuously lacked, so they deferred to Rosemond's choice of alternatives.

There is, of course, a plausible objection to this interpretation. In rebuttal, it might be claimed that Rosemond fell victim to the control of anticipated reactions: that he did not dare propose any alternative he thought the commissioners might reject. On this hypothesis, his success with the commissioners would not be a reflection of the influence he wielded as a recognized expert; rather, it would simply be an index of his ability to estimate what they would accept without boggling. There is, it must be admitted, no way to disprove this contention directly, for it does fit the reported facts and thus possesses the semblance of credibility. On the other hand, Rosemond did persuade the City Planning Commission to press for a new municipal building south of Lee Avenue just one year after his predecessor had convinced the commissioners that such a choice would be foolish *in terms of their own declared values.* This points to the deference laymen pay the advice of experts, even when the evidence given by two successive experts manages to lead to contradictory conclusions. It also lends a particle of confirmation to the proposition that Rosemond used his expertise to influence the commissioners.

As the narratives suggest, there was more to both urban renewal and public housing than persuading commissioners which options to choose. In order to accomplish his policy objectives, Rosemond had to publicize and dramatize urban renewal through his articles in the *Herald* and a series of appearances before a number of critical elite publics.

When Harley Court seemed stillborn as a result of the Negro revolt, Rosemond's sly strategems and indirect threats prevented the Arcadia Housing Authority from stampeding to an alternative he regarded less desirable. It is sometimes forgotten that higgling and chaffering are costly: they are greedy in the demands they make on an individual's time. Alone among all those who eventually supported urban renewal and Harley Court, Rosemond had the time (and was paid to devote it) to further these programs. Not only this; he also possessed the critical knowledge of the appeals required to annex the legitimating sanctions wielded by the groups that joined status and social deference. Rosemond was hardly innocent of the huckster's art: he varied his sales pitch to achieve the maximum response from each audience he confronted. To the business organization he advertised the sheer economic rationality of urban renewal; to the architects the esthetic gains to be harvested from rescuing a flagging area from imminent decay; and to the League of Women Voters the delectable pleasures of waging genteel politics in behalf of the oppressed. The result, as we have seen, was an irresistible coalition. No massive "power elite" sprang into existence of its own volition and class interest; in each case Rosemond and Lowndes consciously riveted together and managed a coalition of the praiseworthy.

Only in a peculiarly Hobbesian universe do people seek political power to the neglect of all other rewards provided by social organization. Businessmen gain the bulk of their material and psychological satisfactions, not unexpectedly, from acting like businessmen. To engage at all intensively in politics, they have to be prepared to shift time, always a precious resource, away from their business concerns and social activities and invest it in an alien and remote world of intrigues, controversies, and crises that they do not quite understand. And, as Whyte (1956) has shown, no businessman wants to get hauled into any dispute if it will reflect adversely on his organization, as it almost always does. He can acquire the credentials of "good citizenship" and "public leadership" merely by making sonorous pronouncements endorsing largely uncontested goals already formulated for him by politicians eager to trade on his esteem and social position.

For Rosemond and, to a lesser extent, Eric Lowndes, political activity was seen in somewhat different perspective. The city planner was a professional and the sources of professional satisfaction are varied: his own self-image, the admiration of his colleagues and teachers, his professional standing as a "doer" rather than as a "talker," and the like. All these rewards are mediated by successfully completing such concrete projects as Harley Court and Dewy Bottom. Thus he had high incentive to use his available resources to influence others in support of his preferred decision outcomes. His opportunity costs were low since his time was already paid for by public funds. Though a businessman, Lowndes was concerned with a much broader market than Arcadia alone and thus had less to lose if by some unexpected contingency he became embroiled in a hot controversy. As mayor, he occupied a political role and could claim the support of a legitimacy earned through his popular election. Like Rosemond, he was a vigorous man, ready to exploit personal resources to achieve concrete and measurable goals. His political position and prerogative gave Rosemond a formidable ally to handle negotiations with the councilmen, and his access to the business community helped sustain the support and loyalty of Arcadia's businessmen.

One cautionary note: This is not to say that all city planners will become energetic innovators, nor that all businessmen will stoutly forward change. Far from it; many are undeniably stodgy, perceive no payoff in change, and are concerned largely with the preservation of routine service functions. On the other hand, the experience in Arcadia seems to indicate that urban political structures can be remarkably plastic. Its businessmen, commonly regarded as stubborn brakes on political change, were not frozen into perpetual reaction by a Bourbon political and economic ideology. They could be enlisted by skilled political leadership to support legitimate goals and programs that would have terrified their ancestors three decades ago. This sort of political system provides a congenial matrix for the innovator and a hospitable environment for the builders and managers of coalitions.

CLASS INTEREST: AUTONOMOUS OR OTHER-DIRECTED? One cardinal postulate of stratification theory is that preferences on specific policy choices are logically inferable from an individual's position in the social structure. There are many variations of this central notion. Hunter and the Lynds, it will be remembered, held that top business leaders are jealous of their economic and social dominance and tenaciously resist any policy choice that might jeopardize their preferred position. In another and more grandiose version, business leaders are supposed to cleave to an ideology, a set of internally consistent "ideas," which they hold in common. The creed upholds the inviolability of "private enterprise" and nostalgically hankers after an aristocratic society which was already decaying when many contemporary businessmen were born. It is this treacly ideology that is supposed to lead to a set of conclusions telling businessmen how to line up on a particular issue. In either case, a network of shared values is supposed to suture business leaders together and heal all transient rifts when business interests are pinched by adversity or are worried by demagogic politicians.

In testing the hypothesis in Arcadia, let us place to one side the obvious point that businessmen rallied to lend their prestige and status to urban renewal and public housing, alternatives utterly repugnant to the creed as it is usually formulated. Evidently these choices were not tested for logical consistency with the tenets of "free enterprise" dogma before its putative adherents decided to throw their lot in with the radicals. Let us ignore, too, the obvious fact that businessmen lined up on different sides of each issue mentioned in this study. This is interesting enough, but it has been commented on by other authors. Rather, the most interesting feature of status politics in Arcadia was that business leaders could not agree on *any specific alternative* until the politicians told them what they could get, and at what cost. Every businessman the *Clarion* polled in 1954 thought a new municipal building would be a fine idea, but there was no consensus on where to build it. Indeed, the Chamber of Commerce and the Merchants' League pleaded with the politicians to present them with a single tangible alternative they could support. No businessman expressed himself in favor of urban renewal and Harley Court until politicians showed them how these programs made sense in terms of their own personal appetites for "civic leadership," increased status, taking part in great events, and serving some abstract "general good." In the division of political labor that prevailed in Arcadia, politicians were evidently expected to mill down ideas and transform them into concrete proposals which could be offered for sale to various elite publics.

POLITICS: A ZERO-SUM GAME? What lends the stratification theory of politics its distinctive anguish is the pathetic assumption that politics is a tense and pervasive zero-sum game. For A to win, B must lose. Yet, in Arcadia, politics seems to be entirely marginal in the life of its citizens.[8] Fully three-quarters of the registered adult population shunned the most simple and least costly of all political acts, that of casting a ballot; and the number of people who participated directly in all three issues could be reckoned in the hundreds. It is difficult to conclude with the Lynds and Hunter that apathy and inactivity are the stark fruits of terror and intimidation. Only a very ingenious sophist could maintain that the many citizens in all demographic strata who failed to vote in the bond elections were somehow disturbed and cheated by the eventual outcome. And no one has any right to assume that the upper-class opponents of the bond issue lost or gained any more than the lower-class and Negro opponents.

In examining the other two issues, the picture becomes murkier still. Some obviously were injured when the city decided to go ahead with public housing: a number of realtors suffered external costs; forty Negro homeowners lost future rents; Councilmen Hulme, Strowd, and Alton saw another golden citadel of free enterprise crumble in the dust, as did a registered nurse and an office-machine salesman. Those who gained were the chief protagonists: Rosemond, the members of the housing authority, and their cohorts on the Council; the Negroes who eventually secured subsidized housing; and, doubtless, a small number of intense Liberal spectators. Substitute a few names on this roster and the same story can be told for urban renewal.

In the light of these data, it is really difficult to take the Lynds-Hunter explanation of political apathy seriously. It could hardly be claimed that the lower classes were fooled as to their "objective interests" by elite propaganda in view of the broad upper-class support for Harley Court and Dewy Bottom. This would logically imply that the status elite was not swayed by its own class propaganda—certainly a most ingenious paradox. It could also imply that public housing is somehow inimical to the interests of the poor, a conclusion no less paradoxical by usual standards.

Once, it is true, executives and owners ruled the company towns as though they were feudal fiefdoms. They made their political dominion effective through their economic control over credit and prices charged at the company store, a control facilitated by Pinkertons and open ballots. But, with a scrupulously secret ballot, impersonal personnel practices, labor unions, and, of course, the support exhibited by owners and managers for liberal legislation, this pattern of control now seems extinct (Dahl, 1959). Indeed, except for the *opéra bouffe* campaign of the Negro Home Owners' League, no evidence of rule by terror could be uncovered in Arcadia.

Conclusion

Perhaps the best way to conclude is with a touch of irony: the events reported in Arcadia represent a straightforward inversion of the stratification theory of politics. In the stratification theory, businessmen originate specific decisions to further their class interests and rely on the mercenary support of obsequious politicians. In Arcadia, politicians innovated policy choices and had their acceptability certified by the visible support of top businessmen.

That this compressed explanation "fits" the small clutch of reported cases is no decisive evidence. The hypotheses are admittedly coarse; they require refinement and definite statement; and demand much additional testing. And Arcadia might just be a sport from a normal pattern. In any case, any network of hypotheses will fit *some* set of facts. What marks a sensible person off from zanies and outright lunatics is the latters' inability to test cherished hypotheses against new, and possibly inhospitable, data.

FOOTNOTES

1. In a 1947 charter referendum, Arcadia's commissioners were supplanted by a nonpartisan City Council elected at large and a city manager. Since the installation of the new governmental structure there have been 8 biennial elections for the Council. Of the 24 winning candidates (some have succeeded themselves), 20 have lived in the wealthy precincts tucked in the southwest corner of the city; 3 in the adjoining college colony; and 1 in a newly annexed middle-class precinct. Negro and lower-class candidates have run in all elections. They generally pile up a handsome vote in their own precincts but poll poorly everywhere else.

   The ousted commissioners had drawn the bulk of their electoral support from Negro and lower-class wards in return for directing the flow of municipal services, including jobs, to the faithful precincts. By so doing, they had brought down upon themselves the displeasure of indignant wealthy civic reformers. The organization that finally unhorsed the commissioners was spearheaded by the Junior Chamber of Commerce, the League of Women Voters, and the Women's Club, all associations of predominantly upper-class clientele and leadership. Most of the votes cast for adoption of the new system of government were concentrated in the wealthier precincts. The movement, in effect, was an upper-class revolution.
2. It is not known whether the change was due to different cost estimates, a covert decision to choose one of the less expensive options, or possibly because he calculated that the chances of passage were inversely related to the size of the issue.
3. The Corporation Council had ruled that outstanding bonds on the Sports Arena had to be redeemed before any new building could take place.
4. This may seem an extraordinarily audacious arrangement for a bureaucratic hierarchy. Saunders and Rosemond had agreed that the city planner's primary responsibility was to the City Planning Commission in the case of dispute. Since Rosemond seems to have controlled the choices the Planning Commission made, these rules of combat gave him a good deal of organizational autonomy.

5. Bearden's second of this motion may not have been quite so irrational as it seems. He knew that the Bragg Street location could not possibly get a majority, and Ferrabee had announced he was prepared to wait two or three years to "do the right thing." The Bragg Street site was bound to fail, and if he had proposed the Mosby Avenue location immediately thereafter, the results might have been the same. This adroit stratagem would have left the field open for the selection of the Sports Arena, since all but two would have voted for it in preference to Hulme's plan. Whatever his intention, the ingenious ruse collapsed; his adversaries exploited parliamentary procedure to postpone making a decision on any site. The only bargain made was to bargain more.
6. We do not know who discovered this gimmick. Some have credited Avery Holmes with the innovation; others, the corporation counsel.
7. The developments of the week following would indicate that Robinson was bluffing. He knew he had three stalwart advocates on the Council. Bearden, Lowndes, and Mayor Ferrabee assured him they would not defect. He had already written Strowd off, and Alton and Hulme were intransigent. Bostwick had wavered, to be sure; but both Rosemond and he gambled he would choose an objectionable site rather than scuttle public housing. Robinson tried to convince Bostwick, so to speak, that all other bridges had already been burned in order to prevent his seeking another.
8. Let the reader beware that we are marching far out in front of our data in this section. To clinch the points we make here (or perhaps modify them), we would need a sociological survey of Arcadia describing the distribution of information and attitudes as to all the issues reported here.

REFERENCES

Dahl, Robert A. (1959), "Business and Politics: A Critical Appraisal of Political Science," *The American Political Science Review,* **LII:1,** 1–34.

Herson, Lawrence J. R. (1957), "The Lost World of Municipal Government," *The American Political Science Review,* **LI:**2, 330–345.

Hunter, Floyd (1953), *Community Power Structure.* Chapel Hill, N. C.: University of North Carolina Press.

Lasswell, Harold D., and Abraham Kaplan (1950), *Power and Society.* New Haven, Conn.: Yale University Press.

Lynd, Robert S., and Helen M. (1929), *Middletown.* New York: Harcourt, Brace

Lynd, Robert S., and Helen M. (1937), *Middletown in Transition.* New York: Harcourt, Brace.

Simon, Herbert A. (1953), "Notes on the Observation and Measurement of Political Power," *Journal of Politics,* **XV**:4, 500–516.

Whyte, William H. (1956), *The Organization Man.* New York: Simon and Schuster.

Wood, Robert C. (1959), *Suburbia: Its People and Its Problems.* Boston: Houghton Mifflin.

Chapter 7

Roles of the Planner in Urban Development

*by Robert T. Daland and John A. Parker **

THIS CHAPTER attempts to explore the assumption that the urban planner is located near the center of an important communication network which functions to influence major decisions affecting urban development. In this sense planning may be viewed as a social control process, or as a major factor in the development and administration of specific controls over development.

It is recognized that many roles are played in the governmental scene which have a direct bearing on urban development, and that other roles in the political arena have indirect effects on urban growth. In this study the particular roles of the planner are isolated within this milieu, and their relationship to other roles are described. These roles are viewed not only as patterns of behavior and expectations, but also in terms of the factors which create them, both personal and environmental. They are also viewed in terms of actual developmental out-

* The authors gratefully acknowledge the considerable contributions of Frederic N. Cleaveland, co-director of this study from 1955 to 1957 and continuing as consultant, and Peter H. Nash, co-director from 1957 to 1959. Important contributions have been made by ten graduate students in planning who have undertaken master's theses within the framework of the study. The authors are particularly indebted to former research assistants Robert M. Griffin, Jr., and Lucien C. Faust, whose contributions have been of invaluable assistance to all participants in the study.

comes. The correlates of particular roles and role behaviors are indicated as far as possible.

Conceptual Approach of the Study

Urbanization is not the result of cosmic forces of organic growth following immutable laws of nature which can be observed but not influenced by human endeavor. Within limits man can control his environment. If the control of urban development is the result of a system carefully designed to improve the rationality of decisions in terms of the major goals of the entire community, we can call this social control system "planning." We are a long way from the time when we can say that we have an ideal, or even an adequate system of social control through planning. But the need for problem solving where urbanization occurs has produced increasingly successful efforts toward this end.

In order to improve systems of urban planning still further, it is paramount to learn precisely what are the functions or roles that "planners" are now performing within the complex of roles which guide and control the location and character of private and public urban development. Where governmental planning departments have been established, they operate near the center of a communications system consisting of the governmental organization which is designed to create and effectuate public policies. Because of the crucial importance of governmental policy in every aspect of urban life, nongovernmental decision makers form a part of this communication network. We are therefore concerned in this study with the roles of planners both in the governmental system of decision making and in the wider realm of decisions about private investment.

Ideally, to evaluate the impact and worth of planning processes on urban growth we should have a complete description of the distribution of influence within each community, in both governmental and private agencies, so as to assess the particular influence exerted by the planners. We would need detailed information on all important developmental decisions: who participated, to what degrees, and the place of planners in each decision process. Such completeness cannot be achieved. We can, however, observe the major differences found within the process of developmental decision making among various urban communities and compare these with the roles which planners of these communities are actually found to be playing.

These inquiries can be used as the basis for analysis of the rationality and potential of "planning." Having assessed these factors, conclusions can be drawn concerning the kinds of educational programs needed to supply professional personnel qualified to assist decision makers concerned with achieving orderly growth patterns in the Piedmont Crescent. A whole new dimension will be added to the inquiry by carrying out similar studies in areas outside the Piedmont for comparative purposes. While a few such comparisons can be made here, it is hoped that the present study will provide the analytical techniques through which the broader problem of planning in an urban society can be explored.

Planning, Planners, Roles, and the Planning Process

To understand the key concepts used in this chapter and our model of roles with which planning practice in the Piedmont Crescent will be compared, two areas of planning "theory" may be distinguished. One concerns the effort to explain how planning is done in reality. It is closely related to the sociology of decision making, role analysis, and to theories of political action. This study is most concerned with this relatively untilled area. The other area has centered around attempts to build a model of rational planning against which to measure planning activity. Considerably more progress has been made in this direction. Each area of emphasis must be developed, since progress in each is in part dependent on the development of the other. Taken up first is our conception of what rational planning is, and then our model of the nature of the planning process is presented. We develop a vehicle for describing the roles of the planner by observing the variations from this model.

A convenient concept of rational decision making applied to planning is found in Meyerson and Banfield as adapted from the literature of administration and sociology (see Simon, 1947, p. 67; Parsons, 1959, p. 58; Meyerson and Banfield, 1955, pp. 314–322). The decision maker considers all the alternative courses of action which lead to the ends he seeks to attain within the limits of the possible, he evaluates the consequences of each course of action, and selects the course of action which will maximize the ends valued most. In short, he applies a scientific method to the solution of problems. It is important to note that this model of rational action depends on the existence of some agreement on the most valued ends. In a planning arena such as the community which operates on the basis of some form of democratic, or at least pluralistic, practice, there may be no consensus as to ends most sought. Therefore, planning cannot be purely rational. That is, the nonrational forms of decision making for the community cannot be replaced entirely by the planning mode of decision making. To put it differently, there are three modes of decision making and thus three possible mechanisms of decision in city planning: the market place, politics, and rational planning. Since there may be a considerable conflict of ends in the community, rational planning can operate only as an adjunct to the market place and politics, within the area in which consensus as to ends has been, or can be, achieved. The public planner may find that opportunities for improvement in his community are limited to therapy, and that long-range community-wide planning is not acceptable. While we know that such situations exist, we are not prepared to say to what extent they exist, or to what extent public planners may have resigned themselves to therapy. We do know of instances where the community has been willing to consider and take favorable action upon planning proposals that would be ignored in other communities as being "impractical" or "utopian." But at this point we need not explore the interesting question of the relation between utopian and therapeutic planning.

What we can do is explore the factors that may require the planner to compromise the utopian approach by analysis of all his roles. One of these is his professional role in which he pursues the rational model of planning as far as possible. The others, however, necessitate compromise with this model.

Planning, then, is the closest approach that the planner can make to a rational process of decision making, departing from the purely rational approach whenever progress toward community goals demands nonrational decisions and practices. Planning includes the analysis of the nonrational factors in the planning environment so that the maximum scope of rational planning can be determined.

The "planner," as used here, is the professionally trained expert employed to provide the intellectual leadership toward rational planning. He is recognized as a professional through his education, experience, and his membership in the American Institute of Planners. This terminology excludes many who do "planning," such as elected officials, planning board members, department heads, budget officers, or civic leaders. He may be employed by an official planning agency, a private organization, or act as a consultant.

Perhaps the key concept around which this analysis centers is that of "role," borrowed from the literature of social psychology. This literature is rich, and provides a multiplicity of role concepts. Our concept of role is synthesized from this body of material, and its elements will be familiar to all students of role. (An excellent analysis of the role concept is to be found in Gross, Mason, and McEachern, 1958.) In our approach to describing the function of the urban planner within the political system of his community, we assume that there are many roles played by actors in the political arena, and that among these are the particular combinations of roles played by the planner. Since our object is the description of function in a system whose elements are by no means completely catalogued, the role concept appears to be a useful tool.

No single simple method of measuring role has been developed. However, different dimensions of role may be measured through three distinct approaches. One component of role derives from cultural norms of the particular social situation existing in the political arena. An effort may be made to measure this component through investigating the expectations and perceptions reported by persons who interact with the planner. While this relatively small group of individuals may not represent the true voice of "society"—which some authorities claim prescribes role—it does provide an operational definition of the group most able to perceive and expound the role of the planner.

A second component of role stems from the personality of the role player himself. Personal differences account in large part for differences in the behavior of different persons holding the same role in a particular social situation. In order to study this dimension of role we have sought the perceptions and expectations of the role player himself.

The third dimension of role may be observed from the point of view of the behavior of the planner as he plays his role. His behavior reflects, in part, the perceptions of himself and others concerning his role, but it has other sources as well. It is the result of accident, unanticipated consequences, health factors, or changes in the political or economic character of the community, as well as of the rational images in the minds of the persons concerned. This behavior, which some refer to as "role playing," "role enactment," or "the dynamic aspect of role," may be empirically observed. In the final analysis, even this source of information is perceptual, just as were the first two sources. But in this case the perception is that of the trained observer in social science, and so may be relied on with as much confidence as the perceptions of the actors in the arena themselves can be relied on.

Students of role tend to think of individuals as holding a specific "status" or "position" in a social system, which is actually a combination of "roles," each associated with certain behavioral norms. The individual planner's position involves such roles as father, husband, church warden, and voter, in addition to his occupational role as planner. Since we are investigating only the planner's role *as a planner* in a governmental system, we may think of his position or status as that of "planner," and then proceed to describe several behavior patterns and associated norms and expectations as the component "roles" of the position of planner. For example, we may think of the distinctive activities of planners associated with their functions as makers of plans, promoters of plans, protectors of the planning organization and staff, and political innovators of policy.

In using these role concepts, we describe the patterns of role combinations found among planners of the Piedmont Crescent, and then wherever possible we investigate the correlates of particular role patterns. Specifically, we are concerned with the impact of planning on governmental decisions, and through these decisions, on the development of the community. Ideally and ultimately we would hope to correlate the roles of planners with other administrative and political roles in the urban community in order to reproduce the entire fabric of functions (combinations of roles) which interact to produce governmental decisions relating to urban development.

The planning process is visualized as activity conducted with the planner as a principal participant, much of it involving interaction with others in the planning arena. In order to have a tool for describing and comparing this process in different communities, a model of role is constructed with which each planning effort can be compared. We begin by postulating that the planner plays four basic roles under the usual circumstances. In particular cases it may be that the major burden of one or more of these roles may be performed for the planner by someone else, but even in such a case, the liaison with the other actor constitutes the vestige of role performance. These four include the planner as institutional leader of his organization, professional planner, instigator of political innovations, and promoter of citizen education in planning. Each of these basic roles may be played differently by individual performers. The professional role, for instance, may emphasize the design approach, or a preoccupation with social and economic analysis.

These functions, or roles, of planners are not only categories of activity which may be investigated, but they also relate to specific sets of relationships planners maintain with others in the political system. For this reason they are not merely arbitrary classifications of activity, but constellations of behavior patterns with definite functions in distinct social subsystems. Specifically, the reference group of the planner in his *institutional role* consists of the administrative organization of which the planning agency is a part. The reference group of the planner in his *professional role* is the planning profession, and specifically the American Institute of Planners and other organizations. The reference group of the planner in his *political innovation role* is the community leadership structure. His reference group with respect to his *educational role* is the urban community at large which he is obligated to "plan." His behaviors toward these groups vary, and occasionally conflict. The conception indicated here, while independently developed, bears considerable similarity to the "role sector" analysis discussed by Gross, Mason, and McEachern (1958), and is consistent with it. That study has helped clarify our model.

As an institutional leader, the planner must fulfill the maintenance needs of the planning agency. A firm and adequate base of operations from which the other roles may be played is essential. The maintenance needs include keeping a competent staff on the job, giving it proper training, seeing to its morale, and directing it in performing the workload of the agency. More important, however, they include defending the status of the agency and structuring its relationships within the community both inside and outside the formal governmental machinery. Students of administrative leadership have termed the latter activity "institutional leadership." (The best discussion of institutional leadership is contained in Selznick, 1957.) Very briefly, the planner must be accepted as a significant part of the governmental machine if the goals of planning are to be achieved. He must have channels of communication for obtaining information relevant to planning. He must develop the confidence necessary to obtain a budget adequate for planning. He must attend to the sufficiency of the legal basis for planning and the controls crucial to planning. He must locate his allies and his enemies, and he must understand the forces that shape policies in his community.

Concurrent with securing his institutional base, the planner is concerned with the professional aspects of planning. These comprise the technical activity ultimately producing "plans": research, analysis, and design. In playing this role the planner is increasingly influenced by the model of rational action indicated above. However, he is also motivated by planning "practice" as it has been conveyed to him through professional channels of education and indoctrination. The myths and mores of planners bridge the gap between the necessity for reaching conclusions and the imperfect ability to do so through purely rational means. Since plan making necessitates some assumptions as to goals, the professional role involves goal discovery and calculations as to plan acceptability where no clear goal consensus can be found. A plan is produced as the result of this professional activity, but it is not necessarily the plan that ultimately emerges from the planning agency, since nonprofessional considerations may modify it as the planner plays his nontechnical roles. In pursuing his professional role, the planner will tend to maintain certain "standards" with reference to what is "good" planning and "democratic" planning. He looks to the doctrine and practice of the planning profession.

A fine line exists between planning as a professional activity and behavior intended to produce acceptance of proposals by persons in the community with the influence and authority to act. This behavior involves promoting proposals as a specific, conscious political innovation. It may include the use of strategy, timing, persuasion, or even pressure. It involves identifying all the actors with a specific interest in a proposal, evaluating their relation to it, and predicting their reaction. It frequently involves the pulling in of such persons (in some cases because of their knowledge of the subject, in other cases in an effort to win over potential opponents) as key participants in the planning process. It draws on the capital established through the role of administrator of the planning organization. But just as it approaches the border line of organizational activity, it is also intimately related to the professional role.

Acceptance depends on the contents of the plan, the methods by which it is produced, and the methods used to communicate it. The planner can modify the plan for the purpose of improving its acceptance chances. These modifications may conflict with "professional" standards. When this occurs, we conclude the decision was an aspect of the nonalternative role of political innovation. The distinctiveness of the political innovation role arises from the fact that a reasonably well-defined group of "influentials" may be identified whose support is crucial to most political innovations of interest to the planner. This role refers to the planner's conscious or unconscious adaptation to influentials, be they a power clique or a veto group.

A final role concerns the long-range effort to modify the area of tolerance of the broader community. That is, the planner is limited in what he can do and what he can successfully propose, not only by the behavior of affected interests, but also by the degree of perception of the consequences of the proposal. He may deal with influentials in improving understanding of planning proposals on a person-to-person basis. But the influentials are themselves limited by the basic attitudes and values of the community at large. As the planner seeks to educate the community on the consequences and potentialities of planning, he seeks to modify the area of tolerance for new ideas, specifically by enlarging it. Ultimately he will be able to propose what initially was clearly unacceptable. The specific techniques include the usual public relations channels such as speeches, personal contact of the planning staff with the citizenry in the office or in the field, stimulation of the formation and activities of neighborhood planning groups, publication of educational pamphlets, press releases, and perhaps more dramatic means of publicity on occasion.

These roles are normally played concurrently rather than sequentially, though in emphasis they may have sequential variations. A new planning agency, for example, may need to concentrate on organization building. Later it can concentrate on professional work. In some situations education may have to precede political innovation, and in others political innovation may be desirable initially. It is assumed that the particular combination of role emphases will vary with every different planning arena.

Research Approaches

Since the object of this study is to describe the roles of the planner as an aspect of social control over urban development, several kinds of information are needed. Planning necessarily operates within a physical, social, and political arena of action, and a description of the environment of planning is required. Since the planner himself has considerable influence in shaping planning as a tool, particularly in the formative stage in which planning still finds itself, it is also necessary to evaluate the background of each planner which influences his behavior in his role. Finally, it is necessary to obtain information on the substance of planning programs and the behavior of planners in carrying them out. Correlations among these three types of information will answer many of our questions concerning the existing and potential roles of planners.

There is no one technique that can be handily applied for gathering these sorts of information. It may be noted that they fall into two general categories—factual and perceptual information. It has long been recognized that objective facts do not explain behavior beyond a certain point. In a relatively new activity such as planning, the perceptions of the planner's roles held by planners and others are considered crucial determinants of these roles.

In this study both types of information were collected in structured and semistructured interviews conducted by graduate student assistants in the Department of City and Regional Planning of the University of North Carolina.[1] Pretests were conducted for all the interview schedules, and considerable effort was devoted to perfecting these instruments. This approach provided a mass of information concerning planning as of the time of the interviews. Interviewing was conducted in the Crescent cities during 1958, 1959, and 1960.

In order to observe the roles of planners as a dynamic process over time, intensive case studies were conducted in six Crescent cities including Raleigh, Durham, Greensboro, High Point, Winston-Salem, and Charlotte. In these case studies planners' roles were observed in connection with specific decision processes. In this way the permutations and changing trends in planning roles could be observed. The cases provided both factual and perceptual information, and in most instances were conducted by the same investigator who did the interviewing in each city. A final source of information has been the files of the Department of City and Regional Planning of the University of North Carolina. Over a period of years the many contacts of the department with the Crescent cities left a body of important data which has been freely drawn on. In addition, all members of the staff of the department have had considerable personal experience with the planning departments of the Crescent cities as supervisors of student projects, consultants, or in one case as planning director. Much of the work on the roles of the planner has taken the form of specific studies, often completed as masters' theses.[2] The research approaches of theses have relied heavily on historical-descriptive, decision-analysis. role-analysis, and participant-observation techniques.

Organization of the Study

The findings of the study are presented under four headings. First, the factors affecting planner behavior are discussed, including both environmental and personal sources of influence. Second, the planner's overt behavior in playing his roles is considered, including his many relationships in the planning arena, his strategies, and his allocation of effort to various activities. Third, an effort is made to evaluate the impact of planning on urban development through attention to several indicators. Finally, conclusions are drawn concerning the nature of planning as a social control, and the apparent effect of different role patterns on planning outcomes.

Planning Roles: The Factors That Mold Them

The Urban Environment

From the description of the Crescent in Chapter 1, it is clear that physiographic features and resources of the area have had an effect on the urban environment. The soil and climate of the Crescent have made possible the development of its three major industries—tobacco, textiles, and furniture manufacturing. The site of Salem, now Winston-Salem, was systematically selected, primarily on the basis of fertility, by the early Moravian settlers. The mild climate contributed not only to the cotton and tobacco development, but also to location of other industries. High Point, for example, is one of the five largest furniture centers in the country. This is due in part to the climatic conditions conducive to rapid growth of timber and to its proper drying in a relatively humid area.

Once these factors began to attract population to the area, it became necessary to establish communication routes and governmental centers. Greensboro, located at the approximate center of its county, was chosen as the county seat. Location of the Forsyth County seat at Winston was an important factor in the growth of Winston-Salem. Raleigh was carefully chosen by the legislature and designed as a new town to be the state capital in a central location in the state. This occurred in 1792—long before the center of the state's population had moved this far west. The specific site was chosen because the Wake County seat was already at this location. Charlotte got its start with a gold rush and the coming of the railroad. High Point was located by the intersection of an early plank road and the Charlotte-Greensboro railroad. Durham came into being when a station was established in the eastern part of what was then Orange County as the North Carolina

Railroad was being projected westward along the divide between the Neuse and Cape Fear rivers.

Charlotte and Raleigh depart the farthest from the pre-eminence of tobacco, textiles, and furniture in the Crescent's economic pattern. Charlotte is predominantly a center of trade and finance, being the major wholesale trading center between Washington and Atlanta. Raleigh has long been a governmental center with substantial employment in the state and federal governments in addition to local government employees. There is a heavy concentration of educational institutions in the Crescent cities. The concentration of these institutions in the eastern end of the Crescent has been the basis for the Research Triangle development which has a high potential for further economic growth.

All of the Crescent cities studied have gone through the waves of governmental reform typical of the country, ultimately establishing city-manager forms of government, now the predominant form in this population group. In all of the six major Crescent cities except Charlotte, the manager plan was associated in one way or another with the development of the planning program. This has produced a climate more favorable to planning than previously existed.

Planning is not exclusively governmental. Accordingly, the overall leadership pattern of each community is of concern to the planner. The development of some of the cities as one-industry or two-industry towns has tended to concentrate leadership in the hands of a relatively few dominant economic influentials. The consequence of this situation for planning, therefore, depends on the attitudes of these leaders toward community development. These attitudes have changed over time. In such cities as Winston-Salem and Durham the current generation of leaders welcomes planning as essential to the proper development of the community. In other cities such as Raleigh and Charlotte leadership is more widely diffused, yet there is no less an appreciation for planning. Support for development programs is organized around such institutions as the Chamber of Commerce and the press. The chief significance of varying sorts of leadership patterns is that planners must employ different means of community liaison in different situations.

Within the broad context of planning, several environmental factors can be summarized which help shape the roles of the planner in the Piedmont Crescent. A history of relatively rapid population and economic growth provides the need for planning as a function of government. The rich educational resources of the Crescent, particularly at the University of North Carolina, have pointed out the potentiality of planning as a technique of public policy. The relatively aggressive business leadership of the Crescent cities, in competition for expanding and diversified economies, has accepted planning as a tool toward these ends.

The Planner's Legacy

Among the factors molding the roles of the planner is the past record of the planning program in the city concerned. A strong predecessor who established the program on firm ground can greatly facilitate the task of his successor. Likewise untrained specialists serving as directors of planning may pursue narrowly focused programs and greatly complicate the task of a professionally qualified successor whose concept of his role is considerably broader. Perhaps the greatest handicap to a newly appointed planner is the inheritance of a recently completed plan, prepared by a consultant who is no longer on the scene to follow through on his proposals.

All of these situations were revealed in Crescent cities. In several cities the planner followed able predecessors who had succeeded in establishing themselves and their programs. Views of their successors concerning the scope of the planning program, while not in conflict, were quite different from those of their predecessors. In other cases the planner, inheriting a weak program, found it necessary to change he image of the planner created by his predecessor before he could proceed with his own concept of the job.

The Planner's Influence

There is substantial evidence that the planning director himself has considerable impact on his own role and that of his successors. The degree of this influence is not measurable, but it can be seen in the correlation between the approach of the planning department and the views of the planner. It can also be seen in the perceptions about planning reported by those who work with and observe planners in action.

The variations among planners as individuals may be summed up under the headings of education for planning, planning experience, motivation, and perceptions of the planner's role. A considerable variation exists in the amount of formal education which planners have had. A survey of the membership of the American Institute of Planners (Faust, 1959) indicates that a little less than half had less than a year of graduate training in planning, while a little more than half had a year or more of graduate training. Of the professional planners in public agencies in the six Crescent cities, nine out of sixteen held graduate degrees in planning at the time of the survey, and two had completed all the work for the master's in planning except the thesis. This suggests that the level of education of the Crescent planners is above that for the country generally.

The amount and kind of experience in planning is also significant. The six Crescent planning directors had an average of six years each as director or assistant director of a planning agency, with experience at this level ranging from two to thirteen years. The type of previous experience included local, state, regional, and federal employment.

Planners tend to be consistent in reporting their motivations to become planners. The membership of the American Institute of Planners was asked (Faust, 1959) to identify the strongest, next strongest, and least strong motivations to enter planning from a list of seven.[3] The two leading responses of a total of 1,415 were "social improvement" (376) and "design" (317) as the strongest motivations. The same two led the list as second strongest with "design" first (278) and "social improvement" second (270). The two items most frequently listed as least descriptive of motivation were "career" (398) and "government and political" (244). Substantially the same picture emerges when the Crescent planning directors are taken as a group. "Social improvement" and "design" are almost exclusively the first and second choices.

One of the more meaningful indicators of the impact of the planner on his role is his own role perception. This is a subject on which every planning director has spent some thought. It is thoroughly discussed in every planning school, and is a favorite subject of discussion when planners forgather.

In a study of perceptions held by Crescent planners, a considerable variation was found from a clearly predominant major pattern. The majority of the sixteen planners (including six planning directors) interviewed reported that they spent too much time on routine administration of planning controls, and too little time on long-range planning, public relations, communication, and coordination. In assessing their own competence, the majority felt that they were relatively strong in administration, public relations, and knowledge of government, while a majority also felt themselves to be weak in statistics and design. When asked "what obstacles do you encounter in attempting to carry on your planning activities," most of the planning directors cited obstacles that would require skill in administration and public relations for solution.

Thus the planners feel their greatest strengths to be in administration and public relations. Since they perceive that the primary obstacles to the success of their programs are those relating to support both inside and outside of city hall, it appears that the Crescent planner holds realistic role expectations.

If the planner recognizes that he is not playing the role that he deems proper, it is safe to assume that when the opportunity arises he will move in the "correct" direction as he sees it. Preliminary indications are that this direction is away from the more routine administration of controls (which many of them feel could be adequately handled by an able administrative assistant), and toward what are to him the more challenging tasks of public relations, coordination, and comprehensive planning.

The Behavior of Planners

The most concrete way to describe and define the planner's role is to observe him in action. Since direct observation is usually not feasible, it is necessary to collect information on certain facts which can be taken as indicators of his actual performance. Three key categories of facts have been chosen, including the use of time, relationships, and strategies of planners. In the present study this information was sought from planners and from the persons with whom they work most frequently.

Use of Time

All planners in the six Crescent cities were asked to estimate how much of their time was spent on various aspects of their duties. While information obtained in this way cannot be considered entirely accurate, the main outlines of planning effort as indicated by the use of time can be compared. The list of activities on which planners spend their time was classified according to three of the four categories of role [4] explained earlier. These include the professional (technical), institutional (administrative and organization building), and educational roles. The fourth category, political innovation role, while no less important than the other three, is concerned with approach and cannot be measured in terms of time. Performance of the political innovation role would influence the way in which a planner goes about his responsibilities as a professional, administrator, and educator.

The use of time of planning directors varied from 33 to 68 per cent of time devoted to the technical aspects of planning. This range indicates considerable variation in the style of operation of planning directors. The directors reporting the lowest and highest percentage of time devoted to planning per se both had well-staffed agencies. The "low" man was director of a new program and came from a nontechnical undergraduate background, while the "high" man directed a well-established program and came from a technical undergraduate background.

Directors spent from 7 to 59 per cent of their time on institutional activity. Two possibilities can be offered to explain this great difference, assuming the data represent the true situation. The degree of maturity of the several agencies varies markedly, ranging from fourteen years of continuing operation under able direction in an atmosphere of enthusiasm and support, to agencies just getting started in communities where strong support for planning has been scattered or intermittent. Alternatively, the director may choose to invest different proportions of effort in institutional affairs because of different personal valuations of the relation of planning to other governmental and political processes. These possibilities will be explored later.

Directors spent from 5 to 25 per cent of their time on public relations and educational activity, with the mature agencies devoting the greatest amount of time to this activity and the less well-developed agencies devoting the least.

Information on how planners use their time was compared with planners' perceptions of their roles. Most of the planning directors felt that they spent too little time on long-range planning studies and on public relations, and too much time on routine administration of planning controls.

These data on use of time and on role preferences of planning directors are highly suggestive but not definitive. They were collected in cities of similar size, and we do not yet know that they would be typical of larger planning staffs. In fact, the demands on the Crescent planning director and his frustrations appear to be closely associated with size of professional staff. Larger cities, capable of supporting staffs of sufficient size to permit specialization in several areas (such as long-range planning, current plans, and zoning administration), provide opportunities for concentration on those aspects of particular interest to the individual planner, as well as greater intra-agency opportunities for promotion and change of emphasis for individual staff members. In contrast, the planner in the smaller city, as well as his one or two professional associates, has to be a "jack of all trades," ready at all times to plunge in where he is most needed, and postponing, if necessary, work on long-range plans, public relations, and many of the (to him) more appealing but less tangible aspects of his responsibilities. This problem becomes even more acute when the planning budget is inadequate to attract and retain a staff of the size and caliber needed, resulting frequently in a rapid turnover of the professional staff, accompanied at times by positions unfilled for months at a time.[5]

There is impressive evidence in the literature of public administration that young, insecure programs need to spend more of their effort on institutional and educational roles, while more stable programs can afford to concentrate more heavily on professional and political innovation ones. On the other hand, planning schools and planning literature have tended to stress long-range planning as the primary goal of the planning program. This is stressed so much, in fact, that the typical planning director who is not making tangible progress toward his comprehensive plan finds it necessary to apologize to other professionals, including his staff, unless work on the comprehensive plan is progressing according to schedule. At the same time, there is evidence to suggest the serious consequences of concentration on technical work and political innovation before an acceptable climate of opinion and institutional base has been established. This is not to suggest that the four roles should not be pursued concurrently, since they are intimately interrelated. It is possible, however, to maintain a different balance among them at different stages of the program.

Relationships in the Planning Process

The relationships that planning directors maintain with other actors in the political arena are very numerous, and often subtle. The Crescent planning directors had established some sort of relationship significant to their program with some forty-five different categories of actors. These tend to vary considerably as the involvements of the department vary from time to time. Broadly speaking, however, the patterns are similar from city to city.

A high frequency of contact is maintained with managers, mayors, public works officials, urban-renewal officials, planning commissioners, realtors, developers, and the press. Any other findings would have come as a surprise. In these categories contacts were maintained on a daily or weekly basis. A low level of contact frequency was reported by most cities with such categories as the city council, state and federal officials, industrial and business leaders, civic groups, and community leaders. Since the frequency of the contact is no reflection of its importance, however, this information does not go far in describing the roles of the planner.

The forty-five categories were grouped in such a way that contacts primarily concerned with the four roles could be counted. Professional and political innovation contacts were much more frequent than institutional and educational ones, but all four occurred at roughly the same level in all cities. Of all the relationships for institutional purposes, the majority tended to occur weekly or oftener. Educational relationships tended to occur less often than weekly. The only category in which the pattern varied significantly from city to city was the political innovation one.

In the great majority of cases communication between the planning director and other actors occurred on a two-way basis. This was particularly true of the contacts with high frequency, such as those with the city manager and other municipal departments. The actors who most commonly initiated communications with the planning department on a one-way basis were reported as bankers, realtors, developers, representatives of civic clubs, and the press.

A considerable variation exists in the degree to which the planning director customarily sees other actors socially after office hours. The actors most commonly among the planner's social friendships are the manager, the director of public safety, planning commissioners, state officials, planners from neighboring local planning agencies, and architects. In only a few cases did business leaders or members of the press appear in the list of friends.

Few conclusions can be drawn from these very crude data. They seem consistent with the image of the planner as striving to act on a technical basis and to maintain the great bulk of his contacts with other members of the city's administration rather than with the public generally or with specific groups affected by planning activity. If this image is accurate we may infer that the planner's influence on the broader aspects of developmental policy are exerted through other members of the administrative organization of the city, and particularly the city manager. This is not to reflect on the importance of his influence which, though indirect, may also be crucial. In the last analysis it is the combination of relationships in a particular city that is most revealing, and these have been explored through case studies.

Strategies of the Planner

The strategies employed by Piedmont planners are chosen, sometimes deliberately and sometimes only after experience, as a compromise. The two factors between which some middle ground must be found are the planner's perception of the total influence structure in his community, and his perception of what he would like this structure to be. Some planners tend to operate as though decision makers in the community can be expected to resolve questions on the same rational basis used by the planner—that is, by formulating goals and taking the planner's advice on how best to implement them. Others act as though this approach is not "practical" and seek the best available levers for promoting the cause of sound planning.

In the selection of channels there is a tendency to try formal governmental arrangements first. If existing institutions do not serve the purpose, recourse is had to informal procedures. In every Piedmont city, planning has tended to be more and more accepted over the years. As this process occurs, the range of strategies available to the planner has increased. Moreover, planners have been quick to learn by experience what techniques are unrewarding in their city. Thus the influence of the planner has increased concurrently with greater skill in utilizing the influence available.

These generalizations may be illustrated by the experience of the six cities with respect to selected matters of strategy. These matters include choice of technical work to be performed, political innovation methods, approach to building confidence in planning, and public relations behavior.

There is a strong feeling among many planners that a major element in the technical work of planning is the long-range aspect of the planning program. The considerations which have impelled planners actually to launch into such a program have varied. In several cities in the Crescent, planning was instigated in the community when the presence of serious developmental problems was recognized. Planners were imported to solve specific problems. The pressure of the work which understaffed planning programs were expected to do tended to prevent them from serious effort toward the comprehensive approach.

When they found themselves able to devote time to it, comprehensive plans were begun.

Most Piedmont planning directors have been given a free hand in selecting the elements of their technical programs. In several cases, however, this freedom was academic since developmental decisions basic to planning were imminent. In this situation the planner's response most frequently was to immerse himself in trying to obtain the wisest decision even if time was not available for a complete study of the problem. In a few cases, however, planners attempted to postpone the decision until necessary basic planning could be done. This effort occasionally met with some success.

In the majority of the Crescent cities the planning director maintains intimate relationships with the city manager in fact as well as in the hierarchy shown on the organization chart. The strategy of handling the city council varies widely. Most commonly relations between planner and council are formal, and flow through the channel of the city manager except where the manager has designated the planner to make direct representations in his behalf. In some cases the planning commission is an alternative channel, particularly on matters with broad policy implications.

One of the key strategic decisions of the planner is the degree to which to inject himself and his department into public or intragovernmental controversies over policy. Where the planner's acceptance as a policy adviser is low, he has tended to avoid controversy and assume the role of provider of technical information to decision makers. Where it is strong, he has undertaken commitments to particular solutions of current problems within whatever area of freedom the managers and planning commissions allow. Four strategic stances can be observed. The first avoids any semblance of controversy and involves purely factual studies on noncontroversial subjects. The second, and more common, involves factual studies of controversial subjects and the giving of opinions on facets of the problem when formally requested by official bodies. The third involves specification of alternative solutions, or plans, indicating the pros and cons of each. In the final approach the planning director commits himself to a specific plan he deems superior to all others, and attempts to commit others to the same plan. A planner may select one or another of these approaches as they suit the situation at hand. His calculation is based on the effect of the tactics chosen on the status and acceptance of the planning department. In the great majority of cases, the planner assumes a personal commitment to a particular solution, but frequently he limits the degree to which he reveals this choice until the decision process has matured further. Thus, for example, he may take the third stance early in the process, and take the fourth as the time for decision approaches.

A final strategic consideration concerns the degree of emphasis that the planner devotes to broad community education concerning the potentiality of comprehensive planning as a device to guide urban development. In general, four approaches to this activity are employed, including publications and press releases directed toward the public generally, personal appearances of planners at meetings of civic groups of all kinds, orientation of public school teachers, and personal contacts with the public at the planning office. The impact of this work can be expected only after a period of many months or years, and for this reason it tends to be given a low priority in the face of more current pressures. Moreover, it contains the pitfalls of possible interpretations of community problems and policies which may be unpopular with city officials. Despite these difficulties, a high proportion of the planning programs include a conscious public-relations emphasis.

Reaction, Support, and Achievement

There is no such thing as not planning. When a problem is perceived, someone will begin to plan. The question raised here is: What is the effect on the community of establishing a continuous, professionally staffed planning agency? There is no way of giving a conclusive answer, but the impact of planning may be judged by observing the following indicators. First, the evaluations of planning by people who have significant and continuing contacts with the planner in the Piedmont cities have been recorded. Second, the response of the communities to the planning agency has been measured in terms of financial support. Finally, the accomplishments of the planning program have been compared insofar as possible. Each of these approaches has its shortcomings, yet each adds something to answer the question.

Planning Perceptions of Community Leaders

In each of the six Crescent cities a series of questions was asked of the fifteen or twenty persons identified as most closely concerned with the planning program, other than the planners themselves. One hundred and six nonplanners were interviewed. Thirty of these were governmental employees (including managers and heads of departments). Thirty-nine were present or former appointed and elected officials (including mayors, city councilmen, and members of planning or urban-renewal commissions). Thirty-seven were leading citizens who had not held public office. Among the 76 respondents not employed by government, the major occupational groups represented were realtors, contractors, and developers (15), industrial executives (15), finance executives (14), business executives (14), professional men including lawyers and architects (10), and newspaper editors (8).

The panel of persons who interact with planners was selected by asking planners and all others interviewed in each city to list ten people in the community whose support they considered essential for the success of any proposal relating to physical development. Those most frequently nominated were classified as top leaders. The respondents were then divided into three categories including top leaders of the community (27), city and county employees (30), and all others (49). Where the roles of city employee and top leader were both played by the same individual, he was classified as a top leader for this purpose. This tended to separate the full-time and professional department heads from part-time elective officials whose role was a function of their position in the influence structure of the community. The answers to the questions provided two kinds of information. First, they indicated the reactions of the respondents to the planning program of the city and its director. Second, they have been grouped in such a way as to measure the perceptions of planning roles held by the persons interviewed.

Respondents were asked, "Do you think the planning program here is representing the public interest of the community?" Virtually all the respondents in all the cities thought so with varying degrees of emphasis. A very few had some reservations and felt that occasionally something was done not in the interest of everyone, or that sometimes the planner was ahead of the community which did not recognize its own best interest. The unanimity of this response correlates very well with the question, "Do you feel that you are kept sufficiently well informed on planning activities in this community?" No more than one or two persons in each city among the group questioned felt that he should have been kept better informed. These few seemed to have some particular category of information in mind which they felt a specific need for. A few felt that while they were adequately informed, the public probably was not.

In evaluating the planning program as such two questions were used: "What is your opinion of the effectiveness of the planning program here?" "How would you evaluate the effectiveness of your planning director?" The response to these questions was generally enthusiastic in the six cities. The criticisms of planning directors and programs included such comments as "ineffective," "uncompromising," "unrealistic," and in most cases produced no pattern in a particular city.

In sum, among those most familiar with planning in the community, the favorable reaction was most impressive, and usually enthusiastic. Even the persons who had some serious reservation about a particular planning director agreed that the planning program was essential in the public interest.

The responses to the questions listed above plus two others were analyzed to derive a composite perception of the roles of the planner as held by those most concerned with the planning program. The two additional questions concerned those qualities which the respondent would seek in a planning director, and those skills and attitudes he felt should be inculcated in planning school. All of the statements made in the open-ended questions were classified according to the role with which they were primarily concerned. It will be recalled that the four dominant roles are political innovational, educational, institutional, and professional.

By counting the number of comments relating to each role and expressing this as a percentage of the total number of comments, the degree of emphasis put on each role was established. For the six Crescent cities the average percentage of comment from observers of planners indicating the institutional role was 35. The average percentage indicating the professional role was also 35. Political innovation and educational roles were both indicated at an average percentage of 15.

The kinds of variation indicated above characterized the entire group of respondents in each city, but even greater fluctuations appear when the responses are grouped according to top leaders, city hall employees, and others. In some cities all of these groups evaluated the roles in about the same way. In others, substantial differences appear.

Another approach to evaluating the impact of planning on community leaders was to ask them their opinion of the publications of the planning department. In this case, each city produced predominantly favorable replies. The sprinkling of criticisms included such comments as "somewhat too theoretical," "idealistic," "devoid of conclusions or recommendations of a useful kind," "too technical," "didn't reach the public," "were too few," and "not understandable to the public." In general it is clear that the criticisms concerned the ability of the reports to communicate rather than the subject matter, coverage, accuracy, or other qualities. The dilemma was posed between reports too technical and detailed, on the one hand, to be meaningful to the layman, and those too generalized and theoretical, on the other, to be translated by him into conclusions concerning his own community. In another sense, the responses to this question indicate a concern with the public education role of the planner.

Data of the kinds indicated above do not provide a definite picture of how the communities view planning. They do suggest, however, some important variations among perceptions of the planner's roles from city to city, and from group to group within a city. Undoubtedly, one of the very important factors determining perceptions of the planning roles is the experience of the city with the incumbent planning director. Where some very distinctive personality trait or some particular approach to planning appears, role perceptions are affected by it. Recognized deficiencies in the planning director draw to the attention of community leaders the need for the missing quality. Where some special competence is recognized, this also affects perception of roles.

Despite the comments here relating to criticisms of the planning director, it should be noted that the predominant response to all of the questions cited, and in all the cities, has been a favorable one. Even in the cities where a history of sharp involvement on the part of the planner in controversial questions is known, the planner has been able to maintain a high level of popularity among the group polled. In answer to the question seeking evaluation of the planner himself, for example, the phrases, "excellent man," "highly effective," "superior," "exceedingly able," and "highly able" constantly reappear. The planner in the Piedmont Crescent has convinced both the official and nonofficial leaders of the communities that planning, roughly along the lines of existing programs, is indispensable to the good health of the city.

Funds for Planning

One measure of the planning consciousness of a community is the level of budgetary support that it gives to the planning program. This comparison does not tell us anything about the quality of the planning program, but it is the best measure of where planning stands when it competes with all the other financial needs of the community.

The six largest Piedmont Crescent communities spent just under $300,000 for professional planning services in 1958. A small portion of this ($6,000 exclusively to planning departments) was spent on consultant services, which indicates an unusually heavy reliance on the public planner in the Crescent.

The dollar total of expenditures is less significant, however, than the per capita comparison used here. It should be noted that two of the six planning agencies serve both the city and county. In these cases the per capita calculation is based on the total population of the county that includes the city, and on the total budget provided by both jurisdictions.

The mean per capita expenditure in 1958 for 223 cities of the United States and Canada was 49 cents (ASPO, 1959). The similar figures for the major geographical sections were: Canada, 89 cents; Far West, 81 cents; Northeast, 39 cents; Southwest, 39 cents; Middle States, 34 cents; Southeast, 33 cents; Northwest, 29 cents. Per capita expenditures for the six Crescent planning jurisdictions (Charlotte and Mecklenburg County, city of Durham, city of Greensboro, city of High Point, city of Raleigh, Winston-Salem and Forsyth County), based on 1960 population, averaged 46 cents.

This is a clear indication that the Crescent cities support planning at a higher level than the average of any of the major regions of the country with the exception of Canada and the Far West. This finding is the more striking in view of the fact that when the counties of the United States with the largest populations are ranked according to per capita effective buying income, the Piedmont counties containing the cities in question rank from 144 to 180 of a total of 200 [6] (*Sales Management*, 1959).

Within this context the six Crescent planning jurisdictions have startlingly different levels of per capita expenditures (based on 1960 population figures) for planning, ranging from far above ($1.03) to far below (14 cents) the national and regional averages.

Planners' salaries in the Crescent range both above and below the national average. In a survey reported in 1959 by the American Society of Planning Officials, seventeen planning positions were listed for North Carolina Crescent cities (ASPO, 1959). Of these, seven were above the mean for the nation while ten were below. All of the planning directors were below the national mean except the two serving city-county agencies. These appeared in the highest quartile of planners' salaries in counties with comparable populations.

Output and Accomplishments

Accomplishments of the Crescent's planning agencies have differed under the regimes of the various directors. Most of the trained planners came up with at least one aspect of the comprehensive plan (some of them preliminary) as well as a substantial number of more specialized planning studies. The majority of those whose education was in fields other than planning concentrated on special studies of particular interest to city officials. Most of the planners had been major participants in annexation studies. Comprehensive land-development plans are currently being given high priority.

The true test of accomplishment of a planning agency may be described as the extent to which its program influences decisions in such a way that development takes place in accordance with the recommendations of the agency. An attempt has been made to identify types of plans that have been prepared under the different planning regimes in six Crescent cities. The extent of impact of these plans is difficult to determine. One can, however, outline the factors which appear to be involved in commanding local attention and respect, and consider the extent to which favorable conditions and consequent progress have been attained in six Crescent cities.

Favorable climate for accomplishment by a planning agency is partly a function of the planner himself (his personality, persuasive powers, and the extent to which he succeeds in building confidence in his program), partly a function of the chief executive, or city manager in the case of the Crescent cities, and partly a function of the community and its leadership. Continuity of service of a planner and a sympathetic manager may also be crucial factors. The Crescent cities in which planning is most solidly entrenched and having the greatest impact on day-to-day development are those in which respected planners and able, enthusiastic managers have been working side by side for a number of years.

In summary it may be said that accomplishment of a planning program in terms of tangible results is not entirely dependent upon the planner himself. However, the planner's contribution to accomplishment is a major one, and is strongly influenced by the extent to which he emphasizes his institutional, educational, and political innovation roles.

Conclusions

There is not likely to be dissent to the proposition that the major function of the urban planners is to assist the community to make more rational decisions on matters of physical development. Some will argue that his function is broader than this, but we may validly confine our attention to this area of general agreement. In performing this function the planner's unique contribution stems from his special perspective. His perspective differs from others in the decision arena in that he has special technical skills, he employs a long-range view of development, and he utilizes these elements to view the community in its entirety. We seek then to understand the roles played by the planner in making his particular contribution to the process of deciding how the community will grow.

Roles of the Planner

It will be recalled that the conception of the present study is based on four key roles of the planner relating to institutional leadership, public relations and citizen education in planning, professional activity, and political innovation. It is a basic assumption here that these four roles are essential to the performance of the planning function, but we have not assumed that they must be performed in the same way in every community. Rather our approach has been to try to perceive the differences in role performance among cities and at different times in the same city, and then to relate these differences to the factors in the planning environment which seemed to produce them. We have not even assumed that the four roles must necessarily be performed by the planner himself, and under some conditions they have in fact been performed at another point in the politico-administrative system of the community.

Let us consider first the institutional role. Essentially this involves building confidence in the planning institution, that is, confidence in the planning department and its staff and confidence in the process that planners employ. This confidence may be viewed as of two kinds, internal and external to the planning staff. Internal confidence is built on effective administration of the planning department. It includes such matters as effective supervision of staff work, training the staff, sound budgetary and personnel decisions, and maintenance of staff morale. Since planning staffs of the Crescent cities are all small in size, this responsibility has not produced significant problems. Every planning director recognizes his responsibility for internal administration, and has earned the confidence of his subordinates. The professionalized nature of planning tends to cement the solidarity within the planning staff.

The more significant element of the institutional role, however, concerns external confidence building. This is a role which every administrator must play to some degree and it involves the maintenance of relationships with other governmental units within the municipal administration. That is, it is an "administrative" role. It may also involve, however, the establishment of contacts with the "political" elements of the community, both formal and informal. It may produce relationships with the city council, mayor, interest groups, or informal leaders of the community. In short, it demands whatever relationships and strategies may be required to assure an acceptance of the planning institution.

The institutional role appears in several styles in the Piedmont Crescent. For the earliest plans the role was not played by anyone, since these were purchased from outside consultants who left the community on presentation of the plan. In an incipient sense we may say that confidence in the planner was supplied by the early private organizations which hired the consultants, and later by the city governing bodies. But the real point is that because the institutional role was nonexistent, the plans were not implemented to any great extent.

With the establishment of permanent professional staffs, an institutional base was provided for planning. The mere presence of the staff, however, and the existence of planning activity did not prove to be adequate in gaining acceptance of planning. One approach toward gaining acceptance of planning involves spreading the confidence-building efforts among several potential bases of support. It requires that the planner himself "carry the ball" for planning, and develop himself as a power in the community decision-making process.

A second approach has been to rely primarily on the support of the city manager. This has been used only in those cities where the planner is under the direct supervision of the manager rather than of the planning commission. This organizational situation, however, does not solve the problem of institutional leadership, and depends on the attitude of the manager toward the planning function.

If the planner is successful in playing the institutional role under one of these patterns, it follows that the over-all strength of planning in a community is greater when there is not a frequent turnover in the office of planning director. Turnover is affected by such considerations as salary, planning budget, and acceptance of the planner's advice. These, in turn, are functions of the confidence which the community places in the planning institution. This circularity of cause and effect is one of the facts of life of any administrative operation. One of the more important sources of strength in planning, then, is the history of planning in the community concerned.

Closely related to the institutional role, but differing from it in important respects is the educational-public relations role. This involves promoting the understanding of planning among nonleaders who do not participate directly in the decision process. Ultimately this activity will affect the acceptance of the planning institution, but this effect will be long in coming. The importance of this role will vary with the degree to which the public has an impact on community decisions, though ideologically it is important in every case in order that the planning process be "democratic."

The variations in the educational role of the planner involve different degrees of emphasis on communication with "the public." The media employed are substantially the same in each program, including personal contact at the planning office, speeches and presentations to community groups, radio and television appearances, distribution of publications, and releases to the press. It is of interest to note that in the Crescent cities in which nonplanners perceived this role to be the most important, it has been historically the weakest.

Probably the two most important dimensions of the professional role concern the planner's degree of identification with the planning profession, and the scope of the technical work done in the planning office. While it is perfectly possible for a planner to be highly identified with the national profession and his own community at the same time, this is not always the case. Several Crescent planners who have a strong commitment to the planning profession have not developed the kind of roots in their community which prevent their leaving for a substantially better job. Others are oriented primarily to the local scene and do not solicit or perhaps even entertain promotion to jobs in larger cities which would be considered "better" by their primarily profession-oriented associates. This difference bears no established relation to the quality of the work done by the planner. It may, however, seem to produce a difference in the planner's selection of the kind of work to undertake. The profession-oriented planner tends to put greater value on the comprehensive approach and on coming up with a plan within a few years. The local-oriented planner on the other hand may be more concerned with work of immediate service value to the community and with affecting day-to-day developmental decisions. This does not mean he does not take as long-range a view as other planners, but that he applies this long-range perspective to different objects of planning, namely those closer to fruition as decisions in the political arena, and tends to postpone the major tasks of the comprehensive plan.

The other dimension concerns the type of technical work done, and bears a relationship to the matter just discussed. The choice of technical work, however, is affected by many variables in the community, among which only one is the orientation of the planner himself. In most Crescent cities the planners have made substantial progress in the development of a comprehensive plan—a function performed by a planner or not at all, and the planning department participates extensively in the preparation of the capital budget, signifying the degree to which planning becomes integrated with the administrative process.

The most important variable in the performance of the professional function, however, is the relationship between staff size and the scope of technical work. In several Crescent cities the lack of budget and other support for planning prevented developing a staff capable of meeting the planning demands of the city, particularly in such specialized areas as highway planning or urban renewal. In these cases reliance was placed on the use of consultants, once the planner had demonstrated a need for these planning services. The shortage of planning personnel and lack of competitive salary scales contributed to the inability of recruiting larger planning staffs. Where one of these situations keeps the planning staff small, the technical role of the planner becomes more a matter of coordinating the planning done by the departments and by consultants. This change in role, in turn, affects the experience and competence of the planning staff in the future. As alternative planning resources develop, the municipal staff is less likely to fulfill an expanded technical role. For example, the cities having the least occasion to do regional planning are not likely to move into this area of technical work because of the establishment of an active regional planning commission supported in part by these cities. A liaison function develops, but not detailed planning work.

Finally, the political innovation role was defined as the injection of new ideas into the political-decision process. Every planner is an innovator in the sense that he creates ideas in the course of his technical activity, produces plans, and proposes methods of implementation. This is part of the professional role as we use the term. The process of *conveying* these ideas to those points in the leadership structure of the community where they will be successfully forwarded to emerge as outcomes is considered political innovation. In performing this role, two basic approaches appear in the Crescent. In some cities the planner prepares the ideas he has produced in the form of proposals which he publicly and formally conveys to the official decision centers consisting of executives, governing bodies, and planning commissions. He makes his own defense of these plans. The innovation may or may not be made public, since the manager or planning commission may decide not to forward the plan to the governing body. In any event, the planner is identified as the proponent and innovator. The effectiveness of this approach clearly depends on the degree to which the institutional role has been successful. It was pointed out above that this varies considerably. A planner with great prestige may operate in this fashion with considerable success. The other approach involves planting the seeds of political innovation in the right places, cultivating them and fertilizing them as appropriate, in the hope that they will take root and grow. It they do, some community leader becomes the proponent and takes credit for the innovation. In some cases the planner has relied on planting the seed at one or two strategic points, such as the city manager or a top leader in the informal influence structure, or perhaps a member of the city council. In others, the technique has been to broadcast the seed to all the leadership elements of the community as much as possible. As a result some of these leadership elements begin to take up the idea, encourage other elements to give it support, and eventually the pressure rises on the formal governmental bodies until a favorable decision is reached. Frequently some combination of the Chamber of Commerce, the press, and a councilman or mayor has created the conditions which forced formal consideration of the innovation.

Patterns and Problems of Role

Among the eleven planning regimes in the six cities during which a planning director has had a substantial tenure of office, several combinations of roles appear. In some cases there has been little if any emphasis on the institutional and public education roles, and relatively little political innovation. The professional role has been performed in all of these cases with continuing technical activity, and sometimes imaginative spot planning. In several cases all four roles have received considerable attention and the result may be thought of as a balanced program with respect to these roles.

While it would take many more cases to prove the point, it is suggested that there may be a natural history of development for a small planning staff generally along these lines: when first organized almost exclusive emphasis is placed on the institutional and educational roles in order to produce the optimum fit to the conditions of the particular political arena at hand. When a firm basis of acceptance develops, the emphasis on institution building is reduced. The educational emphasis continues, but in time it can be reduced more slowly as the community becomes more sophisticated in the ways of planning. As these two roles begin to require less attention, professional work can be rapidly expanded. This is necessary in any event since the planning department must prove its usefulness as a part of confidence building. The early work undertaken by the staff will be chosen carefully from this point of view. Comprehensive planning, ideally initiated at the outset, progresses slowly, partly because of lack of time and staff to do everything at once, and partly because of the problem of acceptability. Finally, the political innovation role begins to expand as acceptance rises, and as innovations become fully analyzed and ready for presentation. The director of planning will relegate his professional role to able subordinates as the political innovation role expands.

Exclusive emphasis on professional work, inadequate professional basis for political innovation, and a weak institutional base are suggestive of the pitfalls that have appeared as Piedmont planners play their roles.

This is not to suggest that the planner has complete control over the roles which he and his staff may play, though it has become apparent that he does have a considerable area of flexibility. Other factors shown to be highly important include his personal limitations, the expectations of leading actors in the governmental arena, particularly city managers, and the attitudes of community groups toward community problems. Some reflection of these variables can be gained by a summary comparison of different perceptions of the roles of the planner. Most of the planning directors reported in one way or another that their hope was to get ahead with comprehensive long-range planning. This is what they have been trained to do. Their professional reference group demands it of them. They feel that whether the community knows it or not, they cannot function effectively without the framework such a plan would provide, and that they owe it to their community to prepare such a plan with key persons participating in its preparation, to acquaint the decision makers with its purpose and validity, and to get it accepted and periodically reviewed as a guide for the community in reaching policy decisions. That the planner's goal is not always clearly understood by others, particularly in relatively new planning programs such as those in the Crescent cities, was partially borne out in responses of nonplanners to questions relating to expectations concerning the planner's role. While numbers of respondents replied in terms that gave evidence of their respect for such qualities as "imagination," "vision," and "ability to see beyond day-to-day problems," some of these same individuals and many others emphasized the need for "practicality" and "realism."

This emphasis could be construed to mean that many of the observers of planners questioned place a low value on what planners consider to be their primary job. However, the almost unanimous vote for technical competence in planning (most of the respondents appeared to recognize planning as a profession, only a few assumed the planner to be primarily an engineer or administrator) as an essential characteristic of the effective planner, suggests that the concern for realism may not have been directed in opposition to long-range planning, but represented a plea for carrying comprehensive plans beyond broad generalized proposals to specific and tangible recommendations which can be understood, and which give some promise of realization within the foreseeable future.

Planners' responses provided substantial evidence that they perceive their job as one in which they would like to devote more time to long-range planning, public relations, and communication, and less time to the routine administration of controls. This suggests that at least this aspect of the institutional role is one which they play unwillingly, and because of necessity rather than choice. It also suggests that planners in under-staffed agencies may be attracted to larger agencies where specialized personnel is employed to cope with these details, thereby freeing the planner's time for developing his professional, educational, and political innovation roles along with the broader aspects of his institutional role.

More specific conflicts arise when the city manager perceives the planner as primarily an administrative assistant, a traffic engineer, or a site planner rather than in the broader perspective in which the planner views himself. Some developers view the planner as primarily an administrator of controls, while some civic boosters feel the planner's job is to promote new industry.

The significance of these conflicts goes beyond whatever personal frustration they bring to the planner. They demand of the planner a choice between spending effort on what he considers to be the proper concern of planning, or giving in to demands of the manager or special interest groups. That is, there is a conflict between the demands of the professional role and the demands of the institutional role. This conflict goes far to explain why, in the role combinations noted above, the professional role tended to be high where institutional and educational roles were low and vice versa.

Similarly there is a potential role conflict between the political innovation and institutional roles. Planners will not forward political innovations when their judgment is that to do so would seriously endanger the confidence placed in the planning institution. A choice must be made between institutional gains and the more risky future gains which might follow from an innovation effort. In practice the effect of this calculation is more often to delay, rather than to prevent, a specific proposal.

Some Implications of the Findings

This study was initiated with the notion that planning constitutes a social control over community development by contributing importantly to the decision stream which produces developmental decisions. The time has come to comment on this proposition. It seems quite clear that in the Piedmont Crescent planning has slowly but perceptibly moved closer to the center of the decision process in an increasing number of policy areas. This has happened as acceptance of the planning institution by the communities has increased. The governmental agents and agencies in particular have shifted to a greater reliance on the planning departments for policy advice.

Acceptance tends to increase to the degree that planning activity is considered "useful" by the actors in policy making. The reputation of usefulness is gained less by the quality of long-range planning than by "practical" work on short-range projects. This suggests that there may be an innate necessity to build the planning program from short-range spot-planning work, through projects with larger implications and intermediate perspectives, and ultimately to the long-range comprehensive plans which the planner is trained and anxious to provide.

The governmental planner's dilemma has generally been to choose between the idealism and imagination of utopian planning and the obligation to plan within the range of tolerance and understanding of his public employer. It has even been suggested that the governmental planner cannot be a utopian and should leave this role to the consultant or the private planning agency, or the planning philosopher. This study suggests that the degree to which the governmental planner may aspire to his ideal is in considerable degree a function of his success in the three nonprofessional roles.

Conclusions of the order just suggested, however, cannot be confirmed without a broader study of planning programs than has been possible here. The most urgent need is to investigate in detail the roles of the planner in representative communities of larger population, including metropolitan planning programs. Cities with varied forms of organization need study to extend the present findings beyond the confines of council-manager governments. Further exploration of the sources of the values held by planners is needed. In particular this suggests an intensive look at the role of the planning schools in the formation of the planner's value system as it relates both to goals and strategies of operation.

Of what significance are the findings of this research to the officials and citizens of the Crescent cities? Organized planning programs have become an established and accepted function of government at the local level, and there is growing interest and activity in regional planning, involving several governmental units.

A successful planning program depends largely on the caliber of the planning director and on the support made available to him to build up his program. Because of the demand for planners, who operate within a nation-wide market, recruitment efforts should be made on a nation-wide basis. In addition to professional skills, ability to build and maintain confidence in the planning program and to communicate effectively are of primary importance. Any competent director of planning must be given the help he needs, in order to release his time for the long-range aspects of the planning program, for public relations and communication.

In order to insure continuity of planning personnel, salaries must be reviewed and revised upward, so as to compete favorably not only with neighboring cities, but with opportunities offered elsewhere in the planning field open to professional personnel with the skills, abilities, and experience sought.

Support for planning in the Crescent and in the state is considerably ahead of the Southeast but is below many other regions of the country. This situation will need to be rectified if the Crescent is to continue to attract and retain first-rate planning personnel.

FOOTNOTES

1. The following graduate students studied the planning programs in six Crescent cities: Dennis E. Daye, Conrad C. Haupt, Jonathan B. Howes, James A. Kelley, Ralph W. Miner, Jr., Richard H. Sears, Jr., George M. Stephens, Jr., and James E. Stuchell.
2. These include: Dennis E. Daye, "The Responsibilities and Limitations of the Planning Director in a Council-Manager Form of Government: An Exploratory Analysis Based on a Case Study of Greensboro, North Carolina" (1958); Robert M. Griffin, Jr., "Planners in Public Agencies: An Exploratory Study of the Role of the Urban Planner" (1958); Richard H. Sears, Jr., "The Responsibilities and Limitations of the Planning Director in a Council-Manager Form of Government: An Exploratory Analysis Based on a Case Study of Southtown and Farrell County, South State" (1958); George M. Stephens, Jr., "The Responsibilities and Limitations of the Planning Director in a Council-Manager Form of Government: An Exploratory Analysis Based on a Case Study of Charlotte, North Carolina" (1958); Lucien C. Faust, "An Analysis of Selected Characteristics of the Membership of the American Institute of Planners" (1959); James A. Kelley, "The Role of the Planner in High Point, North Carolina" (1960); George J. Monaghan, "The Functions and Achievements of City Planning Agencies: The Development of a Questionnaire" (1960); James E. Stuchell, Jr., "The Role of the Urban Planner in the City Government of Raleigh, North Carolina" (1960); and Conrad C. Haupt, "The Role of the Planner in Durham, North Carolina" (1961).

   Several other master's theses have contributed valuable background material to the role of the planner study. These include: Seward Weber, "The Planning Function in Medium-Size Cities" (1952); Pamela R. Jewett, "Problems of Commercial Relocation: A Case Study of the Church Street Redevelopment Project, New Haven, Connecticut" (1958); Valentins Rupeiks, "An Investigation of Planning Commission Members in Piedmont North Carolina Crescent Cities" (1959); Cynthia E. Gubernick, "The Importance of the Decision-Making Process to City Planning and Urban Development: A Case Study of Winston-Salem, North Carolina" (1960); Jonathan B. Howes, "The Planner's Perception of His Role: A Pilot Study" (1961); and Ralph W. Miner, Jr., "The Role of the Urban Planner as Seen by Community Leaders and Public Officials: A Pilot Study" (1961).

3. (1) *Social improvement motivation:* a way to improve the total environment of all citizens of the community. (2) *Scientific motivation:* a way to provide decision makers with accurate information and advice on which to base decisions. (3) *Government and political motivation:* a way to participate in the political-administrative community organization, with regard to the public interest in physical land development. (4) *Design motivation:* the way to effect physically a more visually pleasing and esthetically satisfying environment. (5) *Coordination motivation:* a chance through communication to identify community goals and to coordinate community efforts toward their realization. (6) *Conservation motivation:* an opportunity to channel community forces so as to obtain the maximum social return from limited economic, land, and leadership resources. (7) *Career motivation:* planning combined the benefits of a profession sufficiently rewarding financially, of high status, and great social utility.
4. These categories include such activities as: *professional*—development and administration of controls, data collection and analysis, plan preparation, urban-renewal work; *institutional*—departmental administration, nonplanning activities performed for city government; *educational*—public relations, citizen education in planning; and *political innovation*—coordination with key nonplanners.
5. Planning agencies in the six Crescent cities, representing a total of 65 years of staff operation, have had 14 planning directors (only one city has retained the same director since the inception of its program) and 18 assistant directors. The average term of office for the directors and assistant directors has been 4.4 and 3.6 years respectively. Half of the former incumbents left their positions for higher paying jobs in larger cities. The other half are equally divided among those who now serve their profession (as faculty members in planning schools or working directly for AIP) and those who shifted to other positions within the state.
6. Durham County is not included in the list as it did not fall in the top 200 counties. The per capita effective buying income of Durham County, however, places it within this range.

REFERENCES

American Society of Planning Officials (1959), "Expenditures and Staff of Local Planning Agencies," *Planning Advisory Service, Information Report No. 122, May 1959.*

Faust, Lucien C. (1959), "An Analysis of Selected Characteristics of the Membership of the American Institute of Planners," unpublished master's thesis, University of North Carolina, Chapel Hill.

Gross, Neal, Ward S. Mason, and Alexander McEachern (1958), *Explorations in Role Analysis: Studies of the School Superintendency Role.* New York: John Wiley and Sons.

International City Managers Association (1960), *The Municipal Year Book.* Chicago.

Meyerson, Martin and Edward C. Banfied (1955), *Politics, Planning and the Public Interest.* Glencoe, Ill.: The Free Press.

Parsons, Talcott (1949), *The Structure of Social Action,* 2nd ed. New York: McGraw-Hill Book Company.
Sales Management (1959), *Survey of Buying Power,* May 10, 1959. Sales Management, New York.
Selznick, Philip (1957), *Leadership in Administration: A Sociological Interpretation.* Evanston, Ill.: Row, Peterson and Company.
Simon, Herbert A. (1947), *Administrative Behavior.* New York: The Macmillan Company.

Chapter 8

The Roles of Top Business Executives in Urban Development

by E. William Noland *

THAT TOP BUSINESS EXECUTIVES participate in various ways in the decisions made as a city changes and grows is realistically surmised by everyone, yet the exact patterns of such participation have been examined little more than casually. To study this phenomenon in detail in the Piedmont Crescent, a sample of business firms in four cities—Burlington, Charlotte, High Point, and Winston-Salem—was chosen for the purpose of taking a close look at the roles their presidents played in urban development.

Such a study poses many questions which in turn are indicative of the variety of approaches that research in this area could take. Is the executive's leadership in community affairs and in the decisions that are made as the community changes and grows limited to politically neutral causes, as Lundborg (1950) claims is substantially true? In short, is the executive's life a series of innocuous "do's" and "don't's"? What are our chances of investigating the political participation of business executives against the backdrop of other types of participation, in order to examine the Marxian position that businessmen are dominated by politicians and bureaucrats, or Veblen's insistence that

* Acknowledgment is made of the valuable assistance provided to this study by the following research assistants: Charles M. Bonjean, Emory Kimbrough, Jr., and Robert G. McDonald. Professor Alfred M. Denton, Jr., of Salem College, assisted with the interviewing in Winston-Salem.

government is dominated by business, or the neo-pluralist view that political decisions can be understood only by attentiveness to a multitude of factors and foci? (See Dahl, 1960.) Are the attitudes, values, and ideologies of the businessman which express themselves in resistance to regulatory law born of the belief that the economic costs of regulation are high? Or must we agree with Lane (1954) in his insistence that the economic costs of regulation are relatively low but the psychic costs are high? Is there any basis in the contention, again substantially Lane's, that regulation changes the businessman's ideology by damaging his self-image, generates frustrations by depriving him of his customary choices, and creates anxieties by introducing new uncertainties into an already unpredictable environment?

To what extent might a businessman's participation in community affairs be a reflection of his changed conception of the nature of leadership, that leadership is a relationship among the traits of the leader himself, the characteristics of his followers, the nature of the firm in which he works, and the over-all social, economic, and political milieu in which his firm operates? (See McGregor, 1960, pp. 182–185.) Is it not conceivable that this broad view of leadership as a relationship has a bearing on his augmenting his leadership role in the firm with a leadership role outside the firm? Could it not be true that certain leadership patterns of the businessman, insofar as his participation in community affairs is concerned, are compensatory in nature, in that "strategies of independence" (Bendix, 1956) which present-day industrial workers have a chance to develop within their firm may be thought by him to be counterbalanced in some measure by his activity outside the firm? Phrasing it differently, if authority is increasingly collectively exercised, if management has become an expression of many wills rather than one, might not the executive see in participating in certain types of community affairs the chance to recoup some of his power and authority losses, or a means of re-enforcing his position in the group decision-making process?

Can certain types of community participation (for example, serving on the board of a hospital) be viewed as representing an escape from the demands of the firm, in the individual psyche versus organization needs framework? (See Argyris, 1957.) That is, is such participation diversion or "play," unencumbered by feelings of responsibility to the community or that such behavior has any sort of "payoff" for the firm? Or do certain types of participation in community affairs by an executive denote a concern on his part for conformity? Is it true, as we are led to believe by some of the writings of Whyte (1956),

Riesman (1950), and others, that our culture has shifted from a success-oriented one, where the watchwords have been productivity, industriousness, and achievement, to an adjustment-oriented one, where the emphasis is on fitting in with the group? Is executive behavior in the community-affairs area a reflection of such a desire to conform? Is it inappropriate to carry competitive practices over into the community arena? Is competition in civic affairs, in contrast to the firm, taboo?

These questions are far-ranging and suggest a great many approaches which might be taken in the study of the business executive and his role in urban affairs. By analysis of executive opinions and behavior, the present study seeks to establish under what conditions, at what level, and to what degree the business executive is an active participant in civic affairs in Crescent cities. Theoretical implications of the findings, especially those that shed light on the kinds of questions raised above, are alluded to in the course of this research report. However, the task of systematically examining the results in a theoretical framework is not undertaken here.

Investigations of this kind have import for policy makers in urban affairs. They give insights into the way in which leaders from the business community approach civic-affairs tasks. Furthermore, knowledge of the relationships of the community-participation patterns of top business executives to their personal and job characteristics, the characteristics of the companies in which they work, and the characteristics of the communities in which the firms are situated provide policy makers with some notion of who in the business community are potential sources of strength in civic affairs and under what conditions they are likely to participate.

The Research Context

As a prefatory note, it is well to recall the self-image with which the executive tends to approach the variety of roles he plays and to take note of the interdependence between industry and community. The executive's role in urban affairs must be seen in the context of all roles he plays—producer, promoter and planner, risk reducer, cost reducer, leader of a social group, preserver of custom and "the company," community leader, institution builder (Noland and Bakke, 1949, pp. 129–138), and propagator of free enterprise.

As a *producer*, the executive must associate with himself those who have productive competence; as a *planner and promoter*, he must hire people who not only have technical skill but give evidence of being likely to remain with him, of being adaptable to new tasks, of having the capacity for growth, of being the possessors of those personal attributes which will make them want to undertake tasks with enthusiasm and energy. As a *risk reducer*, the executive sees himself as the guardian of the stockholders' money, a task that calls on him to minimize risks at every turn. In doing this he focuses on employing workers he can count on in terms of health, devotion to job and company, and over-all attitudes of service and integrity. As a *cost reducer*, the executive is profit-minded; his interest here lies in obtaining the greatest productive and teamwork capacity for wages which going standards demand.

As *leader of a social group* or an organization of human beings, the executive displays a multitude of preferences having to do with worker attributes and sources of labor supply. He emphasizes social alikeness in his people; he sees that whether one of his group will be labeled an "in-grouper" or "out-grouper" will depend in substantial measure on similarity of attitudes between him and his associates regarding such phenomena as religious and political tendencies, place of residence, citizenship, nationality, and education. He seeks new employees by consulting his own people—supervisors and workers; he has a certain distrust of institutionalized sources of labor, such as employment agencies and newspaper advertising, and even of educational institutions for certain types of workers. As a *preserver of custom and "the company,"* the top executive proves himself to be highly ethnocentric. The pattern his company has followed in getting to its present position is the best in most respects or his company would not have experienced such a measure of success. His employees must believe this too, so they are to come by it naturally because they are the "right kind of people" (hence the emphasis on hiring with care), or they are to be made into this kind of people through fair treatment and effective symbolization (for example, company banners, insignia, slogans, programs, campaigns, etc.).

These first six of the nine roles appear to be predominantly internal in nature, yet their possible extension outside the plant into the community needs to be examined. The remaining three—community leader, institution builder, and propagator of free enterprise—are substantially external, but, conceivably, have an internal quality stemming from their dependence upon the first six roles.

As a *community leader*, the executive is extending his role as leader of a social group inside the plant into the larger community. In so many ways, as the community goes, so goes the plant. Social conflict in the community, for example, can be as damaging to the firm as social conflict within the work plant, and the executive realizes it. This is not to say, of course, that the executive is inclined to put his community-leadership role ahead of his enterprise-leadership role. However, the executive's concern for his part in community life is real, and likely constitutes a major segment of his self-definition of importance. As an *institution builder*, the executive equates his stature in the community to the stature of the institution he has built. The company he heads he regards as predominantly the work of his hands, and he wants it to be respected. To have others identify him with a good institution puts him far along a respect-laden path. As a *propagator of free enterprise*, he identifies the progress of his company and, in turn, his own progress with the individual, competitive economic system which, in his mind, has characterized American life from the beginning. Rugged individualism inheres in such a system, he reasons, so he gathers about him people who believe in such a concept and who, through hard but meritorious effort, will strive to reach the top in much the same fashion as he has striven.

The interdependence of an industrial plant and the community in which it is located is so well documented in the literature and so broadly experienced as nearly to constitute a sociological truism (Miller and Form, 1951, Chapter XXI). The areas of community-industry interdependence are many. To touch on a few, it may be noted that the location of an industrial plant is often affected by the ecology of the community and the action of its citizens relative to whether and where they want it. In another sense, the plant site is a function of community living patterns. Given a plant site, informal work organization within the plant impinges on community affairs, but at the same time a community has an informal organization which helps determine consumer and employee response to company performance. The economic well-being of the community may be related to the growth of one or more firms and at the same time the economic success of a plant can hinge on community good will.

In a formal governmental sense, the community and the industrial concern can interact in other ways and engage in a multitude of reciprocal relationships. The family structure involves still another basis of viewing industry-community relationships. It gives the community a certain type of work force which may, in turn, determine the nature of the industry that locates there. The church and comparable institutions help set the stage for a certain type of labor-management relationship. While industrial plant supervision, rules and regulations, as well as over-all employment policy, must thus conform in some measure to the culture patterns extant, it is also possible that some firms function more autonomously in the urban milieu, and the plant supervisory hierarchy dovetails with the community power structure. In these many areas of industry-community interdependence—community ecology, community living patterns, technological change, plant and community power structure, informal organization in both the plant and community, company economic survival, community good will, municipal government action, family structure in the community, religious and other institutional behaviors, and culture patterns—things get done and changes come about. The specifics of the part top business executives play in all this begs for examination.

The Research Model

The *dependent variable* in the study is executive behavior. It consists of two parts: membership in voluntary associations, and participation in community affairs. To get at the first of these two, interviewees were asked to provide a complete list of organizations and associations to which they belonged during the past five years or during the time they had lived in the community if it happened to be less than five years. Officerships in associations were noted. From the data on associational memberships a four-point scale measuring "degree of participation" was derived. Five types of associations were used: social (e.g., the country club); religion (e.g., Layman's League; Superintendent of Sunday School); job (e.g., Engineers' Club; Manufacturers' Association); community building (e.g., Chamber of Commerce); and societal welfare (e.g., Red Cross).

To measure participation in community affairs, thirty items, based on preliminary investigation of typical activities in the four cities studied, were submitted to the interviewees. These thirty items were grouped into seven categories: economic, community betterment, livability, education, political, philanthropy, and desegregation. Participation was measured on four levels: "active, open"; "open, through 'lieutenants' "; "behind-the-scenes informal"; and "not at all." The "not at all" response was further divided into "no opportunity," "no time," "just didn't," "none of my business," and "no interest." From the responses, a participation score for each executive on each activity was obtained.

The *intervening variable* is executive attitudes and opinions. Attitude and opinion areas found to be sufficiently related to the dependent variable to be included in the analysis are: opinions about the adequacy of selected city characteristics; bases for choosing activities in a community in which to participate (e.g., time, interest); participation in community affairs expected of top executives by type of firm (e.g., commercial bank, laundry, trucking company); participation in community affairs expected of top executives by characteristics of the firm (e.g., size, type of ownership, locus of consumption of product); attitudes toward holding public office; and opinions regarding the benefits accruing to a firm from its top executive's participation in community affairs and from its gifts to philanthropy. There were other attitude and opinion areas in which data were collected which proved to be unproductive of anything resembling significant association with the dependent variable.

The three *independent variables* are: executive characteristics (e.g., age, education, rate of advancement within the company, wife's patterns of participation in community affairs); company characteristics (e.g., size, growth picture, unionization); and community characteristics (e.g., size, growth picture, degree of business diversification). Complete lists of these will unfold as this chapter progresses.

To measure the association of the dependent variable with the intervening variable and the three independent variables, a score for each item was devised. Thus, each interviewee has a score on each of the five types of associational membership and on each type of community activity in which he participated; he also has a score for each attitude and opinion item (e.g., "opinion of quality of governmental management" ranges along a seven-point scale; "liberal-conservative" position is broken into seven parts). Each characteristic of the firm whose top executive was interviewed is categorized, and, though relatively rough, these categorizations were considered adequate for the level of community analysis being employed. Chi-square was used to determine the presence of significant relationships between the various components of the independent variable and the numerous items which made up the intervening variable and the independent variables. The .05 level of significance was used throughout. Certain other ways of relating scores were used also, especially where chi-square was not significant at the .05 level but came close to it, so that what appeared to be productive results could meaningfully be obtained by pointing up "trends" and "consistency of pattern" among related items.

A feature of the analysis scheme was the comparison throughout of the interviewees who were "leaders" with those who were "nonleaders." Leaders were determined by asking all interviewees this question: "Who are the people who really get things done in your city—whose help and/or sponsorship you would want to have if you were to try to carry out some project in your community? Write them in order of influence." This procedure gave a "nucleus" of leaders ranging in size from 25 to 40 in each of the four cities covered. An averaging of ranks, followed by appropriate iterative procedures, gave a final list of 70 leaders, distributed as follows among the four cities: Burlington, 16; Charlotte, 21; High Point, 18; and Winston-Salem, 15. Of these, 51 were interviewed, and they turned out to be distributed as follows: Burlington, 13; Charlotte, 16; High Point, 10; and Winston-Salem, 12.

The Data and the Sample

Data on four of the five variables were collected by interview: executive behavior, executive attitudes and opinions, executive characteristics, and characteristics of the firm. From appropriate other sources came the data on the characteristics of the community. There were 105 distinct interview items in all. Three hundred and six company heads were contacted; 298 definite appointments for interviews were arranged; 297 interviews were completed, of which 290 were usable.

Business firms were sampled rather than individuals; then the heads of these firms were interviewed, 278 in all. Twelve professional people were interviewed also. The primary bases for the selection of firms were (1) size in terms of number of employees and (2) type of product. One hundred and sixty-nine of the 278 firms employed more than 100 people and constituted approximately 70 per cent of the total number of firms in this size category in the four cities. The remaining firms, 109 in all, employed less than 100 workers and constituted approximately 2 per cent of the total number of such firms in the cities covered. One hundred and twenty-eight of the executives were from industrial firms, 83 from commercial organizations, 67 from service businesses, and 12 were professional people. On all items of the study on which the collection of data made sense for professionals as well as executives, the two groups were so nearly identical in behavior as to justify their being combined into one, totaling 290.

Practically all of the interviews were held during the summers of 1958 and 1959. They ranged from fifty minutes to four and one-half hours. Data processing—computation of distributions, percentages, and chi-square—was done on UNIVAC 1105.

Findings

Results of the investigations are presented first in the framework of opinions and preferences of executives in regard to participation in community affairs and then in terms of executive behavior and selected variables of participation.

Opinions on Executive Participation in Community Affairs

The attitudinal aspect of the investigation seeks to get at considerations of this kind: What do executives consider to be legitimate activities in community affairs in which to devote their time and effort? What are the activities they feel they are entitled to shy away from or participate in minimally? In short, what do executives expect of themselves and of one another relative to participation in community affairs? Answers to these questions are sought by examining executive opinion on the extent to which selected community characteristics, firm characteristics, and their own executive biases prompt participation in community affairs. Also considered are executive opinions as to the benefits accruing to their firms from their participation in local affairs and from their financial contributions to community philanthropic activities. Finally, opinions on their participation in local affairs on a committee level, as an officer of a voluntary organization, and on a political office basis are contrasted.

ADEQUACY OF SELECTED CITY CHARACTERISTICS. Interviewees were asked to give their opinion of the adequacy of each of eight city characteristics (Table 8-1). In general, executives rated their cities lower as a "cultural center" than on any of the other seven. This was true of both leaders and nonleaders, but despite its low ranking overall, it was one of the better items in differentiating between these two

Table 8-1. Executive Opinion of Adequacy of Selected Community Characteristics

	RANK OF CHARACTERISTIC: LEADERS VERSUS NONLEADERS				
	LEADERS' RANKING	NONLEADERS' RANKING	COMBINED RANKING	RANKING BY LEADER-NONLEADER DIFFERENCE (ACTUAL)	RANKING BY LEADER-NONLEADER DIFFERENCE (RELATIVE)[a]
Governmental management	7	7	7	5	6
City as a cultural center	8	8	8	$2\frac{1}{2}$	4
Educational system	5	3	4	7	7
Civic-mindedness	2	2	2	4	3
Professional services	1	1	1	8	8
Economic base	4	5	5	6	5
Attractiveness	6	6	6	1	1
Progressiveness	3	4	3	$2\frac{1}{2}$	2

[a] Weighted using leaders' estimate of importance as base

categories of interviewees. Executives were quite critical of the quality of "governmental management" in their respective cities. This item ranked seventh among the eight in "adequacy," with leaders and nonleaders in substantial agreement. "Attractiveness" consistently fell in sixth place in the adequacy ratings. However, it was the best of all items in differentiating between leaders and nonleaders.

At the other end of the continuum, "professional services" as a city characteristic consistently ranked the highest of all eight, but it was of no value whatsoever in differentiating between leaders and nonleaders. The "civic-mindedness" item consistently ranked second in adequacy. In general, leaders attributed a higher degree of civic-mindedness to the people of their respective cities than did the nonleaders.

In summary, professional services, civic-mindedness, and progressiveness of the cities were adjudged to be good by the executives interviewed; on the other hand, attractiveness, governmental management, and the city as a cultural center were rated poor. This disparagement of the last three characteristics seems to bespeak relatively high pessimism regarding the political and esthetic adequacy of the cities involved. Perhaps the downgrading of these items and the high evaluation given civic-mindedness and progressiveness appear to be contradictory. Yet might it not be true that the executive's definition of the last two has a large "economic orientation" component: perhaps it is sufficiently palatable to the head of a business firm to operate in a city which appears to promise at least adequate economic growth even though its over-all attractiveness in other realms leaves much to be desired.

The best items in the over-all picture for differentiating between leaders and nonleaders were attractiveness, progressiveness, adequacy of city as a cultural center, and civic-mindedness. In general, leaders ranked their cities higher on these items than did nonleaders.

OPINIONS BY CHARACTERISTICS OF FIRM. Ten company characteristics were used as criteria for determining the extent of participation in community affairs that should be expected of top executives (Table 8-2). Of these, "size of firm in terms of number of employees" was rated the most important. This was true of both leaders and nonleaders, but the former tended to feel it to be less important than did the latter. Since there were relatively more leaders from large companies than from small companies, the dynamics of this response picture appear to run as follows: executives in small companies felt that executives in large companies should participate more than they; executives

Table 8-2. Executive Opinion on Importance of Selected Characteristics of Firm as Determinants of Extent Top Executive Should Be Expected to Participate in Community Affairs

	RANK OF CHARACTERISTIC: LEADERS VERSUS NONLEADERS				
CHARACTERISTIC OF FIRM	LEADERS' RANKING	NONLEADERS' RANKING	COMBINED RANKING	RANKING BY LEADER-NONLEADER DIFFERENCE (ACTUAL)	RANKING BY LEADER-NONLEADER DIFFERENCE (RELATIVE)[a]
Size (number of employees)	1	1	1	$2\frac{1}{2}$	1
Size (capital investment)	4	$3\frac{1}{2}$	4	$2\frac{1}{2}$	3
Age	8	6	$6\frac{1}{2}$	1	2
Type of ownership	7	8	8	7	7
Origin (native vs. in-migrant)	5	7	$6\frac{1}{2}$	9	9
Locus of consumption of product	6	5	5	4	4
Distance of firm from center of city	9	10	10	8	8
Past history of participation	10	9	9	$5\frac{1}{2}$	6
Executive ability	2	$3\frac{1}{2}$	$2\frac{1}{2}$	10	10
Executive willingness	3	2	$2\frac{1}{2}$	$5\frac{1}{2}$	5

[a] Weighted using leaders' estimate of importance as base.

in large companies did not regard their size as a major reason for participating more than executives in small companies.

The executive's ability to participate in community affairs tied for second place in over-all importance, yet the leader-nonleader difference over-all was negligible and earned for the item last place in differentiating ability. In the two larger cities leaders labeled this criterion of less importance than did the nonleaders; in the two smaller cities leaders did the opposite. There appeared to be little doubt on the part of the leaders concerning their ability to lead (despite some expressions of modesty), so this relatively high level of confidence spilled over into their convictions regarding the importance of executive ability when a firm is to be evaluated on community participation. Likewise, nonleaders often expressed the opinion that a major reason for their failure to participate more in community affairs was their relative ineptness at the leadership role, hence their inclination to assign even higher importance to leadership ability than did the leaders.

The executive's willingness to participate in community affairs tied with executive ability to participate in community affairs for second place in over-all importance. It was fifth in leader-nonleader differentiating ability. Leaders in the two smaller cities rated it more important than did nonleaders; and in the two larger cities the picture was sufficiently reversed to give the over-all nod (all cities) to the nonleaders as the higher raters of the item. In general, there appeared to be the sentiment that there is, and should be, a one-to-one correspondence between ability to participate and willingness to participate. Responses to this item and the one regarding ability were so similar and, over-all, ranked sufficiently high as to lend support to this claim: certain company characteristics should predispose executives to participate in community affairs as a kind of obligation, but, in the final analysis, whether executives participate or not depends upon their having sufficient confidence in their ability to participate; then willingness to participate and subsequent actual participation follow a positive decision regarding ability.

At the other end of the continuum, distance of firm from center of city ranked lowest in over-all importance. The two larger cities tended to fall one way and the two smaller cities the other way, with the leaders in the former group rating this characteristic less important than the nonleaders, while the reverse was true in the two smaller cities. The over-all tally was practically even, shaded a bit in the direction of leaders considering the characteristic more important than did the nonleaders. The difference was by no means significant. The most important variable here may be city size: in the smaller city, the downtown area is more easily defined and recognized; in the larger city, distance from the center could be rather meaningless in this context, for a branch of a commercial bank, for example, may be located on the periphery but its identification is probably still "downtown." This item was eighth in its ability to differentiate between leaders and nonleaders.

Past history of firm's participation in community affairs ranked next to lowest in importance over-all, and about average in differentiating ability. In three of the four cities, leaders rated it less important than did nonleaders. The actual and the ideal of this characteristic made it confusing: interviewees puzzled over the notion that what a firm has done in the past often sets the pattern of expectations for the present and future, yet, they argued, this should not be the case. The built-in ambiguity in this item doubtlessly helped make it of little utility.

In summary, when business executives as a group were asked to rank company characteristics according to their importance as factors affecting participation of top executives in urban affairs, the three top factors were size of firm (measured by number of employees), executive ability, and executive willingness to participate. Of less importance were such factors as size of the firm's capital investment, locus of consumption of the firm's products, age of firm, and whether the company is of native origin or not. Of least importance were these: how widely held the ownership was, past history of company participation, and the nearness of the firm's location to the center of the city.

Differentiation between leader and nonleader responses was most pronounced for size of firm measured by both number of employees and capital investment, age of firm, and the locus of consumption of product. In other words, leaders more consistently cited these items than nonleaders.

PARTICIPATION IN COMMUNITY AFFAIRS EXPECTED OF TOP EXECUTIVES, BY TYPE OF FIRM. This question in the interview was aimed at answering three questions: (1) Do business executives differentiate among the three major types of business—industrial, commercial, and service—with respect to what they expect of their top executives by way of community participation? (2) Does what is expected of top business executives by specific company type (e.g., commercial bank) agree with what is expected of top business executives by company characteristics (e.g., size in terms of number of employees)? (3) To what extent do expectations of executives by company type agree with actual executive participation?

A list of thirteen different types of firm, representing all three categories of industrial, commercial, and service, was presented to the interviewee so that he could decide, using a three-point scale, the degree of participation he had the right to expect of the head of the firm in each case. The commercial bank was adjudged to be by far the one among the thirteen which should participate most heavily in community affairs. Next, but a poor second, came the privately owned power company, followed rather closely by the investment banking house and the privately owned bus company. In the middle range fell, in order of degree of expectation, the hotel, the retail clothing store, the manufacturer of ice cream, and the manufacturer of machine tools. The least was expected of the trucking company, next to the least of the theater, with the drug store, the laundry, and the dry goods store following in that order. Intercity comparisons on these items revealed a lack of clear-cut patterning.

Responses indicated that business executives do not differentiate among the three major types of business—industrial, commercial, and service—as such: when the thirteen specific types were grouped into these three categories, there were no significant differences in expectations. Furthermore, inconsistencies among cities appeared to be further evidence of a lack of such differentiation by business category. Intercity differences appeared to be a function of extent of presence of firm type and its history of participation.

On the other hand, the item was useful in that it served to verify, at least in some measure, what executives had said regarding their expectations of firms by characteristics of those firms. For instance, the commercial bank, the privately owned power company, the privately owned bus company (the last two were the same company in some cases), and the investment banking house, the four of which most was expected relative to top executive participation in community affairs, were on the average larger, both in terms of number of employees and capital investment, and on the average older than the lowest ranking types of company, dry goods store, laundry, drug store, theater, and trucking company. A big factor in this opinion seemed to be the belief that executives in the larger and older types of firm had always participated in community affairs, so they had had enough practice to make them both capable and willing.

An exception to this picture of consistency between expectations by firm characteristics and expectations by specific firm type appears to be found in the case of the locus of consumption of product. Its fifth place among ten items makes it at least average in importance as a determinant of top executive participation in community affairs. This, then, raises the question: Which type of firm is regarded as having a product consumed predominantly locally, the dry goods store, the laundry, the drug store, and the theater, all of which ranked low in expectations, or the commercial bank, the investment banking house, the privately owned power company, and the privately owned bus company, all of which ranked high in expectations? If we are to insist on consistency between expectations by firm characteristics and firm type, it appears that the latter group is being considered to be that which has the more nearly locally consumed product. A better conclusion seems to be, however, that this item of locus of consumption of product is a "nonconformist," that it was ill-defined in the minds of the interviewees, and that, all in all, it may have had a leveling effect on the total picture (that is, may have tended to reduce the expectations of the high ranking firm types and raise the expectations of the low ranking firm types). Since it was only one of ten items and of little better than average importance at that, its effect in any direction was not likely a telling one.

With regard to the third and last of the three questions, the extent to which expectations agreed with actual behavior of executives, there appears to be a distinct positive relationship. For example, executives in laundries and dry goods stores were lower in participation (with some notable exceptions) than executives in commercial banks and power companies. So it seems that heads of firms who participate heavily create a picture of heavy expectations of them. Interviewees obviously had the difficulty of differentiating between those who have been participating heavily and those who should participate heavily: the two groups overlapped substantially.

As a differentiator between leaders and nonleaders, this item was of little use. With only two firm types—privately owned bus company and trucking company—were leader-nonleader differences of any size. Furthermore, even these two differences were not large and conceivably were accidental. Certainly accounting for them would call for exploration of other variables.

CRITERIA USED BY EXECUTIVES IN DETERMINING EXTENT AND TYPE OF PARTICIPATION IN COMMUNITY AFFAIRS. The basic question here was: Can leaders be separated from nonleaders on the basis of the criteria they use for deciding on their participation patterns in community

Table 8-3. Executives' Criteria for Decision to Participate in Community Affairs

RANK OF CRITERION: LEADERS VERSUS NONLEADERS

PARTICIPATION CRITERION	LEADERS' RANKING	NONLEADERS' RANKING	COMBINED RANKING	RANKING BY LEADER-NONLEADER DIFFERENCE (ACTUAL)	RANKING BY LEADER-NONLEADER DIFFERENCE (RELATIVE) [a]
Time	5	4	4	2	1
Personal interest	2	2	2	5	11
Good of company	4	6	6	6	7
Personal importance	8	7	7	7	4
Civic importance	3	3	3	3	8
Civic obligation	9	9	9	$10\frac{1}{2}$	9
Ability of executive	7	5	5	4	2
Uniqueness of executive's situation	$10\frac{1}{2}$	11	11	9	3
Pressures exerted	$10\frac{1}{2}$	10	10	$10\frac{1}{2}$	5
Importance of person asking executive to participate	1	1	1	1	6
Executive's obligation to person asking him to participate	6	8	8	8	10

[a] Weighted using extent of leader choice of item as base.

affairs? For example, is interest a more important criterion for leaders than for nonleaders? Is time a more important criterion for nonleaders than for leaders? To get at this, interviewees were asked to list the criteria they used for making such decisions and to rank them in order of importance. Eleven such reasons were listed sufficiently often to be included in the analysis (Table 8-3).

Of the criteria receiving most attention, more than one-half the leaders and two-thirds of the nonleaders listed "importance of person asking me" as an important criterion for deciding to participate in community affairs. Consequently, this item turned out to be, for both leaders and nonleaders, the most important of the eleven participation criteria studied (as measured by per cent choosing it—no measure of intensity was used). Personal interest came next in frequency of choice, followed by civic importance in third place. Time was a poor fourth.

Among the criteria receiving least attention was uniqueness of executive's situation, which was regarded as being of negligible importance in making decisions as to whether or not to participate in community affairs. Close behind, as relatively unimportant criteria, came pressure exerted by other people, civic obligation, executive's obligation to person asking him, and importance of an activity in a personal sense. It is interesting to note here that interviewees differentiated between civic importance, one of the higher rating criteria, and civic obligation. The difference is one of being drawn into or attracted to a community activity because of its importance, not of being pushed into it by impingement of obligation. Further evidence of this resistance to obligation appears in the low rating of "obligation to person asking me"; "importance of person asking me" rated high, but "obligation to person asking me" was in eighth position over-all.

It may be of interest to note that good of company, often considered to be an important motivation of executives in their participation in community affairs, rated sixth in over-all importance and seventh as a leader-nonleader differentiator. One hypothesis of the study was that executives would participate in those community affairs which they adjudged to be most relevant to the needs of their companies. Consequently, chi-square was used to explore the relationship between the two variables in each of the following:

1. Participation in airport improvement *against* importance to firm of airport improvement.
2. Participation in provision of adequate water supply *against* firm's needs for water.
3. Participation in fire protection activity *against* the importance to firm of fire protection by the city.
4. Participation in highway location *against* the firm's needs for public transportation facilities for its employees.
5. Participation in traffic control activity *against* the firm's concern with changes in street patterns and traffic handling.
6. Participation in zoning activity *against* the importance to the firm's operation of planning and zoning.
7. Participation in police protection activity *against* importance of city police protection for the firm's operation.
8. Participation in stream pollution elimination *against* importance of sewage disposal for firm's operation.

With the exception of the very first one of these items, that having to do with airport, there were no significant relationships, which seemed to indicate that the primary bases for participating in certain types of community affairs are not those having to do with the executive's concern for the needs of his company or the belief that such needs will be served best by such activity.

Among the best differentiating criteria for leaders versus nonleaders were time and ability. While only fourth in over-all attention, time was the best of all eleven criteria for separating leaders from nonleaders. To leaders time was not as important a consideration as it was to nonleaders. Conceivably this relationship is a function of size of company. (There were relatively more leaders than nonleaders in large companies.) But size of company, in turn, is related to division of labor and task specialization: leaders can find time for community affairs more easily than nonleaders because they are heads of large companies whose type of organization permits such finding of time. Ability of executive to participate, while of only average importance over-all, is second in differentiating usefulness. As was revealed above, nonleaders emphasized ability more than did leaders.

The list of criteria which were poorest in differentiating between leaders and nonleaders is variable according to the city being examined, but there were some criteria on which agreement was more characteristic than disagreement between the leaders and nonleaders. There was such close agreement between leaders and nonleaders on the importance of personal interest as a participation criterion (it ranked in second place over-all) that it was a useless differentiating item. The same was true of civic importance—it ranked third in over-all importance but was far down in eighth place as a leader-nonleader differentiator.

In short, it appears that both leaders and nonleaders find "importance of person asking me," personal interest, civic importance, time, and ability the most important criteria for deciding on community participation, in that order. Of these five, time and ability are relatively more important considerations for the nonleader than for the leader and rank high as items for separating the one category from the other. Each of the items, personal interest, executive's obligation to person asking him, civic obligation, and civic importance, was regarded so similarly by leaders and nonleaders as to make it a poor differentiator. "Importance of person asking me," the top ranking item in over-all importance for both leaders and nonleaders, is no better than average when it comes to the job of separating one group of interviewees from the other: it ranked no better than sixth in relative differentiating power.

EXECUTIVE OPINION REGARDING BENEFITS ACCRUING TO THEIR FIRMS FROM THEIR PARTICIPATION IN COMMUNITY AFFAIRS. Seemingly an inexplicable paradox, in three of the four cities leaders were less convinced than nonleaders of the merits of participating in community affairs. In fact, chi-square measures of the relation between this item and the five associational membership areas and the seven activity areas gave further evidence that participation in community affairs in general was executive behavior "without their corporate heart in it." Of these twelve measures of relationship, eight were significant at the .05 level or better, and six of the eight were negative. In the associational membership areas of religion ($P = .001$), job ($P = .05$), and societal welfare ($P = .05$), the most active participators were the most skeptical regarding benefits to their firms resulting from participation. In the activity areas of economic ($P = .001$), community betterment ($P = .01$), and political ($P = .05$), the most active interviewees were the least optimistic about how much they were helping their firms by such activity. There were two significant positive associations between extent of community participation and belief in the benefits to firm resulting from such participation: those executives who ranked high in the social associational membership areas were strong believers in the rewards of such activity ($P = .01$), and those who were most active in educational activity were convinced of the merits of such participation relative to the good befalling their firms as a result of it ($P = .01$). It would seem, therefore, that executives associate participation in social and educational affairs with their job of advancing their own companies, but find reasons other than company betterment for other types of participation.

Participation in the other ten areas apparently was regarded by executives as having no or, at best, little relevance to promoting company development; in fact, the significant negative relationships seem to indicate that possibly most executive participation in community affairs is motivated by interest in self or community per se, and that executives often entertain substantial skepticism relative to the contribution their community participation makes to their firms. This is not to claim, or even imply, that executives feel that their participation has a negative effect on the welfare of their companies (except, of course, in those cases where community participation, overdone, results in a debilitating neglect of company assignment); rather, it is to say that the more active executives are the more skeptical they are that their companies will benefit from such activity—yet such skepticism does not seem to deter them. Doubtless it is a matter of perspective: "The more I participate in community affairs," the leader often said, "the more informed and realistic I become relative to the payoff limitations for my company such participation has."

EXECUTIVE OPINION REGARDING BENEFITS ACCRUING TO A FIRM FROM ITS GIFTS TO PHILANTHROPY. Here the picture differs sharply from that found in the case discussed immediately above, benefits to firm from executive participation in community affairs. In three of the four cities leaders were more willing than nonleaders to claim that gifts to philanthropy benefit their firms. The thinking here seemed to be that gifts to philanthropy are tangible and their contribution can be measured, and that participation of executives is taken for granted, is far less tangible, and is hard to measure.

This item, gifts to philanthropy, was not as closely associated with associational membership and activity areas as was executive participation. However, three of the twelve participation areas gave chi-square measures that were significant at the .05 level or better. In general, those who were the strongest believers that contributions to philanthropy promoted the firm making them were also the most active executives in political activities ($P = .05$), religious associations ($P = .02$), and in social clubs ($P = .01$).

EXECUTIVE ORIENTATION TO POLITICAL PARTICIPATION: ATTITUDES TOWARD HOLDING PUBLIC OFFICE. Examination of executives' attitudes toward political activity consisted of two parts. First interviewees were asked to rank in order of desirability the following: (1) participation in community affairs as a rank-and-file member of a committee or organization designed specifically to promote and carry out some activity; (2) participation in community affairs as an officer in a voluntary association; and (3) holding political office. Of the 202 of the 290 interviewees who were willing to make one of these choices in clear-cut preference to the other two, nearly one-half of them (99) preferred to serve their community as an officer in a voluntary association. The other two choices turned out to be of about equal popularity: 47 voted for rank-and-file participation, and 56 preferred to hold political office. Thus the story is one of only a little more willingness, if any, by leaders than by nonleaders to hold political office (chi-square computation gave $.10 < P < .20$).

Second, executives were asked to compare the distastefulness of controversy arising in political office with that in other types of activity, such as in the church or charitable organizations. Among leaders who were willing to commit themselves on this item, 68.6 per cent (24 of 35) were not averse to any kind of controversy: they liked a good fight. The corresponding figure for nonleaders was 58.9 per cent (112 of 190). Three of the 35 leaders responding to this item (8.6 per cent) found all kinds of controversy distasteful, while 31.6 per cent (60 of the 190) of the nonleaders providing replies were of that sentiment. One-third (6 of 18) of the executives who found public office controversy distasteful but other types of controversy not were leaders. However, 25 per cent (2 of 8) of the executives who found public office controversy not distasteful but did find other types of controversy so were leaders. In short, it appears that leaders in general resist controversy less than do nonleaders, but the resistance of the former group to the political office type of controversy is as great as, and possibly greater than, that of nonleaders.

Of the twelve relationships between this item, distastefulness of different types of controversy, and the associational membership and activity area variables, seven were significant at the .05 level or better. Leaders in the community-building type of associational membership, and in the community-betterment, political, and philanthropy activity areas did not resist public office as much as nonleaders. However, in the job and societal-welfare types of associational membership, and in the economic type of activity area, the relationship was the reverse: leaders here appeared to dislike more than nonleaders the holding of public office. The rationale here seems to be that leaders in the first four areas have had the chance to realize (or at least believe) that success in these endeavors has a political component: the political activity aspect is obvious; community building, community betterment, and philanthropy—all comprising community welfare—are seen to depend on the machinations of a community political structure. By contrast, leaders who are specifically job-oriented as to associational memberships do not feel that political participation will have a payoff; social club membership and political activity are perhaps more nearly substitutes for one another than complements to each other (that is, if one is active in one area he does not choose to be active in the other); and business activity, like job membership, represents the type of orientation that finds no time for active politicking.

Executive Behavior and Participation in Community Affairs

In this second aspect of the investigation, the participation patterns of executives are examined in the framework of selected executive, firm, and community characteristics. The emphasis thus shifts from attitudes and opinions to the actual behavior of business executives.

EXECUTIVE CHARACTERISTICS. With minor exceptions, leaders compared with nonleaders were younger, better educated (as measured by amount of formal schooling), had been in their jobs a shorter length of time, had more often spent all their executive life in the present company (that is, a one-company man), were more conservative, were more Democratic in political affiliation or identification, and had wives who were more active in community affairs. Leader age and education characteristics, and particularly their company career patterns, varied noticeably among the four cities studied.

In general, wives of leaders were more active than wives of nonleaders in all five associational memberships. This was significantly true in the social category and substantially true in societal welfare and community building. However, the participation of wives in religion and job-related associations was nondifferentiating: the participation of wives of leaders was slightly greater than that of wives of nonleaders in these two areas, but the differences were negligible.

Of the 281 executives who were willing to place themselves on a 7-point Liberal-Conservative scale (they were asked to use their own definition of the two terms), 35.9 per cent claimed to be in the middle position (fourth from either end), 39.9 per cent were conservative (right of center—positions 1 through 3 from the right), and 24.2 per cent were liberal (left of center—positions 1 through 3 from the left). In the over-all picture, leaders were more conservative than nonleaders.

With respect to political affiliation or preference, leaders were more Democratic than were nonleaders. The question used here contained four categories: 100 per cent Democratic (i.e., always registered Democratic and always voted Democratic); selective Democratic (i.e., registered Democratic but sometimes voted Republican); selective Republican (i.e., registered Republican but sometimes voted Democratic); and 100 per cent Republican (i.e., always registered as Republican and voted for Republican candidates only). By such a categorization, there was a high incidence of selective Democratic. Of the 273 executives who responded to this item, 73.6 per cent fell into this category, 12.8 per cent were 100 per cent Democratic, 8.8 per cent were selective Republican, and 4.8 per cent were 100 per cent Republican.

Comments received in this connection indicate that among business executives, and even among the top leaders, questions are being raised about the appropriateness of blind adherence to the Democratic party line; "kicking over the traces" is much in evidence. The chances of developing an effective two-party system in the area represented by these four cities appear good. It seems likely that, as present leaders are succeeded, the business segment of the political picture may become substantially less Democratic. There is little evidence, however, that these political rebels are inclined toward seeking political office themselves, so the trend may never develop.

This item, political affiliation or preference, was a good predictor of social and community building associational memberships (*P* in both cases was .001) and of political activity. The 100 per cent Democrat was more likely than those of weaker Democratic persuasion to pick these three areas for heavy concentration.

CHARACTERISTICS OF FIRM. In all four cities, leaders came more from large companies than from small companies. Size of company was highly associated with executive participation in social associational memberships ($P = .01$) and economic activity ($P = .01$). In other words, executives in the large companies were more given to social participation and in activities of an economic development nature than were executives in small companies.

More executives in large companies than in small companies were founders of their companies or members of the family of management, in contrast to having been outsiders originally. Executives in the larger firms tended to advance less rapidly than executives in the smaller firms. Executives in the larger firms did not consider holding public office quite as distasteful as did executives in the smaller firms.

Of the eleven criteria executives used for determining whether or not to participate in various community affairs (for example, time, personal interest, good of company, etc.), some were useful in differentiating between executives in large and in small companies. Time, good of company, and ability of executives were rated lower by executives in the larger firms than by executives in the smaller firms. However, interest was a substantially more important criterion to executives in the large companies than it was to their counterparts in smaller firms. Civic obligation appeared to be substantially more important to executives in middle-sized firms than to those in either small or large organizations.

On a percentage basis, there were more leaders in the older firms than in the younger firms. Age of firm was a good predictor of social-type associational memberships: executives from the older companies were more active in this area than were executives from the younger companies. The chi-square measure of association between age of company and associational membership of the job, community building, and societal welfare varieties gave a *P* of .10 in each case. Although these results were not significant at the adopted level, .05, the direction of the relationship was consistently the same throughout all three items, pointing to the likelihood that the executives of the older companies were more active than those of the younger companies in these respects. The older the firm, the more often its head was a founder or member of the family of management, the younger on the average was its head, and the less distance the head had moved to reach the top.

While tests of relationship produced no significant differences between leaders and nonleaders, if there was any association between rate of growth of company and the leadership patterns of its top executive, it appeared that there was greater likelihood that leaders would be found in the faster growing firms than in the slower growing ones. However, while this company characteristic differentiated between leaders and nonleaders poorly, it proved to be a good predictor for the job-oriented associational membership area and the political activity area. Executives in the slower growing companies were less active in these two respects than were executives in the faster growing companies.

There seemed to be no significant relationship between an executive's pattern of participation in community affairs and the locus of consumption of his firm's product. Among the four cities differences in the locus of consumption of product appeared to be a function of differences in distribution by type of business in which leaders were found. Locus of consumption of product was found to be closely related to the community-building type of associational membership: leaders in firms whose product was consumed primarily locally were high in this kind of community participation. However, the categories of buyers of product (individuals, other companies, and government) proved to have no significant relationship to any patterns of executive participation.

On a percentage basis, slightly more leaders were found in companies that were close in. The influence of commercial banks, whose heads consistently were high participators, doubtless was a telling one here. A commercial bank, and especially the office of its president, is still downtown, despite the frequent plethora of branches often quite removed spatially from the center of the city. This item, based on chi-square computations, was a good predictor of participation in economic and political activities: heads of firms located downtown were on the average heavier participators in these two areas than were heads of firms farther out.

No substantial relationship was found between a firm's use arrangement (that is, whether it owned or rented its physical plant) and the community-participation patterns of its top executive. Interestingly enough, executives in companies that own their physical plant were more active in social associational memberships than were executives in companies that rented. It seems likely that these two correlated items were each related to a third, age of firm, and possibly to others. For instance, more of the older firms than younger firms owned their property, and, as was pointed up earlier, executives of older firms were more active in associational memberships of a social nature than were executives of younger firms.

In general, site size was not significantly related to executive leadership. However, this item turned out to be a good predictor of social associational membership and political activity: executives in companies with large sites were more active in these two areas than executives in companies with small sites. Here again it would be foolhardy to claim a causal relationship: the answer likely is to be found in the possible association of other variables, to which this one was related, with executive participation.

With respect to a question on anticipated expansion, there seems to be a slight relationship in the direction of finding leaders in those companies that were anticipating expansion. This item was not a good predictor of any specific type of executive participation.

According to per cent distribution, there were more leaders in native companies than in branches or subsidiaries of national concerns. This item proved to be a fair predictor of executive participation patterns in two areas: executives in native firms were more active in political activities than were their counterparts in branches and subsidiaries. When this item was related to the eleven reasons executives gave for participating in community affairs, discussed earlier, there appeared four seemingly significant associations. Executives in branches or subsidiaries paid more attention to good of company and personal importance as bases for determining their participation than did executives in native companies. By contrast, executives in native companies gave a higher importance rating to time and ability of executive than executives in branches and subsidiaries.

Concerning type of ownership, there appeared to be a slightly better chance that leaders would be found more often in closely held companies than in widely held ones. This item had its best predictive value in the area of philanthropic activity ($P = .10$): executives in closely held companies participated more in this area than executives in widely held companies.

The percentage of leaders in unionized companies (12.7 per cent) was found to be less than the percentage of leaders in nonunionized companies (17.6 per cent). Of the 55 companies in the sample having a labor union, only 7 had heads who were leaders. However, this finding merely points to a possible relationship: chi-square computation gave a $.10 < P < .20$, a less than satisfactory level of significance. Two other items, one measuring the length of time the companies with unions had been unionized, and the other asking the executive's evaluation of his company's experience with the union, were unrelated to executive participation patterns.

Another question sought to bring out the extent to which company time was permitted employees for participation in community affairs. There was no significant difference over-all in policy and practice between companies in which leaders were found and those in which nonleaders were found. The nearest approach to statistical significance was among those companies with a policy of complete prohibition of participation during work hours: 19.1 per cent of the nonleader companies permitted no participation by any type of employee, while only 4.5 per cent of the companies in which the leaders were found fell in this category.

An item on the per cent of employees living in town, while not a good one for separating leaders from nonleaders, proved in an over-all sense to be a good predictor of participation of executives in two areas: religion ($P = .02$) and education ($P = .05$). Companies having the highest percentage of their employees living in town were those very companies whose executives participated most in religious and educational functions. The chi-square test relating this item to participation in community betterment and philanthropy gave a nearly significant P of .10 and .20, respectively.

The item relating to plans for moving to another location was not associated significantly with participation of executives in any of the associational memberships or activity areas. Nor was it useful in differentiating between leaders and nonleaders, although no leaders were found in those few companies planning to move away.

Of the 278 executives interviewed, 128 were in industrial companies, 83 in commercial firms, and 67 in service industries. Twenty-four (18.8 per cent) of the industrial executives were found to be leaders; 13 (15.7 per cent) of the commercial executives were leaders; and 8 (11.9 per cent) of the service executives were leaders. On the basis of this distribution, it would appear that industrial firms furnished a little more than their share of community leaders, while service companies furnished a little less than their share. Since it was surmised that type of product or, more meaningfully, type of company classified into the three commonly used categories of industrial, commercial, and service, might be associated with executive attitudes and actual participation in various types of community affairs, chi-square tests of the relationship of this item to several others were run. One such test of association had to do with the attitudes of executives toward the participation in community affairs that should be expected of them. Specifically, the data on executive expectations of the thirteen different kinds of business firms (for example, commercial bank, manufacturer of ice cream, laundry, etc.) grouped into the above three categories, were not related to type of firm of interviewee. The objective here was to see if heads of, say, industrial firms would expect more (or less) of the industrial firms in the list than of the commercial and service companies. No significant relationships were found. This seemed to indicate that the type of firm in terms of its product had no significant bearing on what executives expected of it by way of participation in community affairs.

A check on the above result was made by asking the interviewee the simple question: Do you see differences among industrial, commercial, and service businesses with respect to what should be expected of their top executives relative to participation in community affairs? Responses were related to type of firm represented by the interviewee. Here again no significant relationships were found.

However, when executives were examined by type of firm on criteria they used for determining whether or not they would participate in certain community affairs, some interesting relationships were found. Industrial executives were higher than executives in service and commercial firms in their consideration of ability of executive as a determinant of participation; they were lowest of all three types of executives in the attention they paid to personal importance of an assignment as a determinant of participation. Commercial firm executives were very high on personal importance of assignment, but low on interest and good of company. Executives in service companies were high on interest and good of company, but low in attention paid ability of executive.

COMMUNITY CHARACTERISTICS. Any attempt to uncover association between patterns of participation of top business executives in community affairs and characteristics of their respective communities has obvious limitations when only four cities are being studied. However, data from such a small sample point up seeming relationships (and trends as cities grow) which can serve well as educated guesses for further study.

Size of city appears to be associated with leader attitudes relative to importance of certain company characteristics in determining leadership patterns. In the larger cities, leaders considered size of company in terms of capital investment, origin of company (that is, whether native or in-migrant), locus of consumption of product, and distance of firm from center of city less important, relative to nonleaders' opinions, than did leaders in the smaller cities. Conceivably the larger the city the less important type of company becomes in the minds of leaders as a determinant of their patterns of participation in community affairs. It would appear, therefore, that the larger the city the more business executives who are leaders regard their participation in community activities a private matter for them, unencumbered by affiliation with a particular type of firm. Company characteristics as a city grows become more blurred in their minds: the leader should be a leader, with accompanying expectations, because he is a certain type of person, not because his firm has a great amount of capital invested, sprang up in that city, has its product consumed there, or is located donwtown.

Apparently leaders in the smaller cities were somewhat more self-conscious than their counterparts in the larger cities relative to their ability to participate and the liability of failure. Leaders in the smaller cities considered executive ability a substantially more important determinant of amount of participation in community affairs than did leaders in the larger cities. In the smaller cities there appeared to be the belief that since there were fewer participants, each was under closer scrutiny from a public so near to him. In the larger cities, leaders seemed to take their leadership qualifications for granted: the fact that they were leaders was to them evidence enough that their ability was sufficient to entitle them to be.

Leaders in the smaller cities emphasized willingness of executives as a more important participation criterion than did leaders in the larger cities. Their differing philosophies seemed to be that the smaller city leaders saw participation as something one chooses in large measure voluntarily; the bigger city leaders came nearer to putting their participation on an involuntary basis: "Our city is big, is growing fast, things have to be done to insure sound urban development, so we must participate whether we particularly enjoy it or not." The members of the first group saw their city as still small enough for them to know what is going on, so they are in a position to participate in that amount and in that activity indicated at the time; the members of the second group saw executive willingness not so much as willingness but as obligation. To them their cities to date may have grown haphazardly, but henceforth business executives are in no position to see participation in community affairs simply a function of whim or mood.

However, city size (with related characteristics of growth picture and implied position on the urban-rural scale) does not appear to be associated significantly with career patterns of leaders: leaders in one of the two larger cities were often not members of the family of management and had started well down in their companies, while leaders in the other larger city were inheritors of their jobs and had started near the top. Leaders in the smallest of the four cities were like leaders in the largest in that they were often members of the family of management, started well up in their companies, had not advanced rapidly, and were hanging on to their leadership positions. So the variables of city size and degree of urbanism appear not to be associated with career patterns of executives within their firms.

The two larger cities present interestingly contrasting pictures in the area of political philosophy, political practice, and attitudes toward municipal government. In one city leaders were the most liberal and the most Democratic of all four cities. By contrast, leaders in the other city were the most conservative and the least Democratic of all. Many interviewees in the latter city expressed some alarm over the fact that so many of their city's outstanding leaders were reaching the end of the leadership trail together, that old age and death were forcing such retirement, and that the members of the "young crop" were having to move in before they were quite ready. Conceivably these newcomers to important leadership positions may have more liberal philosophies and do things quite differently.

Many other possible relationships between city characteristics and participation patterns of business executives in urban development beyond the scope of this study come to mind. Among these city characteristics are (1) economic class structure as measured by income; (2) history of the distribution of volunteer citizen efforts in civic affairs among the major categories of activities—economic, welfare, political, cultural, educational, etc.; and (3) history of social, economic, and political pathology—as measured by disharmony and turnover at city hall, labor strikes, bond-election failures, and "abnormal" welfare activity. Still another, which doubtless many would prefer to put in the category of executive or firm characteristics rather than city characteristics, is the record of participation in community affairs of the predecessors of the current business executives under study, for interest in participating in community affairs might be a taste acquired very early at the father's or uncle's knee, or relatively early, from the first days spent in a firm whose history has been one of encouraging its executives to be civic-minded.

In Search of the Community Leader: The Ideal Executive

In terms of over-all participation (that is, that which cuts across social, religious, welfare, cultural, political, educational, livability, job-oriented, general economic growth, and community betterment activities), the company president who is a leader, compared with the company president who is not, is likely to be younger and better educated (as measured by years of formal schooling), to have been head of his company a shorter length of time, to be more nearly a one-company man, and to have a wife who herself is active in civic affairs. He is a little more conservative than his nonleader counterpart, but votes for a few more Democrats because "it is the practical thing to do because my customers expect me to" and "I have no choice in the primary."

The ideal executive as measured by his being a leader in community affairs is characterized by an attitude and opinion complex that differs from that of his less active counterpart, the nonleader. He sees his city as being progressive and its citizens as civic-minded. He claims that his city needs to be changed before it can qualify as a cultural center or as an attractive place in which to live, but he is not as critical on these scores as the nonleader. Relative to characteristics of a business firm as determinants of how much its top executives should participate in community affairs, he places significantly less emphasis on age of company and its size in terms of both number of employees and capital investment, than does his less active associate.

Varying emphasis on certain of the criteria the leader uses for choosing among community activities in which to participate serves to set him apart from the nonleader. While "importance of person asking me," personal interest, and civic importance were ranked one, two, and three, respectively, by both leaders and nonleaders, they were not good criteria for separating the two groups. The fourth ranking item in over-all importance, time, was the best separator, followed by ability (second) and personal importance (fourth). The third ranking item on this differentiator continuum, uniqueness of position, should not be considered here because of its meager choice over-all (that is, only two per cent of the leaders and eight-tenths of one per cent of the nonleaders considered it). In short, the leader, compared with the nonleader, does not consider the job of finding time to participate in community affairs a prohibitively difficult one, is inclined to play down the importance of ability to participate (this may be a reflection of greater self-confidence), and is motivated less selfishly in his selection of activity in that he is less given to choosing what to do because of what it will do for him personally.

In general, the leader does not shy away from controversy, but finds the political variety most objectionable. In fact, while he often insisted that he liked a fight, especially since desirable change and innovation often rest upon strong differences of opinion, his resistance to holding political office was as great as, and sometimes appeared to be greater than, that of the nonleader. In short, a very small part of the leader's interest in the political activity of his community centers around his wanting to hold public office: he is inclined to "let George do it" while he exerts some influence, directly, behind-the-scenes, or through lieutenants, on which George it will be.

Although notable exceptions were found in all four cities, in general leaders came from the larger (measured by number of employees), older, and nonunionized firms. There appears to be a slightly better chance of finding leaders in native companies, fast-growing companies, in those with definite plans for expansion in the foreseeable future, and in firms situated downtown (especially in those in this last category which felt that they could operate equally well downtown and on the periphery). Industrial firms furnished what appeared to be slightly more than their share of leaders, with service companies supplying the least, relatively. This relationship, however, is not statistically significant and, if real at all, should not be attributed to general classification of product per se into industrial, commercial, and service. The answer doubtless lies in other characteristics: industrial firms have a good chance of being older, larger, and faster growing than service companies.

Obviously the characteristics of the business firm listed above as being associated with executive leadership in community affairs often do not complement or reinforce one another: the largest firm may not be old, the fast-growing company may not be native, and the downtown firm may have no plans for expansion. But any firm that is downtown, big, old, native, growing fast, and has expansion plans on the drawing board is likely to furnish its city with a busy civic leader.

Perhaps the most unexpected of all the characteristics of the top business executive was his skepticism regarding the good accruing to his firm from his participation in community affairs. This criterion ranked no better than sixth among eleven criteria for making decisions on participating in community affairs, and was seventh as a criterion for differentiating between leaders and nonleaders. That is, leaders and nonleaders found it equally unimportant. However, executives felt quite different about the merits of gifts to philanthropy as a booster of their enterprises. Here there was a substantial positive relationship between level of leadership and level of optimism about the good to company of philanthropic giving: leaders were the stauncher claimers that gifts to philanthropy benefited their firms.

Measured by associational memberships, the ideal executive had certain distinctive characteristics (using the .05 or better level of significance). The social leader found his city attractive, thought well of its economic base, headed an old firm whose property, situated on a relatively large site, was owned rather than rented, voted Democratic, thought that gifts to philanthropy and participating in community affairs both had a real payoff for his firm, and was married to a woman who herself was active in social affairs. The leader in religious associations headed a firm most of whose employees lived in town, saw his city as being attractive and as having a sound economic base, believed that gifts to philanthropy benefited his company substantially, but questioned the utility of executive participation in community affairs as a promotion device for his firm.

The leader in the job-oriented associations found his city attractive, headed a fast-growing company, shied away from public office, and was skeptical about good to company accruing from executive community activity. The leader in associations aimed at community building found his city attractive, headed a firm whose product was consumed principally locally, had a wife who was also active in community building, voted Democratic, and considered the holding of public office not as distasteful as most. The leader in associations designed for societal welfare saw his city as both attractive and progressive, was married to a woman also active in this type of association, questioned the good realized by a firm from having its top executive active in community affairs, and resisted holding public office.

By activity area, leaders differed from nonleaders in several easily recognized ways (again using the .05 or better level of significance).

The leader in activities promoting the economic growth of the community headed a branch or subsidiary downtown, shied away from holding public office, and questioned the advantage to company of executive participation in community affairs. The leader who focused primarily on community betterment thought well of activities at City Hall, did not resist holding public office, but was skeptical of the good to company of executive participation in community affairs in general. The leader in livability activities had no distinguishing trait or affiliation. Leaders here were a heterogeneous lot, with no related, or even consistent, patterns of attitudes or behavior in other areas.

The educational leader headed a firm most of whose employees lived in town; he was among the strongest believers in the good befalling a firm from its executive's wide participation in community activities. The political leader headed a fast-growing, native firm, located downtown on a relatively large site; he voted Democratic, did not shy away from public office as much as others, thought gifts to philanthropy good for his firm, but questioned the payoff to company of executive participation in community affairs other than political. The leader in philanthropic activity came from a closely held company and thought relatively kindly of holding public office. The desegregation activity area proved to be so nebulous and ill-defined that it was difficult to discover its leaders and, consequently, impossible to describe meaningfully their characteristics. Few if any executives felt that their activity in this area was sufficient to give it leadership status.

In summary, it appears that the decision of an executive on what community activity to participate in, on what level, and how much, is substantially a private matter. It is dictated only minimally by the executive's conception of his company's needs, for actually he often questions the effectiveness of his community activity in promoting his firm. There is evidence that he participates because of a generalized feeling of "ought to," because he feels that he is among the most capable of those available to lead, because a friend who respects him and his stature and who himself is an important person asks him, and because he simply wants to. However, certain *personal traits and background factors* (e.g., age, career pattern) predispose one executive to be more active in community affairs than another. Executives in certain *types of firm* (e.g., big, old) are more inclined to assume, or at least fall heir to, community leadership positions than their counterparts in other establishments. Some *city characteristics* (e.g., size) appear to determine certain attitude complexes and need systems which, in turn, dictate expectations of executive behavior in community affairs.

REFERENCES

Argyris, Chris (1957), *Personality and Organization.* New York: Harper & Brothers.

Bendix, Reinhard (1956), *Work and Authority in Industry.* New York: John Wiley and Sons.

Dahl, Robert A. (1960), "Business and Politics: A Critical Appraisal of Political Science," in *Social Science Research on Business: Product and Potential.* New York: Columbia University Press. Pp. 35–36.

Lane, Robert E. (1954), *The Regulation of Businessmen.* New Haven, Conn.: Yale University Press.

Lundborg, Louis B. (1950), *Public Relations in the Local Community.* New York: Harper & Brothers. Pp. 68, 76, 78, 94, 206, 210. *See also* Dahl (1960).

McGregor, Douglas (1960), *The Human Side of Enterprise.* New York: McGraw-Hill Book Company. Pp. 182–185.

Miller, Delbert C., and William H. Form (1951), *Industrial Sociology,* Chap. XXI. New York: Harper & Brothers.

Noland, E. William, and E. W. Bakke (1949), *Workers Wanted.* New York: Harper & Brothers. Pp. 129–138.

Riesman, David (1950), *The Lonely Crowd.* New Haven, Conn.: Yale University Press.

Whyte, William H., Jr. (1956), *The Organization Man.* New York: Simon and Schuster, Inc.

Chapter 9

Negro Political Participation in Two Piedmont Crescent Cities

by Bradbury Seasholes and Frederic N. Cleaveland *

IN RECENT YEARS increased participation by Negroes in the political sphere has contributed to making race relations in the United States a major problem of national and international concern. The school desegregation decisions of the United States Supreme Court in particular have stimulated popular interest in a wider field of Negro civil rights. The work of the Civil Rights Commission in the area of Negro registration and voting has raised anew the question of control exercised by white citizens over Negroes in political, economic, and social behavior. And "sits-ins," Freedom Riders, "wade-ins," and "kneel-ins" have pushed this question of control into areas of activity where heretofore race relations have hardly been an issue. Psychological studies have probed the effects of race discrimination and segregation. Because Negro-white relationships are the most clearly defined in the South, this region has become the major focus of attention, although similar relationships in other regions have also been the object of concern.

* The authors gratefully acknowledge the valuable contributions of all those who participated in the comparative community studies of Durham and Winston-Salem, North Carolina. In particular the following joined in the planning of these studies and the gathering of data employed in the research on which this chapter is based: Professor Robert E. Agger, William J. Crotty, Jr., Cynthia Gubernick, and Stanley A. Pearl.

Implicit in the upsurge of interest in race relations is an underlying recognition of "the American dilemma"—the lack of correspondence between the Jeffersonian ideology and the reality of a color line in our society. Equally implicit is the corollary to this "dilemma," that changes in established social patterns tend to occur only with extreme difficulty, often occasioning severe conflict and sharp cleavage among groups in a community in transition.

In view of this growing interest in the problems of race, it is surprising to find that little academic study of Negro political activity has been undertaken. The study of Negro and white political participation at the community level in the North Carolina Piedmont setting aims to help fill this research gap, with an eye toward providing a quantitative profile of the politics of each race and identifying some of the factors associated with interrace differences in political behavior. The choice of two Piedmont cities made possible both a contribution to the over-all objective of the Urban Studies Program—increased understanding of the processes of an emerging urban region—and exploitation of information already culled by other research scholars in the Program in the attempt to analyze the patterns of behavior uncovered.

Within the Piedmont, Winston-Salem and Durham were chosen for study because, despite a large number of similarities shared with other cities in the Crescent, they do differ from each other in ways that have bearing on the kind of political system each supports. Before initiating a discussion of Negro political participation, then, it is important to set down pertinent information about the two cities, to provide a backdrop against which this participation may stand forth more clearly. Without some sense of the cities, the inter- and intracity differences uncovered by this study cannot be adequately understood.

The Two Communities

Durham and Winston-Salem lie about one hundred miles apart, separated in the east-west Piedmont chain by Greensboro. Durham is situated near the fall line of the Appalachians, while Winston-Salem lies farther west, just short of the highlands that herald the Great Smoky Mountains. These geographical facts have through the years been amplified into social facts. As Pfouts demonstrated in an earlier chapter, the cities are parts of two distinct trade areas, one oriented to the east, the other to the west. East and west have distinct meanings to North Carolinians in terms of race relations as well. East of Durham and Raleigh is the area of North Carolina most typically "deep South" in character, with a predominantly agricultural population, containing a significantly larger than average proportion of Negroes compared to the state as a whole, and with a significantly lower than average per capita income. To the west of Winston-Salem, particularly in the mountains themselves, are areas populated almost entirely by whites. In many instances, these counties were sympathetic to the Union cause during the Civil War, and to this day they prove unexpectedly prone to vote Republican in local and state, as well as national elections.

Durham and Winston-Salem fall somewhere between the two extremes of these eastern and western patterns of life in North Carolina, for they are situated in the Piedmont, removed from the farthest reaches of the state. In one important respect, however, size of Negro population, there is a reversal of the expected relationship. Durham on the eastern edge of the Piedmont, much closer to North Carolina's "black belt" counties, would be expected to have a significantly larger proportion of Negroes than Winston-Salem. In fact the 1960 Census figures reveal approximately the same percentages of nonwhites in both cities. Indeed within the city limits Winston-Salem showed a slightly larger proportion of nonwhites (37.1 per cent) than Durham (36.3 per cent). The implication of this fact for the political behavior of Negroes in the two cities bears examination.

Size of Negro Population

An especially intriguing facet of Southern politics is the seemingly incongruous link between the proportion of Negroes to whites and the character of the politics of a region. In a number of studies it has been shown that the greater the proportion of Negroes in Southern political districts, the greater the tendency for a political system inimical to Negroes to exist and to maintain itself over time. (See for example Key (1950), pp. 513–517; Heard (1948), pp. 251–278; and Price (1957), pp. 49, 93–103, *et passim.*) The cause lies, of course, in low election turnout and otherwise minimal participation by Negro citizens in politics. This in turn reflects Negro-white differences in income and education, the economic dependency of Negro tenant farmers (leading either to abstention from politics or to voting as the white owner suggests or is presumed to want), and social pressure against Negro participation ranging through threats of physical harm.

The study of Negro politics in the two Piedmont Crescent cities provided some opportunity to observe how much the inverse relationship between the proportion of Negroes in a population and the amount of Negro participation holds in a totally urban context. To the extent that the relationship depends on the lower income and education of Negroes, the fact of an urban, rather than rural or small town, environment should have little bearing. In the cities, however, there is less danger, real or assumed, of physical harm to Negroes who are active in politics. While economic dependence of Negroes on whites is characteristic of both the urban and rural South, it is unlikely that this dependence is either as strong or as personal in the city as in rural areas. Furthermore, political control of Negro employees in manufacturing establishments may be no greater than control over whites; in this situation the presence of labor unions may well be the key defense against intimidation. On the other hand, for Negro women the position of domestic in the city has overtones of the owner-tenant relationship characteristic of the rural countryside. In the last analysis, however, the crucial element of control is greatly diminished in an urban setting, for in the city considerable support can be mustered for virtually any political candidate, thus it is nearly impossible to discover how any one Negro votes. By contrast, precinct returns in many rural areas are often so one-sided that deviation might subject apparent insurgents to thorough investigation, and the possibility of sanction.

Besides the relative size of Negro populations, a number of other aspects of Negro life in Durham and Winston-Salem form key parts of the milieu of Negro politics in the two cities. Of particular importance are employment characteristics.

Employment of Negroes

In the areas of employment with high potential for white employee contact with Negroes, Winston-Salem appears to be the more progressive of the two cities. Among the great majority of industrial jobs, however, Negroes still do not hold positions of rank equal or superior to those held by any white employee with whom they come in contact. Yet industry does not ignore the problem. The Reynolds Tobacco Company, in Winston-Salem, has organized one entire factory building around Negro labor, so that technically it may be said that some Negroes in that plant hold ranks superior to whites working elsewhere for the same company. This policy has permitted an upward extension of the job ceiling for Negroes in the city, while maintaining segregation. Negroes employed in other buildings of this company are limited to the traditional custodial jobs. In Durham, the major tobacco company, Liggett and Myers, has followed the older practice of using Negro employees only in unskilled positions.

In both cities opportunities open to Negroes for upward mobility in the labor ranks in major industries other than tobacco have been extremely limited. Erwin Knitting Mills in Durham and two textile works in Winston-Salem (both named Hanes, but owned by two branches of that family) fill their low-wage, unskilled jobs almost entirely with white women.

Winston-Salem also has a major furniture factory and a large electronics plant. In neither are Negroes occupying the more highly skilled industrial positions, or foremen's positions. On the other hand, the electronics firm, a branch of Western Electric, has hired some Negro personnel at the white collar level. This action cannot be interpreted as a significant break in prevailing employment practices, however; rather it represents efforts by a firm holding United States Government contracts to fulfill contract requirements of hiring without racial discrimination. At the time of the study, this influence of the federal government on employment policy had little direct impact in Durham, for there were no major national concerns with defense contracts in that city.

The federal government has had some influence in both cities in easing the discrimination pattern in other ways. Through direct employment in the Post Office and the Employment Security Commission (the state unemployment service, administered and in part financed by the State of North Carolina), a small number of Negroes have been able to obtain such jobs as interviewer and typist.[1]

Each of the city governments has taken some steps toward improving Negro employment opportunities, and again we must impressionistically conclude that Winston-Salem has been the more liberal in this respect. At the time of this study each city had Negro policemen and firemen; Winston-Salem had taken the lead in both instances. The number employed in this manner was very small but the fact that any were employed is a source of pride and hope for Negro residents.

The employment picture in all-Negro establishments is decidedly better in Durham. This city has long been recognized as a "capital" of Negro business, primarily because of the presence of a large bank and what is often cited as the largest Negro insurance company in the world (Walker, 1945, p. 46). In both cities Negro teachers make up an important, though numerically small, segment of those working in essentially all-Negro establishments. The largest proportion of Negroes employed relatively independent of whites are small shopkeepers. In neither city is there much evidence of great prosperity among this group engaged as grocers, barbers, florists, and so forth.

Institutions of Political Influence

The avenues leading to political effectiveness are many and intertwined in complex fashion. The urgency with which people view the need to mold the commonweal in their own image has led to a welter of well-established organizations designed to implement that sense of urgency. Governments are such organizations. In societies of sharp and evenly matched struggles for power, elaborate governmental machinery arises to give some predictable form to the struggle and to give the victor at any instant in time the powerful psychological weapon, legitimacy, with which to extend his current advantage spatially and temporally. Partisans vying for control of government organize to press their cause more effectively—as political parties, loosely allied around issue positions, or as interest groups more narrowly dedicated to influencing issue outcomes. Other groups in society, organized around nonpolitical goals, on occasion find a political consensus within their membership and are transformed temporarily into political interest groups.

In Durham and Winston-Salem Negroes have utilized all of these avenues—formal government, political parties, interest groups, and social organizations—to one extent or another in attempts to win political objectives. In 1960, direct Negro participation in city government was at about the same stage of development in both cities. Each city had a minimum number of Negroes holding elective office; one councilman out of seven was a Negro. In both cities—as in many urban centers North and South, East and West—the way electoral district lines are drawn plus the normal patterns of residential segregation combine to hold down the numbers of Negroes elected to office. At the same time these factors virtually insure the election of some Negro candidates. Yet in neither city are Negroes living outside the

Negro wards sufficiently numerous to elect one of their own race to office.

In both cities certain appointive offices have been and are held by Negroes. These are positions of multiple membership—boards, commissions, and the like. In cases where such offices hold some potential for acting on racial matters, appointments of Negroes to membership are not sufficiently large to cause any threat to white domination. Thus ad hoc advisory commissions on such matters as building a new hospital are likely to consist of about five Negroes and fifteen whites, regardless of race proportions in the population as a whole or in whatever part of the city population will be affected by these governmental recommendations or decisions. Wherever Negroes are accepted in the city government, it would appear to be in the spirit of token acceptance. It is an important sign of the potency of Negro political action in each city, however, that even token acceptance is felt to be required.

Winston-Salem and Durham have a number of active Negro political interest groups, whose "interest" amounts to modification of the existing social system that works to the disadvantage of their race. The Durham Committee on Negro Affairs (D.C.N.A.) warrants special comment as one of the more influential groups. While its formal membership is not large, its organization is efficient and well-respected by the bulk of Negroes in the city. One observer estimates that the D.C.N.A. can count on a minimum of 60 per cent of the Negro electorate to follow its endorsements, while in most cases 90 to 100 per cent support by Negro voting is likely (Gatlin, 1960, p. 14).

The National Association for the Advancement of Colored People (N.A.A.C.P.) has a chapter in Durham which has been particularly active in legal moves to desegregate the public schools and other public services in the city. In this regard it has played the role most common for that organization's branches in all Southern localities. Its position vis-à-vis the D.C.N.A. is somewhat anomalous because the latter also has a subcommittee specializing in legal action against segregated facilities and other aspects of governmental discrimination disadvantageous to Negroes. There seems to be little rivalry, however. In fact, there is considerable overlap of personnel in the two organizations. Apparently the decision to use the machinery of one or the other group depends on an evaluation of net efficacy by those prominent in both. In legal proceedings requiring large sums of money, considerable legal experience, and national advice, the N.A.A.C.P. is likely to take the initiative. When these considerations do not weigh so heavily, there are definite advantages in using a strictly local organization that lacks the strong negative stigma the N.A.A.C.P. has acquired among Southern whites.

Winston-Salem has no organization comparable to the D.C.N.A. It does have a loosely organized voters' league, the United Civic Organization (U.C.O.), a federation of existing groups that have primary or secondary interests in politics. The U.C.O. does not exist, for all practical purposes, between elections. It is impossible, for instance, to locate any officers of the group except at election time. This instability is not by choice. The U.C.O. was originally modeled after the D.C.N.A., at least in those particular activities relating to election campaigns. But interest and resources, financial and human, have been insufficient to keep it an ongoing operation. Consequently, it is in effect an ad hoc committee formed whenever an election is imminent. The local chapter of the N.A.A.C.P. generally takes the initiative in this periodic resurrection, but the group is not simply an extension or "front" for it. Other Negroes with high stakes in a given election take leading roles in U.C.O. activities—notably those few Negroes who are candidates, and the seven Negro Democratic Party precinct captains. The U.C.O. utilizes a fairly large collection of neighborhood women's organizations as channels of contact to get Negroes registered, pass out endorsement slips, and get people to the polls.

Unlike the D.C.N.A., the U.C.O. does not try to persuade Negroes to run for office, but limits its activities to endorsement of those who have been recruited through other channels. Several Negro leaders interviewed in Winston-Salem appeared to consider this fact a virtue, perhaps believing that lack of active recruitment of candidates removes the epithet of "machine politics" from the organization. In actual fact it is further evidence that full development of the organization as a political force is lacking.

In the absence of any stable, strictly local Negro political interest group, then, the Winston-Salem N.A.A.C.P. chapter is by far the most important organization in the city pressing for Negro political objectives. Its primary aim has been to act through court proceedings, or the threat of court proceedings, to end statutory segregation in public places. In Winston-Salem the implied threat of court action has been a more important force than elsewhere, including Durham, in moving white leaders to seek compromise. Because of this, Winston-Salem N.A.A.C.P. officials have been seen less often in courtrooms and more often in conference rooms with city officials and prominent businessmen. Unlike its Durham counterpart, the Winston-Salem

N.A.A.C.P. has taken an active part in election campaigns. It has also been partly instrumental in overcoming job discrimination in public employment by the city.

In the field of combating job discrimination, however, the Winston-Salem chapter of the Urban League has been the principal champion of the Negro. (This chapter was established directly as the result of white leader initiative following two serious strikes with racial overtones at Winston-Salem tobacco plants during the late 1940's.) Nationally and locally the Urban League is more self-consciously interracial than the N.A.A.C.P., and more narrowly concerned with economic discrimination. In many ways these concerns of the Urban League pose more difficult problems than those facing the N.A.A.C.P., for eliminating job discrimination by private employers is often strictly a matter of negotiation involving no question of law enforcement. The fact that the League also feels that its interracial composition is a desirable end in itself tends to make it more cautious in its behavior. Its Negro officers decline to participate actively in N.A.A.C.P. affairs or in election campaigns because of their concern that such participation might jeopardize the primary goals of the League. This does not mean the two organization are at odds; together they seem to recognize a sensible division of labor, and each applauds the good work of the other. Overlap in activity, and a resulting tinge of rivalry, has occurred only where jobs with the city government were in question. It is noteworthy, however, that in a matter of strong concern to a great many Negro citizens—job opportunities—the principal organization for pressing the issue is almost totally "de-politicized" in the sense of engaging in formal political activity.

As in most Negro communities, the schools and churches are an important part of the political picture, more so than in the white community. The situation undoubtedly exists because teaching and preaching have been two of the highest professional positions to which Negroes could aspire. The influence of ministers and teachers in Durham seems to be less than in Winston-Salem because of the existence of a well-established business class. In Winston-Salem the only two Negroes elected to public office have been ministers. (One of them is also a college teacher.) The president of Winston-Salem Teachers College and his brother, also an administrator at the college, were among the most important Negroes in the city, in the eyes of white leaders. (Other Negro leaders consider this estimate of their influence to be grossly inaccurate, however.) An influential Negro minister volunteered to one of the authors that ministers were in effect the political opinion leaders in that city because there had been virtually no others to assume the role. In his judgment this was an unhealthy situation.

The president of North Carolina College in Durham is also a prominent person in terms of perceived influence. Again there seems to be some overestimation of his power by whites. Several teachers at the college have been active in local community affairs. One became the first Negro councilman in Durham. Another has been a national committeewoman of the Republican Party. In both cities the ability of the schools to contribute strong leadership is hampered by financial dependence on appropriations by the North Carolina General Assembly. In addition, both colleges have received large grants of money from private sources in the cities (such as the Reynolds Tobacco Company), a fact again tending to create an atmosphere of caution at least among administrators of the institutions.

Political influence of Negroes through mass media is slight in Winston-Salem. Its one Negro radio station takes no interest in politics, nor does its counterpart in Durham. The one daily newspaper (white) is moderately liberal on racial questions and has taken editorial stands mildly favorable to Negroes.

In Durham there is a weekly newspaper published by Negroes. In fact, it is designed for state-wide circulation, and does have some sales in Winston-Salem. (An attempt to open a branch in Winston-Salem failed a few years ago, however, because of insufficient subscriptions and advertising.) Most of its readers live in Durham. This paper, *The Carolina Times*, has been an outspoken advocate of strong measures to end segregation and discrimination over a long period. In 1938 its editor was characterized by a Negro sociologist as one of a group of radical leaders more highly race conscious, not economically beholden to whites, and eager to agitate for the right of Negroes to partake equally in the services of the city (Walker, 1945, p. 170). This characterization continues to be valid more than twenty years later. White newspapers in Durham consist of two dailies, both conservatively noncommittal on most race matters, plus a militant anti-Negro, anti-Semitic weekly. By contrast, there is a local labor newspaper which has taken strongly liberal positions on race as well as other matters.

Finally, a brief comment should be made about the political parties. Negroes hold precinct captaincies in both cities, where there are all-Negro precincts, but are a distinct minority within the respective city and county organizations. In Winston-Salem their inability to affect party policy in a significant way has made it difficult to recruit people to take the captaincies, lowered the caliber of those who do serve, and hence weakened an already weak position. In Durham the Negro members have in the past succeeded, in alliance with labor union-affiliated whites, to modify party policy (chiefly with regard to candidate selection). By 1960 this alliance was crumbling under the pressure of race tensions leaving Negroes without influence in formal party affairs. But regardless of relative Negro strength in the party organizations of either city, the basic fact is that the parties are only marginally important in local decision-making. Consequently any intercity difference in party acceptance of Negro participation bears little on the question of Negro influence in the city as a whole.

On balance it would have to be said that Negro political institutions in Durham are stronger than those in Winston-Salem. In both cities Negro access to City Hall is about the same—better than many places in the South, but still not equal to the access of white citizens. In neither city does Negro participation in the local Democratic Party organizations, through holding ward positions, have any real bearing on the course of party policy or of community direction. Strictly political interest groups exist in both cities, but the D.C.N.A. is by far the most effective. Schools and churches are active in both cities, but in Durham their influence is overshadowed by the activity of the Negro business community there. The existence and wide circulation of a militant Negro weekly newspaper in Durham gives that city's Negro population a decided advantage over Negroes in Winston-Salem in the dissemination of normative and informational political material.

A Pervading Ideology: Paternalism

Paternalism is control colored by good will. Negro leaders in Winston-Salem and Durham, and some introspective white leaders too, characterize their cities as "paternalistic." Both cities are often described as run by a fairly small number of influential citizens disproportionately drawn from the upper strata of social position. The "children" in this relationship are both white and Negro. In a paternalistic system the motivation for policy control by leaders is assumed to be the securing and maintenance of the welfare of those controlled. In this way paternalism is distinguishable from control exercised in strict self-interest, or even in malevolence (as in some instances of military occupation).

In community situations where leaders are in a position to exercise paternalistic control, the tendency actually to do so probably varies with their evaluation of the need of those controlled to have them do so. That is, paternalistic behavior by leaders tends to be more common toward those they consider to be incapable of wise self-rule. This means that in the South paternalism is likely to be stronger toward Negroes than toward nonleader whites, even though both groups may be subject to it. Participation in decision making by Negroes and by nonleader whites is tolerated and sometimes encouraged, as long as decisions reached on the whole seem wise (that is, agree with how the leaders themselves would probably have acted in any case), and as long as this participation does not threaten to erode the basic power position of the dominant leaders.

This picture of paternalism is too stark to apply fairly or realistically to Winston-Salem or to Durham. But it is fair to state that impressionistically the two cities appear to lie further along toward the paternalistic end of a continuum than do most American cities of their size. And it also appears that Winston-Salem is further along the scale than Durham. The history of each city is studded with the names of prominent families who contributed vast effort and immense sums of money to the shaping and enrichment of community life. In Durham the big names have been Duke, Watts, and Hill; in Winston-Salem, Reynolds, Hanes, and Gray. In each city private philanthropy has enriched the cultural life with both tangible and intangible monuments. Duke University was for a quarter century foremost among these monuments. More recently Winston-Salem achieved its educational monument and vaulted to new heights of civic prestige and status as new leaders succeeded in transplanting Wake Forest College from its small-town setting near Raleigh to the rolling hills of the Reynolds estate. This achievement, coming more than two decades after the transformation of little Trinity College into gothic Duke University, is taken by some as confirmation that paternalism has been more vital in Winston-Salem than in Durham during the 1950's.

A more pervasive paternalism in one city in contrast to the other may be expected to have many possible ramifications on the extent of Negro political participation. For example, signs of political atrophy might be expected to accompany heavy doses of paternalism and, conversely, a more active politics is logically possible where such control is less strong. Apathy may be compounded of frustration in the face of effective control, plus the receiving of benefits without having to ask or fight for them. Negroes in Winston-Salem have not been very successful in challenging white leadership in that city, and at the same time have been the beneficiaries of a fairly enlightened white leadership policy on racial matters—policy that led to early desegregation of the public schools, for example.

In contrast to Winston-Salem, community leadership in Durham is much less securely in the hands of the old type of first-family leaders. Firms dominating employment in the community tend to be absentee-owned. The second ranks of leadership appear harder in opposition to Negro objectives, more fearful, or more contemptuous, of Negro goals. Moreover, they seem determined to reinforce their own positions of control with less concern for the good will that characterized Durham's old guard. The Durham Committee on Negro Affairs undoubtedly has played a role in this situation, probably as part cause and part effect. That is, its growth has tended to alarm Durham whites, leaders and nonleaders alike, perhaps encouraging white leaders to conclude that paternalism is a luxury they can no longer afford under conditions that threaten the very fabric of their control. And, in turn, the D.C.N.A. may have experienced growth because of a sense of frustration on the part of Negroes over the results achieved through participation, plus, in Durham's case, little compensating progress by virtue of white good will.

With this backdrop we can proceed to a consideration of some of the broad determinants of Negro political participation, determinants whose effectiveness is assumed not to be limited to these particular cities. The basic fact requiring explanation is that Negroes in Winston-Salem and Durham, like Negroes elsewhere in the United States, are less active in politics than are white citizens. In this study it turned out too that Winston-Salem Negroes participate less than Durham Negroes, while whites in both cities participate to about the same extent.

Selected Social Characteristics and Political Participation

On the basis of other research into political behavior, it is likely that the race and city differences identified in this study of Durham and Winston-Salem can in part be explained by social facts that are not distinctively attributable to Negroes, or especially associated with any given city. For example, greater amounts of schooling are known to be associated with greater political participation. Negro-white differences in participation may partially boil down to Negro-white differences in amount of schooling. In this research an examination has been made of the effects on Negro and white political participation of four such social characteristics—income, age, and sex, in addition to schooling. The results proved to be more complex than had been anticipated, but in most instances these complexities stimulated provocative speculation about the nature of these variables and their possible differential effects on the two races.

The General Political Scale

In order to explore the relationship between social characteristics and political participation, it proved essential to devise some means for measuring political participation. For that purpose we have developed what we call "the general political scale" (GPS). We assume that a number of acts of political participation are related to one another to the extent that they can be visualized as different points along a continuum ranging from no participation to maximum participation. To say that this group of acts forms a scale is to say that they can be ordered in such a way that if a respondent reports that he has performed any particular one of the acts, this fact will be highly predictive of which of the remaining acts he has performed.[2]

Five pieces of information were used to form the GPS employed in this study and to categorize the whites and Negroes of Winston-Salem and Durham. Two items were related to activity in formal organizations, and the remaining three items were based on the extent respondents discussed certain public questions with others. The five items of the scale provide a fairly good spread, as seen in Table 9-1. This listing also shows the rank ordering of the items, indicating which types of activity imply the greater and lesser political interest and over-all political activity.[3]

The items of a scale are a few points along a continuum made up of many points; and so it is with the GPS. In this study the main interest does not focus on the five specific types of behavior which make up the GPS, but rather in the relatively high to relatively low degree of political participation which is measured by the scale. Respondents in this study have been assigned to categories according to the rarest of the five types of political activity they reported. For example, someone reporting that he has worked on a community prob-

Table 9-1. Spread of Responses to Questions Comprising General Political Scale

QUESTION	NATURE OF "PLUS" RESPONSE	PER CENT ANSWERING "PLUS"
(2) Worked on community matters through organizations	"Yes"	14
(3) Discuss party affairs with party officials	Either "often" or "once in a while"	25
(1) Organizational membership	One or more memberships	55
(4) Discuss local government affairs with friends	Either "often" or "once in a while"	61
(5) Discuss school affairs with friends	"Often"	79

lem through his activity in formal organization (the rarest activity of the five) is assigned a GPS score of six, while the person answering negatively to all five types of activity is assigned a score of one. The score of six means that the respondent reported doing the rarest of these five acts in the GPS and that he has probably also done the four other acts; but still more important, it also signifies the high probability that he performs a host of other unspecified political acts that would fall below our rarest act in a scale that ordered the whole universe of political acts. In short, we conclude that someone with a high score on this scale is a "high participant" in politics in a general sense.[4]

The extent to which each race in each city participates in politics, as measured by the GPS, is shown in Figure 9-1.

Income and Political Participation

The relationship between a man's income and his likelihood to participate in politics can be viewed on two levels. First, income is a fairly accurate gauge of a person's social standing. Money can be, and often is, used to buy social standing through the accumulation of material goods. And social standing, once achieved, generally makes the accumulation of money easier. The relationship between income and participation at this level is actually one between social standing and participation. This in turn may reflect the desire of that small minority with high status to hold on to the economic and social roots of their status, against the interests of a vast majority in a society whose formal political system emphasizes majority rule and equal participation.

On a more prosaic level it must be remembered that aside from status considerations money offers concrete advantages in the political game. One must have spare time to participate, and the greater the income the more time and flexibility in work scheduling one is likely to have. (This is a tendency, not an invariable rule, as many an over-

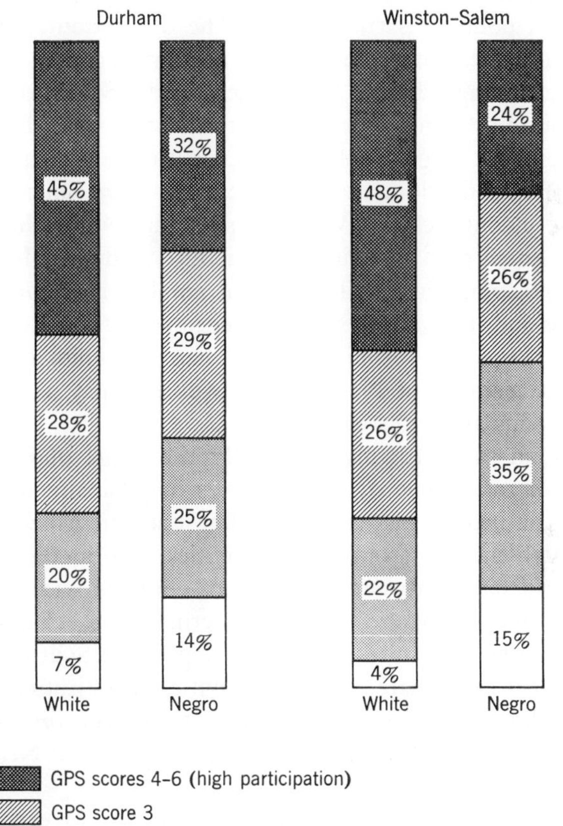

Figure 9-1. Degree of political participation.

worked executive or professional will testify.) High income provides economic leverage with which to exert power and influence. Money can be contributed to candidates and parties, an important form of political activity in itself. It provides the means to obtain the knowledge necessary to operate effectively in politics, through formal education, perusal of the mass media, and so forth. A substantial income is generally needed to compete successfully for elective office. It takes money to join and to maintain membership in social organizations that may be political in nature, all or part of the time.

In studying Negro political behavior it is especially important to distinguish between income as an index of social standing and income as the concrete wherewithal to purchase goods more directly connected with political participation. The distinction is significant because income does not appear to be as accurate a gauge of status among Negroes as among whites. Particularly in the South, the segregation-discrimination system distorts the pattern of income distribution to a marked degree. Large numbers of occupations are denied Negroes regardless of qualification, and those remaining are bunched at the low end of the income scale. Where Negroes and whites hold similar occupations, equal pay for equal work is rarely found. In certain wage or salary positions this is the result of employer exploitation. In the professions and small businesses the Negro professional or entrepreneur tends to charge less for his services than his white counterpart, reflecting the inability of Negroes as a whole to pay as much for services and goods as whites can.

In addition to narrowing drastically the range of incomes obtainable by Negroes, some of these factors help disrupt a close correlation between income and social standing that one expects in white society. High income from illicit activities, low income from professional work, high status resulting from contacts with whites regardless of income, all play a part in undermining a reliable relationship between income and status. Because Negroes in Southern cities carry on more than their share of illicit activities—prostitution, the numbers racket, moonshine—*source* of income rather than *amount* appears to play a part in subjective categorizing of Negroes by Negroes into social classes.

In light of all this, there is some reason not to expect equivalent rates of political participation by whites and Negroes of equivalent income if income is viewed solely as an index of social standing. But if it is considered as well as the resource from which activities more

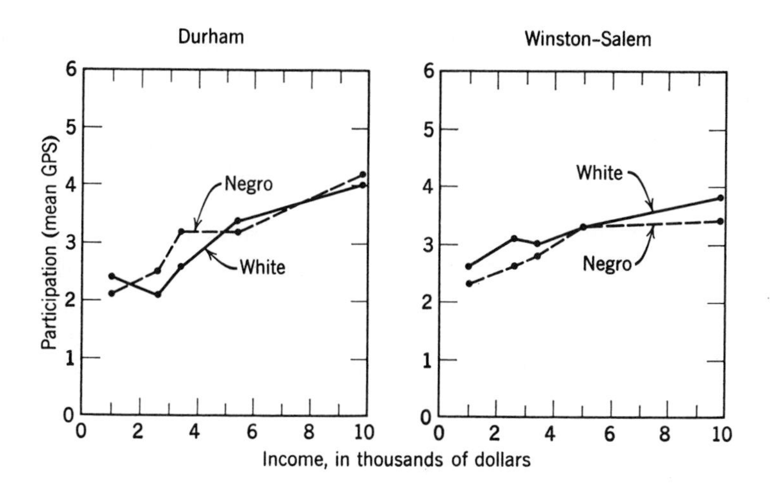

Figure 9-2. Relationship between income and political participation.

directly connected to politics are financed, there is less expectation of a race difference when income is controlled.

As Figure 9-2 shows, the data for Negroes and whites in Winston-Salem and Durham do no violence to the general hypothesis that income and participation are positively related. There is a decided similarity among all four graph lines, and these lines not only have similar slopes, but cut through about the same range of average participation scores. In short, a good amount of Negro-white difference in participation is accounted for by income differences. A closer statistical look at these data proves sobering, however. Plotting mean GPS scores masks a large amount of variation entering into the calculation of the averages. The correlation between income and participation for each race in each city is actually quite modest, ranging from .22 to .27 on a scale whose limits are 0.00 and 1.00.[5] Although the gap between the lines for whites and Negroes never seems great, visually, there is a statistical difference between the two races among those earning $2,000 or less in Winston-Salem. In the preceding section Winston-Salem was characterized as a city in which Negroes lack an ongoing political organization, a fact which puts that group at a disadvantage relative to whites in the same city, and also relative to the more highly organized Durham Negro population. The lack of continuing political stimulation is likely to have a greater effect on marginal participants than on those who have accustomed themselves to community activity. It is reasonable to suggest that low-income Negroes, lacking direct and ongoing political stimulation, would drop off in rate of participation at a faster rate than a similar group (say in Durham) subjected to such stimulation. This may be what is happening to the Negro population in Winston-Salem.

Although the correlations between income and participation are clustered quite close together in size, the figures for the two white groups are higher (.27 in Durham, .24 in Winston-Salem) than for the Negro groups (.23 and .22, respectively). This interrace difference is sufficient to conclude that the fact that in Negro society social standing and income are not so closely tied has some effect. But this effect is small in comparison to the over-all tendency for variations in income—both as wherewithal and as a shorthand for status—to be associated with varying degrees of political activity.

Education and Political Participation

The positive relationship between years of education completed and amount of participation of various sorts is a commonplace finding in social research. But what exactly is it about formal schooling that brings about this relationship? Does formal schooling have the same effect on any segment of a population, regardless of such factors as race?

One answer is that participation, especially in politics, requires a body of facts—facts about what issues are abroad, what alternatives exist to resolve them, the consequences of these alternatives, the attitudes of particular candidates toward these alternatives, modes of implementing personal preferences among the alternatives, and so forth. The assumption is that the major component of apathy is ignorance, ignorance of issues and the personal stake one has in them, and ignorance of ways to make preferences bear on the outcome of issue conflicts.[6]

A second possible answer views the school experience in the broader sense of a socializing experience. In this sense the school experience is seen as an instrument society uses to inculcate persons growing into adulthood with patterns of expected behavior. Thus school becomes (along with the other major institutions of society) a teacher of norms, a preparation ground for "real life."

These two interpretations of the school experience—as the accumulation of factual information on the one hand, and the assimilation of societal norms on the other—are not mutually exclusive. Schooling undoubtedly involves absorbing a mixture of factual and normative data. The proportions of the mixture is what is of interest, because it could bear on Negro-white differences in the relationship between education and political participation. If schooling is foremost a matter of fact accumulation, we might expect the generally accepted inferiority of Negro public schools throughout the South to be reflected in less knowledge about politics and hence less participation than in the case of whites, at any level of schooling reached. Both races would show an increase in participation the more schooling attained, but the rate of increase would be slower for Negroes. If schooling is primarily a matter of socialization it might be hypothesized that Negro participation actually declines the more education received, because what is gradually learned in Southern Negro schools is in part the prevailing norm of political behavior for that race, "noninvolvement." Noninvolvement is generally not taught in such schools in a formal sense—Negro teachers like most others are steeped in the folklore of American democratic ideology; but noninvolvement is often more subtly (and probably unwittingly) transmitted from teacher to pupil by indirection. Negro teachers tend not to be aggressive in their personal, political lives, and thus serve as examples to students who hold them in general esteem. Vocational counseling stresses readily available Negro occupations, underplays political solutions to job restrictions. And a host of school activities are performed on a segregated and usually discriminatory basis without any sign of effort by Negro school personnel to change the situation.

The assimilation of these negative norms is not important enough to determine the over-all direction of the relationship between education and participation for Negroes, but conceivably it does tend to neutralize both the effect of other, positive, norms assimilated (such as the dominant norms of democracy) and the effect of fact accumulation on political participation. This way of looking at education may at least serve as a tentative explanation of what in fact was found in Winston-Salem and Durham. Figure 9-3 shows the actual correspondence in these cities between years of schooling completed and average amount of participation, expressed as mean GPS scores. (It should be remembered that the data are for adults whose formal education has gone as far as it is probably going to go.) The curve for Winston-Salem Negroes is remarkably flat as one proceeds from those with no formal education through those who went no further than high school. At the same time the participation average of the white population increases. This lends credence to the hypothesis about Negro assimilation of the norms of noninvolvement. The flat line may represent the net effect of fact accumulation plus negative norm assimilation. In Durham, the Negroes seem to respond to differences in education in about the same way as whites through the end of high school, their participation increasing slightly the more schooling they have had.

The most striking aspect of Figure 9-3, however, is the dramatic upswing of Negro participation at the college level. A plausible explanation of this gives a reverse twist to the hypothesis concerning norm assimilation. It is possible that college instruction of Negroes provides a break from the accommodation pattern, and is more attuned to preparing Negroes for a type of interaction with whites quite different from that which Negroes with less education can expect—interaction more closely based on mutual respect than on subservience. In some cases this preparation is reinforced by being taught in part or entirely by whites and/or attending college outside the South.

Taking a different tack, these findings possibly reflect the types of Negroes who choose and are able to attend college. These Negro students may be uncharacteristically unaccommodating in personality and motivation. The college population is in large part self-selective

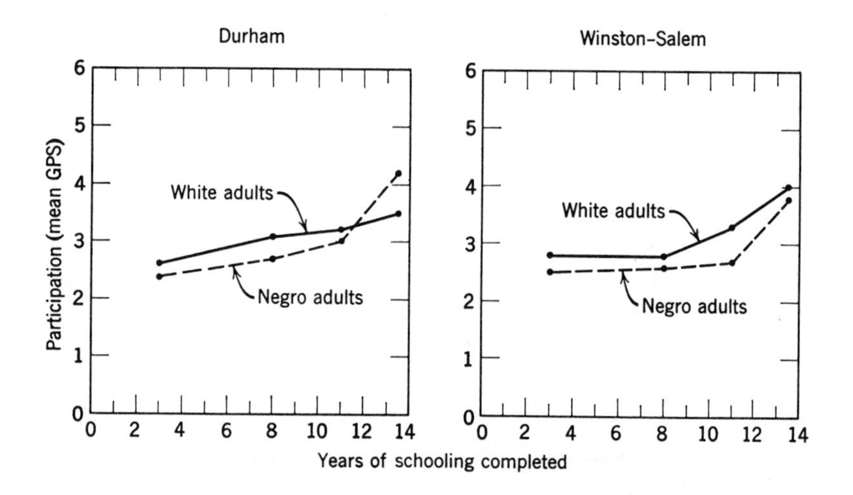

Figure 9-3. Relationship between education and political participation.

—the colleges can only select from those who apply—and undoubtedly includes a disproportionate number of what some whites have irreverently labeled "strivers." The decision to go to college indicates for many Southern Negroes a determination to break through the segregation-discrimination system, a determination that leads the individual to maximize an important avenue of social mobility, education, and that is consciously or incidentally manifested in high political participation.

As with income, the strengths of the relationships between education and participation for each race in each city are modest at best. The correlations are:

Durham Negroes	.27
Durham whites	.17
Winston-Salem Negroes	.21
Winston-Salem whites	.24

These figures indicate that in Winston-Salem the relationship is nearly the same for both races. In Durham, however, there is a substantial race difference, with Negroes higher and whites lower than in the other city. The intercity Negro difference meshes neatly with the impressions about the two cities described in the preceding section. That is, in the city with greater opportunity for independence from white control one might expect a more positive relationship between education and participation. This could be because the mixture of fact accumulation and norm assimilation may be weighted more heavily toward fact accumulation in such a city, or because the norms assimilated may lean more heavily toward those emphasizing democratic ideals, or both.

The drop in strength of relationship for whites from Winston-Salem to Durham could be the result of white reactions to Negro political activity. Possibly the more normal Negro political behavior becomes in a Southern city, the more abnormal white political behavior becomes. Thus the low figure for Durham whites may reflect either an unusually active group with little formal schooling, or an unusually inactive group of the highly educated, or a combination. There is reason to think that challenges to white political power may characteristically stimulate two quite different kinds of political responses: (1) lower-class whites, more limited in education, may respond with relative hyperactivity; (2) conversely, many people whose sentiments are considered liberal or moderate on race matters—that is, people who tend to be disproportionately highly educated—are likely to respond by disengaging from active political involvement. Figure 9-3 lends support to part of this speculation: Durham whites of more than high school education fail to show the marked increase in political participation that occurs with all three other groups.

Age and Political Participation

Recent studies of voting and other forms of political behavior have commented on the tendency for the relationship between age and participation to assume a "hump" shape. Political involvement is very low until a person reaches adulthood, increases to its peak in middle age, and then declines as the individual reaches old age. (See, for example, Campbell, Converse, Miller, and Stokes, 1960, pp. 493–498.) This suggests incomplete political socialization (or politicization) at the age at which one's legal rights to participate come into fullest play (age 21 or 18), a maximizing of interest and involvement roughly concurrent with one's height of earning power, and a decline traceable perhaps in part to physical deterioration and perhaps in part to a disillusionment with the efficacy of politics. Except that Negroes may be more subject to this disillusionment, there is little in this interpretation to suggest that the age variable would have different or special effects on Negroes than on whites. The "hump" interpretation does not conform well with the age and participation parameters for Winston-Salem and Durham. In Durham more Negro respondents were between 45 and 64 years old than white respondents, while of course that Negro population participates less in politics. In Winston-Salem there were, to be sure, more old respondents (65 years old or more) in the Negro sample than in the white sample, but the difference was made up among young, not middle-aged, white respondents.

Another way age can bear on participation is often referred to as the "generational effect" (Hyman, 1959, pp. 139–151). This interpretation holds that current levels of political activity reflect the particular times in which individual citizens have reached maturity. For example, 50-year-olds today were just at the job-hunting stage of their lives when the Great Depression occurred. This fact may have led them to be more involved in politics—no matter how old they happen to be when a given survey is conducted—than persons reaching the job-hunting stage either before or after the Depression. Here it is not age per se that is crucial, but rather the era in which adulthood was attained. This way of looking at age quite definitely suggests potential Negro-white differences. Major events in the last 50 years have not particularly affected whites alone. The two world wars, the Depression, and the cold war, for example, had important ramifications of roughly like character on all Americans. Changes in race relations that these events brought on—better jobs and migration to the North in the two wars, greater unemployment for Negroes during the Depression—had far more impact, objective and psychological, on Negroes than on the vast white majority, even though the latter too were affected.

But in this same 50 years there have also been a number of events bearing more specifically on Negro political activity which could be expected to modify the age-participation relationship for that race. Among them are repeal of the poll tax (1920, in North Carolina), Supreme Court disallowance of the "white primary" (*Smith v. Allwright*, 1944), and a general breaking down of segregation on a number of fronts—the major professional sports, the armed forces, and the public schools (in some Southern states, including North Carolina).

From this recent history we would expect that it is physically and psychologically easier for the 20-year-old Negro to become active in politics today than it was for the Negro who reached that age of emerging adulthood in 1930 or 1940. This should lead to an increasing gap between the political performance of Negroes and whites the older the groups are. Should the "hump" concept also play a part, one would anticipate finding the Negro hump sagging more than the white hump, somewhat as in Figure 9-4.

Figure 9-4 also gives the actual age-participation graphs for Winston-Salem and Durham. As can be seen, there is only slight resemblance between the hypothetical model and the Durham data, and no resemblance between it and the Winston-Salem data. Unanticipated deviations are as follows: elderly Durham whites, younger Winston-Salem whites, and elderly Winston-Salem Negroes are more active than expected under the "hump" hypothesis. In addition both Negro groups, especially Negroes in Winston-Salem, are more active than predicted by the "generational effect" hypothesis.

These deviations seem capricious in the absence of any plausible theory to explain them and particularly in the absence of between-city or between-race consistency. In fact, a very low correlation between age and participation is implied by these data. But because of

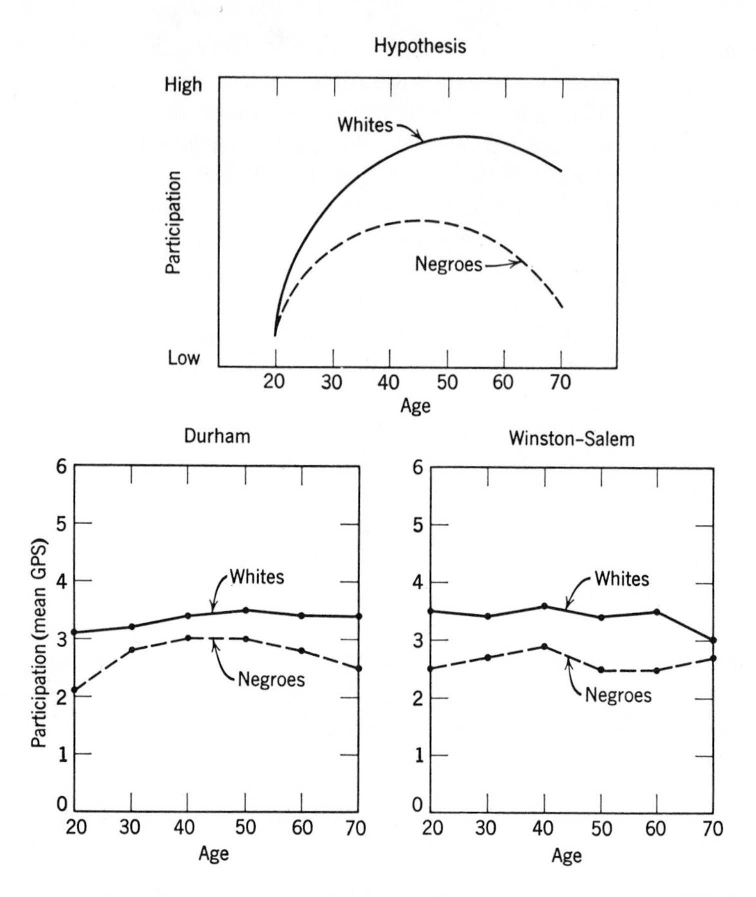

Figure 9-4. Hypothetical and actual relationships between age and political participation.

the hump shape of the predicted relationship the usual statistical methods of indicating strength of relationship cannot be used.

The most important insight to be derived from this information about political activity by various age groups is the apparent rejection of the generational effect—the era in which one enters adulthood does not appear to have an important effect upon later levels of participation. Americans may learn their enduring political preferences at a crucial age in their lives, but their attitudes toward political action appear much more to be constantly shaped by current factors. This, at least, seems to be the case for Negroes and whites in these two cities.

Negro social life in the United States has often been pictured as more matriarchal than white social life. The evidence, however, bears mainly on the patterns of behavior within families. In a disproportionate number of Negro families the father, for one reason or another, is absent. Nearly twice as many Negro families are "broken" in this sense. Even in Negro families where the husband is present, there is a greater tendency toward female domination. The Negro woman in the urban South can often obtain better paying and more stable employment than her husband because of the good market for domestic help. Even when her job is not as good (in any sense) as her husband's, she tends to contribute more, proportionately, to the total family income than her white counterpart does.

The term "matriarchal society" has meaning extended well beyond intrafamily affairs, however. If Negro women are more likely to "rule the roost," does it follow that they also play a larger political role than white women, other things being equal? On an impressionistic level there seems to be no clear-cut answer to this question for Winston-Salem and Durham. In Winston-Salem, only two of the twenty individuals most often listed as influential in community affairs by knowledgeable informants were women.[7] One ranked fairly high on the list, was very well informed, and active in local politics. (She ran unsuccessfully as a candidate for the Forsyth County Board of Education in May, 1960.) The other was only marginally important, judging both from her rank on the list and her lack of information about the political scene. This second woman, however, did outline in sketchy form what appears to be a fairly effective political network that relies on neighborhood women's organizations to do such campaign chores as distribute leaflets, telephone or contact other people in person, and so forth. These clubs periodically subject themselves to rudimentary coordination through the actions of the United Civic Organization, described in the first section. Their political role ought not to be overstressed, however; they are first and foremost "garden clubs," that is, clubs organized for socializing. But they do turn political every so often, and there is no comparable network of male organizations. Thus in Winston-Salem men dominate the top decision-making positions within Negro society, but Negro women may be particularly influential at a level of more immediate contact with the general Negro population.

Social class probably affects variations in the influence of either sex.

The higher the social status of a Negro family unit, the more likely it is that it will conform to white, or American, patterns of behavior, with the female withdrawing from income-producing activity, and the male assuming a stronger role in most family affairs. Middle-class status is virtually essential for the Negro who is perceived as a leader in the community, judging from the occupations, income, and education of persons named as leaders most often in this study. It is also important to note that Negroes who are perceived as leaders by either race must be able to deal with whites from some position of relative strength. This is always difficult because of a dominant white conviction that Negroes are incapable of effective leadership. This difficulty must only be compounded when white male contempt for female abilities in political matters comes into play.

Such pressures, then, hinder the development of Negro female community leadership, despite any underlying matriarchy that may exist in the general Negro population. Again, in Durham there were no women listed among the twenty most influential Negroes. One woman who was expected to be named—she had been a Republican national committeewoman—was conspicuously absent. In contrast to Winston-Salem, Negro women's clubs play a less important part in the political life of Durham, probably because the Negro residential areas are already well-organized on a block-by-block basis by the Durham Committee on Negro Affairs.

If a stronger political role for Negro women does not appear at the leadership level, it still might emerge in the more modest political activities of the population at large, activities the GPS is designed to gauge. As background to the survey data some discussion of the role of white men and women in politics is necessary. Politics in America has traditionally been a man's game. Statutory exclusion of women from voting and other forms of political activity reflected in a formal, legal way the informal norms keeping women "in their place." As in other situations where systems of social norms are strongly held, the elimination of the formal barriers has not been accompanied by immediate widespread use of new freedoms. In part this can be the result of a continuation of informal, negative sanctions, and in part the result of a psychological internalizing of the politically passive role men once insisted on.

The other side of the "politics-is-a-man's-game" phenomenon is a tendency for men with only marginal interests in the stakes of politics to participate anyway out of a sense of "civic duty." This is particularly true in the case of voting and informal discussions. According to Lazarsfeld, Berelson, and Gaudet (1948, p. 48), "Sex is the only personal characteristic which affects non-voting, even if interest is held constant. Men are better citizens but women are more reasoned: if they are not interested, they do not vote."

Since the major voting studies have relied on samples that are overwhelmingly white in composition, the possibility must be entertained that their findings apply more, or only, to whites. Hence it would be expected that white women in Winston-Salem and Durham participate less than white men. But if matriarchy in Negro society has political ramifications, we would anticipate that Negro women are more active than Negro men, or at least approach more closely the level of activity by men.

Figure 9-5 summarizes the extent to which sex and political participation are related in the two cities. The two races in Winston-Salem conform quite well to theoretical expectations. Among whites, males participate in politics more than females, while there is no statistically significant difference in participation levels between Negro men and women. The Durham data are perplexing because they appear to be a reversal of expectations and of what was found in Winston-Salem. The male-female difference for Durham whites is significant, but only at the .10 level. The percentages differ very little from those of Winston-Salem whites. The group that stands out, then, as deviant from expectations is the Durham Negroes. This group, rather than behaving according to expectations for a Negro population, conforms strongly to the "normal" pattern established by the two white groups and observed in other major studies of political participation.

These findings tentatively suggest slightly different norms for whites and for Negroes: the norm for whites, and hence the social norm, is somewhat greater political participation by men than by women; but Negro culture appears to introduce a mild coutertendency producing a norm that results in about equal political participation by both sexes. This assumes that the Winston-Salem Negro behavior is more typically Negro than the Durham Negro behavior, that Durham Negroes have narrowed the gap between white and Negro cultures to a greater degree than have Negroes in most other Southern cities, including Winston-Salem. Such an assumption is consistent with the over-all picture of the two cities drawn in the beginning section.

Actually the Winston-Salem data do not lend particular reinforcement to the idea of Negro matriarchal behavior. The figures indicate

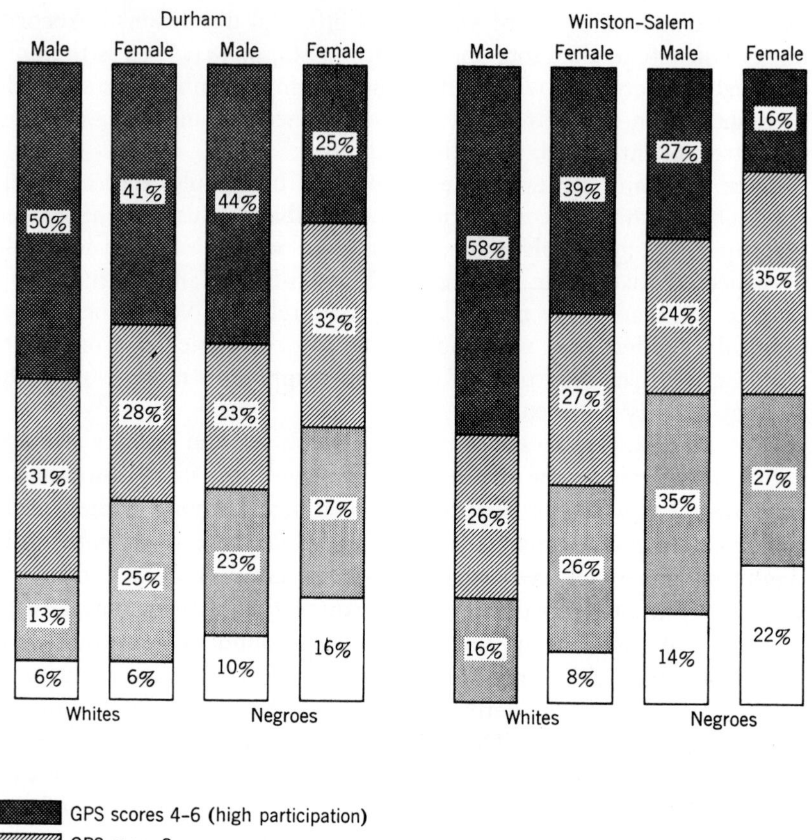

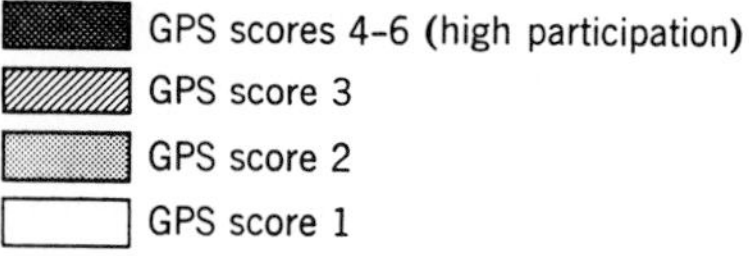

Figure 9-5. Relationship between sex and political participation.

rough equality of participation by virtue of unusual male inactivity, rather than female hyperactivity. In light of the information gleaned from the four groups it seems less tortuous to discuss these results as indications of differential strength of patriarchy in matters political, a prominent facet of American politics, rather than to frame the results in terms of matriarchy. In any case the key point that emerges is the relative immunity of Winston-Salem Negroes to the dominant behavior pattern for the two sexes in the region and the country as a whole. The data do not conclusively demonstrate that matriarchal tendencies in some parts of Negro life spill over into the political sphere. But the Winston-Salem findings leave this still a definite possibility.

Community Attachment and Political Participation

Differences in income, education, age, and sex appear to affect the predispositions of people to become actively involved in politics, and we have seen that when Negroes are compared with whites, variations in education and sex seem to result in consequences that mirror cultural distinctions between the two races. But participation needs a locale—people take part in politics in some specific, defined community. Even for those people who concentrate their political interests and activity on other than local affairs, political involvement often tends to begin at the local level and then spread to other levels. Accordingly integration with the local community, or attachment to it, has been viewed as a catalyst creating conditions in which predispositions to political participation—predispositions growing out of such factors as income and education—are transformed into concrete political acts.

Psychological attachment can be thought of as a function of such objective matters as whether or not a person owns a home in the community, how long he has lived there, how many kinfolk live there, and whether or not he is a "native" (born there). This study attempted to gauge attachment by securing this type of objective information and also by asking more direct, attitudinal questions. At one point respondents were asked to rate their city on a scale from "excellent" to "poor," and at another point they were asked whether they would like to move away.

Of these six variables, each of which is presumed to relate to attachment to the local community, only two, home ownership and number of kin living nearby, proved to be relevant to levels of political participation in Winston-Salem and Durham.[8] And in both of these instances an important race difference was discovered.

Home Ownership and Political Participation

The theoretical basis for assuming that home owners are likely to participate in politics more extensively than renters or buyers is obvious: home owners have more of a stake in society as a whole, and in

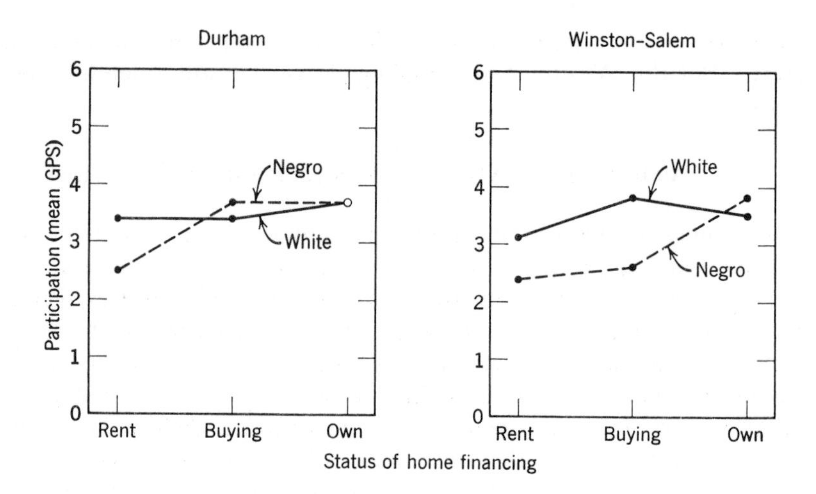

Figure 9-6. Relationship between home ownership and political participation.

their local community in particular. Houses are physically rooted in a single city; and the owner's emotional attachment to his house (and the multitude of experiences for which it provides a focus) quite reasonably leads him to emotional involvement in the community where it is located. As Figure 9-6 shows, this assumption holds up for three of the four groups in this study: except in the case of Winston-Salem whites, political activity increases as one proceeds from those renting to those owning homes. The major Negro-white gap occurs among the renters, where for Negroes political activity drops off sharply. (Because only a very few Negroes in Winston-Salem are in the process of buying, the visual gap between Negro and white buyers is less important than it appears in the graph.)

Of course, these findings may simply mirror the economic positions of the respondents. To see whether this is so, the same relationship was tested with income controlled. Within income categories all comparisons of participation levels between renters and owners plus buyers proved statistically significant.[9] In sharp contrast, in only one of six income category comparisons between white renters and owners plus buyers did any significant difference emerge. This occurred among Durham whites of incomes between $3,000 and $6,000.

This race difference underlines the strong likelihood that home ownership means more to Negroes in these cities than to whites. First, owning a home is rarer among Negroes. In Winston-Salem 27 per cent and in Durham 29 per cent of those Negroes interviewed owned or were buying their homes. The figures for whites were 72 per cent and 58 per cent, respectively. Home ownership by Negroes, because it is uncommon—and particularly because of Negro insecurity in a society dominated by whites—is less likely to be taken for granted once attained.

Why do Negro home owners turn to political action as a means of protecting this particular stake in their community? Literally hundreds of city ordinances and supporting regulations have direct bearing on either the ownership of a house or its importance as a status symbol. Zoning regulations can enhance or threaten the psychological value of owning a house in a particular location. Property tax rates, methods of tax evaluation, requirements for sewage disposal, street paving, lighting—all can strike at ownership itself. Urban renewal and highway development plans can threaten any house or improve the neighborhood in which it is located.

It would be a mistake, however, to interpret the relationship of home ownership with political participation solely in these immediate terms. If home ownership is an especially tangible symbol of status, we can expect that the possession of other such symbols would likewise be associated with participation. The tentative conclusion to be suggested here is that the ownership of a house, with its accompanying relatively high status connotations some of which are derivable from location, ties a person to the city where he is, perhaps much more even than do other status symbols. In short, it gives him an attachment to the city that in turn entails more than the average amount of political participation. Because ownership apparently has more status significance for Negroes than for whites in Winston-Salem and Durham, their political activity appears to be more closely tied with ownership.

Number of Kin Living in Area and Political Participation

Whether or not a person has kinfolk living in the same city, and how many, may affect his emotional attachment to that city; but if this is the case the attachment is of a type that apparently does not lead to heightened political activity. This, at least, seems to be true of all but the Winston-Salem Negroes who, in Figure 9-7, show an increase in political participation the more relatives live nearby until the category "many" is reached. The other three groups act in just the oppo-

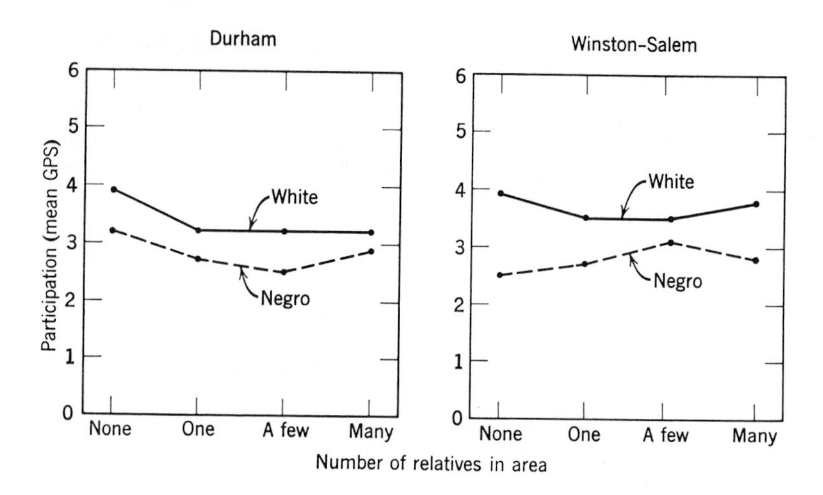

Figure 9-7. Relationship between number of kin living in area and political participation, residents of eleven or more years.

site way. Once again there is reason to view the activities of Durham Negroes as atypically close to white patterns of behavior. Conjecturally that behavior seems to reflect the use of political activity as a substitute for the kinds of social interaction people with nearby relatives can count on—casual assumption of compatibility that is reinforced by frequent informal visiting. This leaves unexplained why whites and Durham Negroes with many relatives close by are more active.

If the Winston-Salem Negroes are more typical of their race, the low participation by those with no relatives in the Winston-Salem area could mean that this group includes a large number of in-migrants from farther south, but this theory assumes that the number is considerably larger than in Durham. The low participation might also be related to the dynamics of out-migration. Among those who have no relatives living in their city are an undetermined number whose families and kinfolk have moved away from them, rather than vice versa. Old people have seen their children (and nephews) grow up and leave the city for greater opportunities elsewhere. The less ambitious, or the more cautious, Negroes have watched others in their extended families gather up their belongings (often meager) and head for the industrial centers of the Northeast, Midwest, and West. This interpretation implies that out-migrants tend to be more active politically than those who remain; that this type of out-migration occurs more often among Negroes than among whites; and that it occurs more among Winston-Salem Negroes than among Durham Negroes. Since this study has no information about out-migrants these implications must remain plausible but unproven.

From studying the effects of home ownership, number of kin nearby, and noting the lack of effects of four other variables on political participation, we can only conclude that "community attachment" has many faces. The concept simply does not seem to hold together, at least in this study. The concrete index of one form of attachment, home ownership, did prove to bear consequences consistent with the presumed relationship between attachment and participation. But that variable can as well be treated in its own terms without making it serve as an index of some other variable. And while examination of the effects of having kinfolk close by turned out to have bearing on differences between Negroes and whites in Winston-Salem and Durham, these effects do not tie in well with the concept of attachment; the results can be explained as well or better in other terms.

Negro Perceptions of the Political Process

We have examined some reasons why Negroes participate in politics in ways different from whites. But toward what ends is Negro political activity directed? What political channels seem most helpful to them in achieving these ends?

The characteristics of the dominant Southern social system have influenced Negroes to take a view of the political process quite different from that of other groups. On the one hand, the impact on them of the system of segregation and discrimination has created and raised to prime importance a complete set of political issues centered on overcoming these hindrances to equality. On the other hand, many of the common agents of political action have become suspect to Negroes because of their role in sustaining that system. For example, although the occupational profile of the Negro population suggests that Negroes would rely heavily on labor unions as agents to gain political goals, their dissatisfaction with union attitudes toward Negro members has tended to raise serious doubts about the utility of their acting through organized labor in the South. Similarly, participation in political parties in the South has not only seemed useless to Negroes, but has also been actively resisted by whites in most areas.

Perceptions of what issues are abroad, what goals are desired, and what the effective channels of action are, vary from person to person according to his education, income, age, and so forth. They also vary, presumably, with his familiarity with the political process. Analysis of how Negroes in Winston-Salem and Durham view the political scene can, therefore, be fruitfully pursued through comparison between low and high participants in the political process.[10]

Issues and Goals

Respondents in the study were asked, "What in your opinion are the most important issues, problems, or projects facing (Winston-Salem) (Durham) at the present time?"[11] Table 9-2 gives a tabulation of the responses. These responses are categorizations of open-ended answers. Accordingly, in picking one answer as attracting a large response it must be conceded that a different method of classification might have resulted in quite a different distribution of percentages.

The most striking discovery is the inability, or refusal, of large numbers of respondents to name any issues at all. This is particularly true of the low participants, as we would imagine, and especially in Winston-Salem, where different question wording put the respondents under less pressure to produce some sort of answer. Such withdrawal from the issues of the day is undoubtedly both cause and effect of the low levels of participation reported by these Negroes. It is more remarkable that 11 per cent of high participants registered no answer to the question about important issues. Part of this may be laid to such extraneous matters at coding and punching errors, respondent refusal to give an answer, and falsification of answers leading to classification on the GPS scale as high participants. Another part can be laid to the core influence of a sense of duty associated with political participation regardless of substantive interest.

Those Negroes stating issues showed a great deal of consistency. In Durham there is considerable emphasis on basic needs for decent material living: jobs, housing, and city services. This is slightly more marked among the low participants, who are likely to be lower in socio-economic standing and, therefore, tend to have more reason to complain. In Winston-Salem something of the same pattern occurs. It is curious that high participants in Winston-Salem put less emphasis

Table 9-2. Issues Considered Most Important by Negroes in Durham and Winston-Salem

	DURHAM		WINSTON-SALEM	
	LOW GPS	HIGH GPS	LOW GPS	HIGH GPS
Proportion of respondents naming no issues	35%	11%	46%	13%
Proportion of respondents naming one or more issues	65	89	54	87
	100%	100%	100%	100%
Total number of issue mentions	329	201	186	75
Percentage of issue mentions dealing with:				
getting new industry	5%	6%	0%	0%
recreation facilities	7	8	3	1
housing	15	13	25	25
better job opportunities; unemployment	20	20	26	17
modernizing downtown area	3	2	0	0
taxes	4	5	0	0
school segregation	14	17	20	25
segregation aside from that involving schools, jobs	4	7	3	3
schools, aside from segregation issue	5	6	7	12
city improvement (streets, fire and police protection, etc.)	16	8	7	13
other	8	8	9	4
	100%	100%	100%	100%

on the problem of job opportunities vis-à-vis low participants than is the case in Durham. Compared to the situation in Durham, job opportunities for lower-class Negroes in Winston-Salem are better, and for higher-class Negroes worse.

School segregation is not uppermost in the minds of most of the Negroes in the two cities, but it is still prominent within the whole range of issues. Its primacy for high-participant Negroes in Winston-Salem may result from the fact that at the time of the survey (summer, 1958) Winston-Salem was nearing the end of only its second year of minimal school integration, a venture undertaken by parents and supporters who without question fall into the high-participant category.

Why do Negroes seek school desegregation? For some it is an end in itself, a chance to disprove the white contention that Negroes are inferior. But there is indirect evidence that for most Negroes desegregation of public schools is desired as a means to a more general material betterment. A large part of the appeal of an unsegregated education is the advantage that it is presumed to offer in later employment. White schools are generally better than Negro schools, in the first place, and in any case most employers are likely to think of them that way. When better job opportunities can be obtained without integrating schools, most Negroes—in Winston-Salem and Durham, at least—seem willing to forego the integration. In this study Negroes were asked to rank the desirability of four different goals by the method of matched pairs. This method involved forcing a choice between better job opportunities and public school integration. Faced with an "either-or" choice, the majority of the Negro respondents chose job opportunities.

In summary, a sizable number of Negroes in Winston-Salem and Durham apparently have few or no political matters on their minds. For those who are conscious of various issues, job opportunities, housing, public school integration, and to a lesser extent better city services, stand out as the most important. There is general consensus between low and high participants on what the main issues are, but the latter tend to place greater stress on the school situation. In turning to a discussion of how Negroes in these two cities evaluate the agents for political action in the local political system, it will be useful to keep in mind both this broader consensus and the subsumed difference in stress on the school issue it incorporated.

Political Agents and Goal Achievement

To whom do Negroes look for help in improving the life conditions of their race? Do they count on their own political and economic strength to gain their objectives, or have they come to hope for benevolent action by whites? Negro respondents were asked to rank six groups as to "which is doing more to help Negroes in (Winston-Salem) (Durham)": businessmen, labor unions, the city government, the political parties, the N.A.A.C.P., and one other Negro-oriented interest group. (In Durham, the D.C.N.A. was specified. In Winston-Salem the Urban League was used in light of widespread unawareness of the U.C.O.) The six chosen were assumed to be among the most prominent political channels of activity, or "agents." Admittedly, others, such as the churches, could profitably have been included.

The average rank assigned to each of the six is given in Table 9-3. To a political analyst the striking aspect of the rank order is the prominence given an interest group, the N.A.A.C.P., and the low esteem afforded the political parties.

The confidence expressed in the activity of the N.A.A.C.P. is clearly evident. Judging from this expression, there appears little justification in Durham or Winston-Salem for Southern whites to claim that the N.A.A.C.P. is out of tune with the thoughts of the general Negro population. Support for the organization and confidence in its work has increased steadily with its successes in the public school segregation cases. This is not so much because the Negro population was previously more timid, but on the contrary because the legalistic approach of the N.A.A.C.P. seemed too cautious.[12] As this approach began to bear substantial results, the dissatisfaction melted rapidly. By 1960 renewed signs of impatience with the organization were appearing, signs implicit in the growth of the "sit-in" demonstrations and "Freedom Riders."

Table 9-3. Ranking of Political Agents in Terms of Helpfulness

"Which of the following would you say is doing more to help Negroes in (Durham) (Winston-Salem)?"	AVERAGE RANK			
	DURHAM		WINSTON-SALEM	
	LOW GPS	HIGH GPS	LOW GPS	HIGH GPS
N.A.A.C.P.	2.0	1.8	2.3	2.5
D.C.N.A.	2.5	2.3	...	...
Urban League	...	...	3.1	2.7
Labor unions	3.6	3.4	3.7	4.3
Businessmen	4.2	4.5	4.1	4.1
City government	4.3	4.6	3.4	3.1
Political parties	4.3	4.5	4.2	4.3

The esteem of the N.A.A.C.P. in Durham and Winston-Salem seems somewhat unusual, given the emphasis Negro respondents placed on job opportunities. N.A.A.C.P. activity in the economic area has not been remarkably successful, nor has the group given particular attention to job equality. Of the seven groups listed in Table 9-3, five besides the N.A.A.C.P. have had important roles in the question of employment discrimination, although not all have taken helpful roles. The self-defined task of the Urban League is almost entirely that of opening new job possibilities. Yet its work has been either so unsuccessful or unheralded that Negroes in Winston-Salem give the League little credit for helping them. It ranks a low second in Table 9-3, mainly because many Negroes answered "Don't know" a disproportionate number of times when the League was compared with other groups.

This incongruence between most-desired goal and perceived most-helpful group may result from the fact that so little has been accomplished in the job area—hence an unwillingness to give much credit to groups attempting to deal with job opportunities. Another possibility is that the N.A.A.C.P. is admired for its successful work in school integration, and integration is highly valued as a goal for the race, but not as a personal goal. Or possibly, the N.A.A.C.P. is rated highly as an emotional reaction to white attacks upon it, attacks interpreted as thrusts against Negro aspirations in general.

The lack of substantial difference of opinion between low and high participants underlines the consensus of approval accorded the N.A.A.C.P. in the Negro population. Privately, white leaders seem aware of this consensus, even though it is sometimes expedient for them to state otherwise in public.

The Urban League is appreciated more by high than by low participants in Winston-Salem. Part of the mediocre ranking given it by low-participant Negroes must be attributed to its slow progress in the economic sphere. But another factor contributing to the low ranking may be found in the operating methods of the organization. The Urban League is not a mass-membership organization depending on membership fees for funds. As a participating agency in the United Fund, it receives most of its money indirectly by means of a pre-established proportion of contributions made to the Fund as a whole. With this arrangement the League has felt less compulsion toward spectacular successes and less need to trumpet those successes it has achieved. This quiet approach is considered imperative in order to maintain over-all community support through the United Fund, and to maintain its strictly biracial character, described earlier. To keep the League's "community service" stance, the Negro personnel have had to assume political neutrality in public, a factor which again diminishes the likelihood that the organization will become well-known or well-liked among the Negro population, particularly in its lower-class, low-participant component.

As mentioned earlier, the Durham Committee on Negro Affairs is under no such constraints and speaks out in a strong voice for Negro rights and privileges in all fields, political, social, and economic. Its high rank is therefore not surprising. Objectively it has done more in Durham for Negroes than the N.A.A.C.P., but the latter is ranked higher. Clearly respondents tended to be more familiar with the N.A.A.C.P.; it is also probable that in evaluating the local chapter they were influenced by their knowledge of the activities and successes of the national organization.

The low opinion of the city government in Durham is in some ways remarkable. For most of the post-World War II years that city has had a government which could be described as "liberal" in matters of race relations. The mayor has been considered generally sympathetic with the desires of the Negro population. He has enjoyed generous support from the D.C.N.A. and other Negro organizations in his campaigns. His city council has never been strongly "liberal," because it is elected by wards rather than at large. But this is also the case in Winston-Salem, where the city government was viewed more favorably by Negro respondents in this study. In Durham city government officials have proceeded cautiously in dealing with the demands of Negroes. While they have been able to maintain Negro voting support, they have apparently won little or no enthusiasm from these constituents. Concessions to Negroes instigated by the city government in Durham match those made by Winston-Salem's city government, but these concessions have nearly always come later in Durham and with greater reluctance.

In an area of the country where labor unions are disliked by those outside the so-called working class and treated with caution even by those within, the ranking of unions as the third most helpful of the six political agents in Durham deserves comment. Negro tobacco workers in that city are unionized for the most part. Moreover, Durham's white unions have added strength to the liberal coalition that has continued to elect the mayor described above. There have been attempts, with varying success, to unite the voting strength of the unions with that of the D.C.N.A. in support of other city and county candidates. As previously noted, the local labor newspaper has taken strongly liberal positions on race as well as other matters. These union efforts apparently have tended to impress Negroes favorably, even though they seem to have had little effect on the attitudes or behavior of rank-and-file white union members.

The low ranking of labor unions in Winston-Salem can be attributed to the fact that the city's industries are not unionized (with one exception). In a pretest, several respondents indicated allegiance to the labor-union movement, but expressed inability to give high rank to something that barely existed. In the one plant that is unionized, those few Negroes who are employed hold service jobs or white-collar jobs, neither of which is affected by the union. It is interesting that low participants rate unions somewhat higher than high participants do. This probably reflects a loyalty to unions consistent with the socio-economic positions of the bulk of low participants. Such loyalty is most likely to distort evaluation when respondents lack much objective information on which to base their judgment.

In both cities businessmen have also been assigned low rank among political agents. It is true that businessmen in these cities, and particularly in Winston-Salem, have gradually made a number of concessions to Negro customers since World War II. For example, retail managers have increasingly instructed their clerks to treat Negro customers politely (wait on them in order, thank them for purchases, and so forth). In more and more shops Negroes are permitted to try on apparel before purchase; and in many retail establishments and business houses separate drinking fountains for the two races have been removed. Each concession has come in response to Negro pressure, to be sure, but once the change was made, there have been no attempts at subterfuge or circumvention. The record of large manufacturers is ambivalent. For the most part job discrimination has been rigidly maintained. Yet some of the most prominent businessmen in Winston-Salem initiated the move to bring in a chapter of the Urban League, and the League's Board of Directors continues to bristle with many of their names. All stores and factories in both cities still maintain separate toilets for the two races. At the time the survey reported in this study was completed, no eating establishments were attempting to serve both races.

On the whole, then, while changes have occurred in attitudes and practices of business establishments regarding Negroes, respondents were apparently not greatly enough impressed to view businessmen as a major source of assistance to Negroes in working for their objectives. Furthermore the Negro populations of both cities are heavily lower class, and in all likelihood share a general lower-class distrust of businessmen, white or Negro.

It is quite apparent from the general ranking that Negroes believe the political parties to be of minimal utility in helping them in their own cities. Low ranking could be the result of Negro feeling that the political parties are not relevant to their goals, or could in a more active sense mirror a realization that the parties—especially the dominant Democratic Party—oppose the particular solutions to issues that Negroes prefer. In the South as a whole, the virtual monopoly of party power in the hands of the Democratic Party has come about by the party's opposition to Negro betterment, especially when such betterment requires a breaking down of segregation. In addition one major consequence of a one-party system of this type is the absence of any coherent party ideology that can be identified with or against the interests of Negroes. In Winston-Salem and Durham candidates supporting widely divergent positions on race-relations issues have won Democratic Party nominations in primaries. Some have been Negroes.

To try to answer whether low ranking of the two parties is due to lack of enthusiasm or to more sharply negative feelings, Durham Negroes were asked a set of questions designed to relate their feelings about four major issues. The questions were: "Would you say the Democratic (Republican) Party has been helpful or not very helpful in solving the problem of school segregation . . . of getting better job opportunities . . . of getting better city services . . . of determining how high or low taxes should be?" A tabulation of the answers is given in Table 9-4. The percentages shown are based only on those respondents who stated an opinion. Excluded from the calculation are those who were noncommittal, who refused to answer, or said they did not know.

As in the general ranking, these noncommital respondents constituted a large element in the over-all picture. The percentage of low participants falling in the noncommittal category ranged from 29 per cent to 36 per cent on the questions about the Democratic Party and from 35 per cent to 40 per cent on the Republican questions. Among high participants the equivalent percentages were smaller: 16–31 per cent and 15–33 per cent, respectively. High participants are most certain about party helpfulness on job opportunities, least certain about their helpfulness on taxes. Low participants are best able to gauge the Democratic Party's helpfulness on school segregation and least able on taxes. Low participants' opinions on the helpfulness of

Table 9-4. Helpfulness of Political Parties in Four Problem Areas *

	Democratic Party Has Been Helpful		Republican Party Has Been Helpful	
	Low GPS	High GPS	Low GPS	High GPS
Job opportunities	76%	69%	28%	43%
School integration	60	50	39	45
City services	71	79	40	59
Lower taxes	60	57	16	19

* Percentages are those saying party has been helpful, when answering. Excluded from the calculation are those who were noncommittal, refused to answer, or said they did not know.

the Republican Party is roughly the same from problem to problem.

Although such a large number of respondents were noncommittal about the helpfulness of the two parties on these four matters, those who did state opinions made some interesting distinctions, issue to issue and between parties. There is general optimism about the Democratic Party. This fact, plus the large number of noncommittal answers, leads to the conclusion that the low general ranking of "the political parties" resulted more from a feeling of irrelevance than of dissatisfaction. But the Democrats are downgraded somewhat on school integration. High participants are particularly cautious in giving the party credit for help in this area. Nor is much enthusiasm kindled for either party on taxes. It appears that Durham Negroes believe city services have been improved and that the Democratic affiliation of the city government is well perceived.

On the Republican side, high participants are more willing to credit that party with being helpful than low participants are. The opposite is the case in the evaluation of the Democratic Party. Remarkably, the Republican Party is given substantial credit for being helpful in getting better city services, despite the fact that no Republican has ever held office in the city government. Perhaps the respondents answered less in terms of the physical services than in terms of who provides them. To them fire and police protection (for example) may have improved simply because Negro policemen and firemen now serve Negro residential areas in Durham. In turn, introduction of

Negroes into such jobs may be attributed to national pressures from the then (1959) Republican administration, tenuous as such a link may objectively have been.

Viewed broadly the results shown in Table 9-4 may be subject to a simpler explanation. What may be occurring here is an interplay between an ordering of issues according to how much progress is seen to have been accomplished in recent years with a basic preference for the Democratic Party over the Republican Party. Thus, given a conviction that the former party is in general more helpful than the latter, the helpfulness attributed to either party varies with perception of how much headway has been made on any one issue or problem. Where either party has a clear ideological image on an issue a final adjustment has been made. Consequently the Republican Party was viewed in 1959 more favorably on a civil rights issue, school desegregation, and the Democratic Party on what can be construed as an economic issue (although "job opportunities" also encompasses basic social issues as well). With a large portion of their interest in better job opportunities focusing simply on reducing unemployment, one suspects that old New Deal loyalties still remain strong.

Our data show strong allegiance to the N.A.A.C.P. and the D.C.N.A. Yet Negro preferences for specific individuals as their political agents is often more striking than for groups. Consensus on candidates for state and local offices in both Winston-Salem and Durham has frequently been overwhelmingly. Bloc voting is sometimes a reprehensible consequence of machine politics, a combination of unthinking loyalty, purchased votes, and corrupt ballot counting. But it is patently clear that bloc voting in these two cities has been perfectly rational for Negroes. It demonstrates the importance of racial attitudes of candidates to Negro voters, the infusion of nearly all public issues with the overriding question of segregation, and the scarcity in most cases of candidates with liberal attitudes on race. Negro voters need to find out which candidates are liberal in this regard, and both the U.C.O. and the D.C.N.A. have served as machines to this extent, by endorsing candidates and informing Negroes of the endorsements. The D.C.N.A. has done a far better job of communicating such information, but Winston-Salem has taken no backseat in ultimate electoral results. Table 9-5 cites the tallies for mayoralty elections in both cities in 1957, to illustrate the point.

When given a chance to choose between more than one liberal, or when forced to make a selection between two candidates neither of whom offers an acceptable choice, Negroes in both cities have shown

Table 9-5. Negro Bloc Voting, Mayoralty Campaigns, 1957

RACIAL MAKE-UP OF PRECINCTS	WINSTON-SALEM: DEMOCRATIC PRIMARY FOR MAYOR		WINSTON-SALEM: GENERAL ELECTION FOR MAYOR		DURHAM *: DEMOCRATIC PRIMARY FOR MAYOR		DURHAM *: GENERAL ELECTION FOR MAYOR	
	KURFEES	SPEAS	KURFEES	MORROW	EVANS	BIGGS, HICKS	EVANS	BIGGS
All Negro	1186	37	2195	89	834	46	1862	141
50% Negro					814	678	1712	1367
25% Negro	213	167	446	327	241	204	471	510
All white	2063	2168	3183	4874	767	1321	1369	3042

* Figures for Durham compiled by Gatlin (1960).

a normal inclination toward diversity of opinion. In the Winston-Salem primary for mayor in 1949, just following a period of high racial tension in that city, the two candidates received 41 per cent and 59 per cent of the votes cast in all-Negro precincts, the same division as in the population as a whole. In this case neither candidate's position on racial matters was sharply differentiated from that of the other. The candidate who received almost 60 per cent was Marshall Kurfees. As seen in Table 9-5, Kurfees in 1957 received 97 per cent of the vote in all-Negro precincts in an election where differentiation on race matters was much sharper.

In Durham another indication that bloc voting is a consequence of attitude consensus rather than machine manipulation was observed in two elections in which both opponents were Negroes. In each election only one candidate was endorsed by the D.C.N.A. He did win, but a substantial vote was cast for his opponent (27 per cent in 1957, 39 per cent in 1953). In another election in the same ward, a white candidate faced a Negro and received only 1 per cent of the vote.

Conclusions

From investigation of Negro participation in and perception of the political process in Winston-Salem and Durham emerges a broader sense of the direction in which the Piedmont Crescent and the so-called New South are traveling. Negro political participation is increasing faster than white participation because of striking changes occurring in such politically relevant personal characteristics as income and education. A marked sex imbalance is likely to diminish as better job opportunities for Negro men develop in the Crescent cities, both contributing to a shift toward the dominant American pattern of male preoccupation with politics and toward an increased over-all level of participation by Negroes.

Even though Durham is not presently growing at the rate of Winston-Salem and other Piedmont Crescent cities, it bears a number of characteristics that make it useful as a predictor of the future course of race relations and Negro political life in the Crescent. The proportion of absentee-owned manufacturing, the increasing economic independence of its Negro population, the greater impersonality of race contacts resulting from this relative independence—all these characteristics are to be found in the kinds of urban communities outside the South that the Piedmont Crescent cities seem destined to resemble. These characteristics have had an impact on Negro politics in Durham, giving rise to stable political organization in response to the necessity of waging political "battle" under nonpaternalistic circumstances. Such a situation seems in prospect for the region as a whole. It is too early to know whether the host of organizations that have arisen to direct "sit-ins" and other types of protest have the staying power to survive and become permanent features of the political scene in the Crescent and elsewhere. But this is a possibility.

While the prospects for increased participation are clear, those for greater diversification of political choice and behavior are more uncertain. Except possibly in national affiliation, Piedmont Crescent Negroes seem firm in their attachment to the Democratic Party. Signs of nascent Republicanism are as yet too feeble to be considered clear indicators. The civil rights actions of Eisenhower's two attorney generals had their effect on the loyalties of some of the more sophisticated Negro citizens, but the Republican Party currently has no positive image to project to Negroes.

Political choice at the state and local level remains severely limited so far as Negroes are concerned because so many issues in Crescent cities continue to have racial overtones. To be sure there are increasing choices between race liberals and conservatives, choices not to be found in other parts of the South. But as long as racial attitudes of candidates have potentially major consequences in wide-ranging policy decisions, Negroes cannot feel too free to let other criteria—economic liberalism or conservatism, competence, incorruptibility, and so forth—affect their electoral choices to the extent these criteria affect the choices of other segments of the population. In the decades to come many of these racial overtones will disappear as one form or another of desegregation becomes accepted as commonplace. But the bloc voting that currently results from such overtones is likely to persist for some time into the future. Experience with the ethnic political behavior in other parts of the country demonstrates that real need for ethnic cohesion at one period of history breeds patterns of political loyalty that extend far beyond the demise of that need. Boston Irish still vote overwhelmingly "for the green" long after the close of the era in which they, like Negroes today, were a despised and distrusted minority.

The hope, then, for greater diversification of electoral choice lies in the proliferation of candidates who are liberal on racial matters but who display a variety of attitudes on other matters of policy. One can only be cautiously optimistic about the speed with which this will transpire in the Piedmont. The day is far off when Negroes will be found running against other Negroes in any campaigns except those involving all-Negro wards. But the number of instances of several white liberals running against each other is definitely on the rise. In some cases this situation aids conservative candidates by splitting the opposition vote. It is, however, less and less true that these instances occur through conscious maneuvering by conservative elements.

The increase in Negro political participation deserves to be counted among the various forces pushing the Piedmont Crescent and North Carolina toward greater acceptance of liberalism, or at least moderation, in race matters. As Negro participation increases, the number of candidate alternatives acceptable to Negroes on the basis of racial attitudes should also increase. In turn the opportunity for a more diversified expression of nonracial political goals through electoral choice will be magnified. Thus the trend in patterns of political behavior toward becoming more like white and over-all American patterns should be accelerated.

The promise of the Piedmont, then, is more Negro participation in politics with greater diversity of choice. It is a promise that someday may render comparisons between Negro and white political behavior redundant.

FOOTNOTES

1. Eight Negroes worked for the Winston-Salem Commission, and four for the Durham one, as of 1957. In 1957 the Winston-Salem Post Office employed seven Negro mail handlers, four carriers, and three clerks. This is in contrast to having none on the payroll (except custodians) ten years earlier (Harvey, 1957, pp. 11, 13). Durham Post Office figures are not given.
2. The particular approach to scaling employed here was developed by Louis Guttman in connection with the well-known American Soldier Project (Stouffer et al., 1951).
3. A major consideration in the selection of particular items, or pieces of information, to form a scale is the "spread" among the items, or the extent to which each is separated from the others. If the subjects under study do two things about as often—for example, if (hypothetically) 21 per cent contribute to political campaign funds and 23 per cent work for party candidates—the ranking of one type of behavior over the other in the prospective scale becomes more dubious. The evidence is strong that they are "tied," that is, they are interchangeable insofar as their value in measuring political activity is concerned. This equivalence generally leads to a marked increase in the number of deviations from a perfect scale pattern and forces the analyst to reject the scale. Consequently it is preferable to choose scale components which are well spread out over the continuum. If five items are used the analyst tries to select five forms of political activity which about 16⅔ per cent, 33⅓ per cent, 50 per cent, 66⅔ per cent, and 83⅓ per cent of the subjects under study report doing. This ideal spread of course can only be approximated, since the way respondents will answer cannot be accurately foretold.
4. It will be noted that the GPS offers little insight into many political acts that hold particular interest for students of politics and community affairs—running for office, being appointed to office, lobbying, campaigning, and the like. All of these acts clearly fall at the extreme upper end of the political activity continuum. A study focused upon people engaged in such activities would be a study of a political elite, for the mainstream of politics catches but a very few in its current. This research, in contrast, is designed to study the many. Political activity in this context is admittedly rudimentary in nature, as illustrated by the range of activities employed to construct the scale. Furthermore, the cities under study are located in a region characterized as relatively apolitical, at least in the sense of active party competition. One partyism tends not only to lower general levels of political participation, but also to divert what participation does exist into nonparty channels.
5. Correlations for this study are measured by the statistics known as Tchuprow's *T*. See Hagood and Price (1952, pp. 170–171).
6. Giving an interesting twist to this line of thinking, Downs (1957, pp. 260–276) suggests that the rational man with full information about how the political system works may well consciously avoid accumulation of facts about specific issues in conflict, as a waste of time and energy.
7. This may reflect the sex bias of the informants, most of whom were men. But this very bias adversely affects women's chances for community leadership.

8. The negative findings for rating of the community, desire to move, length of residence (without and with control for age), and natives versus nonnatives are reported in some detail by Bradbury Seasholes in a manuscript in preparation.
9. It was necessary to combine buyers with owners, and to use broad income categories, because of the small sizes of the sample subgroups.
10. Respondents with a GPS score of 3 or less are classified as low participants.
11. In Durham the word "three" was inserted before "most," resulting on the average in more (rather than fewer) issues being named by each respondent. In an attempt to minimize the effect of the use of different wording in the two cities, the percentages in Table 9-2 have been based on the total number of issues mentioned by respondents, instead of on the total number of respondents.
12. Garfinkel (1959, p. 8) makes this observation in comparing the relatively greater appeal to the Negro mass of Phillip Randolph's "March on Washington Movement" of 1941.

REFERENCES

Campbell, Angus, Phillip E. Converse, Warren E. Miller, and Donald E. Stokes (1960), *The American Voter.* New York: John Wiley and Sons.

Downs, Anthony M. (1957), *An Economic Theory of Democracy.* New York: Harper & Brothers.

Garfinkel, Herbert (1959), *When Negroes March.* Glencoe, Ill.: The Free Press.

Gatlin, Douglas S. (1960), "A Case Study of a Negro Voters' League: The Durham Committee on Negro Affairs in Municipal Elections," *Research Reports,* No. 2, Political Studies Program, Department of Political Science, University of North Carolina, Chapel Hill.

Hagood, Margaret J., and Daniel O. Price (1952), *Statistics for Sociologists.* New York: Henry Holt.

Harvey, Samuel D. (1957), "Community Relations in Winston-Salem, North Carolina," unpublished monograph, Winston-Salem Urban League.

Heard, Alexander (1948), *A Two-Party South?* Chapel Hill, N. C.: University of North Carolina Press.

Hyman, Herbert A. (1959), *Political Socialization.* Glencoe, Ill.: The Free Press.

Key, V. O., Jr. (1950), *Southern Politics in State and Nation.* New York: Alfred A. Knopf.

Lazarsfeld, Paul F., Bernard Berelson, and Hazel Gaudet (1948), *The People's Choice.* New York: Columbia University Press.

Price, H. Douglas (1957), *The Negro and Southern Politics.* New York: New York University Press.

Stouffer, Samuel A., et al. (1951), *The American Soldier,* Vol. 4. Princeton, N. J.: Princeton University Press.

Walker, Harry T. (1945), "Changes in Race Accommodation in a Southern Community," unpublished Ph.D. dissertation, Division of Social Sciences, University of Chicago.

Part Three

Social Correlates of Urban Growth and Development

by John Gulick

PART THREE portrays various aspects of life in the cities of Greensboro, Burlington-Graham, Durham, and Raleigh—in other words, in the eastern half of the Piedmont Industrial Crescent. Although the material was obtained in the course of three studies which were conceived and executed independently of each other, it often touches on the same issues in the same localities. Since these parallel findings turn out to be consistent in some important respects, our confidence in generalizing from them is augmented.

The ensuing chapters deal with a wide variety of personal actions, attitudes, and circumstances. Are any of them peculiarly characteristic of the Piedmont Industrial Crescent or of the Southeastern region? Can, on the other hand, any of them be seen as being characteristic of North American cities in general which are of comparable size? This is an appropriate place in which to raise some specific questions along these lines, and the reader can, from his own experience, supply many answers.

It will be well to recognize explicitly an epistemological limitation which applies to nearly all of Part Three. The information was obtained by formal interviews, structured largely in terms of closed-end questionnaire items, and it is therefore purely verbal in nature. The data are, in effect, statements which were made, on the multiple-choice principle, by the informants about their feelings and actions. Although we can assume that most people consciously try to be truthful under such circumstances, we also know that their vision of the truth can easily be affected by wishful thinking, idealizations, and being requested to express standardized opinions on matters to which they ordinarily give very little thought. Without direct observation which requires personal acquaintance and great expenditures of time, there is no really reliable way either of locating or of correcting for such biases, and such techniques can, in practical terms, reach only a small fraction of the number of people whose statements are the substance of these chapters. One pays one's money and takes one's choice. In this case, our choice involves our recognition that, strictly speaking, the only facts that we have to offer are the various types of response which various numbers of people gave. We then take these responses at face value and describe and analyze them as if they were items of observed behavior (in the case of responses about actions) and as if (in the case of statements of opinion) there were no such things as inconsistency, indecisiveness, and vagueness of attitudes and feelings. Ideally, such a procedure should be subject to any necessary corrections derived from research by participant observation. In our case, we and the reader must as much as possible leaven our conclusions with common sense and comparative knowledge.

We have no reason to believe that the findings in these chapters are not representative of the Crescent as a whole, except in one respect. All the information in Chapters 10 and 12 was given by white persons, and much of it may well not be representative of the opinions and actions of the Negroes who constitute approximately one quarter of the population in the cities involved in the research. In Chapter 12 attention is drawn to the probable reflections of this selectivity on the class composition of the interviewed population, and we can be sure that if the Negroes were included, many of the distributions discussed in this chapter and in Chapter 10 would be considerably different.

There were two primary reasons for not soliciting information from Negroes: (1) serious biasing effects of using either white or Negro interviewers were suspected but could not, at the time, be controlled for; and (2) the Institute for Research in Social Science was in the process of planning a special Negro research project in the area. This project has since been put into operation, and one phase of it has involved the use of part of the Greensboro questionnaire which was used to gather material for Chapter 10. In other words, exactly comparable material on Negroes and whites in Greensboro will before long be available, but this takes us beyond our present concerns. Information from Negroes is included in Chapter 11.

Some striking correspondences between Chapters 10 and 12 tend to confirm general impressions of the Crescent as an urban area:

1. Its nonnative population is recruited very largely from the immediately surrounding area and from smaller towns than the prominent communities of the Crescent. Regionality and homogeneity are hallmarks of this urban area. These are obviously not characteristic of American cities of comparable size which are growing more rapidly by reason of immigration from all parts of the country. But it is not so obvious how, for example, the neighborhood and friendship patterns of Greensboro may differ from those of Fresno or San Jose, California.

2. Prominent among the well-educated, upward mobile residents are newcomers from outside the region. To some extent related to this is the fact that the upper class in the Crescent is not pre-empted by old, local families. This latter point is clearly implied in Chapter 12 and is demonstrated in findings supplementary to those in Chapter 10. (See Gulick and Bowerman, 1961, Appendix.)

3. The generally upward mobile and middle-class character of the Crescent is exaggerated by the exclusion of information on Negroes, but even if one corrects for this exclusion, we here see phenomena which are not peculiar to the Crescent alone but are nation-wide trends. It should be noted that while there is a marked tendency semantically to promote blue-collar workers into the middle class, this does not necessarily imply any decrease in consciousness of and concern for social differentials.

4. Continued industrialization, which, willy-nilly, will probably be at a relatively slow pace, will tend to perpetuate the rather positive

type of urbanization characteristic of the Crescent. Yet it must not be too slow if the Crescent is to keep pace with the region.

Is the aura of bland satisfaction which is imparted by Chapters 10 and 11 purely an artifact of the questionnaire situation? Possibly there is an element of artificial exaggeration, but the relatively stressless processes of newcomer adaptation in the Crescent, which do not necessarily apply in more rapidly growing and heterogeneous cities, need to be taken into account also. But beyond this, we may question whether there is anything particularly regional about this quality. We may see here a reflection of the times in which the research was done —the late 1950's—a time in the United States as a whole which has been widely noted for its prosperous complacency. While roughly 6 per cent of the United States population lives in cities of the same range of size as those discussed in Chapters 10, 11, and 12, similar living conditions are found in both smaller and larger cities and even in many suburbs of the really large metropolitan areas. Indeed, thanks to industrialization and concomitant saturation by modern transportation facilities and the mass media of communication, the Crescent can be looked upon as being a series of suburbanized small towns, replete with suburban values and social patterns which are found among far more than 6 per cent of the population of the United States. It remains to be seen whether, without the irritations of metropolitan commutation, the people of the Crescent will see as a problem the "urban devastation" of the parking lot for which Greensboro was recently immortalized (Mumford, 1961, plate 47). Or will the strong familism of the Crescent, as illustrated in Chapter 10, which also may be a nation-wide phenomenon (Haller, 1961, pp. 621–622), provide a sufficient haven from such threats?

While the South is supposed to be particularly strongly church-oriented, and Chapter 10 would support this stereotype, the close relationship between religious and other social participation would not at present seem to be a characteristic peculiar to the South or to the Crescent. For,

> . . . it is only too evident that the religiousness characteristic of America today is very often a religiousness . . . (which is) a way of sociability or "belonging" rather than a way of reorienting life to God.
>
> The other-directed man or woman is eminently religious in the sense of being religiously identified and affiliated, since being religious and joining a church or synagogue is, under contemporary American conditions, a fundamental way of "adjusting" or "belonging." (Herberg, 1960, p. 260.)

These statements, written with the entire United States in mind, are wholly consistent with the findings of Chapter 10, although our questions did not attempt directly to probe the difficult issue of the depth of sincere religious commitment.

In the balance, the social correlates of urban growth and development in the Crescent seem more to reflect patterns of the national culture as a whole than they do particular, regional specializations.

The preceding part of this introduction can be taken as an indication of some of the Piedmont Industrial Crescent's prominent "urban thoughtways," to which reference was made in Chapter 1 of this volume. What implications do they have for the control processes connected with urban development policy? While no "scientific" answer to such a question is available, we can make a pair of educated guesses.

First, policy makers should not expect the "average citizen," as delineated in Part Three, necessarily to be the initiator of any grassroots ground swell of enthusiasm for any far-reaching urban-development policies. The already existing appropriate authorities see present problems and the threat of future ones more clearly than the layman, and it is they who must continually initiate leadership in their solution. This is not to say that the public is incapable of perceiving such problems and taking action, for there are instances on record of public arousal and resulting action, but conditions usually must become very bad indeed before such arousal crystallizes—with much waste of effort and funds as a result. As will be seen in the following chapters, despite their complaints about such things as traffic problems, most of the people are generally satisfied with their lot and not generally inclined to take any action concerning their complaints.

Second, the leadership of urban planners, in its necessary task of seeking public support and interest, must be "practical" if it is to be persuasive. However much we may sympathize (as this writer personally does) with the esthetic orientations of urban planners, we must recognize that the average citizen is not primarily moved by such considerations. The following chapters indicate the likelihood that as long as new jobs and opportunities for upward social mobility are available in the Crescent, people will continue to migrate to its cities regardless of other conditions in them. Pressures for improvements over and beyond those concerned with job opportunities are not likely to develop "spontaneously." The urban planner at his best must avoid the temptation to succumb to the operations of Parkinson's Law in proposing solutions to exaggerated hypothetical problems in the future; at the same time, he must be alert to immediate present problems, such as building proposals whose execution would be certain to create even worse traffic problems or to obliterate all possibilities for playgrounds or parks. Granted that long-range planning—provided it is not dogmatic and inflexible—is necessary, public support of it must be built gradually by means of more immediate step-by-step procedures.

None of this should be taken to imply that the people of the Crescent are to be talked down to as if they were shortsighted children. They are not, but, as the following chapters show, they are people whose time and energies are devoted largely to work, family life, social activities, and some personal relaxation; people who, rightly or wrongly but along with most of their compatriots, expect municipal and other authorities "to do their duty" in regard to taking care of public needs. Compared to the average citizens of cities in the underdeveloped parts of the world today, they are very public spirited indeed and capable of effective support and action on problems which are intelligently set forth to them. Attempts, however, to win their support by lectures from condescending experts or to bamboozle them with grandiose abstract schemes are very likely to fail, or worse, to cause confusion and distrust of all efforts on behalf of controlled, farsighted urban development.

REFERENCES

Gulick, John, and Charles E. Bowerman (1961), *Adaptation of Newcomers in the Piedmont Industrial Crescent,* Urban Studies Program, Institute for Research in Social Science, University of North Carolina, Chapel Hill.

Haller, A. G. (1961), "The Urban Family," *American Journal of Sociology,* **LXVI:** 6, 621–622.

Herberg, Will (1960), *Protestant, Catholic, Jew,* rev. ed. Garden City, N. Y.: Doubleday Anchor Books. Copyright © 1955, by Will Herberg. Reprinted by permission of Doubleday & Company, Inc.

Mumford, Lewis (1961), *The City in History.* New York: Harcourt, Brace, and World.

Chapter 10

Newcomer Enculturation in the City: Attitudes and Participation

by John Gulick, Charles E. Bowerman, and Kurt W. Back *

THE RESEARCH reported on in this chapter was conceived in the context of certain long-held notions about the nature of urban life in the United States. In brief, these notions are that the city constitutes an unfavorable environment for social life, and as evidence for the validity of this notion, statistics on the high rates of urban crime and other social ills have been amassed in the literature. We do not deny that these social ills exist in cities in general, or in the cities we studied in particular, but we are very conscious that the proponents of the traditional urban stereotype have generally ignored the fact that most

* Robert E. Agger was a senior participant in this study before and during the Durham survey. In the writing of this chapter, Back prepared the sections on the reasons and decisions to migrate and on personality characteristics. Bowerman and Gulick shared responsibilities for analysis and writing of the remainder of the sections, with Gulick taking responsibilities for organizing the chapter and preparing the final draft. John W. Ruff supervised the interviewing in Durham and the coding of the Durham schedules. Angell G. Beza supervised the interviewing in Greensboro and did the machine analysis of the data for both surveys. David A. Gover collected and analyzed the data on the marital satisfactions of employed women.

For an expanded version of this chapter, including numerous tables, see Gulick and Bowerman (1961).

city dwellers are not demonstrably either the victims or the perpetrators of such social ills.

What, then, of this majority? Are they rootless, frustrated, and anomic pawns in an anonymous mass? Are they, by way of compensation perhaps, hard-driving and manipulative in personality; or, by way of another form of compensation, do they feel compelled to join every possible association in their ken in the urgent desire to fill the vacuum caused by too few close personal relationships with a large number of superficial ones? The urban stereotype would suggest an affirmative answer to these questions.

In general, our findings do not support this urban stereotype. While this cannot be taken as a refutation of the stereotype, it emphasizes the possibility that it may be appropriately applied only to certain kinds of city dwellers anywhere, and that it may be less prevalent in some kinds of city than in others. One of the theses of this book is that a particular kind of urban growth is taking place in this increasingly industrial section of the Middle South. In what follows we shall set forth certain correlates of that growth as they are reflected in social behavior. This social behavior appears to be characteristic of this particular urban area, and there is some evidence that it is not peculiar to it alone. More we cannot say at the present, although the facts should certainly be clear by now that there are many different kinds of urban settlement in the United States and that urbanization is a many-faceted phenomenon which cannot be assumed to have the same effects everywhere and under all conditions.

Since migrants (or "newcomers") to a city must make a series of new adjustments there, since most cities' populations consist very largely of newcomers (or nonnatives), and since they are obviously primary agents in urban growth, our analysis has been conducted to a large degree in terms of the length of residence of our informants in the cities in question. Furthermore, a whole section of our material is concerned with the motivations and conditions of migration.

Our information was obtained by house-to-house interviews in Durham in the summer of 1958, and in Greensboro in the winter of 1959–1960. For this purpose, 42 residential blocks in Durham and 54 in Greensboro were chosen by means of random sampling. An effort was made to conduct interviews in every household, with some systematic exceptions, in each block. There were, of course, some refusals, and there were cases of households where no one could ever be found at home. Nevertheless, 602 interviews were completed in Durham. Of this total, 258 were with men and 344 were with women.

The great majority of these people were married, but for the most part, each person represented a different household. The median ages of the men and women were 44 and 43 years respectively. Somewhat less than one sixth of the people interviewed in Durham were 60 years of age or older. In Greensboro, interviews were conducted in 509 households in each of which a married couple was present, and a separate interview was completed with both the husband and the wife —making a total of 1,018 persons interviewed. The Greensboro sample was slightly younger than the Durham one, the median ages of the men and women being, respectively, 41 and 37 years. About one tenth of the people in the Greensboro sample were 60 years of age or older.

Speaking generally, from a composite picture of both cities, we can indicate some further characteristics of the people who were interviewed. In terms of occupation, they would conventionally be thought of as upper- to lower-middle class. Between a quarter and a third of the men have professional or managerial positions, and about half of them are in clerical, sales, service, and skilled labor occupations. A quarter of the men are college graduates, and about a fifth of the women are. Approximately one-third of the men and women did not complete high school. The median family income is between $4,000 and $5,000 a year, and in somewhat more than a third of the cases, the wives contribute to the family income by full-time or part-time work outside the house. Over 75 per cent of the households are located in single houses, but there are some apartment dwellers. Last, they are overwhelmingly Protestant in religious affiliation.

The methods of interviewing were somewhat different in the two cities. In Durham the interviewers asked questions from a mimeographed schedule on which they recorded the answers. In Greensboro, the informants themselves filled out a printed questionnaire, the interviewers' function being largely that of clarifying any problem of interpretation which might arise. In designing the Greensboro questionnaire, we had the benefit of knowing the strengths and weaknesses of the Durham schedule. Consequently, while the two instruments are in many respects comparable in coverage, the Greensboro questionnaire also diverges to some extent in content and in the phrasing of certain questions. The Durham survey, in other words, became in some ways a pretest of the Greensboro one. When we compared the results of the two surveys, we discovered that in a number of comparable respects (such as those which have been indicated above), the two samples are quite similar to each other. For these reasons, as well as those of space, the remainder of this chapter will present detailed information very largely from Greensboro only. While detailed information from Durham will occasionally be introduced, the major characteristics of that city's sample will be indicated by pointing out to what degree the Greensboro characteristics are similar to them.

Characteristics of Newcomers as Migrants

Forty-three per cent of the Greensboro sample had lived there for at least 20 years, but only a fifth were born in that city, and another 10 per cent had moved there before the age of 15 and remained there since. At the other extreme, almost 10 per cent of the sample had moved to Greensboro within the past year. Over a fourth of both the men and the women had been there fewer than 6 years. The city can therefore be characterized as having a fairly even balance between newcomers, oldtimers, and natives resulting from a steady growth over a long period of time.

As would be expected, the newcomers are represented more heavily in the younger age groups. Thirty-five per cent of those people who had lived in Greensboro under 6 years were under 35 years of age. Since age is related to migration and also to many of the other characteristics which we wish to compare by length of residence, we have held age roughly constant in the analysis of characteristics of migrants to Greensboro by dividing the sample into two age groups—those under 35 and those 35 and over—giving the distribution by length of residence shown in Table 10-1.

In regard to the places from which the Greensboro migrants moved, 63 per cent of the men moved from other parts of North Carolina—most of them from within 50 miles of Greensboro—and another 23 per cent moved from other parts of the South. The smallest percentage of migrants from North Carolina is not found among the most recent migrants in general but among the most recent migrants who are 35 years of age or older. These are, correspondingly, the people of whom proportionally more have come from outside the South. The same pattern is found among the Greensboro women and, in general, in Durham.

Another interesting characteristic of recent migrants to Greensboro is their amount of education. Only 17 per cent of the recent migrants

Table 10-1. Greensboro: Length of Residence by Age and Sex

	MEN		WOMEN	
	NO.	%	NO.	%
Under age 35				
Under 2 years	48	9.4	58	11.4
2 to 5 years	32	6.3	40	7.9
Over 5 years	39	7.7	58	11.4
Native	52	10.2	44	8.6
35 years of age and over				
Under 2 years	24	4.7	17	3.3
2 to 5 years	30	5.9	25	4.9
6 to 20 years	104	20.4	106	20.8
Over 20 years	90	17.7	87	17.1
Native	90	17.7	74	14.5
Total	509	100.0	509	99.9

(within the last 6 years) under 35 years of age failed to complete high school, compared with 37 per cent of those under 35 who came over 6 years ago and 28 per cent of the younger natives. In further contrast, 53 per cent of the natives over 35 years of age did not complete high school. To state these results in another way, migrants in general have more education than natives, and the younger recent migrants have more education than the older migrants. If this trend (noticeable also in Durham) continues, the characteristics of urban centers in the Crescent may be expected to change, with the "transfusion" of young, well-educated migrants.

Many of the younger recent migrants are newly married, some of them having married since moving to Greensboro. Yet 74 per cent of the couples who have been there under 2 years have children, compared with 88 per cent of the rest of the couples under 35. Recent migration has not involved living with parents. Only one of the young couples who have been in Greensboro less than 3 years have a parent or parent-in-law living with them in the same household. It will be seen later, however, that many of them have parents living within distances of easy communication.

Questions were asked about religious affiliation and attendance. As would be expected, older couples are more likely to belong to a church and to attend services than are the younger couples, and the women go more often than their husbands. It is of interest, however, that within each of the age groups, membership and attendance vary only slightly by length of residence. There is a very slight increase in frequency of attendance among younger couples by length of residence, and the same can be said for the older women. The greatest difference is among the older men; 58 per cent of those who have been in Greensboro under 6 years attend church services twice a month or more, compared with 73 per cent of those who came earlier. On the other hand, only 53 per cent of the older native men attend as frequently. It should be said that these variations occur within a fairly "churchy" group, since the frequency is high for all groups.

These results lend support to the contention that church-going is one of the effective ways in which a person can become acquainted in a new community. Our newcomers apparently joined early and attend often.

With respect to type of residence, the majority of the young newcomers first take up residence in an apartment or duplex. The proportion reduces sharply after 2 years, and even more after 6 years, when most people are found in single houses. The age difference is striking in this regard. Whereas only 37 per cent of the "under 2-year" migrants who are less than 35 years old live in a single house, 79 per cent of those over 35 are single-house dwellers. In part this reflects the needs of larger families, but lack of capital is probably the main factor. In regard to urban satisfaction, this may be a significant point, since the general community orientation of a family may be greatly affected by its housing facilities. Those living in apartments cannot be as highly "home centered" as those living in a single house of their own, and they are more likely to seek their satisfactions in relationships with job and people. Possibly this is a characteristic of age as well, with older people increasingly turning to upkeep of house and grounds as a source of satisfaction and as an anchor in the community.

Along the same lines, only two of the younger families claim ownership of their homes, although the percentage of those who are in the process of buying them increases with length of residence. Among the older couples, a larger proportion of them who have been in Greensboro over 20 years own houses than do natives, probably reflecting an economic differential between older migrants and natives.

Occupational differences among the men, by length of residence, are quite striking. Out of 67 men classified as professional or technical, only 5 are natives. One-fourth of the younger men of less than 2 years' residence are in this occupational category, as are a third of the young men who have been in Greensboro from 2 to 6 years. On the other hand, those in the managerial, official, and proprietary occupational classification are of longer residence, mainly in the older group. Newer migrants are also more likely to be clerical or sales workers, while those who came more than 10 years ago are more apt to be craftsmen or operatives. Eighty-two per cent of the men over 35 plan to stay on in the same job. The recently arrived younger men, however, are less likely to be stable in their job plans, with only 61 per cent of those who moved less than 6 years ago planning to stick with the present job, compared with 79 per cent of those who have been in Greensboro longer or are natives.

Reasons for Migration

Most discussions of urban growth assume that the principal reasons for migration are economic. Our data from both Durham and Greensboro support this assumption. When asked for the principal reason for moving to Greensboro, 45 per cent of the male respondents answered "job offer," another 18 per cent listed "better economic opportunity," and 18 per cent said it was a necessity, often a job transfer. Two-thirds of the women listed one of these three reasons as primary. Among all the reasons listed, educational opportunity was indicated in only one out of seven cases and only 5 per cent of the respondents indicated dislike of their former place of residence as a reason. A few moved because a parent was moving, and 40 per cent of the women listed move of husband as a reason. It is interesting that one-fourth of the women put marriage as a reason for moving. Unfortunately, we cannot tell if they moved to find someone to marry or because the person they planned to marry lived in Greensboro.

When asked for reasons for not wishing to leave their former place of residence, the respondents listed friends and family in about equal amounts. Women were over twice as likely to mention these things as were men, again emphasizing the importance of the job sphere in the total life interests of men. Women were also three times (30 per cent) as likely to mention that they did not want to leave the old place because they liked it. Surprisingly, only 10 per cent of the men and 15 per cent of the women mentioned having a home as reason for not wanting to move. Since these reasons are mainly noneconomic, the apparent conservatism of women seems to derive from their being more involved in the life of the community and less in direct economic pursuits. They are more likely to consider the personal relationships of a place in thinking about a move.

Since we are dealing only with people who did move, and for whom economic considerations appeared to be supreme, we should not forget that those who did not move either had fewer economic opportunities, or were possibly more influenced by some of the noneconomic factors.

Decisions to Migrate

It might be supposed that a decision which has such important consequences on the life of a person or household as moving would be considered for a long time and only undertaken after considerable deliberation. In fact, however, the typical migrants seem to feel few qualms about moving. Several questions about the period which led up to the move point to the same conclusion. The migrants were asked, "How long, before deciding to move, did you think about it?" Almost two-fifths of the men made up their minds in less than a month, and the majority took less than three months. The women took slightly longer. Both men and women usually agree that it was the husband who first brought up the subject of moving. However it seems that it took the women longer to come to a decision to make the actual move once the subject had been brought up. This conforms with the finding that women are more reluctant to leave, being more concerned about leaving friends and family. However, the majority of both men and women report that the decision itself came easily.

If a decision is a product of long deliberation, it may be discussed at length, and alternatives may be considered. Neither seems to have been particularly the case with our respondents. The respondents in Greensboro were asked whether anybody tried either to discourage or encourage them to move. To both questions a large majority gave negative replies. Similarly, only a fifth considered moving to any other place than Greensboro. On the other hand, only a minority reached Greensboro with the definite decision to stay, and even now only one third of the in-migrants definitely expect to stay for good. This does not mean, however, that they are unhappy with their move.

Nine out of ten, knowing what they do now about Greensboro, said that they would decide again to move to it if they had the chance.

The casual approach to migration becomes comprehensible if we remember that for this group residential mobility plays a role secondary to that of decisions about occupations. It is primarily the economic opportunities which form the attractions of the city, and deliberations and decision making were probably concerned much more with the job conditions and less with the particular features of the city in which the job was located. Results from the Durham sample, where questions were comparable, support these conclusions in Greensboro almost identically.

The predominance of economic factors in decisions to move does not automatically mean that all migrants feel that migration is forced on them by necessity. Among the more recent migrants, particularly, there are explicit statements of a favorabe attitude toward migration. This may well be due to the fact that many of these people have professional occupations which in themselves often entail migration for the sake of advancement. Or, to put the matter in another way, *there are indications in our findings of the emergence of positive attitudinal and emotional adaptations to the fact that migration is an integral aspect of many contemporary occupations.*

General Community Satisfaction

Having given some consideration to the origins of the newcomers and to their reasons for moving, we may now turn to a consideration of the various aspects of the attitudes and social activities of our urban samples as a whole.

The respondents in Greensboro were asked four questions each of which was intended to elicit answers which would indicate degree of general satisfaction with Greensboro as a place in which to live. One question asked directly how satisfied (or unsatisfied) they felt they were. The second asked how much they felt they would miss Greensboro if they had to move away. The third asked how often they wished they did not live in Greensboro, and the fourth asked how often they felt Greensboro was a wonderful place in which to live. The responses to these questions were highly consistent with each other. The four items were scaled to produce ranked scores ranged from 0 to 7 with a median score of 4.87. For analysis of the relationship between other items and community satisfaction, scale scores 5, 6, and 7 were combined as high satisfaction, scores 3 and 4 for medium satisfaction, and 0 to 2 as low satisfaction. Forty-nine per cent of the men and 62 per cent of the women were in the high-satisfaction group, 29 and 17 per cent were in the medium group, and 22 and 21 per cent, respectively, were rated as having low satisfaction.

In general, the percentage of informants expressing high satisfaction increases with length of residence. For example, it is 28 per cent among the men under 35 who have lived in Greensboro less than 2 years, contrasted with 44 per cent among the native men in this age group. Among the men over 35, there is the same pattern of increase with length of residence, but in general more of the older men express high satisfaction than do the younger ones. Thirty per cent of the most recent migrants over 35 express high satisfaction, as opposed to 70 per cent of the native men. The low level of general satisfaction among the younger men is not related to job satisfaction in itself, for their level of job satisfaction is not lower than that of the older men.

It is interesting to note that the big increase in satisfaction for older couples does not occur until after 6 years of residence, after which it remains about the same. Younger couples possibly adjust more readily to a new community, or maybe the difference between older and younger couples' rates of "adjustment" is a product of the type of migrant attracted at different ages. In all but one comparison, the women are more likely to express a high degree of general satisfaction than men. Whether this is because modern urban living is more stressful for men than for women or because women simply respond more readily to extreme positive statements in regard to satisfaction, we do not know.

For both men and women, there is a U-shaped relationship between general satisfaction and education. Fifty-nine per cent of the men and 89 per cent of the women with 6 or less years of education are in the high satisfaction category. This percentage declines with increasing education to 41 and 50 per cent of the men and women, respectively, who completed high school but went no further. It then increases with some college education and completion of college to 59 per cent and 70 per cent of the latter group. The nature of our occupational and values structure may be such, as some studies indicate, that people with less than a high school education have fewer aspirations and consequently fewer dissatisfactions; that those with college education have high aspirations which they are able to achieve in large measure; but that those with only a high school diploma acquire the aspirations but are unable to achieve them in sufficient measure to be truly satisfied with their existence.

The number of children a couple has in itself appears to have no relationship with general urban satisfaction. However, those couples who have no children are more frequently highly satisfied than those with children, but this statistical finding is affected by the high satisfaction of older couples whose children have grown up and left home. We do not know whether their high satisfaction is due to absence of children in itself. For those who have children, the age of the children seems to be related to general satisfaction. Both men and women all of whose children are under 6 years of age have the lowest percentage satisfied of any group. These are more likely to be newcomers, and it may be that small children make it more difficult to establish those community contacts which lead to a satisfactory adjustment in the new location. At any rate, there are other factors in the low satisfaction of the most recent newcomers. In cases where all of the children are over 13, the per cent satisfied is quite high, and those couples with children at varying ages in between are only slightly lower. Without more detailed analysis of our data it would be hazardous to venture further interpretation, but it is suggested that family structure is very possibly a factor of importance in determining general satisfaction, particularly for the newcomer.

Very few of our families have other adults living in their home. Even in these few cases, however, there are no important differences in general satisfaction between those with relatives in the home and those without. Nor is report of a major illness in the family during the previous year related to satisfaction. Interestingly enough, chronic illness or permanent physical disability of the spouse appears to decrease satisfaction considerably, whereas report of such an affliction to self does not affect satisfaction.

Our sample is predominantly Protestant. However, 81 per cent of the 32 Jewish respondents in it fall in the highly satisfied group, compared with 53 per cent of the 38 Catholics and 55 per cent of the Protestants. Church affiliation is related to general satisfaction. The percentage of highly satisfied men who are affiliated with a church is 12 per cent greater than that of those who are not affiliated, and for women the difference is 20 per cent. The drop-off in percentage satisfied among the men shows up sharply among those who attend church less than once a month, while the percentage satisfied among the women decreases among those who attend less than twice per month. It is clear from these two bodies of data that there is a significant relationship between urban satisfaction and church relations. Church-going may in part be an expression of satisfaction, but, on the other hand, many kinds of satisfaction may find their source in religion and the associations formed in the church.

Community satisfaction shows a definite relationship with the occupation of the husband. Sixty-two per cent of the men in the professional, managerial, and proprietary category are highly satisfied, compared with 42 per cent of the men in clerical, sales or skilled occupations, and only 34 per cent in semiskilled and laboring. Employment of the wife is related to lower satisfaction for both husbands and their wives. Degree of expressed job satisfaction has a high relationship with general satisfaction. Fifty-six per cent of the men who like their jobs very much have high general satisfaction, compared with 30 per cent of those who are neutral and 23 per cent of those disliking their jobs. The comparison for employed women is very similar.

To summarize other relationships briefly, those people in Greensboro who are most likely to express high general satisfaction are: (1) couples who have lived in their present house for a relatively long time; (2) couples living in single houses; (3) those owning their home; (4) individuals rating themselves as upper or upper-middle class; (5) those coming from other than lower-class families; (6) those feeling that they are adequately paid for their work; (7) those who say they can buy all the things they really need plus a few luxuries; (8) those couples in which the wife is not employed; (9) those men (but not women) who had lived a relatively short time in the place from which they moved to Greensboro; (10) those men who moved to Greensboro from outside the South.

In Durham a single question on general satisfaction, the same as the first of those used in Greensboro, was asked, and it yielded similar results: namely, a preponderance of expressions of medium to high satisfaction and a definite increase of high satisfaction with increase of length of residence.

In addition, a long series of questions which sought to find out what aspects of living in the community were most likely to be associated with general satisfaction or dissatisfaction were asked in Durham but not in Greensboro. As might be expected, since the subject is a common source of ironic humor in the culture at large, the most frequently expressed complaints related to economic aspects of living such as shopping and traffic facilities (an acknowledged public problem in Durham) and amount of available money to spend. However, although the generally dissatisfied people more frequently expressed dissatisfaction with these aspects of life than did the generally satisfied, it was not economics which primarily distinguished the generally dissatisfied from the generally satisfied. Rather, it was the very high frequency among the dissatisfied of complaints concerning social relationships (church affiliation, frequency of contacts with friends, and the kind of people associated with) which distinquished them from the generally satisfied. These complaints (which suggest intrapersonal as well as interpersonal problems) occurred at least twice as frequently among the dissatisfied than among the satisfied, and more than half of the dissatisfied complained about lack of sufficient contact with friends.

Amid overwhelmingly frequent expressions of general satisfaction, there are some negative factors. Newcomers tend to be less frequently satisfied, generally and specifically, than oldtimers. Specific dissatisfactions, such as they are, recur in consistent ways. There are economic factors, such as traffic conditions and inadequate shopping facilities, which are related to the community as a whole, but they do not deter most people from saying that on the whole they are satisfied. The fact that relatives and friends are not near enough is another relatively frequent source of dissatisfaction. It is most frequent among newcomers, and for them, but largely for them only, the community is deficient, although the deficiency has been caused not by the community but by their migration. Third, a sense of having too few friends (regardless of place) and of lack of "fellowship" are factors for dissatisfaction among some.

It is among people affected by the second and third sets of factors that we may assume that the elements of dissociation, rootlessness, and anomie are most likely to occur. However, the second factor is likely to be only temporary if the newcomers remain in the city. The third, which does not seem to vary with length of residence, is, it may be suggested, possibly more a function of personality orientation than of lack of community adaptation. On the whole, it would seem that expressions of general satisfaction and dissatisfaction are expressions of a product of more specific sentiments and that the causes of these sentiments are anchored primarily in the individual. "General community satisfaction," therefore, would appear to be more a general sentiment or feeling tone rather than an attitude toward the community as some sort of entity or unitary organism.

We now turn to considerations of various dimensions of the urban social life of individuals.

Several questions were asked of both the Durham and the Greensboro samples about the degree of satisfaction with their marriage. On one of these questions, "Considering everything, has marriage been, for you: very unhappy, somewhat unhappy, about average, quite happy, extremely happy," 3.7 per cent of the men and 2.9 per cent of the women in Durham gave one of the two "unhappy" responses, while about 40 per cent of each sex said they were "extremely happy." In Greensboro, 8 per cent said they were unhappy and 35 per cent were extremely happy. The distributions for the two cities are fairly close, but the slightly higher degree of unhappiness in Greensboro may be due to the fact that the data were collected more anonymously by the type of questionnaire used there.

A scale of marital satisfaction was constructed from the responses of the Greensboro sample to the seven items about satisfaction with marriage. These items formed a quasi-scale with scores ranging from 0 to 10. Table 10-2 shows the relation between the marital satisfaction scale and the scale of general community satisfaction, with scores on each scale combined to form high, medium, and low groups. There are considerable differences in the level of community satisfaction between those with highest and lowest marital adjustment scores. (Kendall's Tau for this table is .134 for men and .153 for women. The chi-square value is significant at the .005 level.) Since marriage and com-

Table 10-2. Degree of General Satisfaction with Community, by Marital Satisfaction: Greensboro

MARITAL SATISFACTION		COMMUNITY SATISFACTION (IN PERCENTAGES) LOW (0–2)	MEDIUM (3–4)	HIGH (5–7)	TOTAL %	TOTAL NO.
Men	High	17.2	23.7	59.1	100.0	215
	Medium	23.4	30.4	46.2	100.0	158
	Low	30.5	33.1	36.4	100.0	118
Women	High	14.9	17.3	67.8	100.0	202
	Medium	16.7	15.2	68.1	100.0	138
	Low	33.3	19.1	47.6	100.0	141

munity form two important spheres of life satisfaction, it would have been surprising if we had not found these two variables to be related. Unfortunately, our study was not designed in such a way as to shed any light on the causal connection between these variables. We would suspect that in part they are both dependent on other personal and situational factors. However, we would suggest that these two basic types of satisfaction interact with each other in a circular manner such that dissatisfaction with one tends to decrease satisfaction with the other, which in turn decreases satisfaction with the first, and so forth.

Our Greensboro data also show that there is some relationship between length of residence and marital satisfaction. Natives have lower satisfaction on the average than migrants in both the under 35 and over 35 age groups. The most recent migrants have higher average marital satisfaction scores than those who have been in Greensboro over 2 years. This may be in part due to recency of marriage, but it may also be because they are more likely to appear in the upper occupational categories, which generally have higher scores. Although we have shown that marital and community satisfaction are related for most couples, this finding suggests the possibility that for some couples entanglement in community interaction over a longer period of residence may be a negative factor in marital adjustment. Increasing interaction with groups and activities outside the family provides opportunity for divided interests and differences of opinion between the husband and wife, and one or both may become less dependent upon the other for support and companionship since there are more relationships with others outside the marriage. The effect of community participation may therefore depend on whether it is in common and therefore adhesive, or independent and disruptive.

Additional conclusions from our data regarding the marital adjustment of the wives are as follows:

(*a*) Middle-class wives have better marital adjustment, on the average, than working-class wives.

(*b*) Wives with low marital adjustment are more apt to see a job as an escape mechanism, where they can avoid duties and responsibilities of household activities and personal boredom.

(*c*) Wives prefer the role they are playing at present. The vast majority of those who are working say they are doing so because they want to and not because they have to, while those who are housewives say they prefer not to work.

(*d*) The marital satisfaction of employed wives in our sample is somewhat lower ($\bar{X} = 4.82$) than that of nonemployed wives ($\bar{X} = 5.98$). This difference is statistically significant at the .01 level.

Relatives

Recent studies indicate that people in cities have a larger amount of interaction with relatives than has usually been assumed on the basis of the old stereotypic image of the city dweller. We might expect that a city like Greensboro would have a greater emphasis on kinship ties than the larger cities like Detroit and Buffalo which have been studied. In the Detroit study (Detroit, 1956, p. 22), 43 per cent of the sample have parents living in the Detroit area. Our study (see Table 10-3) indicates that 52 per cent of the *living* parents are within 50 miles of Greensboro. However, since both parents of 28 per cent of the sample are dead, only 37 per cent of the sample have a parent living in the area. Another 25 per cent of the living parents are within a radius of 50 to 200 miles, however, so that the differences between our study and the Detroit study may be due to the size of the area covered. The Detroit study found that 75 per cent have brothers or

Table 10-3. Percentages of Relatives Living in or around Greensboro

		PER CENT WITH RELATIVES			
SUBJECTS WITH:	NO.	IN GREENS-BORO	WITHIN 50 MILES	TOTAL IN OR AROUND GREENS-BORO	50–199 MILES AWAY
Both parents living	409	28.6	17.1	45.7	25.2
Mother only	244	35.2	15.2	50.4	19.3
Father only	79	26.6	22.8	49.4	20.3
One or both parents	732	32.9	18.9	51.8	24.5
Brothers and/or sisters	927	43.8	28.2[a]	58.4	...

[a] Includes 126 cases, or 13.6 per cent, who also have brothers or sisters in Greensboro.

sisters in the area. In Greensboro, 58 per cent of our sample who have siblings have at least one brother or sister living within 50 miles. We did not ask about the number living within the next 150-mile radius, but since there were a number of parents living within that distance it is likely that our figure for the larger area would have been at least up to the figure for Detroit. Another possibly relevant point is that the Greensboro sample has a higher proportion of professional and managerial people than does the Detroit sample which is heavily weighted by craftsmen and operatives. In Buffalo, a significantly larger proportion of professional and managerial people than manual workers have no relatives in the city (Litwak, 1960, p. 392). Because of the differences in areas covered, it is impossible to make completely accurate comparisons between the studies. Our findings nevertheless support the conclusion that urban dwellers are not without a supply of close relatives living within a short travel distance.

The proportion of parents living in the area is a function of length of residence in the community (see Table 10-4). In some cases parents may have moved to Greensboro because their children were there. Study of the age differences, however, makes us suspect that most of our subjects with parents in the city came with their parents originally.

As indicated in Table 10-4, there is considerable interaction with parents despite physical separation from them. Differences in amounts of visiting with mother and with father are slight. Furthermore, the majority of the subjects indicate an interest in seeing their parents more frequently than they do. Most of the others say that they see them frequently enough. Our evidence certainly does not suggest strong alienation from parents.

There is some relationship between ties with parents and the scale of general satisfaction with life in the city, discussed previously. The most satisfied people are more likely than not to have parents living in Greensboro or in the immediate area around Greensboro. They are more likely to see their parents frequently and to state that they "feel close" to both their mother and their father (if living). Contrary to the findings of other studies that the in-law relationship is more likely to cause difficulty for the wife, there is no relationship in our data between the degree of closeness the wife feels for her in-laws and her urban satisfaction, while there is a fairly strong relationship between these two variables for the husbands.

Somewhat fewer persons have siblings than have living parents in the area, possibly a reflection of selective migration out of the region. In regard to preferential patterns of interaction with siblings, 42 per

Table 10-4. Relationship with Parents by Age and Length of Residence: Greensboro

	PER CENT OF PARENTS IN GREENSBORO OR WITHIN 50 MILES		MOTHER			FATHER			PER CENT WHO WOULD PREFER TO VISIT PARENTS MORE OFTEN	
	MOTHER	FATHER	DAILY OR WEEKLY	MONTHLY OR MORE BUT NOT WEEKLY	ONCE A YEAR OR LESS	DAILY OR WEEKLY	MONTHLY OR MORE BUT NOT WEEKLY	ONCE A YEAR OR LESS	MOTHER	FATHER
Under age 35										
Under 2 years	28.3	30.1	23.2	34.7	16.8	19.3	37.3	16.8	62.1	63.8
2 to 6 years	36.8	31.0	15.9	43.5	10.1	12.7	45.5	14.5	69.6	65.5
7 to 20 years	57.5	56.9	41.4	32.2	12.6	36.1	36.1	11.2	60.5	65.3
Over 20 years or native	95.3	86.0	83.7	8.1	3.5	70.8	11.1	9.8	36.5	49.9
Age 35 and over										
Under 2 years	13.3	10.5	3.3	43.3	30.0	0.0	42.1	42.1	80.0	63.2
2 to 6 years	21.9	29.2	18.8	28.1	21.9	16.7	29.2	25.0	81.3	75.0
7 to 20 years	29.5	29.5	16.5	21.1	22.6	13.8	20.7	19.5	78.8	78.2
Over 20 years	57.1	56.3	25.6	30.8	5.1	30.0	26.7	6.7	71.1	66.7
Native	96.5	95.7	65.9	11.0	0.0	71.7	15.2	0.0	46.8	52.1

cent of the people under 35 have contact at least once a week with brothers who live in the area, and 48 per cent have such contact with sisters who live in the area. Comparable frequencies among the people over 35 are 26 per cent and 33 per cent. Daily contacts with siblings are the same among both age groups—about 5 per cent of the people being involved.

Responses to questions as to whether relationships with brothers and sisters in general were very close, quite friendly, neutral, or negative, weighted by the number of siblings put in each category, were overwhelmingly positive, and did not seem to be particularly affected by the physical closeness of the sibling. The chief differences were that while the men expressed about equal warmth for their brothers and sisters, the women expressed somewhat more warmth for their sisters than for their brothers and considerably more warmth for both than did the men.

In an attempt to assess the extent of ramified kinship contacts, two questions were asked concerning attendance at large family reunions —often of the descendants of a couple who lived several generations previously. Notices of such reunions are not infrequently printed in the local newspapers. About one-half of the informants said that they never attended them, and the remainder were about equally divided between those who attended reunions once a year and those who attended them less often than once a year. These differences in attendance showed no relationship with degrees of general satisfaction. In regard to attitudes toward reunions, 103 men and 142 women said they enjoyed them to such an extent that they, in the phrase of the question, "would not miss one for anything."

In Durham, by way of comparison, about one-fifth of the newcomers (0–6 years) have relatives also living in Durham, about two-fifths of them have relatives living in the place from which they moved to Durham, and three-fifths of them have relatives living elsewhere. About one-third of the natives indicate that they have relatives living elsewhere than Durham. Very few of the newcomers have relatives who live in the same block or neighborhood as they, and only about one-sixth of the natives do. As in Greensboro, while the most recent newcomers are not wholly deprived of contacts with relatives, the localization and intensity of contact with relatives tend to increase with increasing lengths of residence.

Subjects in Greensboro were asked to compare the amount of time spent with relatives and with friends, and to give their preferences.

Fifty-three per cent of the men and 47 per cent of the women said they spent more time with friends than with relatives. Conversely, 24 and 34 per cent, respectively, of the men and women spend more time with relatives than with friends. Regarding preferences, if given a choice, about 45 per cent of each sex said they would like to divide their time equally between friends and relatives, with the remainder almost equally divided as to direction of preference.

We have some indications of preferential differences in terms of differing ages and lengths of residence on a group basis. Among the following groups, there are more people who say that they would like to spend more time with relatives than there are people who say that they actually spend more time with relatives: the men under 35 who have lived in Greensboro no more than 6 years, and the men and women over 35 who have lived in Greensboro from 7 to over 20 years but are not natives of Greensboro. It is interesting that the women under 35 who have lived in Greensboro for less than 6 years do not express this preference; however, many more of them actually spend more time with relatives than do the men in this category, and so their level of deprivation is less. Over half of the men and women over 35, mentioned above, say that they actually spend more time with friends than with relatives, whereas barely a quarter of them say that they spend more time with relatives. These people probably miss a number of their relatives, as suggested by their preference, but most of them are in the most generally satisfied category.

Those who say that they actually spend more time with relatives than with friends are the native men and women under 35, the women under 35 who have lived in Greensboro over 20 years, and the native men and women over 35. These people have the largest number of close-living relatives and it is interesting that, when given a choice, fewer of them say they would like to spend more time with relatives than they actually do. This shift is particularly noticeable in the younger age group who possibly feel at times that they have a surfeit of relatives. In this connection, the figures for the native women under 35 are interesting, since they illustrate some extremes. They are equal with the native women over 35 in that 45 per cent say they spend more time with relatives—this being the highest frequency of this pattern among the groups. Only 21 per cent of them say they spend more time with friends, which is the lowest frequency of this pattern. Regarding preference, however, only 18 per cent of them say they would like to spend more time with relatives than with friends, only 18 per cent of them say they would like to spend more time with friends than relatives, and 64 per cent of them express an equal preference for friends and relatives which is the highest frequency of this pattern. Those groups in which more people say they would like to spend more time with friends than say they would like to spend more time with relatives are: all four of the groups of men under 35; all of the men's groups over 35 except those who have lived in Greensboro over 20 years who constitute the oldest age group of men and have experienced the greatest loss of relatives through deaths. The only group of women in this category are those who have lived in Greensboro from 7 to 20 years and who, along with their men, indicate the highest rate of interaction with friends as opposed to relatives (67 per cent). The difference between preference for friends and for relatives, in favor of the former, is greatest among the native men under 35 and among the men who have lived in Greensboro less than 2 years. The latter group of men have fewer close-living relatives than almost any other group and they are therefore, presumably, primarily dependent on friends whether they like it or not.

While relationships with friends would appear to be more important to the inhabitants of Greensboro, in a number of respects, than relationships with relatives, the latter can hardly be belittled. The Greensboro sample is hardly a kin-deprived group. Contacts with kinsmen are frequent, even among the most recent newcomers who have fewer close-living relatives than the natives and less recent newcomers.

Friends

Investigations into the important subject of friends and friendship are made very difficult by the fact that people define friends and friendship differently, so that it is impossible, at least in survey research, to have complete confidence in responses to terms which do not have a standardized meaning.

In both Durham and Greensboro informants were first asked how many friends, unspecified as to type or place of residence, they felt they had. The responses in both cities, in which the majority said they have 40–50 or more friends, suggest to the investigators that "friends," in this connection, probably carried the connotation of "acquaintances who are friendly."

In order to arrive at a more accurate estimate of friends, rather than merely friendly people, we asked the Durham informants how many "very close friends" they had. Of the men, 45 per cent said that they had 11 or more, and 34 per cent of the women gave the same response. Fifty per cent of the men and 58 per cent of the women said that they had between 3 and 10 very close friends, inclusive. There were no significant differences on the basis of length of residence.

In Greensboro, each informant was asked: of all his friends, "how many would you consider as really close friends, in the sense that you can confide in them, feel that they really understand you and your problems, and that you could depend on them in a crisis." Of the men, 37 per cent, and of the women 28 per cent, said that they have 10 or more such friends. In regard to having between 3 through 9 such friends, 48 per cent of the men and 52 per cent of the women responded. As in Durham, there are no significant differences in terms of length of residence or age group.

However, as might be expected, the number of friends who also live in Greensboro does vary significantly with the length of residence of the informant. From Table 10-5 it becomes clear that although the most recent newcomers are the most "deprived" of friends living in Greensboro, a considerable number of them have made at least some such friends, and the proportion increases steadily with length of residence. There is an increasing city-wide localization of friendships, in other words, although they never become completely localized. However, as will be shown in the next section, most of most people's closest friends do not live in their immediate neighborhood.

There is a good relationship between the number of friends living in Greensboro and the level of general satisfaction of the respondents. Only about one-fifth of the men and women who indicated that they have no close friends living in Greensboro are in the highly satisfied category. Most of these are recent migrants. By contrast, 57 per cent of the men and 73 per cent of the women who indicated that all of their closest friends live in Greensboro are in the highly satisfied category. In general, incidentally, there seems to be a stronger relationship among the women than the men between high general satisfaction and concentration of close-living friends. It has already been shown that the frequency of most generally satisfied people is low among the most recent newcomers, and it would therefore now appear that the paucity of close-living and accessible friends among these people may be an important factor in their general dissatisfaction. Counterbalancing this, however, is the fact that newcomers indicate

Table 10-5. Distribution of Places of Residence by Length of Residence and Age of Respondents: Greensboro

		PERCENTAGE WITH FRIENDS LIVING IN GREENSBORO		
		ALL OF THEIR FRIENDS	¼ OF THEIR FRIENDS	NONE OF THEIR FRIENDS
Under 35 years of age				
0–2 years	Men	2.1	42.5	40.4
	Women	7.0	41.3	29.3
2–5 years	Men	25.0	28.1	6.2
	Women	22.5	33.5	12.5
6–20 years	Men	34.2	13.1	5.2
	Women	50.0	13.7	5.1
Native	Men	42.3	1.9	3.8
	Women	65.1	2.3	4.6
Over 35 years of age				
0–2 years	Men	4.1	41.6	41.6
	Women	0.0	29.4	52.9
2–5 years	Men	10.0	43.3	20.0
	Women	8.0	32.0	32.0
6–20 years	Men	24.0	24.0	1.9
	Women	18.9	21.6	3.7
Over 20 years	Men	21.8	14.9	2.3
	Women	40.0	10.5	1.1
Native	Men	57.9	6.8	0.0
	Women	54.1	8.3	0.0

that they have acquired rather numerous new friends in the city after their second year of residence. Somewhat over half of the newcomers to Greensboro, in fact, indicated that they had acquired "some" close friends within 6 months after their arrival. For most newcomers, then, "rootlessness," insofar as it is imparted by absence of friends, is a rather short-lived state of being. As we have indicated in the preceding section, the relationship with friends is a more potent factor in this matter than is the relationship with kinsmen, although the latter is by no means negligible. An interesting sidelight on this whole matter is provided by the responses to this question which was asked in Durham: "If you were in need of a lot of money, to whom would you turn?" Sixty-two per cent of the men and 42 per cent of the women gave the "rationalistic," "impersonal," "contract-type" answer that would be expected in an urban population, namely that they would turn to a financial institution. Nevertheless, 21 per cent of the men and 41 per cent of the women said that they would turn to a relative, but only 7 per cent of the men and 4 per cent of the women said that they would turn to a friend—perhaps supporting the old adage that to borrow from a friend is to lose a friend.

Friends and kinsmen together presumably constitute the core of an individual's personal relationships, and the people in our samples are, in general, by no means deprived of them. In other words, it cannot be said that the lives of these people in two cities of, admittedly, moderate size are enveloped in an impersonal atmosphere. One of the theses of the authors is, in fact, that "urban impersonality" is not *the* central characteristic of life in the city but is, rather, an added dimension of social participation there. An attempt was made in Greensboro to find out something about the extent of this dimension. Each informant was asked "how often in your daily life do you talk to or have other dealings with people you do not know personally?" While only about a dozen persons out of 1,018 indicated that they never have impersonal contacts, there are noticeable differences between the men and the women in this matter. Seven out of every ten men, as opposed to three out of every ten women, have impersonal contacts every day. Eighty per cent of the men and half of the women have such contacts very frequently if not daily. Three-quarters of the men, and almost as many women, apparently usually enjoy such contacts, and only 7 per cent of the sample definitely dislike them. These findings hardly convey the impression of an urban population which is miserably lost in an anonymous mass. It should be noted, however, that the quality of sentiment in this connection varies inversely with degree of general satisfaction. Half of the small number of men who indicate a dislike of impersonal contacts are in the generally dissatisfied category, as opposed to 18 per cent of the men who indicate that they enjoy such contacts very much.

One last point on friends and on the matter of personal and impersonal contacts is in order. In both Greensboro and Durham the great majority of people said they felt that they had about the same number of friends as other people of their acquaintance. However, among the most recent newcomers there was a tendency for more people to say that they had fewer friends than said that they had more friends than others. In Greensboro, while somewhat more people said that they would like to have more friends than said they had as many as they wanted, the great majority said that they were satisfied with the intensity of their friendships.

Neighbors and Neighborhoods

Our findings on neighbors and neighborhoods appear to be consistent with some from the Middle West (Useem, Useem, and Gibson, 1960) and from Rochester, New York (Foley, 1952), namely that "neighboring" involves a number of frequent, sociable activities but that intense, intimate relationships are not generally included in these. In the former study, good neighbors are described as being "friendly, but not friends" (Useem, Useem, and Gibson, 1960, p. 73). In Greensboro, the informants were asked a series of questions about neighbors used in Foley's study, and so we have some precisely comparable material in this connection. Thirty-seven per cent of the informants indicated that none of their best friends lived within five blocks of them, while in Rochester 38 per cent indicated this (Foley, 1952, p. 30).

Table 10-6 summarizes some of the findings on neighboring in Greensboro and compares them with Foley's results in Rochester.

The major differences between the two cities appear to lie in informal visiting and group outings. Whether these differences are due to the demonstrable fact that Greensboro's climate is less severe than Rochester's or to the supposed contrast between "southern hospitality" and "northern reserve," or to some other factor, we do not know. In Greensboro itself, the contrast between men and women in regard to asking neighbors for advice is notable. On the whole, the differences within Greensboro are more clearly related to differences in sex

Table 10-6. Comparison of Neighboring in Greensboro and Rochester, New York

LENGTH OF RESIDENCE	BEST FRIENDS WITHIN 5 BLOCKS: PER CENT HALF OR MORE	EXCHANGE THINGS: PER CENT OFTEN AND SOMETIMES	ASK ADVICE: PER CENT OFTEN AND SOMETIMES	VISIT INFORMALLY IN HOMES: PER CENT OFTEN AND SOMETIMES	HAVE GROUP PICNICS, OUTINGS: PER CENT OFTEN AND SOMETIMES
Greensboro					
Men					
Under 2 years	8.5	56.9	27.8	55.6	27.8
2–5 years	6.5	56.5	27.4	53.2	21.0
Over 5 years	13.7	63.9	40.1	61.9	34.2
Native	18.8	60.9	36.2	52.5	24.6
Women					
Under 2 years	16.0	60.0	55.4	64.0	32.4
2–5 years	18.5	58.5	47.7	66.2	33.8
Over 5 years	15.0	69.2	50.8	67.6	29.0
Native	19.8	71.2	41.9	63.2	32.5
Rochester [a]	23.0	59.0	26.0	39.0	17.0

[a] Foley (1952, p. 30).

than they are to differences in length of residence in the city. Neighboring activities, in general, would appear to begin very soon after arrival in the city and to be maintained at a fairly constant rate thereafter. There are no outstanding differences between natives and migrants except possibly in the matter of localization of friends as far as the men are concerned.

We found a small but consistent relationship between general community satisfaction scores and the items on neighboring. For example, the per cent of women having high general satisfaction scores was 62 if half or more of their best friends were within 5 blocks, but 49 if none were within that area. Sixty-six per cent of the women had high satisfaction scores if half or more of their social visits were in the neighborhood; 42 per cent if none were in the neighborhood; 70 per cent if they sometimes or often visited informally in homes of their neighbors; 47 per cent if they rarely or never did. These relationships were in the same direction, but smaller, for the men. People who engage minimally in various neighboring activities are not necessarily generally dissatisfied people, although most of the generally dissatisfied people probably are also minimally engaged in neighboring activities.

In Durham, 65 per cent of the men and 71 per cent of the women said that they are very satisfied with their neighborhoods, the frequency of this sentiment increasing somewhat, but not strikingly, with increasing lengths of residence. Definite dissatisfaction with neighborhood, while most frequently expressed by recent newcomers, was indicated by only one-tenth of the total sample. More than 9 out of 10 of the people who are satisfied with their neighborhood in general are also satisfied with the "other people" as a whole who live in it. Virtually all of the natives who are satisfied with their neighborhood are also satisfied with it in terms of its nearness to their friends and relatives, despite the fact that most of their friends and relatives do not live in it. As might be expected, the most recent newcomers are less satisfied in this respect; nevertheless, three-quarters of the people who have lived in Durham no more than 6 years, and are satisfied with their neighborhoods in general, are also satisfied with this aspect of it.

From this and previous discussions of personal relationships in Durham and Greensboro, certain conclusions suggest themselves. (1) Kinsmen and, especially, friends play an important part in the lives of the informants, and migration results in temporary deprivation in regard to this relationship. However, accommodation appears to be rather rapid. (2) The fact that most of the kinsmen and friends of most people do not live in their neighborhood appears to have little bearing on the level of satisfaction with interaction with kinsmen and friends, and it appears to have no bearing on satisfaction with neighborhood. (3) Therefore, it would appear that the frequent though rather superficial interpersonal relationships which characterize the urban neighborhood should be regarded as functional, rather than dysfunctional, phenomena. To put the matter another way, urban neighboring, like urban impersonal contacts, can be seen as an additive, rather than an unsatisfactorily substitutive, dimension of social life. Except for the most recent newcomers, it neither takes the place of, nor displaces, relationships with kinsmen and friends.

Formal Associations

We have been considering social relationships which are generally classified as being informal in the sense that, except for the husband-wife relationship, the roles are not defined in terms of charters and

Table 10-7. Percentages of People Having Membership in Formal Associations: Greensboro

LENGTH OF RESIDENCE BY SEX	TYPES OF ASSOCIATION							
	CHURCH	SERVICE	FRATERNAL	PTA	SOCIAL	PROFESSIONAL	OTHER [a]	NONE
Men (No —494)								
Under 2 years	40.2	9.7	15.3	19.4	13.9	23.6	26.4	30.5
2–5 years	41.9	6.4	16.1	11.3	1.6	25.8	14.5	35.5
Over 5 years	62.1	14.2	32.5	31.9	16.8	28.0	23.7	18.1
Native	43.0	8.5	18.3	32.4	19.7	31.0	24.6	22.5
Women (No.—492)								
Under 2 years	40.5	5.4	4.1	28.4	10.8	5.4	8.1	43.2
2 5 years	46.1	3.1	1.5	35.4	16.9	10.8	10.8	27.7
Over 5 years	68.3	13.3	6.0	43.4	33.7	9.2	14.9	18.1
Native	66.1	5.9	4.2	51.7	26.3	11.9	10.2	13.6

[a] Includes veterans' organizations and political clubs as well as other unspecified organizations.

legal codes. We now turn to a consideration of the extent to which our informants participate in formally organized groups. This subject has received considerable attention in studies of modern American society since the formally organized groups in question are indeed very numerous. It has also received attention since it is obviously related to those aspects of the urban stereotype which have it that modern Americans are "compulsive joiners," "organization men," and "other-directed" robots.

In Durham, 45 per cent of the sample belong to no formal associations at all, not counting regular attendance at church services as a type of participation in formal associations. In Greensboro, church association (primarily implying regular attendance at church services) was included in this category, with the results shown in Table 10-7.

Including church association, three-quarters of the Greensboro sample belong to at least one formal association. As in Durham, those with no formal associations are most frequent among the most recent newcomers, but it should be noted that church association is relatively high among even the latter people. This is, as has been pointed out earlier, the type of association which can most easily be undertaken from the very beginning of residence in a new city.

The average number of formal memberships in Greensboro is 2.5 per person, there being only slight variations by length of residence and age. Membership in 3 or more associations, though it occurs among people of all ages and lengths of residence, is most frequent among the migrants who have lived in Greensboro 6 or more years, and second most frequent among the natives. Thirteen per cent of the native men and women and about one-fifth of the least recent migrants belong to 5 or more formal associations. In other words, among some people, but by no means most of them, there is a definite intensification of formal associations with increasing age and length of residence. Interestingly enough, being a native of the city appears in itself to have only a very slight positive effect on intensity of formal association, and we suspect that this effect may operate chiefly in the cases of "socially prominent" natives. All of these tendencies are also present in Durham. An indication of the circumstances under which formal associations were joined is provided by some material from Durham. Formal solicitation was mentioned by 38 per cent of the total sample—most frequently by the men, especially, interestingly enough, by the native men. Forty-three per cent had been asked by friends to join. About a third indicated that they joined because they wanted to support the aims of the association. Only 9 per cent said that they joined primarily because they wanted to meet people, and most of these were not among the most recent newcomers. It must be remembered, however, that church association was not included in these considerations and that one of the recognized motives for becoming involved in church activities in a new place of residence is the desire to become personally acquainted with other people.

The prominence of church association in Greensboro leads us to wonder whether there are any relationships between it and other forms of association. Table 10-8 presents percentages of associational mem-

Table 10-8. Church and Other Forms of Associational Behavior: Greensboro

		PERCENTAGES OF PERSONS WHO ARE MEMBERS OF:									
	NO.	CHURCH	SERVICE	FRAT.	PTA	VETS	POL.	SOCIAL	PROF.	OTHER	NONE
Men											
Church and other	210	100.0	22.9	45.7	49.5	11.9	4.3	27.1	44.8	18.6	0.0
Church and no other	50	100.0	...	...	...	...	...	...	...	...	...
No church and other	130	0.0	6.2	23.8	28.5	15.4	2.3	16.2	36.9	17.7	0.0
No church and no other	118	0.0	...	...	...	...	...	...	...	...	100.0
Women											
Church and other	221	100.0	19.9	9.0	68.7	0.9	0.0	51.6	14.5	20.4	0.0
Church and no other	87	100.0	...	...	...	...	...	...	...	...	...
No church and other	87	0.0	2.3	4.6	70.1	2.3	1.1	24.1	18.4	13.8	0.0
No church and no other	111	0.0	...	...	...	...	...	...	...	...	100.0

bership in terms of four mutually exclusive categories. There can be no doubt that there is a positive relationship between church and other forms of associational behavior. But what does this mean? Are regular church attenders more inspired than others by their religious convictions generally to participate more in associational behavior, such behavior being rather notorious for the amounts of time and energy which it entails? Or is the high frequency of church association a concomitant of a *generally* participant social attitude of which there are various degrees in the urban population? We suspect that both factors may be operative in the situation, but we do not know which one is crucial, if, indeed, either of them is.

Inspecting Table 10-8 we might suspect that the high PTA participation among male regular church attenders may be due to a possibly enhanced sense of duty among them, and it could be added that among the men the rates of involvement in veterans' and professional associations, which are self-interest-oriented, differ less between the church attenders and the nonchurch attenders than do those in other forms of association. Among both men and women, the difference between church attenders and nonchurch attenders in participation in service associations is very striking. There may be a semantic bias here ("service" = "Christian service"), but we had in mind those organizations which currently call themselves service organizations, and do indeed perform public services, but are fundamentally concerned with furthering business opportunities. On the other hand, church attendance obviously has no effect on the women's PTA participation, and it is impossible to attribute the far greater participation of church-attending women in social associations to whatever enhanced religious virtues they may have in contrast to the nonchurch-attending women.

To some extent, Table 10-9 highlights a number of points which have been made in this and previous sections. Church association is a concomitant of high satisfaction, and so is general participation. When the two are combined, it would seem that participation in general has a stronger relationship than does church association alone, for the primary breakpoint in high satisfaction is not between church and no church but between church and other (in which *general* participation is highest) and the other categories.

Now let us look at Table 10-9 in another way. Thirty-six men and 22 women are low in satisfaction and report no formal social participation whatever. These are the most likely candidates in our sample for the status of dissociated, anomic, and unhappy city dweller. They constitute slightly less than 6 per cent of our total sample.

Table 10-9. Church and Other Types of Association by Degrees of General Satisfaction: Greensboro

ASSOCIATIONAL BEHAVIOR	NO.	DEGREES OF GENERAL SATISFACTION % LOW	% MEDIUM	% HIGH
Men				
Church and other	210	18.6	21.4	60.0
Church and no other	50	18.0	36.0	46.0
No church and other	130	23.1	30.8	41.5
No church and no other	118	30.5	33.1	34.7
Women				
Church and other	221	11.3	12.2	73.8
Church and no other	87	10.3	26.4	55.2
No church and other	87	21.8	14.9	50.6
No church and no other	111	19.8	18.0	45.1

About the same number of people (64) are maximally participant but also low in satisfaction. Are these the "compulsive joiners"? In contrast, 286 persons (28 per cent of the total sample) are both maximally participant and high in satisfaction. Are these the tranquilized "other-directed organization men"? Last, 91 persons (9 per cent of the total sample) report no memberships in formal associations and yet are high in satisfaction. Could these include those "inner-directed" and "autonomous" persons in whom Riesman and others, rather hopelessly it seems, would find the salvation of modern urban society? Our questions represent only surmises as to what might be the most likely connections between our quantitative findings (which have their limitations) and well-known intuitional depictions of urban life (which also have their limitations). There is much uncertainty here, but of one thing we can be certain: urban life may not validly be seen in terms of a single, "typical" set of behavioral patterns and attitudes.

Community Involvement and Identification

Apathy and disinterest in public affairs except when they directly affect the individual are supposed characteristics of urban dwellers.

They are presumably associated with a lack of sense of identification with the community as a whole either because it is too large or because it is felt to be basically unsatisfactory, or both.

In Greensboro, two questions were asked concerning public participation. One was, "Did you vote in the last city, school, or county election?" To this, 46 per cent of the men said yes, 47 per cent said no, and 7 per cent could not remember. The comparable figures for the women were: 38 per cent yes, 57 per cent no, 5 per cent could not remember. Similar trends are apparent in Durham.

The second Greensboro question was phrased in this fashion: "Every community has, from time to time, certain problems (such as school problems, tax rates, water fluoridation, annexation, traffic and parking facilities, and many others) which receive publicity and have to be decided. Are you now, or have you been in the last year or so, seriously concerned about such problems? Yes or no. If yes, did you do any of these things about your concern: spoke directly to a public official, wrote a letter to a public official, signed a petition addressed to a public official, wrote a letter to the newspaper, talked to friends?" Only 56 per cent of the men and 52 per cent of the women expressed any concern. Of those concerned, about 80 per cent of each sex had talked to friends, 17 per cent had signed petitions, 22 per cent of the men and 6 per cent of the women had spoken to a public official, 6 per cent of the men and 10 per cent of the women had written a letter to a public official, and 1 per cent of the men and 2 per cent of the women had written a letter to a newspaper. For those who expressed a concern, therefore, relatively few did anything about it, for one reason or another.

By way of comparison, between half and three-quarters of the people in Durham (who were asked a series of questions on this subject) had done nothing about various public problems apart from talking with friends about them. While 9 out of 10 Durham informants said that more money should be expended on various public services, usually only half of them (six-tenths in the case of schools) said that they would be willing to pay more taxes to this end.

Public participation in Greensboro is related to the level of general satisfaction of the informants. Of the voting men, 66 per cent are in the most satisfied category, as opposed to only 34 per cent of the men who did not vote and 40 per cent of those who could not remember if they voted or not. Comparable figures for the women are 76 per cent, 55 per cent, and 48 per cent. In regard to concern with public problems, 57 per cent of the men who were concerned, as opposed to 39 per cent of those who were not, are in the most satisfied category, the comparable figures for the women being 70 per cent and 54 per cent. In regard to doing something about their concern beyond talking to friends, the "doers" are very largely highly satisfied people. For example, five-sixths of the men who had spoken directly to a public official were in the most satisfied category.

This, in turn, is related to age and length of residence. Only 26 per cent of the Greensboro informants under 35 who had been in Greensboro 2 or more years had voted, as opposed to 58 per cent of those over 35. The "doers" about public concerns are very heavily concentrated among the people over 35 who have lived in Greensboro 6 or more years. In general, the natives in both age categories are somewhat less participant than the newcomers of more than 6 years' residence, though definitely more participant than the more recent newcomers. It will be recalled that frequency of high satisfaction increases with age and length of residence.

While level of high general satisfaction might in itself be considered to indicate some sense of positive identification with the city as a whole, and it does indeed seem to impart among some people a greater apparent sense of public responsibility, it is also clear enough that many personal factors which cannot specifically be related to the city itself enter into the matter of satisfaction. Besides this, there are a considerable number of people in both cities who are highly satisfied but indicate no particular sense of public responsibility.

Since public problems can obviously affect personal problems, concern with the former cannot in itself be taken as an indication of a sense of dedication to the whole community or of emotional identification with it, although this may sometimes be the case.

Feeling that in the general culture definite sentiments are attached to the expression "home town," we asked the informants in both cities where they felt their home town was, and about 90 per cent of them answered, respectively, "Greensboro" or "Durham." While there were semantic difficulties with this question, it is nevertheless striking that as many as half of the most recent newcomers in Greensboro named that city while only two-fifths of them answered "place where I was born and raised." Only 11 persons in Greensboro indicated that they felt they did not have any home town.

Among the Greensboro informants further attempts were made to elucidate the matter of identification, the questions being phrased in the hope that the responses might indicate more than mere word association. First, the Greensboro newcomers were asked to what extent they had felt that they belonged and were settled in the place from which they had moved to Greensboro. Sixty per cent of the men and 70 per cent of the women said completely or fairly much so. However, only about 35 per cent of the men and women said that when they moved they felt strongly or very strongly that they were pulling up roots. These findings would seem to confirm the suggestions which have been raised by other data that for many people local adaptation is relatively easy.

"At the present time, do you feel that you 'belong' and are settled in Greensboro?" Only about 11 per cent of the men and women answered negatively and of these only 9 per cent of the men and 6 per cent of the women are in the most generally satisfied category. About 35 per cent of the "don't belong" respondents are found among the most recent newcomers who are under 35 years of age, but there are respondents of this type in all the other length of residence categories except the natives under 35, and only 2 persons among the natives over 35 made this response. Again, we encounter a small core of persons who are dissatisfied and dissociated, but dislocation due to recent migration is only partly a cause of these sentiments. Of those who indicated that they belonged in Greensboro, over half said that they started to feel this way immediately or within one year after moving to Greensboro.

The Greensboro informants, regardless of whether or not they were newcomers, were further asked, "in what place do you feel you *most* 'belong'?" Eighty-three per cent answered "in Greensboro," 8 per cent answered "some other place," and 9 per cent answered "no place in particular." Sex differences are not especially notable, but there is a progression of "in Greensboro" responses from about 50 per cent among the 0–2 year newcomers to about 96 per cent among the natives and those who have lived in Greensboro over 20 years. Somewhat more than a quarter of the "some other place" and of the "no place in particular" respondents are among the 0–2 year newcomers under 35 years of age, but the contribution of the older recent newcomers is only about 10 per cent. The responses to this question are very strongly related to general satisfaction. Only 4 per cent of the men in the "don't belong" category are high in general satisfaction, and only 16 per cent of the women are. The majority of the men and women in the "in Greensboro" category are high in general satisfaction.

Finally, two questions of a "projective" sort were asked in Greensboro in the attempt to assess the extent to which personal identification with the city is felt. The first asked, "If you read in the newspaper that someone from Greensboro, whom you do not know personally, has been promoted to a nationally important position, your most definite feeling about it would be: . . . ?" Fifty-five per cent of the men and 59 per cent of the women gave one of the "neutral" responses, "This is a fine thing for him, but does not concern me," or "good for him." Eleven per cent of each sex checked the response, "This will put Greensboro on the map" (community identification), and 34 per cent of the men and 30 per cent of the women checked "This makes me feel just a little bigger because I, too, am from Greensboro" (personal identification).

The second projective question asked for their reaction if someone from Greensboro whom they did not know had been guilty of a serious crime. About three-fourths of the persons gave one of the two "neutral" responses to this question ("It's too bad but there are crime stories in the paper just about every day," and "It's terrible that another serious crime has been committed"). Eight per cent gave the "community identification" response ("This is a disgrace to Greensboro"), and 18 per cent checked the "personal identification" response ("This shames me because I, too, am from Greensboro").

Although these are only two of many questions of this type which could have been asked, it is interesting that identification seems to be more pronounced with respect to favorable publicity.

Who are these people who express personal identification? In regard to the good publicity items, the lowest frequency is 19 per cent of the men under 35 who have lived in Greensboro 2–6 years. The highest frequency (44 per cent) is among the native men over 35. Thirty-one per cent of the men and women under 35 who have lived in Greensboro less than 2 years express this type of identification, in which respect they are only one percentage point less than the men and women over 35 who have lived in Greensboro more than 20 years. In other words, though there is some relationship to length of residence and age, it is not very strong. In general, the same is true of identification in terms of bad publicity. The native men over 35 rate highest in this case, with a percentage of 28, followed by 25 per cent of the most recent newcomer men over 35 years of age.

When we look at these responses in terms of general satisfaction, we find some striking facts in regard to the good publicity item. First, highly satisfied people were the most frequent among those who checked either "This will put Greensboro on the map" or the personal identification statement. The men and women reversed themselves on this. Among the men, 53 per cent of those checking "This will put Greensboro on the map" were highly satisfied, while 70 per cent of the women were. On the personal identification response, 60 per cent of the men and 67 per cent of the women were in the most highly satisfied category. Second, only 26 per cent of the men and 30 per cent of the women were in the highly satisfied category checking "This is a fine thing, for him, but I don't see that it concerns me." In itself, this statement has nothing to do with community identification but rather expresses a sense of personal dissociation, and a "sour grapes" connotation could be read into it, too, although this was not originally intended. At any rate, of the people who checked it, more than two-thirds are not in the most satisfied category. These are approximately 58 men and women, a trifle less than 5 per cent of our total sample.

We have found that marital adjustment and accessibility of friends and kinsmen affect the level of general satisfaction among our sample population. We have found that dislocation consequent upon migration temporarily lowers general satisfaction, but that satisfactory adjustments seem to be made fairly rapidly. We have found more highly satisfied people among the most participant people than among less participant people, but we cannot conclude that minimal participation necessarily in itself is an indication of low satisfaction. And the same can be said regarding those who indicate that they perhaps have a sense of generalized "belongingness." On the other hand, we have recurrently found people who number from 5 to 10 per cent of the total who are dissatisfied and dissociated. If there are anomic and rootless persons in our sample, these are the ones. However, except for some negative effects due to recent migrations, this small core is found in all age and length of residence groups. We suspect, therefore, that for the most part, these people who fit best the traditional urban stereotype are the way they are not so much because of the city and what it "does to" them, but rather because of the personal orientations which they have toward life in general, regardless of where they may be living.

And now we turn to a consideration of certain factors of personality which were revealed by our studies in Durham and Greensboro.

Personality Characteristics

In the course of discussing the stress of city life, much has been made of the urban personality. In general, this has implied some disorganization, and the principal references which can be found to this topic treat marginal groups, criminals, and delinquents. Seldom is the common run of city dweller discussed.

As part of our study we attempted some measurement of personality traits of the respondents. Because of the difficulty of obtaining meaningful personality measures on a large scale, we restricted ourselves to projective measures of two traits, affiliation and achievement needs. Striving, fear of failure, and need of success have been interpreted frequently as being principal stresses of the city dweller, while the need for human companionship is supposed to be starved in the cold urban environment. These two traits seem therefore important in an analysis of the urban personality.

The method used was an adaptation of a projective device which is being developed by Willerman and French (French, 1956). The test consisted of questions involving interpretations of some actions of a person, for example "J. E. will usually volunteer for a difficult task because. . . ." The answers to these questions were coded to identify four variables: (1) striving for status, (2) need for affiliation, (3) hope of success in achievement (or, conversely, fear of failure), and (4) confidence in interpersonal relations (or, conversely, fear of rejection). Each variable is measured by the answers to four or five questions. Personality tests administered in survey questionnaires are not, of course, clinical instruments, and they can give only crude indications of inner dynamics. Consequently most of the differences which we will note were rather small, but we will assume that they would be more pronounced if more intensive means of assessing them were to be used.

The first question which arises is the distribution of these personality traits within the population. For brevity's sake, only the data for the men in Greensboro will be presented, especially as the social characteristics are mainly family characteristics. The data for the other groups follow a similar pattern.

The four traits are interrelated and thus there is a common trend for their distribution. That is, the same people exhibit desire for status and for affiliation and also feel confident to achieve both. They are in general people who are successful in the urban setting, having achieved an economic and social status which gives them confidence. Within this common core there are certain differences between the distributions of the different traits.

People who are high in status striving are more likely to be those who have achieved status within the community. They are older, have higher incomes, and are likely to have bought or to be in the process of buying their houses. Correspondingly they are not likely to identify themselves with the working class, although their occupational distribution is not different from that of the people with less status striving.

By contrast, the respondents with high affiliation needs, although similar in many respects, are distinguished by their different way of living. They have higher education and are more likely to have professional and managerial jobs, occupations which are distinguished by the necessity of dealing with people. On the other hand, affiliation need is not accompanied by any purely economic or status characteristic, income, rental status, or age.

While these needs themselves may distinguish people by the way in which they achieve success within the city, the confidence in the satisfaction of these needs distinguishes the degree to which they have achieved it. The people who score high on confidence in affiliation are those who have reached a position where they can have confidence in being accepted. They are older, in the better occupations, have a higher income, own their homes, and do not identify with the working class. By contrast, the people who show hope of achieving success would seem to be those who have most potential for achievement. They have better education, have at least escaped the low-status jobs, and are also buying their homes. But they show no difference in age or class status from those who do not show hope of success and have no great difference in income. They are still trying to achieve success and hence show both tension and confidence in their answers.

The pattern of personality traits is also correlated with the social relations of our respondents. We shall consider both informal relations in friendship groups, and formal relations in organizational memberships and civic activity. The answers to a series of questions on these topics give a picture of the meaning of these four personality traits. Taking the combination of questions into account, the influence of the four traits is close to what we could expect from their social distribution.

"Confidence in affiliation" seems to be an indication of extensive social contacts. People who score high on this trait have easier social contacts with friends, relatives, strangers, and formal social contacts. High scores are related to having friends, having even more contact with relatives, having friends outside Greensboro, having ease in contact with strangers, organizational membership, and having participated in civic activities. It may seem strange that these people report less contact with friends and wish for more chance to see them. Considering the total amount of social contacts, however, this looks more like a wish to be able to do justice to all the social connections the person has than a craving for friends whom he does not have. The high scorers in these variables are close to that aspect of the urban stereotype which postulates a great range and variety of social contacts without very much time being spent on any particular one.

Confidence in success in achievement has a similar pattern in informal relations, except that there is an even stronger relationship to lack of time to see one's friends and desire to see more of them. This is, however, not compensated for by civic participation. We have concluded from the pattern of background factors related to this variable that the high scorers are the people who are still trying to make their way in the city. They have the friendship patterns of the successful group but not yet enough security to have strong social participation in the city. They cannot spend as much of their time with friends. High scores on this trait are probably closer to the picture of the "driven" city dweller.

It seems that both the need for achievement and status and the need for affiliation can find expression in an urban environment. Affiliation needs are rewarded for the successful person in a somewhat diffuse pattern. People who are looking for success are the ones who seem to suffer most from lack of social integration, but they are potentially the ones who will achieve success and satisfaction later.

We have discussed these personality traits as possible cues to the effects of life in the city. Another important, related question is the relation of these traits to mobility. In order to study this we have to treat two kinds of mobility, social and residential.

As a measure of residential mobility (or migration) we shall use the scale of favorable attitude toward moving to which reference was made earlier in the chapter. This gives us an indication of whether a person is willing to change his residence. This willingness may have a different function for the person depending on his general life course. If he has been improving his status, willingness to move may be a sign of optimism, but if his status has been stationary or even deteriorating, moving may only be a futile escape. As a rough index of social mobility, and especially of felt mobility, we shall take a comparison of the social-class status of the respondent's father and of the respondent himself. The questionnaire asked the respondent to rate himself and his parent in one of the five classes (shown here in descending order): upper class, upper-middle class, lower-middle class, working class, and lower class. Comparison of the answers to the two questions can give us an indication of whether the respondent felt that he had improved his status over that of parents, whether he felt it had stayed the same, or whether it had declined. As could be expected, most men (161) thought that the state had stayed the same. Eighty-eight indicated upward mobility and only 26 downward mobility. There was no relation between this mobility and desire for residential mobility.

Because of the small number of the downward mobile persons we shall combine them with the stationary group and shall distinguish upward and nonupward mobile persons. These will then be further divided by their inclination for migration, thus making four groups. We can now relate these groups to personality traits (see Table 10-10).

Each of the two different types of mobility is related to one of the personality traits. Social mobility is positively related to status striving; we see again that these people have achieved the change which they show to be so important to them. Desire for residential mobility is related inversely to confidence in affiliation. These people have throughout shown themselves to be satisfied and effective in their life

Table 10-10. Mobility and Personality, Greensboro Men Only

SOCIAL MOBILITY:	UPWARD MOBILE		STATIONARY OR DOWNWARD MOBILE	
RESIDENTIAL MOBILITY:	FOR MOVING	AGAINST MOVING	FOR MOVING	AGAINST MOVING
Percentages of high scorers in:				
Status striving	48	52	41	42
Need of affiliation	54	49	49	58
Confidence for affiliation	50	61	53	67
Hope of success	54	40	47	47
Community satisfaction	50	71	44	71
Community identification	35	69	34	47
Total	34	53	131	156

in the city and would be expected to have no reason to move away. As their gratification comes from interpersonal relations, social mobility has little to do with this personality trait. Need for affiliation, as distinguished from confidence in satisfying this need, has hardly any relation with mobility.

Hope of success, which has been identified as the driving force in urban life, has an interesting relationship to mobility. There is no difference in this trait according to social mobility, and none according to desire for moving among the socially stationary group. Among the men who have experienced success there is a strong relationship with hope of success. The men who are willing to leave strongly express belief in success; those who are not seem to be more motivated by fear of failure. The people who are successful in their striving and optimistic are willing to move; those who are mainly motivated by fear of failure seem to be unwilling to make any further moves. Both remind one of urban stereotypes: the eternally mobile striver and the anxious protector. Among the extremes of this variable we may find the "anomic city dweller."

Finally, let us consider the relationship of the mobility types to the two community scales mentioned previously, community satisfaction and community identification. Both scales are positively related to reluctance to move. Community satisfaction is unrelated to social mobility, but community identification is positively related to upward mobility, especially among the persons who want to stay in the city. People who have achieved success in the city identify with it strongly if they want to stay there. As they are the same people who seem to be plagued with fear of failure, it is possible that this identification gives them some security. This is reinforced by the fact that these people show themselves confident of their interpersonal relations. If this is true, it would show that residence in the city gives emotional support at least to some of its residents and that the community alleviates the anxiety of the group of people who seem to be most in need of such alleviation.

Conclusions

Contrary to the postulates of the traditional urban stereotype, the inhabitants of Durham and Greensboro are not typically deprived of close, affectional social ties. For the most part, their marriages are satisfactory, and they have a sufficient number of satisfactory relationships with friends and kinsmen. In general, they have made a happy adjustment to the relatively superficial urban neighborhood social patterns and to the necessity of dealing impersonally with many people.

Nonnatives of these cities do at first experience a certain amount of deprivation and dissatisfaction in these respects, but they adapt, or enculturate, themselves rather rapidly and successfully to their new surroundings. The fact that they were drawn to these cities primarily because of hoped-for economic advantages does not mean that their motivations in subsequent behavior are necessarily or primarily economic in nature.

We do not know, of course, about those people who were at one time newcomers in these cities and subsequently moved away; nor do we know anything about those natives who moved away. A survey of such people might yield a quite different image of life in these cities than the one which we have presented. However, it is quite possible that those who moved away were also primarily motivated by economic considerations rather than by urban-stereotypic emotional dissatisfactions. Nevertheless, roughly one-tenth of the people in the population in one way or another do apparently conform to the traditional urban stereotype, but these may well be people who would be unhappily adjusted in any type of community.

The preponderance of high satisfaction, general and particular, among the majority of the population should not be misconstrued. It does not mean that their lives are completely idyllic, free of stresses and anxieties, or unburdened by complaints and problems. It does mean, however, that the characteristics of life in these cities have not prevented them from achieving a reasonably contented existence. This, in view of the prevailing notions in some circles about "the City" and its alleged malevolent effects on the human spirit, is an important finding.

We cannot, of course, claim that Durham and Greensboro are necessarily representative of all other cities of comparable size in the United States; and certainly there are objective differences between them and much larger metropolitan centers (for example, no lengthy commuting to work each day, absence of the huge, multistoried apartment house, and less ethnic diversity). Durham and Greensboro probably are, however, representative of the other cities in the Piedmont Industrial Crescent, and our concern is with the kinds of social characteristics, including growth, which are found in this particular urban complex.

Among the factors which may contribute to the relatively satisfactory nature of social life in the Crescent, two in particular are suggested by our findings.

First, the majority of the newcomers are natives of the Southeast. This means that their moving into the Crescent does not require any serious readjustment in a large number of minute and subtle social conventions which, taken together, constitute a large proportion of the ordinary routines of living. Such newcomers therefore encounter very little that is strange or difficult in the manner of conducting day-to-day activities. Most of their readjustment has to do with becoming familiar with a new physical location and with forming new social relationships. In regard to the former, the changes they experience are probably not drastic. Most of them do not come from open-country farms but from towns and smaller cities which, in regard to such matters as domestic and public architecture and general layout, are really not very different in kind from the Piedmont cities. As far as forming new social relationships is concerned, serious readjustments are necessary, and they can, at first, be a source of stress and dissatisfaction. However, the process is greatly eased for the many newcomers who move from nearby places since they can and do maintain frequent contacts with friends and relatives there.

The second major factor has to do with the increasingly high levels of educational attainment, and concomitantly professional or highly skilled occupations, of the more recent newcomers, both those from the Southeast and most particularly those who move from places outside the region. There is some evidence that such people are, by reason of their training and experience, more and more developing a set of attitudes which make it possible for them to accept positively rather than to resist the necessity of occasional migration. If this is the case, it increases their ability to enculturate themselves quickly and successfully as newcomers.

The social correlates of urban growth in the Crescent may be expected to continue as we have described them as long as that growth itself continues to be relatively slow, to be based on the expansion of businesses which primarily require professional or highly skilled workers, and to be supported by ever-improving facilities for higher education in the Crescent.

REFERENCES

Detroit Area Study (1956), *A Social Profile of Detroit: 1955*, A Report of the Detroit Area Study of the University of Michigan, Ann Arbor.

Foley, Donald L. (1952), *Neighbors or Urbanites?*, Studies of Metropolitan Rochester, No. 2, Department of Sociology, University of Rochester, Rochester.

French, Elizabeth G. (1956), "Development of a Measure of Complex Motivation," Research Report AFPTRC-TN-56-48. San Antonio, Tex.: Lackland Air Force Base.

Gulick, John, and Charles E. Bowerman (1961), *Adaptation of Newcomers in the Piedmont Industrial Crescent*, Urban Studies Program, Institute for Research in Social Science, University of North Carolina, Chapel Hill.

Litwak, Eugene (1960), "Geographic Mobility and Extended Family Cohesion," *American Sociological Review*, **25**:3, 385–94.

Useem, Ruth H., John Useem, and Duane L. Gibson (1960), "The Function of Neighboring for the Middle Class Male," *Human Organization*, **19**:2, 68–76.

Chapter 11

Livability of the City: Attitudes and Urban Development

by Robert L. Wilson *

LIVABILITY IS DEFINED as the sum total of the qualities of the urban environment which tend to induce in a citizen a state of well-being and satisfaction. Those qualities of the environment which contribute toward a positive valuation of that environment may be called factors of livability. The purpose of this investigation was to explore some of those factors which seem to contribute to the general image of a livable city among the population of two Crescent cities. In other words, the study sought to help understand what kind of physical city the people wanted.

Through interviews with samples representative of two city populations, data were collected about hypothetical preferences, aspira-

* Anne Solomon Clavel participated in many aspects of the survey and analysis as a research assistant and contributed significantly to analysis of several open-ended questions. Kurt W. Back advised as consultant during part of the period while the schedule was being designed. Sample design and Greensboro interviewing were executed under the direction of John Monroe of the Survey Operations Unit, then a part of the University of North Carolina, and now a part of the Research Triangle Institute. Earlier work of the author, with F. Stuart Chapin, Jr., contributed toward the development of concepts and of certain specific questions on the schedule, and was supported by the Institute for Research in Social Science and the University Research Council of the University of North Carolina.

tions, and evaluations of existing environment which are of particular interest to city planners.

This work has sprung from multiple motivations. Among the reasons for undertaking this study, in addition to seeking light on the attitudes of people of the Crescent, was the hope that this activity could lead toward a useful tool for city planners in other cities—that this could be a pilot study for development of a "standard" technique of analysis which could accompany other studies ordinarily used by city planners in their work. This chapter will not take up this latter aspect of the work, leaving it for discussion in a monograph elsewhere, which will also include considerable detail not possible to present here.

Who Was Interviewed? And How?

The information reported in this chapter came from interviews with 385 people who generously gave one and one-half to two and one-half hours of their time toward an endeavor which the interviewers explained was intended to "help us to understand how the citizens here feel about certain things affecting the city."

Criteria for selection of Durham and Greensboro as study cities were convenience (proximity to Chapel Hill), relationship to other studies programmed in those cities, and the belief on the part of the researchers that these cities were somewhat different in their livability characteristics.

Stratification of the Sample

Greensboro, the first city studied (summer, 1958), was represented by 211 completed interviews, and Durham by 174 completed interviews (summer, 1959). Within each city, the sample selection process was essentially the same, producing a random sample stratified into four subgroups on the basis of residence location: central city (inside city limits)-higher income areas; central city-lower income areas; fringe (somewhat built-up areas outside the city limits)-higher income; and fringe-lower income.

Approximately one-third of the interviews in each city were in the fringe areas. Of these, about one-third were located in neighborhoods classified on the basis of Census data or independent judgments as "higher than average" in income. A little less than one-fourth of the central-city interviews took place in higher-income areas. Computations after the completion of the survey showed marked differences between strata on such measures as incomes reported by the respondents, and the availability of "urban" services, tending to corroborate the data used for the original stratification.

In brief, the selection process involved dividing the four strata into fairly large districts, randomly selecting subdistricts—usually blocks—from these, randomly selecting households within the blocks, and finally selecting, through a random method, a specific respondent from a list of people aged 18 years or older in each household designated. The interviewer had no choice whatsoever about who was to be interviewed. This was automatically determined for him by the process, designed to assure that within each city each adult had an equal probability of being selected for an interview.

The final result was a sample which is believed to have been reasonably representative of the adult populations (aged 18 or older) resident in the high- and low-income areas in the central and fringe areas of the cities. When completion of the surveys permitted estimates of the total population at the time of the survey, it appeared that in both cities the number of respondents from central, low-income strata was somewhat less than it should have been, especially in Greensboro. In Durham, the central, high-income stratum was also undersampled somewhat. Higher refusal rates and more difficulty in reaching respondents in the central areas contributed to this effect. Practically, the result is that attitudes inferred from the entire 385-person sample without adjustment of the data for this effect give somewhat more weight to the higher-income, fringe areas than would be ideal. In this chapter, when attitudes or other measures are generalized to the Greensboro or Durham population as a whole, appropriate corrections will be made to equalize the contribution from all strata, and this will be stated. However, in most of this analysis comparisons involve only the 385 people within the sample, and the contribution of the central-city, lower-income strata is slightly understated. Caution should be used in generalizing from these samples to the entire city populations.

The reader should also keep in mind that the findings reported in this chapter are based on sample data, which are inherently somewhat elastic in nature. It is not possible to achieve the same degree of precision that would be possible if a complete survey were taken of the entire city population. For the purposes of this study, however, the precision which can be achieved through the sampling process is generally adequate, since the instrument itself is relatively crude.

Characteristics of Respondents

The 385 respondents ranged in age from 18 (youngest included in the sampling) up to several septuagenarians. About 11 per cent were 65 and over, 28 per cent were in the 45 to 64 range, 26 per cent were from 35 to 44, and 22 per cent were between 25 and 34. The remaining 13 per cent were 18 through 24. The Durham sample tended to be a bit more middle-aged, with more people than Greensboro in the 35 through 44 category and fewer in the 25 through 34 group. The completed sample was about 29 per cent Negro, the Durham sample including a somewhat higher proportion than the Greensboro sample.

About two-thirds of the total sample lived in households made up of a "basic" family unit consisting of husband and wife with their children, if any. Another 14 per cent of the households of respondents included this basic family unit plus additional persons (relatives, roomers, etc.). About 8 per cent of the respondents were part of a "part-basic" household which included (only) one parent, one child and/or perhaps other persons. Another 8 per cent of the respondents lived in households consisting of two or more unrelated persons, usually of the same age level. Finally, 4 per cent of the respondents lived alone. Generally speaking, about two-thirds to four-fifths of the respondents came from the sort of "normal" group which is generally envisioned in planning the environmental needs of the city. The remaining one-fifth came from some kind of "special" household which may need special consideration in planning.

Nearly 85 per cent of the respondents were either the heads of these households themselves, or were spouses of the heads of households. The remaining respondents were almost all relatives of the household head—9 per cent of the sample were "second generation" within the household, and most of the balance were parents or siblings of the household head.

Family income of the respondents varied between the strata, of course, since economic judgments were one basis upon which strata were selected. Mean annual income for the sample was about $4,800 for Durham respondents and $6,010 for Greensboro respondents. (When adjusted to correct for differences in sampling rates, the estimate for family income for the total city populations becomes $4,840 and $5,555, respectively.) Standard deviations on these income figures are relatively high. Considerable caution should therefore be used in drawing conclusions about the income differences between the two cities.

Educational experience of the respondents reflected the entire range of possibility. About 10 per cent of the sample reported four years or less of formal schooling. At the other end of the scale, nearly 10 per cent reported college degrees. These were among nearly 30 per cent who reported at least one year of college, and about 70 per cent who reported at least one year of high school. When asked to classify their own social status as "lower," "working," "middle," or "upper," the bulk of the respondents were evenly distributed between "working" and "middle." The remaining 6 per cent thought of themselves as "upper."

Where the Respondents Lived

About two-thirds of the respondents lived within the city limits of their respective cities. These locations were generally characterized by utilities and urban services such as public water and sewer, sidewalks, street lights, curb and gutter, storm sewers, etc. The "fringe" dwellers, on the other hand, were much more likely to have septic tanks, wells, open ditches for storm drainage, etc. Particularly in Greensboro, there seemed to be real differences between central-city and fringe locations. In briefest summary, the central-city respondents tended to live in locations with a higher order of urban service, while the fringe area respondents lived with fewer services and relatively spacious surroundings.

The samples were composed primarily of people who lived in single-family dwellings, about 82 per cent of the Greensboro and 71 per cent of the Durham samples. Only 5 per cent of the composite sample came from structures housing five dwelling units or more. Roughly half of the respondents were living in a dwelling which to some extent they or their spouse "owned," although about half of these were still paying on their mortgage. About 10 per cent in both cities were neither owners nor renters, but lived in a rent-free status with relatives or friends.

The interviewers were asked to rate each respondent's neighborhood on a five-point scale for such things as appearance, upkeep, etc. In the judgment of the interviewers, the sample lived in a wide variety of conditions ranging over the entire scale from worst to best, although the midpoint ("average") ratings and those just below were the most frequent evaluations.

Interview Technique

The interview was conducted by full-time paid interviewers who were hired and trained specifically for this study. Their assignments were in accordance with the principles of random selection described earlier. After locating the households in one of their assigned sampling units, the interviewers, in a door-to-door count, listed all the adults in each household (in order of age, to avoid "arranging" by the interviewer) on a special form. Only those persons whose names fell at predetermined positions on the list were to be interviewed.

The interviewers identified themselves as "from the University of North Carolina," and indicated that the questions concerned "how the citizens here feel about certain things in the city." The interviewer then began the interview, unless it appeared that time would not permit. In that case a later appointment was scheduled.

The interview itself contained several distinct parts. The first, a series of oral questions, dealt with the amount of experience living in other cities and/or on farms, along with reasons for moving to the current location. General satisfaction, likes, and dislikes about the city as a whole were next. City size preferences and questions about the relative importance of certain social and physical characteristics of cities in general followed. A number of questions dealt with the relative importance to the respondent of his neighborhood, compared with the city as a whole, and with his view of the desirable and undesirable features of that neighborhood.

Direct questions were varied by a second part of the interview, called a "game" because of its mechanical similarity to familiar parlor games. A series of alternative choices among various types of residential utilities and services (described on the board) were "bought" with a limited amount of "money" supplied in the context of the game. (Briefly, the respondent had won a free house. The decisions in the game were those necessary to determine the kind of neighborhood in which to build the house.)

A second part of the game was similar, but dealt with neighborhood facilities such as schools and churches, and distance relationships desired between those facilities and the respondent's home. During the course of the game, the interviewer rated the house and neighborhood environment for certain qualitative aspects.

A third major element of the interview utilized a series of photos of miscellaneous neighborhoods. The respondent was asked to indicate by a rating scale the extent to which each of the photos contained certain specified qualities, such as "privacy," "beauty," etc., and to rank the photos in order of preference.

The interview ended with a series of personal questions: attempts to get information about the basic personality of the respondent, social and economic data, occupation, etc. After completion of the interviews, the responses were edited and recorded by coding onto punched cards for mechanical sorting. The punched-card tabulations, in addition to special analyses of open-ended questions, form the basis for the analysis reported here.

Prevalence of the Different

The above sketch of the sample composition is intended primarily to indicate the background from which the attitudes have sprung. Incidentally, it provides an opportunity to emphasize the importance of the "different" groupings in the population. Review of these sorts of data and the larger sample estimates of the U. S. Census suggest considerable diversity within an urban population, even in these relatively small cities. If municipal-planning policies and administration emphasize only the needs of the "father-mother-children" families who own their own single-family home, it may be a mistake. It appears that there is a group of possibly one-fifth to one-third of the adult population which differs significantly from the single-family image. Policies for housing and community facilities, such as libraries and schools, and policies for taxation, housing code enforcement, zoning regulation, etc., might well be examined to see whether they adequately meet the needs of the smaller different groups.

Satisfaction with Current Environment

Inasmuch as satisfaction is an important element in the definition of livability, the extent of satisfaction or the lack of it should be a clue to the relative livability of the environment presently being experienced. "Satisfaction" in this discussion is assumed to be related to expressions of "approval," "pleasure," "liking," and similar feelings.

The interview included several approaches to the measurement of satisfaction: direct questions about satisfaction and likes and dislikes; questions about any desire to move away from the present neighborhood or city; and respondent's ranking of his neighborhood with respect to other neighborhoods in photos.

Direct Questions about Satisfaction

Each respondent was asked the following question:

Would you please look at this card and tell me which of the five statements is closest to how you presently feel about living in (*respondent's city*), all things considered?

The responses available on the card were these: very much satisfied, satisfied, neutral (neither satisfied nor dissatisfied), dissatisfied, and very much dissatisfied. About 43 per cent of the respondents received an alternative form of the card with the order of the five responses reversed. In addition, for Durham, interviews included a similar seven-position scale which ranged from "best possible" to "worst possible" and was used by the respondent to rate Durham "as a place to live."

There were interesting technical problems associated with this kind of question. First, there was some doubt, in the early stages of analysis, about whether the respondents were distinguishing between an attitude of satisfaction with city and neighborhood and an attitude of general satisfaction with life as a whole. After detailed examination of the association between various satisfaction-scale responses, it appeared that the responses were sufficiently different to suggest that people did indeed discriminate between their attitudes toward city, neighborhood, and life in general.

A second problem was associated with differences in response among those persons who used the alternative form of card from which to select their response. Consistently, when respondents used a card where "very much satisfied" was at the bottom of the list, that response was chosen more frequently than it was by the group using the card form as listed above. For instance, the "regular" card, as listed above, elicited the response that people were "very much satisfied" with their city in 24 per cent of the total sample using this form of the card. The alternative (reversed) form elicited a 45 per cent response on this item. Similar, but less striking results obtained in the other questions where the card was used. In all cases, very little difference in the total satisfaction measure was noted. The difference was in the apparent intensity of response within the satisfaction range. After a number of unsuccessful attempts to "explain" this difference, it was concluded that since the use of the alternative card forms had been more or less randomly distributed among the total sample the effect would cancel itself out. No effort has been made to differentiate between the card forms in these data, therefore.

Satisfaction with the City as a Whole

Very little dissatisfaction was expressed in the responses to direct questions; only 3 per cent of the composite sample said that they felt dissatisfied or very much dissatisfied with living in their city. Another 14 per cent were willing to take a neutral stand on the question. This leaves about 49 per cent satisfied and 33 per cent very much satisfied. Thus about 82 per cent, or about four-fifths of the sample, expressed apparently positive feelings about their city as a place to live, by this measure.

From other responses of the neutral respondents, such as their open-ended replies, there is basis for believing that in about half the cases the neutral response is basically negative in its implications. Even if this is true, fewer than one out of five persons expressed any negative feelings at all, and very few of these were explicitly unhappy with their city, if this direct question is a valid measure.

Further insight on this general evaluation of the city is available from the Durham question which used a "best possible" to "worst possible" continuum to rate "Durham as a place to live, taking everything into consideration." Using a seven-point scale, the results were as follows:

Best possible	4.0%
Very good	31.6
Good	44.3
Neither best nor worst	17.8
Bad	1.7
Very bad	0.0
Worst possible	0.6
	100.0%

When this set of responses is cross-tabulated against responses on the "satisfaction" question, they tend to corroborate each other. But there is also sufficient lack of association to suggest that though these are related in their meaning, they are measuring a somewhat different attitude. For instance, those who said Durham is good divided their satisfaction responses between neutral, satisfied, and very much satisfied. The bulk, comprising about five out of eight, were in the satisfied category. The relatively few (only three) people who said Durham was bad agreed that they were dissatisfied. Combining the two measures into a group composed of all who expressed some degree of satisfaction and also expressed a belief that Durham was good to some extent, about 73 per cent of the Durham sample expressed this general approval.

The satisfaction response was definitely related to expression of intent to move away from the respondent's city. Those very few respondents in the composite sample who had expressed definite intent to move were a third of them either neutral or dissatisfied. This is a much higher proportion of dissatisfaction than among those who had no plans to move away. There was no way to check on the satisfaction level of those who had definitely planned to move and *did* move. The extent of dissatisfaction among that group might be considerably higher than one-third. Those people who had no definite intent to move but who had thought about moving were also less satisfied; 40 per cent were neutral or dissatisfied. Of the remainder who had not in the past ever thought about moving, only 11 per cent were neutral or dissatisfied. A clear relationship is found between attitudes of satisfaction and plans or fantasies of moving away from the present city of residence.

When asked to select a preferred "size of place" (assuming complete freedom to choose) from a list of six categories ranging from "in the country or on a farm" up to "a metropolitan city of 500 thousand people or more," a majority (60 per cent) of the respondents chose the size category which included Durham and Greensboro. The 15 per cent who chose the bright lights of a larger city expressed considerably more dissatisfaction about their current city than did the former group (who wanted their present city size). Contrary to some early expectation, those who expressed preference for a smaller city or for a rural setting did not express any unusual dissatisfaction with their current city.

A farm background (as determined by the question "Did you ever live or work on a farm?") did not appear to influence the satisfaction responses. On the other hand, neither the extent of urban experience as measured by the number of different towns in which the respondent had lived, nor the amount of experience with cities outside the South seemed related to an attitude of dissatisfaction. (The small number of cases severely limits the statistical basis for this conclusion, however.)

Unfortunately, the small number of dissatisfied respondents limits the reliability of efforts to study them as a special subgroup. Among a number of characteristics examined, only the age of the respondent appeared to be of significance. A disproportionately large contribution of responses indicating dissatisfaction was made by persons in the age category of 20 through 24.

Negative feelings or dissatisfactions with the city in general might be expected to evidence themselves in open-ended questions such as these which followed immediately after the question referring to satisfaction with the city: "What things do you especially like about living in ___*(respondent's city)*___?" "What things do you especially dislike about living in ___*(respondent's city)*___?"

For the moment, quantity of answer is of interest, on the assumption that extensive dissatisfaction might result in an outpouring of response, especially on the latter question. There appears to be no flood of response. Specific responses to the "like" question outnumbered the specific responses to the "dislike" question in both cities. Within the composite sample, only 60 per cent of the respondents found at least one thing to dislike about their city as a whole, while 90 per cent found something to like. Apparently the amount of negative response was increased by a question specifically oriented to negative attitudes. Yet, even under prodding, 40 per cent of the people could not think of one specific complaint.

From these attempts at estimating the level of expressed satisfaction and dissatisfaction with the total city environment, the main conclusion has been that respondents were generally satisfied with their city. Approximately two-thirds of this sample were so satisfied that they did not articulate any significant complaint about the city as a whole.

Satisfaction with Neighborhood

Satisfaction or dissatisfaction with one's city is one thing. Satisfaction or dissatisfaction with one's immediate neighborhood may be something else again.

At a point in the interview after the frame of reference had shifted from the city as a whole to the neighborhood where the respondent was living, the following question was asked—a repetition of the earlier question except that it referred to neighborhood instead of city:

Would you look at this card again and tell me which of the statements is closest to how you presently feel about living in this neighborhood?

As might be expected, attitudes toward the neighborhood tended to parallel the attitudes toward the city. A fairly high coefficient of association between items was found. Over half the respondents were in complete agreement about their satisfaction scores for the city as a whole and for their neighborhood. Among the remainder, when there were differences between the two scores of the same individual, satisfaction with city was higher in slightly over half of the cases, and the neighborhood ranked higher in the other cases. Only occasionally was there a reversal of judgment (satisfied with city, dissatisfied with neighborhood, or vice versa)—fewer than one-tenth of those who disagreed on their evaluation.

The net effect of the differences is that a higher proportion of the respondents in the composite sample reported dissatisfaction when the frame of reference was their neighborhood rather than when their city was being considered. And fewer were neutral, as shown below.

	CITY	NEIGHBORHOOD
Very much satisfied	33.2%	33.9%
Satisfied	49.3	45.1
Neutral	14.4	12.1
Dissatisfied	2.3	7.1
Very much dissatisfied	0.8	1.8
	100.0%	100.0%

Although the number of cases of dissatisfaction is too small to permit full confidence in the significance of the apparent differences above, it appears that about three times as many people were critical of their neighborhood as of their city.

Questions about likes and dislikes in the neighborhood were asked in a form which corresponded with the previously noted queries about living in Durham or Greensboro. There appeared to be relatively little difference between city and neighborhood versions in quantity of responses. About the same number of people identified likes or dislikes in each case, although there were some differences between the cities in this respect. Except to a slight extent in Durham, the quantity of these open-ended responses did not tend to corroborate the above observations about the relative amounts of satisfaction.

Acknowledgement of serious intent to move from the neighborhood was associated with dissatisfaction with the specific neighborhood. Although the responses are not strictly comparable, it appears that a higher proportion of respondents (about 12 per cent) expressed intent to move from their neighborhood to another neighborhood in the city than expressed intent to move from the city (about 5 per cent). Here there is some indication that there may be more critical response when the neighborhood constitutes the frame of reference.

In these data, and others, there is a basis for believing that different attitudes are expressed when the frame of reference differs—the city as a whole contrasted with the respondent's neighborhood. At this point, it appears that a larger degree of dissatisfaction is associated with the neighborhood scale than with the city-wide scale. If this is indeed the case, it would seem that manipulation of environmental variables at the scale of the neighborhood rather than the city would be somewhat more productive in any effort to increase livability for most people.

Relative Satisfaction with the Two Cities

Estimates of the proportion of each city's total population who would express various degrees of satisfaction with that city are shown below. These approximations have been adjusted for variations in sampling rate, and therefore are applicable to the total population of each city, at the time of the survey. In general, the adult Greensboro population was estimated to have relatively more people who were very satisfied with their city than those in the Durham sample. The former were also estimated to exhibit slightly more extreme dissatisfaction although the actual numbers involved were small. The adjusted estimates expanded to the total population are as follows:

	GREENSBORO	DURHAM
Very much satisfied	43%	23%
Satisfied	39	58
Neutral	14	16
Dissatisfied	2	3
Very much dissatisfied	2	0
	100%	100%

Greensboro seemed to be in a somewhat better position with respect to existing conditions of livability, judging from the more frequent choice of emphatic statements of satisfaction. About 81 per cent of the populations of both cities are estimated to have been at least satisfied with their city environment at the time of the survey.

As judged by expression of intent to move away from their city, the Durham respondents were less satisfied with their situation. Over 8 per cent intended to move, in comparison with about 3 per cent in Greensboro. Greensboro respondents, on the other hand, were more restless about their neighborhood than Durhamites. Twice as many of the Greensboro people were anticipating moves to other local neighborhoods (17 per cent compared with 7 per cent in Durham).

In the samples drawn from Greensboro and Durham there was little to suggest extensive unhappiness with either of the cities as a place to live. Very few people reported serious dissatisfaction, and the bulk of the people expressed some degree of satisfaction. If dissatisfaction is interpreted as a measure of the intensity of citizen desire for "improvement," "reform," etc., we would not expect to find in these two cities any large recognition of need for generalized municipal improvement programs.

The meaning of the precise proportions of dissatisfied and satisfied people in these two cities would be clarified if strictly comparable figures were at hand for other cities. In earlier surveys where respondents were asked to report their satisfaction with various aspects of their city and neighborhood (Branch, 1942; Brewster, Flinn, and Jurkat, 1955; Slayton and Dewey, 1953, pp. 386–410), the proportion of reportedly satisfied people ranged from about 60 per cent up to 90 per cent depending upon the specific aspect of the environment with which the question was concerned. The approximately 80 per cent of the Greensboro-Durham sample who reported satisfaction corresponds generally with the proportions in these other studies.

Significance of Satisfaction

Why be concerned with attempting to identify the extent of satisfaction or dissatisfaction in the sample?

It has been noted earlier, of course, that the quality called "livability," as defined for this study, is a function of satisfaction. On the other hand, dissatisfaction with the city suggests that certain desiderata constituting livability factors may be missing from that city environment. Satisfaction is an indirect measure of the general quality of the city as a place to live. The relatively low range of variation between the two cities and between neighborhoods in each city is of interest. It suggests the possibility that some kind of norm for cities in general might eventually be identified. And it suggests that more sophisticated techniques for examining subtle variations around that presumed norm would be valuable.

However, the planner must look further than for the indirect measure of general satisfaction with the city at large. General satisfaction is undoubtedly a function of many other things in addition to those physical elements with which the planner is primarily concerned. (Responses to questions relating to likes and dislikes made this clear.) Subsequent sections deal more specifically with physical desiderata which contribute partially to the over-all satisfaction levels discussed above.

General Character of the City

What about the kind of city wanted? Should there be a city at all? Is there much consciousness of the city as a total entity? In looking at these and similar questions, the data were examined from the viewpoint that there might be desiderata related to the city as an entity.

Rural Backgrounds

About 55 per cent of the respondents had lived or worked on a farm during some portion of their life—about half of these during childhood only (under 18 years of age). About two-thirds of those with farm backgrounds reported 15 or more years in that farm environment.

However, relatively few people (only about 6 per cent of the entire sample) came directly to their present residence from a farm or rural village. A question designed to determine whether contacts with persons in rural areas have been kept up asked: "Do you presently do any visiting with people who live on a farm?" About 22 per cent of the entire sample reported visiting at least once per month on a farm. About the same number reported less frequent visits, but at least once every six months.

The relative intensity of these ties to the farm may be inferred by noting that of those who do visit, 21 per cent said they "almost always" bring back food from the farm, another 46 per cent bring back food "about half the time" or "once in a while" and 32 per cent "never" bring back food. These responses imply that for a substantial portion of these farm visitors—perhaps a quarter to a half—the relationship to rural people is relatively close and must provide considerable opportunity for continuance of rural values.

It may be of interest to note that the Durham portion of the sample appeared somewhat more rural by the measures discussed above: more people had come directly from the farm, more people had spent more time on the farm, brought more food home, etc. This difference is consistent with this investigator's over-all impression that Durham was somewhat more rural than Greensboro both in its physical character and in the attitudes of the people encountered during the survey.

While background and at least one aspect of current behavior indirectly suggest this kind of emphasis on rural values, a direct question on farm experience resulted in about 45 per cent of the respondents of both cities reporting no farm experience and 50 per cent saying they do not presently do any visiting with people who live on a farm. Are these people from a substantially different background which might suggest a highly urban orientation?

Urban Backgrounds

Nearly three-fourths of the entire sample had lived in their Greensboro or Durham urban area for at least ten years. About 36 per cent had never lived in any city except the one in which they were living at the time interviewed. A large segment of this sample, then, cannot be said to have had much opportunity to experience living in a variety of urban environments. Among this segment, it does not seem likely that there would be any substantial desire for anything radically different from present experience.

To overlook the more mobile population might leave a false impression. Fifteen per cent of the respondents had lived in their respective urban areas less than five years, and one-third of these had been in the area for only one year or less. About 64 per cent of the sample had lived in at least one other city, and 11 per cent had lived in four or more cities. Most of this other-city experience had been within the South (including boundary states of Texas, Oklahoma, Arkansas, Kentucky, West Virginia, Maryland, and Delaware) although one person with non-South experience was found for every six who had lived only in Southern cities. More than half of those with non-Southern experience were Southerners who had moved away and later came back.

If experience is a factor in establishing expectations about what a city should contribute to life, the respondents as a whole in this sample might be expected to respond primarily in the context of (Southern) medium-sized cities, with a substantial seasoning of viewpoints influenced by rural contacts and attitudes. Relatively few of the respondents had significant experience with life in really large metropolitan centers, in older, densely built-up industrial cities, and the more heterogeneous urban populations.

City Size Preferences

Shown below are responses to the question "If you had complete freedom to choose the size of city in which you would live, which of these city sizes would be your first choice?" (A card was used with this question listing examples of Southern cities in each population category.)

	GREENSBORO NO.—209	DURHAM NO.—174	BOTH CITIES NO.—383
Metropolitan city of 500,000 people or more	5%	8%	6%
Large city from 100,000 to 500,000 people	14	3	9
Medium-sized city from 10,000 to 100,000	59	63	60
Small city under 10,000	10	5	8
Small town or village of less than 1,000 people	2	7	5
In the country or on a farm	10	14	12
	100%	100%	100%

Sixty per cent selected the class which included Greensboro and Durham. A quarter of the total sample chose something which could be considered less urban than their present environment. Another 15 per cent answered in the other direction for a more urban setting. These responses are in general agreement with the backgrounds reported above. Even if it is assumed that city size is directly related to urbanity (and there is considerable question about that), this item does not give much basis for arguing that Durham and Greensboro should divest themselves of their urban qualities, nor, on the other hand, that they should seek more urban qualities.

Nonurban Daydreams

In an effort to identify more directly (through reference to fantasy) the aspects of a desirable total city, the Greensboro respondents were asked ". . . If you ever daydream about the ideal kind of place to live, can you tell me where it might be?" The Durham form of the question asked "what kind of place it might be" rather than "where," since the Greensboro question had tended to elicit what seemed to be too many "Florida," "California," and "Hawaii" answers. The wording change seems only to have made the respondents more explicit about why they wanted to go to Florida, California, and Hawaii. About 28 per cent of those who responded did so by mentioning a particular state of the United States. In about one-third of these cases, the state's "climate," "ocean," or "beauty" was mentioned to explain the choice.

More pertinent to the question of city character is the fact that out of 250 respondents only 5 persons said that they daydream about "cities" or "the city" in general, while 36 mentioned in general terms either "suburbs" or "the country." There seemed to be little spontaneous enthusiasm for the city per se, particularly in comparison with the lure of noncity images. However, a number of specific cities were cited (about 30 per cent of the responses), often with a statement of some economic, social, or physical advantage thought to be associated with each city. Evidently the particular advantages were sought in these cases, rather than the fact of a city environment.

Likes and Dislikes

Responses which probably get closer to the fundamental elements of livability came in connection with the question "What things do you especially like about living in Greensboro (or Durham)?" Respondents replied in their own words. Roughly 60 per cent of the respondents gave comments that were specific enough to be coded. (About 25 per cent were generalities about the whole city such as "I like just everything here"; 15 per cent were unable to respond at all.)

The samples from each city were quite similar in their collective replies. In the order of decreasing frequency, the most common answers dealt with things later coded as people, jobs, schools, and stores and shopping.[1] Frequencies ranged from about 20 per cent (of the total sample) who liked the people to 5 per cent who liked stores, and proportions in each category were remarkably similar for the two city samples. In broadest outline, these are probably the categories of livability which really count with the individual citizen. Although useful in understanding the relative importance of physical facilities in relation to the social and economic factors, these categories are obviously too general to assist much in the identification and location of facilities. It seems not unlikely that a similar list might be found in most Crescent cities, if not in most cities in the United States. Citizens will probably measure the city planning and development effort by the degree to which it helps meet personal needs subsumed under these headings.

It would appear to be more helpful to the planner and administrator to ask the question "What are the things you especially *dislike* about living in ___*(respondent's city)*___?" Although fewer usable responses were obtained, the complaints tended to be more specific and therefore of more immediate usefulness. And it was here that some of the differences between the two cities began to show up. Responses about things disliked were coded into the subject categories and ranked below by decreasing frequency of response. The list represents the percentages of people in the total sample who responded in each category.

GREENSBORO NO.—211		DURHAM NO.—174	
Cost of living	19.3%	Streets	20.1%
Government	10.8	Cost of living	10.7
People	9.6	Stores and shopping	10.7
Recreation	9.0	Recreation	9.4
Jobs	4.8	Traffic	7.5
Stores and shopping	4.8	Jobs	6.9
		People	4.4

These lists again call attention to a number of economic and social factors; for example, "cost of living" was a fairly important item, as was the item on problems with "people," involving aspects of human relations. There was some reason to believe that the somewhat higher ranking of "people" in Greensboro has something to do with the segregation issue, which may have been more of an issue there than in Durham.

The interesting Greensboro discontent with "government," which includes references to "city hall" and other comments about municipal operations, may be in part the aftermath of the annexation controversy which had occurred in some areas not long before the survey.

A significant new item which appears on both lists is "recreation." The absence of recreation appears to have been associated with considerable intensity of feeling. As used here the term includes all types of leisure-time activities, utilizing both public and commercial facilities.

Another interesting element seen here is the attention given in Durham to streets and traffic. In another analysis of these same responses, it was noted that considerable attention was given in Durham to "convenience" and "location" of things, giving emphasis to a proposition that movement within the city was of more widespread interest in Durham than in Greensboro.[2]

Some Physical Items Compared with Social Items

Other data on these matters came from a question on ". . . how important each of these things is in making a town an *ideal place to live*, from your point of view." Phrases which had physical implications were ranked high more frequently in Durham than in Greensboro. In order of decreasing importance rating, the Durham sample evaluated the phrases in this rank order:

1. Good roads.
2. Convenient public transportation.
3. Good sidewalks.
4. Plenty of parks.
5. Schools close enough so that children can walk to them.
6. Shopping facilities not too far away.
7. A city where people attend to their own business.
8. { Low tax assessments.
   Quietness of the city (lack of noise).
   The right kind of people in your city. }
9. Friends close by.

10. A city that persons in other communities look up to and hold good opinions of.

11. A friendly city that has the type of people with whom you can stop and chat awhile on the street and visit often.

12. A city where you can be yourself and not have to worry about what people think.

13. A city should have a mixture of all types of persons.

The Greensboro respondents, in ranking essentially similar items, seemed to put greater emphasis on factors such as prestige, social relationships, etc.:

1. Good roads and sidewalks.
2. A town that persons in other communities look up to and hold good opinions of.
3. The right kind of people in your town.
4. A town where people attend to their own business.
5. Convenient public transportation.
6. Friends close by.
7. A town where you can be yourself and not have to worry about what people think.
8. Schools close enough so that children can walk to them.
9. A friendly town that has the type of people with whom you can stop and chat awhile on the street and visit often.
10. Plenty of parks.
11. Shopping facilities not too far away.
12. Quietness of the town (lack of noise).
13. A town should have a mixture of all types of persons.

The differences in ranking of items on the two lists seem compatible with differences noted earlier between samples from the two cities. However, it will be noted that some modifications were made in the phrases between the Greensboro and the Durham surveys. Each reference to "town" was changed to "city" in the Durham version and "good roads and sidewalks" became two separate items. The apparent differences in ranking may be attributable in some way to these differences in question wording.

When the frame of reference is the city as a whole, the picture seems something like this: There is a general satisfaction with these cities which seems to be based largely upon very general social and economic factors which the people like. While these factors are probably rather basic elements of livability, examination of their physical implications is beyond the scope of this study. As dissatisfaction and dislike are explored, negative factors which detract from livability ("unlivability" factors, as it were) begin to emerge. These negative factors are more specific and refer more frequently to physical attributes of the city or to things which can be more closely related to the location and character of physical facilities. In Durham, streets, highways, and other aspects of local transportation are examples of the latter negative factors. In both cities additional recreational facilities would evidently contribute to an increase in livability.

General Character of the Neighborhood

The vocabulary of planning and development includes much reference to a concept of subdistrict within the city—the neighborhood. Unreported efforts of the earlier stages of this study to identify the meaning of this term to various respondents strongly suggested that "neighborhood" identifies areas of varying dimension for different people. Although it appeared fruitless to attempt a rigorous definition of the physical extent of each respondent's neighborhood, some attention was given to the question. Fewer than one out of ten respondents thought of "this part of town" as "having any particular boundaries or limits." Nearly 29 per cent of the entire sample, however, supplied some kind of neighborhood name in response to the question: "If someone you meet elsewhere in Greensboro asks you where you live, what do you tell him?" Another 29 per cent answered with a street address, but when asked whether their part of town had any particular name, they provided a neighborhood designation.

From these and other data it appears clear that the term "neighborhood" has some meaning for people, even though it might be difficult for them to delineate the precise extent of the area implied by the word. For purposes of this discussion it is enough to recognize that the neighborhood is an area which is considerably smaller in physical dimension than the city as a whole, and that the term means something reasonably concrete to most people.

Differences between City and Neighborhood Responses

Built into the schedule of questions was the opportunity to compare two frames of reference: (1) the city as a whole, and (2) the neighborhood. During the early part of the interview the scale of observation suggested to the respondent was always city-wide: "Durham" or "the Greensboro area" or "the city," etc. Later, the frame of reference shifted to "this part of town" and "this neighborhood." In several items, precisely the same questions were asked, but in a different context as far as scale was concerned (neighborhood instead of city).

The intent of this manipulation of scale was to explore whether there was a difference in the attitudes about what is needed to provide livability at these different scales of planning and development. Briefly, the data suggest that there are differences in the way the respondents saw things, depending upon which scale was involved.

Perhaps more important, the neighborhood factors appeared to be more important to the people than the city-wide factors in these Durham and Greensboro samples. For instance, there was much interest (described above) in roads and streets and mobility when discussion centered on the city as a whole. However, when forced to choose between "a very good neighborhood, but located so that it would be difficult for you to travel to other parts of town" and "a less desirable neighborhood, but located so that it would be very easy for you to travel to other parts of town," the respondents were three to one in favor of the good neighborhood, at the expense of accessibility. Further verification of the importance of the neighborhood is indicated by a similar comparison in a forced choice between "a very good house in a less desirable neighborhood," and "a less desirable house in a good neighborhood," which resulted in an even higher proportion–six to one in favor of the neighborhood over the house. These proportions are characteristic of responses from both cities.

In the earlier discussion of satisfactions it was indicated that more dissatisfaction was reported when the frame of reference had shifted to the neighborhood. This was interpreted as evidence of a more critical attitude or keener perception of things at the neighborhood level. Responses on other aspects of the interview tend to confirm this view. The question "What things do you especially like about living in this neighborhood?" elicited responses which were more specific (and therefore potentially more useful) than responses to the same query about "living in Durham" (or Greensboro). Neighborhoods received frequent praise because they contained "friendly," "good," "likable" neighbors (about one-fourth of the responses), or because of the location of stores, schools, churches, bus lines; or because the people do not intrude on privacy ("are not nosy"). An increase in attention to specific locational variables (for example, bus line) is apparent, when these responses are compared with evaluations of the city as a whole.

Similarly, when dislikes at the two scales of reference are compared, comments about the neighborhood are somewhat more numerous and more specific than in the case of the city as a whole. Absence of street lights was cited a number of times, especially in Durham, as was absence of sidewalks. The fact of living in a rented house was cited as a negative factor by from 5 to 10 per cent of the respondents (Durham and Greensboro, respectively). Concern about the use of specific buildings and lands in the neighborhood was expressed in about 10 per cent of the responses. In Durham, streets, sidewalks, and traffic accounted for nearly one-third of the complaints at the neighborhood level. Various aspects of familiarity were mentioned most frequently when the reference was the city as a whole. "Friendliness" and "quietness," on the other hand, received more emphasis in reference to the neighborhood.

When the items about the components of "an ideal city in which to live" were compared with similar items about the "ideal neighborhood" there were a number of differences in rank order. The general effect of the differences was more attention to locational factors in the context of the city; more importance for items bearing on prestige, privacy, and social relationships in the neighborhood context. About one-third of the respondents changed their evaluation of at least one of the thirteen items when they shifted from city to neighborhood.

The above discussion suggests that desiderata for a localized environment called the "neighborhood" were somewhat different from the things wanted for the city as a whole. There was also some evidence to indicate that neighborhood elements are important to most people, that people can articulate their neighborhood needs more readily, and therefore that the neighborhood environment may contribute more directly to livability than does the city viewed as a whole. Subsequent portions of the chapter discuss efforts to assess more directly the factors of livability at this local scale.

Neighborhood Photographs—Clues to Desired Qualities?

In the hope that visual cues in a series of photographs of urban neighborhoods might stimulate useful reactions about desirable and undesirable aspects of those neighborhoods, the respondent was shown a

Figure 11-1. Photographs used in Greensboro picture game. *Top:* Builder's development—"friendliness" and "newness" were the only significant positive qualities attributed to this neighborhood. *Center:* High-density residential area—this was the least desirable picture of two-thirds of the Greensboro respondents, and especially bothersome were lack of space, lack of privacy, and undesirable environment for children. *Bottom:* Durham street scene—friendliest, quietest, and most private of the neighborhoods pictured here.

series of three photographs (see Figure 11-1). While looking at a photograph, he was asked to respond individually to each of a series of words and phrases (such as "privacy," "beauty," etc.) which were descriptive of selected qualities which could perhaps be imputed to the neighborhood pictured. When the interviewer said "privacy," for instance, the respondent, using a card with seven possible alternatives, indicated whether the *amount* of privacy he attributed to the pictured neighborhood was satisfactory to him and if not, how much the absence or presence of that quality would "bother" him ("greatly," "some," "not at all"). After completion of the first series of words and phrases, the second photograph was evaluated, and so forth. The respondent's own neighborhood was next evaluated in exactly the same fashion. Finally he ranked the three photographs and his own neighborhood in order of relative desirability to him.

The series of words and phrases were presented in the form of verbal cues to a number of possible concepts for the general character of environment. There was no attempt to define the physical correlates of these, nor has subsequent analysis sought to do so. To the extent that these verbal symbols are meaningful to the respondent, their ranking indicates the relative importance to him of qualitative aspects of neighborhood development. Analysis so far is encouraging, with respect to the validity and significance of the verbal cues, but more experimentation is needed.

In Greensboro, 15 possible qualities of environment were considered by the 187 people who participated in this "picture game." Combining all Greensboro responses and deriving an "intensity" score for each quality (based on how much the presence or absence of that quality would "bother" the respondent), the relative importance of the 15 words and phrases is shown below and continued on next page, in order of decreasing importance.

Spaciousness
Beauty
A character which is good for children
Exclusiveness
A country-like character
Closeness to nature
Privacy
Greenery
Homeyness
Quietness

Cleanliness
Newness
Friendliness
Crowdedness
Dirtiness

The qualities near the top of the list are those which excited the most concern in connection with the photographs, usually because the respondent did not think the neighborhood depicted would have enough of those qualities to satisfy him. Words at the bottom of the list indicate factors about which there was less concern. Depending upon the particular photograph under consideration, there were variations in detail, but the relative position of most items did not change more than three or four positions in ranking.

When asked to select the best neighborhood, two-thirds of the Greensboro respondents said they liked their own neighborhood better than any of the pictures they had been shown. By examining the responses of these 123 people, it is possible to see some of the factors that make their neighborhoods desirable to them. Most (at least 80 per cent) said that their neighborhood had "just about the amount I want" of the following:

Friendliness
Homeyness
Quietness
Greenery
Cleanliness

In descending order of importance, these are the qualities which generally seemed adequate in their neighborhood setting, and presumably contributed to the existing level of livability.

On the other hand, there was less satisfaction with other items which help to define the missing qualities of these neighborhoods:

Beauty
Exclusiveness
A country-like character
Spaciousness

The last-named items, by this measure, are some of the things which would tend to increase the livability of present neighborhoods for at least two-thirds of the Greensboro sample.

A similar analysis can be made from the negative point of view.

Almost the same number of people (two-thirds of those who played this "picture game") indicated that the neighborhood in the center picture of Figure 11-1 was the least attractive in comparison with their own neighborhood and the other photographs of Figure 11-1. What was the ranking of those things which would "bother" these people "greatly" in the neighborhood shown in the center picture? Lack of privacy leads the list. Concern for spaciousness and the relative lack of desirability of this environment for children follow closely. This area also seemed to lack homeyness and quietness—characteristics which have been seen to be important in the context of the favorably evaluated home neighborhood. In relation to these latter five qualities, newness, cleanliness, and even friendliness seemed of importance to relatively few people.

These data are not generally comparable with the Durham responses. A different series of pictures (with one exception) and a reduced list of qualities were used. The top picture in Figure 11-1 was used in both cities and elicited quite similar responses, although slightly more Durham people tended to respond "just about the amount I want" with respect to qualities implied by the photograph. The Durham data suggest results which are similar in essential outline to those discussed for Greensboro; although contrary to Greensboro results, a photograph taken in Radburn, New Jersey (not shown), was selected by most people as substantially better than their own neighborhoods.

By this analysis some qualities which seemed especially important to most people were space, beauty, and the kind of environment which they perceive as "good for the children." Even in the most popular photograph, these qualities were matters of concern. Evidently the qualities of familiarity, quietness, and even friendliness tend to be perceived as already present in the local environment of a large number of people. This suggests the hypothesis that these are things which can grow up independently of the physical environment. On the other hand, population density ("crowdedness") and beauty are heavily dependent on physical elements, and if not available in a neighborhood they are not easy to add. This seems to be recognized in the earlier finding which noted the emphasis on "desirable neighborhood" over "desirable house" or over "accessibility."

The physical accomplishment of these objectives in neighborhood development is not easy, since these qualitative desiderata are yet to be interpreted in terms subject to ready translation into physical elements. The next section deals more specifically with some of the elements which can be used in building up a residential neighborhood.

One of the major elements of the schedule was a series of two related "games." In a stricter sense, it was not properly a game since there was no competition involved. However, the use of the term was intended to help create a willingness to set aside considerations of social and economic reality impinging upon choices made during the decision making involved here.

Each of the 357 respondents who played the game was instructed to pretend that he had recently won a house on a television program. He was asked to assume that he and his family liked the house, and that it met their needs. However, the house was not yet built, and the sponsor of the program who was giving them the house needed certain information about a suitable neighborhood for the house which was to be located on a tract of land "at the edge of town." To help the winner decide the kind of facilities he wanted, the company had prepared a pair of "game boards" similar to equipment used in many parlor games. This formed the mechanism for the selection process discussed here. The first game included 34 items of utilities and service (see Figure 11-2). Each item had a value in dollars attached. The respondent was given a number of markers to represent an allotment of money ($2,000 in Greensboro, $1,800 in Durham) with which he "purchased" items by placing the appropriate valued markers on the board in the spaces where the items were described. The transactions in this game will be discussed later.

The second game board included references to density and to travel distances and times, and to selected neighborhood and community facilities (see Figure 11-3). The rules for this game were somewhat different; the markers no longer had a monetary value, but served simply as a means of limiting the total amount of choice available. Forty markers were available in Greensboro; 36 in Durham. The respondent was instructed to select first one of the density categories illustrated at the top of the board. This required from 6 to 30 of his markers, depending upon how much elbow room he wanted in the block where he was to live. With the remaining markers he could select as many facilities as he could afford in combination with the degree of accessibility he wanted (time-distance measures). If he wished to have the facilities within a 3-minute walk (category A) it required 5 of his markers (except shopping center, which needed 18). If will-

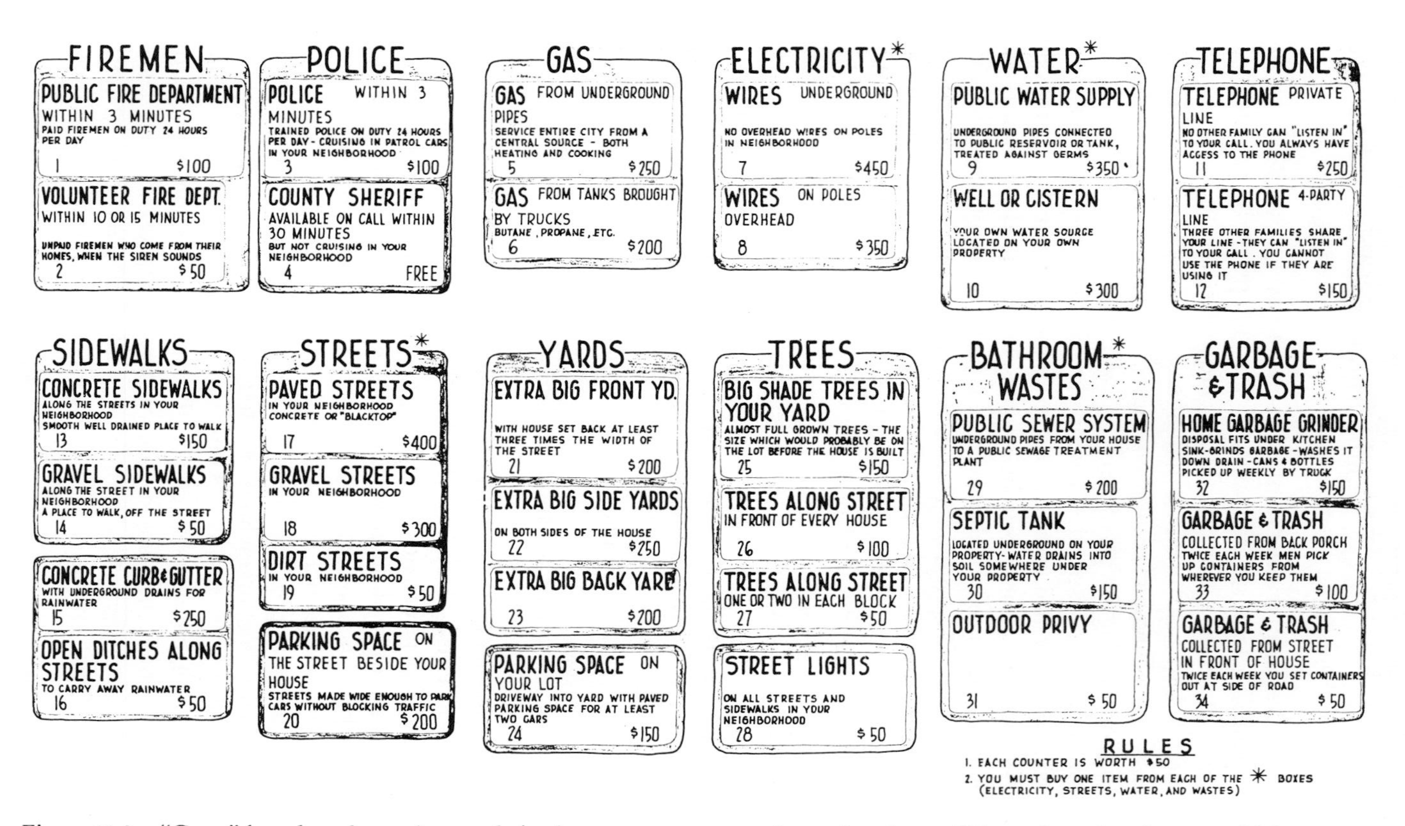

Figure 11-2. "Game" board used to estimate relative importance to respondents of various utilities and services for potential house site.

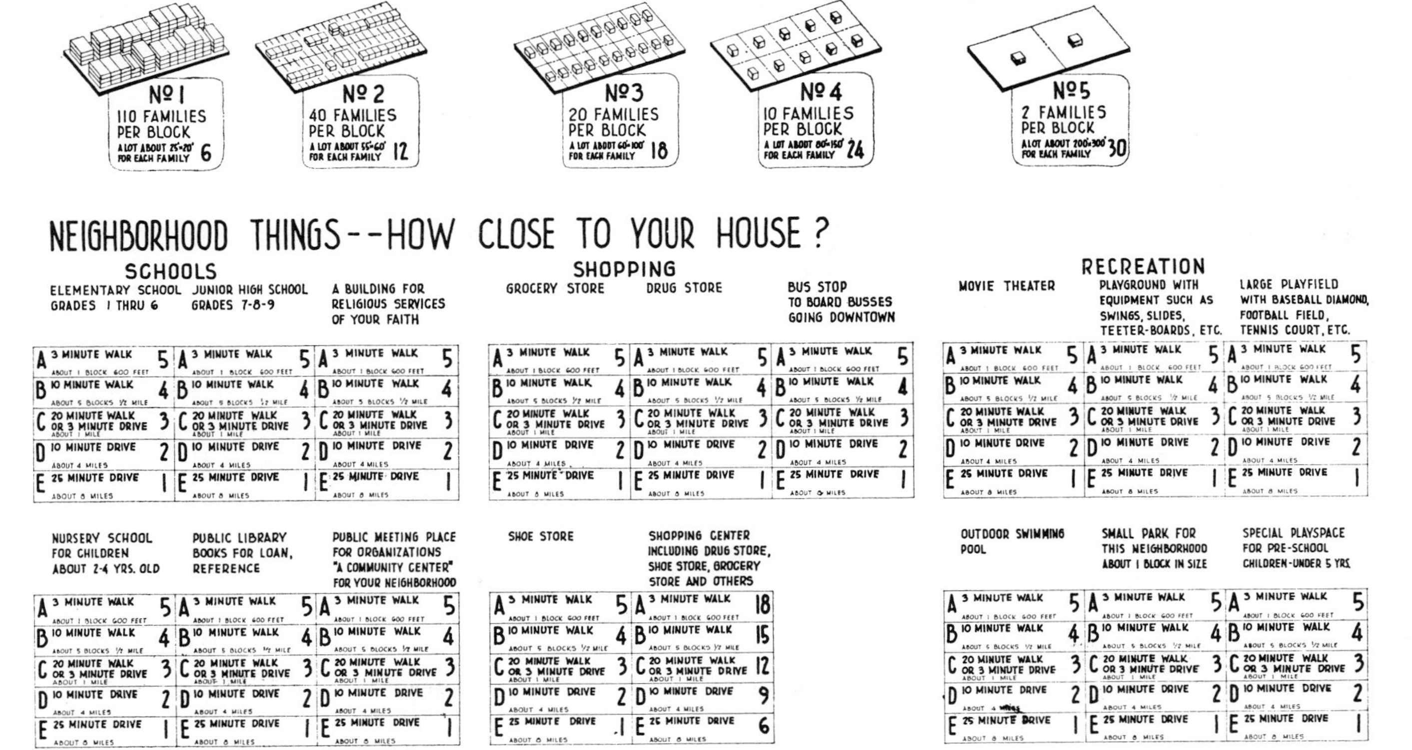

Figure 11-3. "Game" board used to evaluate aspects of neighborhood density and distance relationships. Original, 28×45 inches, included five photographs of building types typical of the five densities at the top of board to assist in conveying concept of relative densities.

ing to travel as much as 25 minutes to get to a facility, he needed only 1 marker—and therefore could have access to *more* facilities but farther away.

Density

Five options were offered with respect to densities (top row, Figure 11-3). The rules forced the respondent to select one of five possible densities, which ranged from 40 dwelling units or families per acre (which typically means at least 3-story apartment buildings) down to 0.7 dwelling units or families per acre, which implies about 60,000 square feet per single-family dwelling unit. The densities illustrated on the board are, from category one through five, about 40, 15, 7, 4, and 1 families per acre, respectively.

Out of 347 respondents only 10 people chose the first two more densely built-up areas with multifamily structures. About one-fourth of the people selected density category number three, which is usually associated with a single-family house on the minimum size lot permitted by zoning and subdivision regulations in many cities. The remainder of the sample wanted even more room for themselves. There appears to have been an overwhelming response in favor of single-family housing types, and against row houses and apartment structures, and for and against the densities associated with these housing types.

PROPORTION OF RESPONSES IN EACH DENSITY CATEGORY (PER CENT)

	1	2	3	4	5	TOTAL %	TOTAL NO.
Greensboro	1.1	2.7	23.2	55.7	17.3	100.0	185
Durham	0	1.9	24.7	35.8	37.7	100.0	162

A portion of the Durham sample was offered the opportunity, after completing this game, to repeat with an unlimited number of markers, instead of 36. When given this additional freedom, a substantial proportion selected a density even lower than their previous choice. Earlier observations suggesting that the Durham sample was somewhat more rural than the Greensboro sample are given further support by the fact that even though the Durham people each had fewer markers to spend, twice as many people in Durham invested heavily in the extremely low-density category, even at the cost of having fewer choices available for facilities. These responses are in accord with findings discussed earlier about frequent references to spaciousness and concern about crowding.

Facilities

Table 11-1 shows the rank order of the "popularity" of all the facilities listed on Figure 11-3. The Greensboro list ranks the selected items based on a total purchasing power of 40 markers. The Durham "A" ranking was chosen by people with only 36 markers available, requiring more difficult decisions presumably. The Durham "B" list shows the rank order of selections by a group of people repeating the game without any restrictions about number of facilities to be selected.

A religious facility is very high on the list of items wanted in the neighborhood. Only in the closely limited Durham "A" group did transportation and everyday needs for food seem more important. In that same severely restricted group, the first 7 items seem to identify

Table 11-1. Rank Order, Percentage of Respondents Who Chose Neighborhood Facilities in Figure 11-3

GREENSBORO 40 MARKERS	DURHAM "A" 36 MARKERS	DURHAM "B" NO LIMIT
1. Religious building	1. Bus stop	1. Religious building
2. Elementary school	2. Grocery store	2. Shopping center
3. Grocery store	3. Religious building	3. Bus stop
4. Junior high school	4. Drug store	4. Neighborhood park
5. Bus stop	5. Elementary school	5. Elementary school
6. Shopping center	6. Shopping center	6. Junior high school
7. Drug store	7. Junior high school	7. Playground
8. Library	8. Movie theater	8. Movie theater
9. Community center	9. Neighborhood park	9. Community center
10. Swimming pool	10. Library	10. Swimming pool
11. Neighborhood park	11. Playground	11. Library
12. Playground	12. Community center	12. Playfield
13. Movie theater	13. Swimming pool	13. Grocery store
14. Playfield	14. Playfield	14. Drug store
15. Nursery	15. Nursery	15. Preschool play space
16. Preschool play space	16. Preschool play space	16. Nursery
17. Shoe store	17. Shoe store	17. Shoe store

from 17 possibilities on the board the core of service needs: bus stop, grocery store, religious building, drug store, elementary school, shopping center, and junior high school. Note the relatively low priority of recreation items and cultural facilities in this list. When the same group was permitted an unlimited number of choices (Durham "B"), the relative importance of neighborhood park, shopping center, playground, and other recreational items was increased. It may be symbolic that with the unlimited "purchasing power" exemplified in this list, the neighborhood shopping center has displaced the grocery and drug stores from the top of the list.

Differences between cities were not especially striking. Public transportation facilities, inferred from the relatively strong position of the bus stop, appear to be more highly valued in Durham. A neighborhood movie was sought by a smaller proportion of people in Greensboro than in Durham.

There is some indication that the selection of different density choices was followed by differences in the pattern of facilities chosen. Within the Greensboro sample, for instance, the high-density people —those who chose number 3 category instead of number 4 or number 5 in Figure 11-3—apparently felt significantly less need than the others for a religious building in the neighborhood, and significantly more need for a library, playground, and playfield.

Time-Distance

After selecting one of the facilities, the respondent placed 1 to 5 markers on the board in one of the spaces marked A through E indicating how close to his home he felt it would be desirable to have that facility located. A range of choice was offered from 3 minutes to 25 minutes in time, combined with from 600 feet to 8 miles in distance.

It is readily apparent in the analysis that time-distance choices have some underlying logic. Items of daily use received higher rankings than facilities which are less frequently called upon. In both cities, for instance, respondents were unwilling to spend much money to have a library close to them. Clearly libraries were not nearly as important to most people as other things on the list. The facilities which large proportions of people wanted close to their home (within less than a 20-minute walk) were the bus stop, elementary school, junior high school, grocery store, drug store, shopping center, and religious building, in order of increasing distance from home.

Two substantially different patterns of response were identified in evaluating the choices made on particular facilities. The most common pattern was a moderate level of response on A followed by a fairly high peak on B, after which response dropped off fairly rapidly. Generally, this seems to have been a pattern for the facilities on which location was not highly critical—things which may or may not be necessary or desirable as part of the immediate neighborhood. Another response pattern characterized reactions to the grocery store, drug store, bus stop, nursery school, and preschool play area. Here choices peaked at A and dropped off appreciably in a relatively smooth downward curve. These apparently are viewed as pedestrian-oriented facilities by the bulk of those who chose them.

The major differences in the pattern of desired distances to particular community facilities did not seem to be associated with differences in choices of residential density. Of course, the higher-density people, who had more "purchasing power" left, had more opportunity to choose facilities having shorter travel time-distance.

Finally, it is of interest to examine the difference between the first, tightly limited, Durham response and the second, unlimited response. This difference may be viewed as the effect of luxury. Here are the things the Durham people moved much closer to their homes *when they had plenty of resources:* a library, playground, neighborhood park, preschool play space, nursery school, bus stop, grocery and drug stores. Of particular interest is the predominance of recreational and cultural facilities in this list. Outdoor recreational areas have been conspicuously absent from the lists of things which were wanted in the local environment. The above finding suggests that perhaps this omission is not a rejection of recreational and cultural facilities but rather a recognition of the budgetary difficulties involved.

Services to the House Site

The alternative utilities and services listed on Figure 11-2 were offered to the respondents in the manner described above, as the first in the series of games. It will be recalled that the respondent received a limited amount of "money" in $50 markers, and that they could purchase items up to the limit of their funds. The play aspect of this device seems to have been reasonably successful, and most of the respondents entered into their task with zest and became thoroughly involved in the decision making.

The general objective here was information about the relative importance of services noted on the board, and of various quality levels of those services. The particular set of alternatives offered is subject to improvement, of course, especially after there has been opportunity to observe the kinds of questions which arise in the use of each item. It may be well to note that an effort was made to fit the items to the range of local conditions—not only in the selection of the items but in the assignment of values to those items. However, with time and further experimentation, it is clear that some of the items and especially the assigned values will need re-examination and possible revision. Nevertheless, the data provide some insights into certain factors deemed desirable for house and site by the Greensboro and Durham respondents. This discussion examines some of the relatively broad implications of the data. Detailed discussion of the methodological aspects of this particular aspect of the research are reserved for discussion elsewhere.

Two general observations, however, can be made about method. First, the respondent's specific experience and current living pattern with respect to these services and utilities do not seem to offer the major explanation for his attitudes. Comparison of experience with selections on these and other items has tended to suggest that other factors are helping to establish attitudes and preferences. Second, the particular values attached to each item are perhaps less crucial than it might appear at first glance. A preliminary analysis which evaluated the effect of these values alone as possible determinants of choice has been somewhat reassuring on that question.

The Bonus Feature

After "spending" his money each person interviewed was asked to respond to a 5-point satisfaction scale with reference to ". . . how you feel about the number of things you were able to buy with your money?" The Greensboro people, with $200 more to spend, seemed to be happier about their "purchasing power." Note that over 80 per cent of the Greensboro residents said they were "satisfied" or "very much satisfied" with their purchases at this point. Only 55 per cent of the Durham people responded in the same way.

Both sets of respondents were pleased when the interviewer announced that the company had discovered "that it has some extra money in its treasury. So it has made another $1,000 ($1,200 in Durham) available for you to spend." The interviewer had already recorded the items chosen up to this point, and after the respondent had completed his "bonus" purchasing, the interviewer recorded these choices also. That the extra money was helpful is indicated by large increases in the number of "very much satisfied" and "satisfied" persons at the completion of the bonus selections, when the question about satisfaction was repeated. Satisfaction was now reported by about 95 per cent of both samples. In general the more money, the more satisfaction with the number of items which could be purchased. This reaction tends to support the author's intuitive belief that most of the respondents were playing the game with gusto, that they were much involved in the decisions, and that they took the activity seriously.

The use of the bonus device provides two measurements of the respondent's attitudes about the relative importance of these items. The first is a "bare minimum" sort of selection, which required some rather hard decisions about how to spend the last few markers. The second level of choice, the $3,000 level, permits some analysis of the luxury items.

Streets, Electricity, Water, and Waste Disposal

Because of experiences during pretesting, it seemed necessary to force certain choices with respect to basic facilities which would otherwise be taken for granted and therefore not be purchased although believed to be necessary and desirable. Choices were required under "electricity," "water," "streets," and "bathroom wastes." The highest level of service was overwhelmingly desired for streets, waste disposal, and water supply. (Around 90 per cent of sample selected the highest level in these areas.) However, there was a 60-40 split on how electricity should be supplied, with the majority favoring poles.

The people who chose lower-quality items in one area were not necessarily the same people who chose lower qualities on others. There appears to be no significant group who consistently bought gravel streets, septic tanks, and wells. There was, of course, a great deal of consistency in the group which selected the high quality of service in these areas.

Police and Fire

There was a high degree of correlation between choice of the high-quality utilities above and the higher-quality fire and police service (Items 1 and 3, Figure 11-2). Here again, about 91 per cent of the respondents selected the higher-quality services.

Basic Services

At least 25 per cent of the respondents in the entire sample chose all of the following items, and they can be viewed as the basic core of utilities and services:

Paved streets
Police
Public fire department
Public sewer system
Public water supply
Street lights
Sidewalks

Telephones and electricity, of course, should be on the list since most people wanted the service, but did not agree about the alternative ways of providing for it.

Amenities

We have noted above the inclusion of sidewalks and street lights as very popular items. In addition, "big shade trees" (Item 25, Figure 11-2) were extremely desirable, ranking even higher than "parking space." Curb and gutter along the streets were highly valued. Larger front and back yards were valued much more than more side-yard space. Of particular interest is the relatively high response on street lights and concrete sidewalks, which are not universally available, especially in outlying residential areas.

Table 11-2 shows the ranking of the entire 33 items (excluding Item 4 of Figure 11-2, which is free) as they were selected by 357 respondents in both cities. Each respondent had $3,000 to spend in making his decisions.

The data from this game serve to confirm earlier observations of the importance residents attach to various aspects of residential site devel-

Table 11-2. Rank Order of "Popularity," Game 1 Items, $3,000 Choices, Composite Sample (Final Choice)

NUMBER OF PEOPLE WHO CHOSE THIS ITEM (NO.—357)	ITEM AND ITEM NUMBER IN FIGURE 11-2
329	Paved streets (17)
327	Police (3)
326	Public fire department (1)
319	Public sewer system (29)
315	Public water supply (9)
307	Street lights (28)
285	Concrete sidewalks (13)
258	Big shade trees in yard (25)
218	Parking space on lot (24)
216	Concrete curb and gutter (15)
216	Telephone—private line (11)
215	Extra big back yard (23)
214	Wires on poles overhead (8)
213	Extra big front yard (21)
144	Home garbage grinder (32)
141	Trees along street in front of every house (26)
133	Wires underground (7)
126	Garbage and trash collected from back porch (33)
125	Telephone—4-party line (12)
101	Garbage and trash collected from street in front of house (34)
99	Extra big side yards (22)
97	Parking space on street beside house (20)
96	Gas from underground pipes (5)
90	Trees along street—one or two in each block (27)
45	Open ditches along streets (16)
33	Volunteer fire department (2)
32	Well or cistern (10)
28	Septic tank (30)
22	Gas from tanks brought by truck (6)
21	Gravel sidewalks (14)
20	Gravel streets (18)
3	Dirt streets (19)
2	Outdoor privy (31)

opment which contribute to health and convenience. Most cities have already accepted the desirability of providing paved streets, water, and sewer systems. However, less consensus is found on whether curb and gutter, underground wiring, and sidewalks are sufficiently desirable to warrant public intervention in the development process to provide these. The data suggest that people in these two samples had a high regard for these amenities of development, and that a more livable city will include more attention to these and other details of the house site.

Conclusions

By and large a major proportion of those interviewed were reasonably well satisfied with their environment, and probably would not see any reason to initiate change, to alter the living situation in which they find themselves. Yet it has been clear in the several different ways of approaching their attitudes used in this study that these people do have preferences and can recognize gradations in beauty, convenience, and many other qualities which can be built into a city. Much of this chapter has been devoted to suggestions of what these qualities and the physical appurtenances of the city ought to be in the judgment of a large proportion of the people queried.

Some of the most fascinating work—exploring the needs and aspirations of those who were not heard from in this chapter—still lies ahead. Clearly our cities as they stand today do not yet fulfill the full range of livability preferences of the majority, so there is an immediate challenge in finding ways of physically attaining livability qualities explored in the Crescent. At the same time, there is a greater challenge in meeting needs on a much larger scale elsewhere where urban agglomerations have lost many of the living qualities the Crescent cities still possess.

FOOTNOTES

1. The figures discussed here are for the first item mentioned by each respondent. Analysis of second and third responses showed them to be essentially similar to the first response. If the second and third responses had been added, the total amount of response in each category would be substantially and proportionally increased. This is the case for all figures given in connection with the "like" and "dislike" items.

2. As will be seen later, there is evidence that citizens of both cities valued streets and highways and other appurtenances of physical mobility rather highly. However, at the time of the surveys there appeared to be somewhat higher standards in Greensboro with respect to street paving, and it is probable that this apparent dislike of existing conditions in Durham was based on an objectively less advantageous situation. In Durham, there also appeared to be substantially more concern with the "condition" of things—maintenance and upkeep, and the quality of facilities.

REFERENCES

Branch, Melville C., Jr. (1942), *Urban Planning and Public Opinion.* Bureau of Urban Research, Princeton University, Princeton, N. J.

Brewster, Maurice R., William A. Flinn, and Ernest Jurkat (1955), *How to Make and Interpret Locational Studies of the Housing Market*, Office of Technical Services, U. S. Department of Commerce, Washington.

Slayton, W. L., and Richard Dewey (1953), "Urban Redevelopment and the Urbanite," in Coleman Woodbury (Ed.), *The Future of Cities and Urban Redevelopment.* Chicago: University of Chicago Press.

Chapter 12

Occupational Careers and Mobility *

by Richard L. Simpson †

MUCH RESEARCH has shown the prevailing patterns of occupational mobility in industrial societies. Most studies have dealt with intergenerational mobility, the movement of sons into different occupational strata from those of their fathers. A lesser number have treated career (intragenerational) mobility, the movement of workers from one stratum to another during their work careers. (A summary of mobility studies with extensive bibliography is given in Lipset and Bendix, 1959.) Several major conclusions seem warranted from the research so far:

* The research reported herein was performed pursuant to a contract with the United States Office of Education, Department of Health, Education, and Welfare, which provided funds through the Institute for Research in Social Science, University of North Carolina, for the major part of the research. Additional support was provided by the Urban Studies Program of the University of North Carolina for a large portion of the research. The University Research Council of the University of North Carolina also supported part of the research.
† The author wishes to acknowledge the substantial contributions of H. Max Miller, David R. Norsworthy, and John R. Earle. Miller prepared part of the interview schedule, and planned and supervised the sampling and interviewing. Norsworthy and Miller devised the coding and punching procedure. Norsworthy and Earle planned and executed much of the IBM analysis. All three did some of the interviewing, along with Douglas Gatlin, Burton Onstine, and Robert O. Pickard. Ida Harper Simpson gave advice and assistance at various stages. The interview program was made possible by the assistance and cooperation of city officials, especially J. D. MacIntosh, Marvin R. McIver, and Jesse R. James of Burlington, Bruce Turney of Graham, and Tom Davis of Raleigh.

1. There is everywhere some tendency for sons to "inherit" the occupational status levels of their fathers. The higher the occupational status of a father, the higher the status of his sons is likely to be.

2. At the same time, there is much intergenerational mobility, more of it upward than downward. Inherent in industrial society is a general upward trend in the occupational status of workers, since new and expanding occupations tend to require more skill and responsibility than the older occupations they displace. (See Kahl, 1957.)

3. Several things in addition to a worker's family background influence the status level of his first job. One is the amount of education he has received. Another is the type of community in which he grew up: the larger the community of origin, the higher his first job is likely to be (Ammon, 1895; Boalt, 1954; Lipset, 1955). Still another is the occupational advice he has received: access to numerous sources of advice increases a worker's chance of obtaining a high-ranking first job (Lipset and Bendix, 1959; Simpson and Simpson, 1962).

4. The first job a worker takes affects his occupational level throughout his career—so much that, according to findings presented by Lipset and Malm (1955, p. 256), "knowledge of the occupational level of a man's first job is a better predictor of his subsequent mature status than is either education or father's occupation."

5. Nevertheless, there is considerable mobility during work careers, and most of it is upward. Workers moved up by acquiring seniority, experience, capital, and better knowledge of available opportunities.

In this chapter we undertake three tasks: (1) to see whether there are differences between the career patterns of workers in two Crescent communities and those of workers elsewhere; (2) to contribute new knowledge about social mobility by examining the effects on careers of some combinations of variables not previously treated in combination, or treated previously but less fully; and (3) to discuss some practical implications of the findings for the social and economic development of the Crescent.

Sample and Research Method

The data were collected by interview from two urban areas of Piedmont North Carolina, Raleigh and Burlington-Graham. The potential sample included all adult white males in the labor force living in randomly selected blocks in the two cities in the summer of 1959. Raleigh is primarily a commercial and governmental center, and the Burlington-Graham area is mainly industrial; the two communities rather than only one of them were studied to obtain a diversified occupational distribution. Defining the sample as all known white male labor-force members in all blocks where any interviewing was done, completed and usable interviews amounted to 380 in a sample of 541, or 70 per cent. The refusal rate was below 5 per cent, and nearly all the missing interviews represent people in blocks where some interviewing had been done, who had not yet been reached when the time and money available for interviewing came to an end. In the absence (as this is written) of detailed 1960 Census data we cannot estimate precisely the amount of sample bias. The sample probably underrepresents people of low occupational and educational status, but a detailed evaluation of the Burlington-Graham sample by Norsworthy (1961) suggests that this bias is slight; the somewhat heavy concentration of white-collar workers is due mainly to the exclusion of Negroes from the sample.

Factors Related to First Jobs

Education and Family Background

Both education and family background were strongly related to the status levels of workers' first jobs, but a worker's own education appeared to have more effect than his father's occupational status when one of these was high and the other was low. Of the workers with white-collar fathers, 77 per cent of the 132 high school graduates, but only 28 per cent of the 36 nongraduates, obtained white-collar first jobs. Of those with blue-collar fathers, 44 per cent of the 97 high school graduates, but only 6 per cent of the 94 nongraduates, obtained white-collar first jobs. (A more detailed tabulation and discussion are given in Simpson, Norsworthy, and Miller, 1960.) Even these figures conceal some of the effect of education by lumping together the college men, most of whom had white-collar fathers, and those who finished high school but went no further. Some of our findings given later will show that the effects of factors other than education were greatest among the uneducated workers and tended to weaken or even disappear among workers with advanced education.[1]

Community Origin and Occupational Advice

Lipset and Bendix (1959) have shown that workers who grew up in large cities are at an advantage in urban labor-market competition, workers from farms are at a disadvantage, workers from small towns are intermediate in urban job chances, and these differences are partially independent of the workers' educational and family status backgrounds. (See also Lipset, 1955.) Simpson and Simpson (1962) have shown for our Crescent sample that access to occupational advice from many sources, especially from people outside the workers' families, is predictive of high-ranking first jobs, and that these relationships are partially independent of the workers' family-status backgrounds. Lipset and Bendix (1959) also note the effects of advice on job chances, and they suggest that one reason for the advantage of native urbanites in urban job markets is their access to superior advice about available job opportunities. In this section we shall pick up where these earlier findings left off, cross-tabulating workers' educational attainment, community origins, and occupational advice to see if they had independent effects on first jobs.

Table 12-1 classifies workers by education (graduates versus nongraduates of high school), community origin (residence during teens in cities larger than 15,000 versus other nonfarm communities versus farms), and number of persons who gave them advice before they took their first jobs (three or more versus two or fewer). The table shows the percentage of workers in each of the resulting categories whose first jobs were nonmanual. The findings suggest that community origin and occupational advice did have separate effects on the status levels of first jobs, whether the workers had graduated from high school or not.

The effects of community origins on first-job levels, with education and advice controlled, can be seen by comparing rows 1, 3, and 5 (high education, much advice); rows 2, 4, and 6 (high education, little advice); rows 7, 9, and 11 (low education, much advice); and rows 8, 10, and 12 (low education, little advice). In all these comparisons the city-bred workers were the most likely and the farm-bred the least likely to begin their careers in white-collar jobs, with one exception: in the group with low education and little advice (rows 8, 10, 12) the workers from small towns were the most likely (13 per cent) to obtain white-collar first jobs, and the city-bred and farm-bred were about even with between 6 and 7 per cent of each having white-collar first jobs.

Table 12-1. Per Cent of Workers with White-Collar First Jobs, by Education, Community Origin, and Number of Occupational Advisers [a]

EDUCATION, COMMUNITY ORIGIN, AND NUMBER OF OCCUPATIONAL ADVISERS	TOTAL (NO.—368)	PER CENT WITH WHITE-COLLAR FIRST JOBS
High school graduates		
1. City, 3 or more advisers	(38)	79
2. City, 2 or fewer advisers	(42)	76
3. Town, 3 or more advisers	(55)	65
4. Town, 2 or fewer advisers	(46)	50
5. Farm, 3 or more advisers	(25)	56
6. Farm, 2 or fewer advisers	(28)	43
Not high school graduates		
7. City, 3 or more advisers	(7)	29
8. City, 2 or fewer advisers	(15)	7
9. Town, 3 or more advisers	(21)	19
10. Town, 2 or fewer advisers	(32)	13
11. Farm, 3 or more advisers	(11)	0
12. Farm, 2 or fewer advisers	(48)	6

[a] "City" refers to places with 15,000 or more population, including their suburbs. "Town" refers to places with fewer than 15,000 population, excluding farms.

The effects of occupational advice on first-job levels, with education and community origin controlled, are seen in comparing successive pairs of rows in Table 12-1 (1 and 2, 3 and 4, etc.). Each successive pair of rows matches workers on education and community origin but varies the number of people who gave them occupational advice. While the differences tend to be slightly less on the average than those created by differences in community origin, and there is one reversal of the usual relationship (between rows 11 and 12, the uneducated farm-bred), these comparisons generally show the predicted favorable effect of occupational advice on first-job levels.

Thus workers from nonfarm backgrounds, and especially those from towns and cities larger than 15,000, were at an advantage in seeking first jobs, as were those who had received occupational advice from numerous people; and these relationships were independent of each other. Similar findings not reported here show the same effects when college graduates are removed from the sample so as to equate the high school graduates more precisely in education. Other findings not shown here indicate that receiving his main occupational advice from someone outside rather than inside his family had the same kind of favorable effect on a worker's job chances as we have shown for having numerous advisers. (Some of these findings are given in Simpson, Norsworthy, and Miller, 1960; others in Simpson and Simpson, 1962; others are available on request.)

Vocational Counseling

Since there is a relationship between receiving occupational advice from numerous sources and obtaining a high-status first job, we might expect the advice to have an especially strong effect when some of it has come from a trained vocational counselor in the school. Usually the counselor sees his task as helping to fit the worker to the *type* of work which best suits his needs and aptitudes, without any necessary reference to the *status level* of the work. Nevertheless, counseling which makes people aware of the range of occupations potentially open to them might be expected to increase the likelihood of their finding high-status jobs, since most people if given the choice will prefer high-ranking to low-ranking work.

Table 12-2 attempts to cast some light on the relation of vocational counseling to the level of first jobs. The attempt is not entirely successful because of the small number of workers who said that they had received counseling and because we have no information about the type or extent of the counseling, but the findings may suggest things worth exploring in more systematic research on the effects of counseling. In Table 12-2 the workers' first jobs are divided into three levels: upper white-collar (executives, business managers, proprietors of large and medium-sized businesses, and major and middle professionals), lower white-collar (clerical and sales workers, lesser administrative personnel, technicians and minor professionals, and small businessmen), and blue-collar. The upper white-collar level corresponds to the top two levels and the lower white-collar level to the next two levels in Hollingshead's index of occupational status (Hollingshead and Redlich, 1958).

Only 81 of the 366 workers who answered the question said that

Table 12-2. Responses to Questions about Vocational Counseling by Status of First Job

QUESTIONS ABOUT VOCATIONAL COUNSELING	STATUS OF FIRST JOB: UPPER WHITE-COLLAR	LOWER WHITE-COLLAR	BLUE-COLLAR
Did your school offer vocational counseling?			
Per cent "yes"	22	31	17
Total No.	(55)	(112)	(199)
(If yes) Did you receive counseling?			
Per cent "yes"	67	59	50
Total No.	(12)	(34)	(34)
(If received) Did counseling influence your occupational plans?			
Per cent "yes"	38	60	41
Total No.	(8)	(20)	(17)

their schools had offered any kind of vocational counseling. These 81 included 22, 31, and 17 per cent of the workers whose first jobs were upper white-collar, lower white-collar, and blue-collar, respectively. Of the 80 who answered the remaining questions about counseling, 45 said that they themselves had received some counseling, and these included 67 per cent (8 of 12), 59 per cent, and 50 per cent of the respondents to this question whose first jobs were upper white-collar, lower white-collar, and blue-collar, respectively. Of the 45 who had received counseling, 22 said that the counseling had some effect on their occupational choices. These 22 included somewhat more than half (12 of 20) of those whose first jobs were lower white-collar, and somewhat fewer than half of those who began their careers in upper white-collar or blue-collar work.

Thus fewer than 6 per cent of the 366 respondents to the initial counseling question and barely more than one-fourth of those who said that their schools had offered counseling were willing to acknowledge any influence of counseling on their own careers. We did not ask about the nature of any effects which counseling might have had, but unpublished results of a study of college students by R. L. Simpson indicate that more than half the students who attributed influence to vocational counseling, when asked to describe the influence, said that counseling merely strengthened plans they had already made. Almost none in this college study said that counseling had changed their career plans, though a sizable minority said that it had made them more aware of the features of certain occupations and may thereby have speeded up their career decisions. From the Burlington-Graham and Raleigh data and from this college study it seems a safe conclusion that vocational counseling as heretofore practiced does not often have a significant effect on career plans or that, if it does, the effects are seldom perceived by the persons affected.

The higher the status level of the first job, the higher was the percentage of workers who said that they had received counseling, among those who said that their schools had offered counseling. This might mean several things. It might mean that counselors did not make much effort to reach students from lower-class backgrounds, though these presumably needed the most help. It might mean instead that the students most likely to seek counseling were those who least needed it. Or it could mean that counseling had favorable effects on workers' occupational chances.

The workers most likely to say that their schools had offered counseling were those whose first jobs were in the lower white-collar group. It is possible that these workers actually came from schools which were more apt to give counseling. This does not seem likely, however, since the workers with upper white-collar first jobs included a larger percentage who had grown up in cities, and a city is more likely than a small town or farm community to offer counseling in its schools. (Thirty-two per cent of our workers from cities larger than 15,000, 19 per cent from smaller nonfarm communities, and 16 per cent from farms said that their schools had offered counseling.) What this finding may mean instead is that workers who began their careers in upper white-collar jobs, since they tended to come from high-status families, had access to all the occupation information they needed without recourse to school counseling, and simply forgot that such counseling had been available to them. Workers who began in lower white-collar jobs, on the other hand, were often from lower-status family backgrounds, and it seems probable that such a person, if he is ambitious, is apt to take advantage of counseling and remember it later. This interpretation is consistent with the fact that the lower was the father's status, the greater was the amount by which workers with lower white-collar first jobs exceeded other workers in the percentage reporting that their schools had offered counseling.[2] It is also consistent with the finding mentioned earlier, that among the workers who said that they themselves had received counseling, those who began their careers in lower white-collar jobs were somewhat more likely than the rest to say that the counseling had influenced their occupational plans.

It would be unwise to put complete faith in these findings. Very few cases are involved and we do not know the exact nature of the counseling to which the workers were referring, although the question indicated "a formal program of vocational counseling." But bearing in mind the need for caution, the findings suggest the hypothesis that vocational counseling has its greatest impact on students whose families are slightly below average (but not extremely low) in status and who themselves are upward mobile into the lower white-collar ranks. Logically these students would seem likely to want information about potential careers and to be unable to get it from their own families and associates. For these students it is especially important that the counseling given them be realistic. Lipset and Bendix (1959) report that nearly three-fourths of the workers in their Oakland survey who had been advised by teachers had been advised to enter professions. Simply urging students indiscriminately to aim for top-ranking professions probably does little good, since many of them lack the financial and perhaps the intellectual resources to become professional men. Perhaps what many ambitious students from modest backgrounds need most is a clear picture of the careers available to them in the middle range of the status pyramid and slightly above. No one needs to tell them that it is a good thing to be a doctor or lawyer—they already know this—but many of them do *not* know of the expanding career opportunities open to people trained as technicians, skilled clerical and lower management workers, minor professionals and semiprofessionals, and the like.

Career Mobility

Rates of Career Mobility

Career mobility refers to the relative standing of a worker's first and subsequent occupational statuses. A worker whose current occupation is at a higher level than his first has experienced upward career mobility; a worker whose current occupation is at a lower level than his first has been downward mobile; and a worker whose first and current positions have been at the same level—whether or not he has changed jobs—has been stationary. Tables 12-3, 12-4, and 12-5 show rates of career mobility for men age 30 and older in our sample. Men

Table 12-3. Current Jobs of Men 30 and Older, by First Jobs

		PER CENT WHOSE CURRENT JOBS WERE					
FIRST JOBS	TOTAL (NO.—311)	PROFESSIONALS	MANAGERS, ETC.	CLERICAL AND SALES	SKILLED, ETC.	OPERATIVES	LABOR AND SERVICE
Professionals	(56)	77	16	7	0	0	0
Farm managers and proprietors	(12)	0	33	8	8	33	17
Managers, proprietors, and officials, nonfarm	(17)	23	59	12	0	6	0
Clerical and sales workers	(68)	18	40	28	7	3	4
Skilled workers and foremen	(13)	15	15	8	46	8	8
Operatives	(91)	3	24	14	20	29	10
Labor and service workers, nonfarm	(49)	14	14	14	20	25	12
Farm laborers	(5)	0	0	0	20	60	20

Table 12-4. Upward and Downward Career Mobility of Men 30 and Older, by First and Current Jobs

		PER CENT WHO HAVE		
	TOTAL (NO.—311)	MOVED UP	BEEN STATIONARY	MOVED DOWN
First jobs				
Professionals	(56)	0	77	23
Managers and proprietors	(29)	14	48	38
Clerical and sales workers	(68)	57	28	15
Skilled workers and foremen	(13)	38	46	15
Operatives	(91)	62	29	10
Labor and service workers	(54)	87	13	0
Current jobs				
Professionals	(71)	39	61	0
Managers and proprietors	(81)	72	17	11
Clerical and sales workers	(47)	45	40	15
Skilled workers and foremen	(41)	71	15	15
Operatives	(49)	31	53	16
Labor and service workers	(22)	0	32	68

Table 12-5. Per Cent of Workers Currently in White-Collar Jobs in Five Studies, by First Job [a]

	STUDY AND FIRST JOB									
	SAN JOSE, 1934		ENGLAND, 1949		OAKLAND, 1949		JAPAN, 1950		CRESCENT, 1959	
CURRENT JOB	WHITE-COLLAR	BLUE-COLLAR	WHITE-COLLAR	BLUE-COLLAR	WHITE-COLLAR	BLUE-COLLAR	WHITE-COLLAR	BLUE-COLLAR	WHITE-COLLAR	BLUE-COLLAR
Per cent white-collar	73	25	77	21	81	35	87	26	92	42
Total No.	(368)	(811)	(498)	(3,097)	(229)	(356)	(1,366)	(1,013)	(141)	(153)

[a] Data for studies other than our own are from Lipset and Bendix (1959, p. 290). The other studies are Davidson and Anderson (1937), Thomas (n.d.), Lipset and Malm (1955), and Odaka (1958). Workers with nonurban first jobs are omitted.

under 30 are omitted since these had not yet had time to accomplish much mobility but might do so later, though the same is of course true of some of the older men. The findings show higher rates of mobility than have been reported in studies conducted elsewhere.

Looking first at Table 12-3, we see the gross relationships between workers' first and current job categories. The pattern resembles those found in earlier research such as the San Jose, California, study by Davidson and Anderson (1937) and the study of Oakland, California, reported by Lipset and Bendix (1959). Among workers with nonfarm first jobs, whatever the level of a worker's first job was, his current job was more likely to be in this category than in any other, with the exception of workers whose first jobs were at the bottom of either the white-collar or blue-collar stratum. These last included workers with clerical first jobs, who were more likely to have moved up into managerial positions than to have stayed where they started, and the initially unskilled, who were *less* likely currently to be unskilled than to be in any other category. (The table shows a similar picture for workers with farm-proprietor and farm-labor first jobs, but our data on these are not very meaningful since there were few of them and the sample automatically excluded such people if they stayed on the farm.)

Despite the pattern just noted, more workers were mobile than stationary. Table 12-4, which summarizes data from Table 12-3, brings this out clearly. Nearly half the workers had moved up and about a seventh had moved down. Rogoff (1953, pp. 26–27) has stated that "studies in career mobility have generally found that no more than 50 per cent of the population moves out of the occupational class in which the first position was held," but this generalization was not true of our Piedmont Crescent sample. The first section of Table 12-4 classifies workers by first jobs and reveals that the only first-job category in which more than half the workers remained stationary was the professional category, from which upward movement was impossible by definition. In all other first-job categories except that of proprietors and managers, fewer than half the workers were stationary and more moved up than down. Even the appearance of greater downward than upward movement among the managers may be misleading, since this group included small-farm proprietors whose current manual and clerical jobs may not really have represented downward mobility. The second section of Table 12-4 classifies workers by their current jobs and shows only two groups—professionals and operatives—in which more than half the current workers had been stationary. In the managerial and skilled categories, more than 70 per cent of the current workers had been upward mobile.

Rogoff does not cite the research summarized in her statement that studies have "generally found" more than 50 per cent of all workers to be stationary, but if we may assume that the research to which she refers is representative and classifies occupations in the usual Census fashion, our findings indicate more career mobility in the Crescent than in other places where research has been done. Table 12-5 gives this conclusion a firmer basis. It compares some of our findings with those of four other studies summarized by Lipset and Bendix (1959), classifying workers by first job (white-collar versus blue-collar) and showing for each group the percentage whose current jobs were white-collar. The various findings are not wholly comparable. For example, our Crescent data are for men 30 and older while some of the others are for men 31 and older, and the occupational classifications used in the five studies are not identical. Despite this, the differences are suggestive and are probably too large to be explained by incomplete comparability of the data. Of the Crescent workers with white-collar first jobs, only 8 per cent had been downward mobile into blue-collar jobs, compared with 23 per cent in England, 13 per cent in Japan, 19 per cent in Oakland, and 27 per cent in San Jose. Of the Crescent workers with blue-collar first jobs, 42 per cent had moved up into white-collar jobs, compared with only 21 per cent in England, 26 per cent in Japan, 35 per cent in Oakland, and 25 per cent in San

Jose. These comparisons strongly suggest that the cities we studied in the Piedmont Crescent have had unusually high rates of upward career mobility and low rates of downward mobility.

Why do we find such high rates of upward mobility? The probable reason is that the Piedmont has been experiencing industrial growth and diversification in recent decades. It still lags behind the nation as a whole but has been catching up; and more upward mobility is to be expected in a newly industrializing or diversifying area, where high-status jobs are being created, than in a mature industrial area, where the growth in high-status jobs is slower because it starts from a higher base. Norsworthy (1961) has described marked effects on certain kinds of mobility in the Burlington-Graham area stemming from the introduction of a single large electrical appliance plant into this traditional cotton-mill town, and it seems likely that the general process of industrial diversification has created the high mobility rates we found in our two-city sample.

If this interpretation is correct and the Crescent has had high mobility rates because it has been catching up industrially with the North and West, we would expect its rates of career mobility to slow down in the near future unless the region can attract new types of industry faster than the nation as a whole has been developing new industries in recent decades.

Education, Family Background, First Job, and Current Job

We now turn from describing mobility rates to examining some factors which help to account for the current occupational levels of individuals. Table 12-6 cross-tabulates workers by education (high school graduates versus nongraduates), father's occupational status (white-collar versus blue-collar), and first job (white-collar versus blue-collar). For each of these worker characteristics, reading from left to right in the order named, a "plus" represents possession of the characteristic favorable to high status and a "minus" represents possession of the unfavorable characteristic. Comparable data are given from the Oakland study reported by Lipset and Malm (1955, p. 257). The numbers in the table show the percentage of workers with each set of attributes whose current jobs were white-collar. Our findings are less trustworthy than the Lipset and Malm findings because our sample was much smaller, and concerning two of our eight groups in

Table 12-6. Per Cent of Workers with White-Collar Current Jobs, by Education, Father's Occupation, and First Job: Crescent and Oakland Samples [a]

EDUCATION, FATHER'S OCCUPATION, FIRST JOB [b]	CRESCENT, 1959		OAKLAND, 1949	
	PER CENT	TOTAL NO.	PER CENT	TOTAL NO.
1. + + +	98	(86)	96	(82)
2. + + −	90	(20)	49	(51)
3. + − +	94	(33)	92	(61)
4. + − −	58	(38)	44	(79)
5. − + +	56	(9)	76	(37)
6. − + −	32	(25)	38	(53)
7. − − +	50	(4)	59	(54)
8. − − −	27	(79)	30	(221)

[a] Crescent data are for men 30 and older; Oakland data are for men 31 and older (Lipset and Malm, 1955, p. 257).

[b] "Plus" refers to high school graduation or more education, white-collar father's occupation, and white-collar first job, respectively.

the table—the two with less than high school graduation but white-collar first jobs—nothing meaningful can be said because there were fewer than 10 workers in each group. Nevertheless some meaningful comparisons can be made, and they suggest that the relative impacts of education and first-job level on current-job level were not the same in the Crescent as in Oakland.

The Crescent data show education more important and first job less important in predicting current job than they were in Oakland. Meaningful comparisons of Crescent workers matched on father's status and first job but varied on education can be made by comparing rows 2 and 6 and 4 and 8. In these two comparisons the differences between the percentages of workers with white-collar current jobs are 58 per cent and 31 per cent, respectively, while the Oakland differences are only 11 and 14 per cent. (The other two comparisons, rows 1 and 5 and 3 and 7, also show greater impact of education in the Crescent than in Oakland but involve too few cases to be trusted.) Meaningful comparisons of Crescent workers matched except for first-job level are rows 1 and 2 and 3 and 4. These show first job making differences of 8 and 36 per cent, compared with 47 and 48 per cent in Oakland. (Again, the two comparisons where our sample size is too small to be trusted show the same pattern, with first job making more difference in Oakland than in the Crescent.) In both the Crescent and Oakland, father's status seemed to have the least effect on current-job levels, though it did have some effect in the expected direction. The meaningful comparisons of Crescent workers matched except for father's status are rows 1 and 3, 2 and 4, and 6 and 8. In only one of these—row 2 and 4, involving workers high in education but low in first job—did father's status make a sizable difference.[3]

When the data in Table 12-6 are summarized somewhat differently, the stronger effects of education in the Crescent and of first job in Oakland come out still more strongly. If the "father's status" variable, which made relatively little difference, is ignored, there are four categories of workers in each sample. Of the workers high in both education and first job, 97 per cent in the Crescent and 94 per cent in Oakland currently had white-collar jobs, and of those low in both education and first job, 28 per cent in the Crescent and 31 per cent in Oakland currently had white-collar jobs; workers in the two studies were essentially alike when they were consistently high or low in these two variables. But among the workers high in education only, 69 per cent in the Crescent but only 46 per cent in Oakland were currently in white-collar positions, and among those high in first job only this situation was reversed, with 46 per cent in the Crescent but 66 per cent in Oakland currently in white-collar positions. The difference made by education when first jobs were high was 51 per cent in the Crescent but only 28 per cent in Oakland; when first jobs were low it was 41 per cent in the Crescent and 15 per cent in Oakland. On the other hand, the difference made by first jobs when education was high was 48 per cent in Oakland but only 28 per cent in the Crescent; when education was low it was 35 per cent in Oakland and 18 per cent in the Crescent. (The table does not show these figures but is the basis for them.)

Thus no matter how we look at the data given in Table 12-6, they show education as the major factor affecting the level of a worker's current job in the Crescent but first job as the major factor in Oakland. This conclusion is consistent with the greater prevalence of upward career mobility in the Crescent.

Table 12-7 shows the relative effects of education and community origin on a worker's chances to move from a blue-collar first job into a white-collar current job. It deals only with workers who were 30 or older, had held blue-collar first jobs, and had not graduated from college; thus the "high education" category includes high school graduates and men who had attended college without receiving degrees. The numbers in the various categories are small, but bearing in mind the resulting need for caution, we may draw two tentative conclusions from these data. The first, which is hardly surprising, is that education made a marked difference in a blue-collar worker's chances of becoming a white-collar worker, regardless of his community origin. The second is that community origin made a substantial difference among the uneducated but did not make a consistent difference among the high school graduates; nearly as many of the farm-bred high school graduates as of the high school graduates from cities larger than 15,000 had risen into white-collar work, and the farm-bred high school graduates had done better than the high school graduates from nonfarm communities smaller than 15,000.

These data suggest that a high school education erased the long-

Table 12-7. Per Cent Currently in White-Collar Jobs, by Education and Community Origin, among Noncollege Graduates 30 and Older with Blue-Collar First Jobs

EDUCATION AND COMMUNITY ORIGIN	TOTAL NO.	PER CENT CURRENTLY IN WHITE-COLLAR JOBS
High school graduates		
City origin	(12)	75
Town origin	(24)	58
Farm origin	(17)	71
Not high school graduates		
City origin	(17)	47
Town origin	(40)	28
Farm origin	(51)	20

run disadvantage of a farm background. In comparison with the workers of comparable education who had not grown up on farms, the farm-bred workers who had finished high school but not college started lower but climbed further to end at about the same place. In contrast, workers from farms who had failed to complete high school not only started lower but were less likely to advance from where they started. (Tabulations showing this are omitted from the chapter but are available on request.)

Our findings thus indicate that education, the most important single predictor of both first and current job level for the entire sample of workers, was even more important for the farm-bred than for others. We cannot guess whether a high school diploma will be enough to equalize the chances of rural and urban youths in the future, as education through high school and even beyond becomes more and more common. It does seem likely that the urban occupational prospects of a farm boy who has failed to graduate from high school will remain bleak.

Summary of Findings

Data from interviews with 380 white male workers in the Burlington-Graham and Raleigh areas of North Carolina's Piedmont Crescent reveal that several factors helped to account for the status levels of workers' first full-time jobs. A worker was relatively likely to obtain a white-collar first job if he was highly educated, came from a white-collar family background, had received occupational advice from three or more people, and had lived during his teens in a nonfarm community, especially one with more than 15,000 population. All of these variables had separate effects on first-job levels, but education had by far the greatest effect. The disadvantage in finding first jobs due to farm origin was strongest among workers who had not finished high school.

Formal vocational counseling in the schools had played little part in shaping the careers of these workers. Only 81 of 366 who answered the question said that their schools had offered counseling, 45 had personally received counseling, and 22 had been influenced by it. The data suggest the hypothesis, without being able to demonstrate it, that counseling has its greatest impact on boys from somewhat below-average status backgrounds who are moving up by taking first jobs in the lower white-collar class.

Nearly half the workers aged 30 and older had moved up into Census occupational categories higher than those of their first jobs, and only about one-seventh had moved down into lower categories. Our Piedmont Crescent workers had experienced more upward mobility during their careers than the workers described in earlier studies made in England, Japan, and California. The high rate of upward mobility in the Crescent area is probably due to its recent industrial growth and diversification. An area which is not yet fully industrialized but is undergoing relatively rapid industrialization is likely to have high rates of upward mobility, since it starts from a low-status occupational base and creates many new, higher-status jobs.

Despite the prevalence of occupational mobility, the first-job levels of workers over 30 were somewhat predictive of their current-job levels. The amount of education a worker had received was, however, the best single predictor of his current job level. In this respect the Crescent pattern differed from that of Oakland in 1949, where Lipset and Malm (1955) found that first jobs had more effect than education on current job levels. The status levels of workers' fathers also had continuing effects on their occupational careers, but these effects were less than those of education and first jobs.

Community origin had a continuing independent effect on job levels only among workers who had not finished high school. Data on current jobs of workers over 30 indicate that the high school graduates who had grown up on farms began in lower first jobs than those of nonfarm high school graduates, but closed the gap by achieving more upward career mobility. Farm origin appeared to impose a permanent disadvantage, and origin in communities larger than 15,000 a permanent advantage, among workers who had not finished high school.

Some Implications of the Findings

If we are right in attributing the high rate of upward career mobility in the Crescent to its early stage of industrialization, an obvious prediction to make is that the mobility rate will slow down as the Crescent enters a more mature phase of industrialism. If more workers start their careers at high occupational levels, fewer can rise. Rogoff (1953) notes that in an advanced industrial economy where the best jobs require high levels of education or technical training, career mobility tends to give way to intergenerational mobility achieved through education. Increasingly, either a worker enters the labor force at a high occupational level by virtue of his education or he may never reach a high level at all. Perhaps this fact helps to account for the substantially greater ability of educated blue-collar workers to rise into white-collar jobs in the Crescent than in the Oakland sample of workers studied by Lipset and Malm. In a region which has lagged educationally behind the rest of the country, our educated blue-collar workers took advantage of the region's late start by moving during their careers into jobs that might already have been held by younger men in a region with a higher general level of education and a prior start in industrial diversification. Whether or not this interpretation is correct, education will remain a requisite for high-status jobs. Its importance may even increase as the region attracts more modern, automated industries with fewer semiskilled jobs and more jobs requiring college education or at least technical training beyond what is now offered in the high schools. Industries like electronics, to name only one, offer little future for the uneducated worker.

In the light of this, the research findings on the differential opportunities of workers from cities, small towns, and farms point to what may be a growing problem. The worker who moves to a city from a rural area is already at a disadvantage if he lacks advanced education. His disadvantage may become even greater if the cities establish special schools to give their own young people technical training beyond high school, as several in the Crescent have already done, while the rural schools give only the traditional curriculum. Since it is probably impractical to expect rural communities to vote money to train their youth to move away to cities, perhaps only some kind of action by the state can help.

Vocational counseling may also offer hope for improving the prospects of farm boys, if it is aimed at increasing their knowledge of realistically available opportunities. Our findings on the effects of vocational counseling were not very encouraging, but this was mainly because so few workers in our sample had been exposed to counseling. It seems likely that greater knowledge of opportunities is one reason for the superiority of native urbanites in urban job competition. Our data and others from the same study (Simpson and Simpson, 1962) indicate that the sheer amount of occupational advice a worker receives is a factor in the kind of job he will get, and that advice from people outside the family is more effective than advice from inside the family, possibly because outsiders are apt to be experts or people with information about specific jobs. Few high school boys have a clear idea of the kinds of careers that offer them the most promise, and this is especially true in a rural community where not many occupations are visible in the boys' environment. All of this suggests that counseling programs designed to acquaint students with the range of possibilities might help, especially if they are coupled with local opportunities for training in fields other than vocational agriculture.

FOOTNOTES

1. Throughout our discussion we shall use the word "effects" loosely, for simplicity of presentation, although we show only relationships among variables and cannot prove causation.
2. These percentages are not given in the table. They are available from the author. Another finding not shown in the table is that when community origin is introduced as a control variable, the finding that workers with lower white-collar first jobs were the most likely to report that their schools offered counseling holds up in two of the three community origin groups, the exception being the workers from farms, among whom those with upper white-collar first jobs were slightly (2 per cent) more likely to report counseling in their schools.
3. We could have evened out the cell sizes and made more meaningful comparisons possible among our Crescent workers by choosing different cutting points for dichotomizing our workers on the three variables, but this would have destroyed the comparability between the Crescent and Oakland data.

REFERENCES

Ammon, O. (1895), *Die Gesellschaftsordnung und ihre natürlichen Grundlagen.* Jena, Germany: Verlag Gustav Fischer.

Boalt, G. (1954), "Social Mobility in Stockholm: A Pilot Investigation," in *Transactions of the Second World Congress of Sociology*, II. London: International Sociological Association. Pp. 67–73.

Davidson, P. E., and H. D. Anderson (1937), *Occupational Mobility in an American Community*. Stanford, Calif.: Stanford University Press.

Hollingshead, A. B., and F. C. Redlich (1958), *Social Class and Mental Illness.* New York: John Wiley and Sons.

Kahl, J. A. (1957), *The American Class Structure.* New York: Rinehart and Company.

Lipset, S. M. (1955), "Social Mobility and Urbanization," *Rural Sociology*, **20,** 220–228.

Lipset, S. M., and R. Bendix (1959), *Social Mobility in Industrial Society.* Berkeley and Los Angeles: University of California Press.

Lipset, S. M., and F. T. Malm (1955), "First Jobs and Career Patterns," *American Journal of Economics and Sociology*, **14**, 247–261.
Norsworthy, D. R. (1961), "Mobility Effects of Industrial Growth," unpublished Ph.D. dissertation, University of North Carolina, Chapel Hill.
Odaka, K. (Ed.) (1958), *Shogukyô to Kaisô* (Occupation and Stratification), Tokyo: Mainichi Shimbunsha.
Rogoff, N. (1953), *Recent Trends in Occupational Mobility*. Glencoe, Ill.: Free Press.
Simpson, R. L., D. R. Norsworthy, and H. M. Miller (1960), "Occupational Choice and Mobility in the Urbanizing Piedmont of North Carolina," a report to the United States Office of Education for the Institute for Research in Social Science, University of North Carolina, Chapel Hill (mimeographed).
Simpson, R. L., and I. H. Simpson (1962), "Social Origins, Occupational Advice, Occupational Values, and Work Careers," *Social Forces*, **40**, 264–271.
Thomas, G. (n.d.), "The Social Survey: Labour Mobility in Great Britain, 1945–1949," an inquiry carried out for the Ministry of Labour and National Service, London (mimeographed).

Part Four

Patterns of Urban Development

by F. Stuart Chapin, Jr.

THE PREVIOUS SECTIONS of this volume having focused on successively different aspects of the dynamics of urban growth, each adding new insights into the impact that urbanization has on a society and its behavior, it is fitting now to turn to the physical environment within which these complex changes are taking place. So, in the first of the two final chapters the spotlight comes to rest on the city itself, in particular on patterns of land development, how they spread out into space, and how intensity of use varies in time and by location. The last chapter gives an interpretative view of the policy implications of findings from the series of studies which have been reported in the preceding twelve chapters.

The fact of increased urbanization in America needs no laboring. It has been estimated that the urban population of the United States may reach 255 millions by the year 2000, more than a 100 per cent increase over the 1960 urban population. It has also been estimated that this population will require 41 million acres of land for urban use, an area better than the size of the six New England states. This would constitute an increase of 147 per cent over the 1950 urban land area in this country (Clawson, Held, and Stoddard, 1960, pp. 110–111).

The South is destined to share in a major way in this unprecedented growth. Each of the major geographic sections of the country is expected to take up sizable areas of open land, but the South is expected to have the greatest absolute increase. By the turn of the century, the expected 75 million urbanites in the South may well take up, in addition to the present 5 million acres of land in urban use, an additional 8 million. This would amount to nearly one-third of the national total.

The square miles of land in urban development in the South will therefore be considerable, but since the major proportion of it will have occurred in relatively recent time, the contrasts will be dramatic and will pose singularly difficult adjustments. If we examine this growth as it is distributed to those urban areas of the South which seem destined to absorb the major proportion of the increase, the impact will be staggering by today's standards. The Houstons and Atlantas will receive much of this growth, but the large number of medium-size centers will share in the expansion. The spread of cities over the landscape, the physical form that the urban environment assumes, will have a great deal to do with the costs of city living for generations to come—the social as well as money costs.

Land development patterns are directly responsible for many of the satisfactions and irritations involved in city living. Patterns that now create traffic headaches, produce crowded living conditions, or result in inadequate open space, by contrast, may well become nightmares in the future. Indeed, experience elsewhere indicates that problem situations created by land development seem to multiply almost geometrically with the growth. So, if land development of this magnitude is imminent and if its impact is so important to the well-being of urban dwellers, it is a matter of great import to study this phenomenon in the most exhaustive way possible now and over time not only to understand more fully the dynamics of urban growth, but also to provide policy makers with insights into some of the variables which affect the choices they must make in reaching decisions on urban development.

Using one cluster of cities in the Piedmont Industrial Crescent as a study locale, Chapter 13 focuses on an analytical schema which seeks to determine how and why land development in any particular locality takes the form it does. It presents an approach to the measurement of land development patterns and then examines land development characteristics of the study area in this framework of study. Finally, using the insights thus obtained, it illustrates the kinds of choices open to decision makers in an urbanizing area—choices that can be positively identified and deliberated on and decisions made in advance of forecast growth.

Chapter 14 is both an epilogue and a summary. Returning to the themes of Chapter 1, it notes the theoretical research which lies ahead and identifies an approach which seems suited to carrying out the work. Combined with these observations is an interpretative summary of the findings from the Crescent studies which have significance for policy makers.

REFERENCE

Clawson, Marion, R. Burnell Held, and Charles H. Stoddard (1960), *Land for the Future.* Baltimore: The Johns Hopkins Press.

Meyerson, Martin, and Edward C. Banfield. Politics, Planning, and the Public Interest. Glencoe, Ill.: The Free Press, 1955.

Chapter 13

Land Development Patterns and Growth Alternatives

by F. Stuart Chapin, Jr., and Shirley F. Weiss *

PATTERNS OF URBAN land development can be studied in the context of aggregations of cities, that is, a regional belt of urbanization, and they can be examined in the more localized setting of the single metropolis or of a cluster of cities. The work of Gottmann (1961) in studying "megalopolis" (the massive pattern of urbanization that exists along the Northeastern seaboard), especially its geographic patterns of population density, suburbanization, and income and the changes in patterns of occupations, rural land uses, and other characteristics, illustrates the first type of investigation. Chute (1956) has identified other small belts of urbanization, including one in the Piedmont Industrial Crescent.

The approach used in this research focuses on the localized situation —an area that might represent the locus of commuting activity for a selected center or cluster of centers. The work undertaken in this study is reminiscent of such descriptive concepts as Burgess' concentric zone hypothesis (1925), Hoyt's sector hypothesis (1939), and Harris and Ullman's multiple-nuclei hypothesis (1945). While possessing

* The authors gratefully acknowledge the valuable contributions of their colleagues, Thomas G. Donnelly and George C. Hemmens, who participated actively in important portions of the research on which this chapter is based. (See Chapin, Hemmens, and Weiss, 1960.)

similarities in the way space can be organized into sector and zonal components, this research goes beyond these concepts and pursues analytically some of the variables which appear to be important in structuring the pattern of land development.

Very recently a few studies have begun to focus more directly on prediction of land-development patterns by means of land-use models. In addition to the pragmatic kinds of approach which have grown out of transportation studies, some investigations of theoretical significance are beginning to appear. Artle's study of Stockholm (1959), Herbert and Stevens' work (1960) for the Penn-Jersey Transportation Study, Garrison's applications of systems analysis and simulation to urban structure (1961), and Wingo's model for studying the structure of the city in the framework of rent concepts and equilibrium theory (1961) are indicative of this deepening interest in models for forecasting land development. Much of this theoretical interest in urban spatial structure can be traced to transportation studies, for example, the work of Carroll and his associates in Detroit (1955) and later in the Chicago area studies (1960). Other approaches are found in the work of Hansen for the Bureau of Public Roads (1959), and Voorhees (1961) and Barnes (1961) on the Hartford Transportation Study. These latter studies have direct ties to transportation analyses, but each has an objective in forecasting future patterns of land development.

While there is this distinct upsurge of interest, in balance it must be concluded that research on urban spatial structure is still in a very formative stage. The Land Development Study of the Five Cities Cluster is intended to shed some additional light on this developing research area. It constitutes a pilot study which has since been greatly extended (Chapin and Weiss, 1962). In the experimental stage of the work reported here, no predictive model is proposed. Rather, this study seeks a systematic approach to describing the spatial pattern of land development and analyzing how and why it takes the form it does. More particularly, the study undertakes to investigate the spread and intensity to the pattern of land development in a cluster of cities, identifying the major factors that appear to influence the form of these patterns. In addition, the chapter discusses the applications of findings from research of this kind in the advance detection of problems and in the study of growth alternatives, indicating the nature of public policy decisions involved in the selection of an alternative.

Land Development Dynamics

It would take repetitive analyses in time to obtain a clear picture of the dynamics of land development. While the present study does not attempt to get into this aspect of the research problem, an approach toward this end has been projected and is briefly summarized here to indicate the conceptual basis on which dynamic studies can be undertaken.

Figure 13-1 shows the 1958 land-development pattern of the cluster of cities being examined in this and succeeding studies. It is an area with a nonfarm population of half a million and a total area in urban land uses of 103 square miles. In the order of the highest to least amount of area taken up in urban land use, the cluster consists of Winston-Salem, Greensboro, High Point, Thomasville, and Lexington. The cities are located on V-shaped segments of the Interstate Highway System with the junction being in Greensboro. Eventually, the open end of the "V" will be closed by still another link in this system, forming a triangle, with the present Five Cities Cluster being at the eastern apex of the triangle. A 1958 intercity traffic survey indicates a marked passenger-car trip movement between High Point and Thomasville and between Greensboro and High Point, with work trips accounting for the bulk of the interaction.

The splatter of urban use of land in Figure 13-1 may be thought of as a single frame of a motion picture recording urbanization in this cluster of cities. Like the effect of a series of pictures of the action from pebbles dropped in a pool and suddenly halted by the camera, it is possible to record at successive intervals in time not only the splatter but also the larger ripples around each city. In following the ripples we can trace the distortion in the outward spread that develops at points where the ripples bump into one another.

This way of viewing the progression of changes in the pattern of urbanization on the land, of course, is oversimplified. If growth followed perfect concentric patterns and splayed out like merging ripples in a pool where two or more patterns make contact, it would be a simple matter to anticipate the growth pattern, and the cities might then take whatever steps each deemed necessary to accommodate this growth pattern. But the dynamics of this growth sequence are influenced by many other factors. The directions and intensity of the growth of a cluster of cities may be affected by a variety of decisions

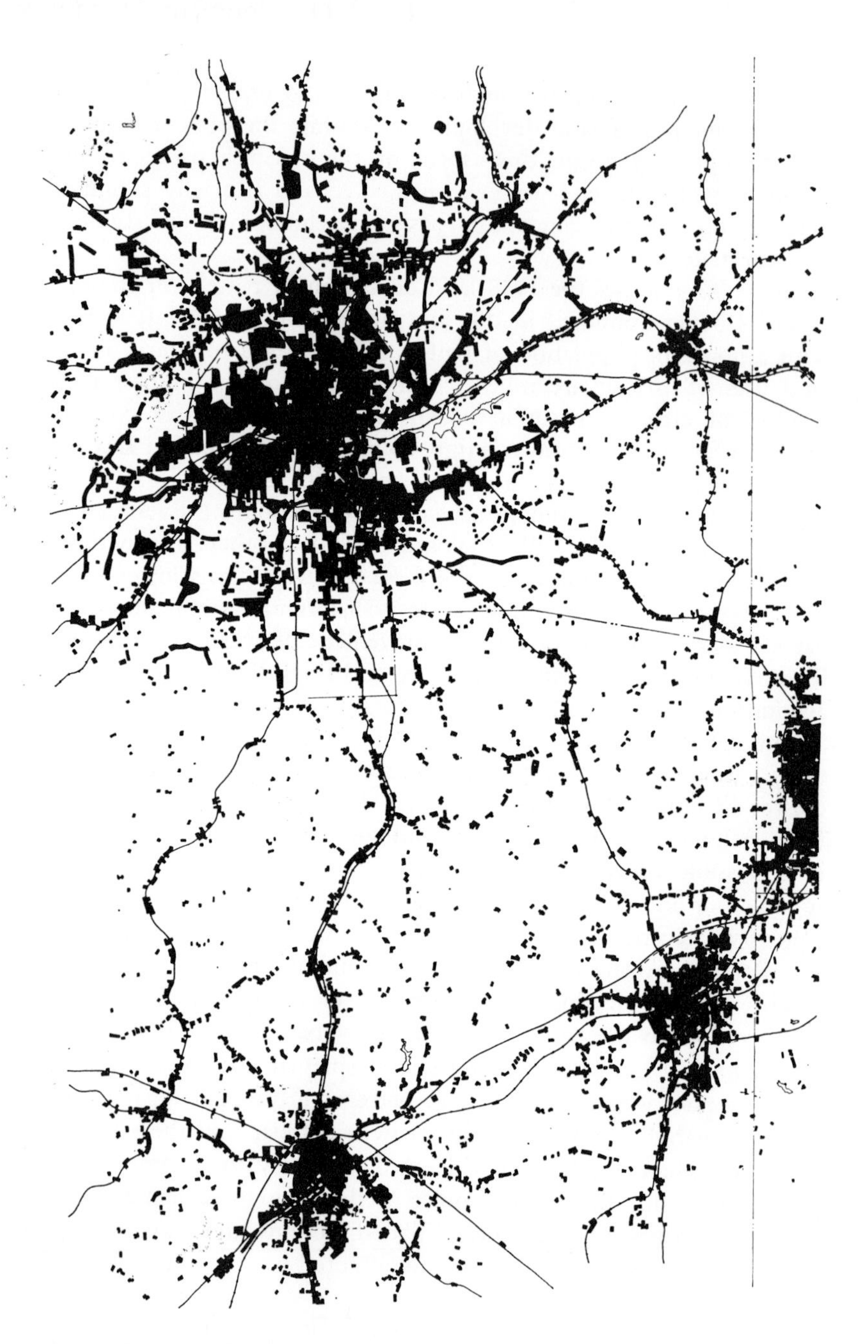

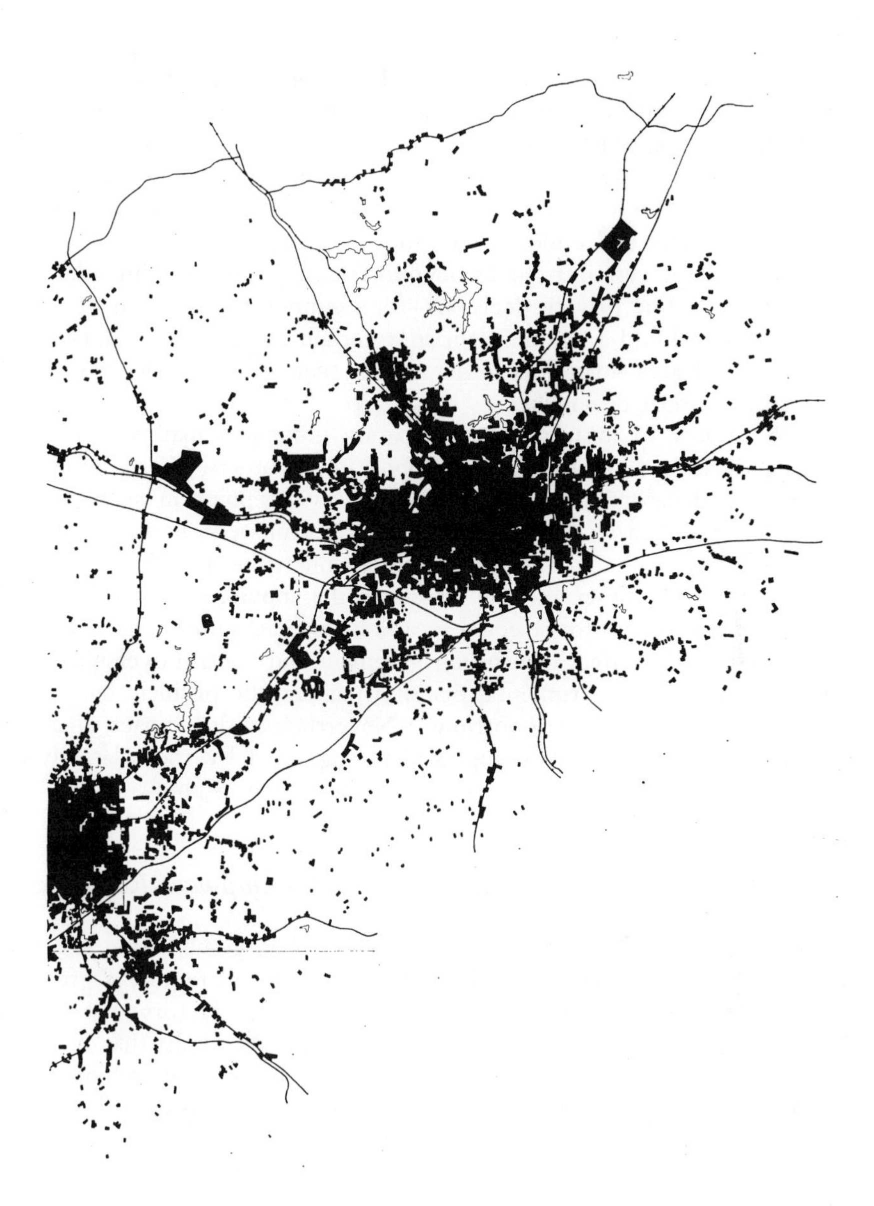

Figure 13-1. Splatter of urban land use in Five Cities Cluster, 1958.

of both a public and a private nature. Thus, the decision to build the Interstate Highway System through this area in a pattern more or less paralleling the Southern Railway introduces forces that may not be consonant with the natural kind of expansion pattern noted above. Similarly, the decisions that cities make individually or unilaterally concerning where and under what conditions they extend their water lines or sewerage system to areas beyond the city limits will introduce other forces. The private decisions—for example, the decision of an industrialist to build a sizable plant in a certain location in or outside the urbanized area—introduce other forces that influence the way in which the pattern develops.

With respect to location, these separate influences may act sympathetically in some sectors and in opposition in others. If the effect of location decisions were considered for every point in space, of course the problem would have no limits. Fortunately, however, the locations where the effect of such decisions might be investigated can be narrowed. By observing the effects of the above-mentioned kinds of decisional variables for selected locations, especially locations which exert a structuring effect on land development and control over which is in the hands of governmental decision makers, the problem can be kept within manageable proportions. Nevertheless, the impact of all of the factors is far more complex than suggested by the relatively simple concept of the effect of dropping pebbles in a pool.

Toward a Land Development Rationale

To sort out the factors that individually and in combination exert an influence on the patterns of land development will require a great deal of research and study. It is unlikely that all factors that are operative in any locality can be identified, nor is it likely that if all factors were identifiable they would function in identical fashion in all urban centers. Nevertheless, it is a premise of the ensuing discussion that in any particular community the key factors are identifiable and that given adequate measures and analytical techniques, it is possible to establish empirically the relative importance of these factors as determinants of the present-day pattern of land development in that urban center. How universal these factors are in shaping the physical spread of cities over the landscape will not be entirely clear until a number of cities can be examined.

We may conceive the land-development pattern of a city at any particular point in time as the cumulative effect of a myriad of decisions and actions by individual entities and groups, consisting of households, institutions, corporate interests, and government. These actions stem from deeply embedded individual and group-held values some of which assume a degree of concreteness and become manifest in the form of specific attitudes and behaviors. The attitudinal bases of these actions have been broadly categorized as stemming from profit making, livability, and culturally rooted values (Chapin, 1957, pp. 67–68). Looking at the complex result, the mass impact on the land of the actions that grow out of these values of many individuals and groups, we may think of these actions in two categories, what we shall call "priming actions" and "secondary actions." We may conceive of land development as a consequence of certain priming actions which precondition and establish the broad framework for the mass of secondary actions that follow and make up the bulk of the pattern observed. Thus, if the decision on the location of major highways may be thought of as a priming action, we may think of this initial action as triggering other secondary actions—first a wave of actions by real estate developers, builders, financiers, and others which then set off still other actions by families, merchants, churches, and others. Taken together the priming and secondary actions are said to produce the land-development pattern.

Such a rationale thus places a premium on discovering and studying how and why priming actions occur. Obviously, if these structuring actions of land development can be isolated and their relationship to the directions and intensities at which development later proceeds, it may be possible to achieve a working knowledge of the impact of all of the factors without ever going through the motions of identifying all of them, even if that were possible.

To pursue this schema, two directions of research development are important—one focusing on the identification of the priming actions and the extent that they influence the pattern of land development, and the other directed at the underlying decisional variables that condition the form that each particular priming action takes. In general, research on the first must precede work on the second. To establish conclusively that any particular kinds of action are key determinants of land development requires elaborate documentation. Thus, it would be important to make studies that trace linked events over time and establish in a time sequence the relationships between events that lead to a particular pattern of land development. Ex post facto case studies that seek to reconstruct the sequence of events may provide sufficient evidence to determine cause and effect relationships. However, participant-observer techniques of the kind used in the study of governmental decision making described in Chapter 6, if utilized in a particular locale over a period of several years, could be expected to give greater insight into the dynamics involved.

The Five Cities study might be thought of as an investigation that is prerequisite to this kind of research. It seeks clues as to what actions should be given intensive scrutiny. Because the present investigation has not yet been cast in a behavioral sequence, at this stage of the work we refer to "factors of land development" rather than "determinants of land development," reserving the latter phrase for findings from the more definitive behavioral type of investigation. In this exploratory search for factors that might provide leads on priming actions of land development, we undertook first to develop a suitable technique to measure the land-development pattern of a city, and we then sought through various statistical tests to relate selected factors to irregularities observed in this pattern. These steps in the research procedures will be taken up before we proceed to a discussion of findings.

Analytical Approach

If we conceive of land development occurring in concentric lines around some central point as suggested by the earlier allusion to ripples in a pool, it is useful to use as a "template" a mathematical representation of the circular normal distribution—reminiscent of the concentric zone theory of growth (Burgess, 1925). At any particular point in time, such a template permits measurement of two characteristics in the pattern—its outward spread from some reference point, let us say, the high value corner of the central business district, and its intensity of development. But in addition, over time it permits analysis of the rhythm of change in these two characteristics. Now, if we use a grid coordinate system as a basis for subdividing the pattern into small units, we can describe both the spread of the pattern and the intensity of development in location-specific terms. To carry this conceptualization still another step, it is not difficult to conceive of each city in the Five Cities Cluster being examined with reference to the circular normal and a composite distribution evolved that not only provides a measurement of the combined regional pattern of land development but also recognizes the interaction characteristics between the cities—reminiscent of the multiple-nuclei concept of urban growth (Harris and Ullman, 1945).

Using such a basis for analyzing the pattern of land development, we can estimate the intensity of development expected in each grid square in the circular normal distribution or in some multiple-form distribution. By comparing the actual with the expected intensity of development over the entire spread of an urban area, we can note and record regularities and irregularities in the pattern. Of special import to the problem in hand, this means of measurement provides a basis for establishing relationships with factors that may be advanced for explaining the irregularities.

By observing any particular set of land-development conditions found to exist at each grid cell, it is possible to establish by multivariate analysis what individual or combination of these factors are significantly correlated with irregularities in the pattern of land development. Thus, we may observe, for example, whether the accessibility of any particular grid unit of land to the major street system of the city has some relationship to the irregularities in the pattern of land development, whether proximity to major employment centers has significance, whether the racial occupancy of the grid cell's environs seems to have a bearing on the observed land-development pattern, or whether some combination of these or other factors have special significance.

What has been said so far concerns analysis of what can be discovered in one frame in the "motion picture" of land development. Supposing the analysis is repeated once each two, five, or ten years. We begin to get a picture of the dynamics of land development and the way factors behave over a period of time. Thus this kind of study pinpoints the priming actions and paves the way for a second phase of the research effort—the investigation of decisional variables that condition the way in which priming actions function.

Land Development Variables

As indicated in the preceding discussion of a land-development rationale, there is a wide range of factors which might be advanced to explain any city's pattern of growth. Indeed, it would appear the range of selection might be so broad that we might despair of ever being certain of including in any particular list the ones which are most crucial. While it is possible that the present investigation has overlooked some important factors, a special effort was made to identify the ones which are widely held to be important. A total of 13 factors was culled in the following manner. First, the authors listed the factors which from experience and observation appeared to them to have some effect on the pattern of land development. Next, this list was supplemented by reference to the general literature and particular studies of the kind cited in the opening section. Then the resulting list was submitted to a dozen professional planners and through a series of questions they were asked to arrange the items in the list in the order of importance. Finally, a selection of the 13 factors noted below was made on the basis of the nominations thus obtained and the immediate practicability of obtaining a suitable measure for each variable.

Because it was expected that some of the variables not only behave differently in different cities but behave differently over time in the same city, some special supplemental tests were devised for one of the cities (Greensboro). For example, it was reasoned that the effect of the availability of sewer and water services on land-development patterns might be more precisely established by relating served areas to the ring of recent development rather than to the entire land-development pattern. To control for time, the analysis of variables in relation to the total land-development pattern was therefore repeated to test the relationship of the same variables with respect to the ring of recent growth in Greensboro (area developed between 1948 and 1958). The Nelson study (1959) provides some useful insights in this respect. Examining for the association between the location of new highways and rings of subdivision activity over a 40-year period, this study suggested that the total pattern of land development might profitably be investigated by periods or rings of development.

The Variables and the Formulation for Multivariate Analysis

In preparation for the multivariate tests, each grid cell which contained urban land development was coded according to measures devised for the following 13 variables:

Location of water areas and areas subject to flood
Location of major highways
Location of major work areas

Location of city's water service area
Location of city's sewer service area
Location of city's fire protection service area
Location of city's police service area
Location of city's school service area
Location of city's zoning jurisdiction
Location of city's subdivision control jurisdiction
Location of areas of mixed land use
Location of blighted residential areas
Location of nonwhite areas

Some of the measures used in the initial investigation were crude and will need to be improved upon in the extension of this research. Because of the complexity of coding measurements for each of these variables, the pilot investigation limited this aspect of the analysis to Greensboro and Winston-Salem.

The kind of multivariate analysis used in this study was a linear form of multiple regression:

$$Y = a + b_0X + b_1W + b_2V + \cdots$$

in which the dependent variable Y is the deviation from the expected intensity of development and X, W, V, . . . are independent variables selected from the 13 listed above.

Measures Used for Variables

Sources and measures used for these variables were as follows. To get at the physiographic capabilities of vacant land for urban development, county soil maps were used. With the assistance of Ralph McCracken of the Soils Department of North Carolina State College of Agriculture and Engineering, a special series of overlays were prepared interpreting soil maps of the counties involved. Areas of flood hazard were delineated and used to identify areas unsuitable for urban development. Although additional information on terrain slopes would be required to obtain a complete picture of land-development capabilities, the pilot investigation considered drainage factors only. In the case of this variable, it is reasoned that land-development patterns will tend to bulge away from, and show indications of retarded expansion in areas where drainage problems exist. Irregularities due to drainage will be most evident at the outskirts of the city, with drainage improvements in the more central areas tending to eliminate open areas by-passed in earlier periods of development. Although omitted in the pilot study due to time limitations, but considered an important variable for future study, is the influence that large vacant tracts held out of development have on the land-development patterns. Functioning as barriers to development, these are tracts tied up in estates, land-speculation schemes, and other restrictive holdings.

The influence of highway location on land development was taken into account by observing the relation of each grid cell to the center of the city and to the network of major radial highways available to take residents of each cell to that central point in the city. Coded first was the mile ring at which the residents of a particular cell would be expected to gain access to the nearest radial which would carry them to the high-value corner in the central business district. Measurements for these rings were made along traveled routes of all radials. After the ring was coded, the travel distance along the most direct route from the grid cell to the point of access to the nearest radial was coded. The two observations thus provided a measure of each cell's accessibility by the shortest actual travel distance (*a*) to the nearest radial, and (*b*) along radial leading to the high-value corner of the central business district. The relationship of each cell to other focal points of traffic generation and their associated travel routes was not directly investigated in this study. However, measurements of the influence of work centers on land development provide an indirect means for taking into account traffic flow systems other than those focusing on the central business district.

A crude measure of the influence of the location of work centers on land development was obtained by determining the proximity of developed areas to all major centers of employment in the city. The distance of each developed grid cell to each of several major employment centers was measured along lines "as the crow flies" and weighted according to size of employment. Had there been unlimited time for coding, travel time along the most direct available route would have been used as a measure for this variable. For purposes of this pilot investigation, the relation to land development of water, sewer, school, fire protection, and police services was estimated by coding whether the developed grid cell was in or outside the facility's service area. It was reasoned that the pattern of land development would show some relationship to the service area if the facility was exerting an influence on the direction and intensity of land development. Similarly, each developed cell was coded as to whether it was in or outside the city's area of zoning and subdivision jurisdiction. Again, it was reasoned that if these local protective devices were having an influence on the spread and intensity of land development, a statistical relationship would manifest itself.

Mixture of land use, evidences of blight, and nonwhite occupancy are three final variables in the list. For purposes of this study, a grid cell which contained a mixture of residential and/or industry and/or business uses was coded as having mixed land uses. To get a rough measure of quality of residential areas, the planning directors were asked in each of the two cities to delimit residential blocks containing (*a*) spotty evidences of need for upkeep (but no blight), (*b*) scattered evidences of blight, and (*c*) continuous incidence of blight. Although not an entirely objective basis for identifying degrees of blight, the material was considered usable for purposes of the initial study. Each developed residential grid cell was then coded according to the quality of development. Similarly, residential areas of nonwhite occupancy were mapped and coded according to whether they contained blocks entirely or partially nonwhite. It was reasoned that if any one of these variables exerted an influence on the spread or intensity of development, it would show a relationship to irregularities in land-development patterns.

Although there may well be other variables that will eventually need to be added to this list and improved measures of some variables will need to be devised, these thirteen variables and the indicated measures of each seemed adequate for purposes of an exploratory study of this kind. Using the measures indicated, the research design thus calls for each variable and differing combinations of variables being correlated with the deviation found to exist between the observed and the expected pattern of land development in each of the two cities. The design also calls for a special test in Greensboro, using the ring of development for 1948 to 1958 in addition to the total pattern of land development in 1958.

Physical Characteristics of Land Development

Before the findings of the multivariate analysis are summarized, it will be of interest to examine our research subject, the Five Cities Cluster, in terms of the raw aggregates of grid coordinate cells. Table 13-1 gives a generalized statement of the distribution of land in urban development among the five cities and according to the inten-

Table 13-1. Grid Coordinate Cells in Urban Use in Five Cities Cluster by Intensity of Development, 1958 [a]

	NUMBER AND PER CENT BY PROPORTION OF CELL IN URBAN USE							
	25–50%		50–75%		75–100%		ALL CELLS (25–100%)	
	NO.	%	NO.	%	NO.	%	NO.	%
Winston-Salem	505	27.0	662	35.4	703	37.6	1,870	100.0
Greensboro	418	31.3	374	28.0	544	40.7	1,336	100.0
High Point	256	41.0	167	26.8	201	32.2	624	100.0
Thomasville	116	43.8	80	30.2	69	26.0	265	100.0
Lexington	120	42.1	96	33.7	69	24.2	285	100.0
Totals	1,415	32.3	1,379	31.5	1,586	36.2	4,380	100.0

[a] Based on an exploratory investigation by Stephens (1960).

sity of use as pictured in Figure 13-2. Although some variation from city to city may be noted, the developed grid cells in the cluster as a whole divide up so that roughly a third falls into each intensity category. The smaller cities have a larger proportion of all developed grid cells in the low-intensity group, the 25 to 50 per cent developed grid cells, and conversely, the larger cities have a larger proportion in the high-intensity group.

We can get another perspective of the over-all pattern of development by looking at the distribution of developed cells by quadrants and concentric tiers. In this analysis tiers are nests of square-shaped zones of 5,000-foot width drawn concentric to the high-value corner of the city. Each tier is like a square picture frame with a width of five grid cells.

Taking the first seven tiers, we note in Table 13-2 that for this circumscribed area of 26.5 square miles Greensboro's cells are 26 per cent developed, with the southwest quadrant having the highest percentage of developed cells and the southeast quadrant the least percentage. Part of the differential rate in amount of development by quadrant is in the availability of suitable land for residential development. Limitations in the amount of land suitable for development stem from physical characteristics, such as areas subject to flood or steep slopes which prevent economic development of housing, as well as ownership patterns which preclude large parcels from being assembled or offered on the market. While ownership patterns were not researched in this first study, reference can be made to the marginal cells coded for flooding. Close-in marginal land, for example, accounts in part

Table 13-2. Developed and Undeveloped Marginal Cells as Per Cent of Total Cells in Quadrant and Concentric Tier, Greensboro, 1958 Land Use [a]

CONCENTRIC TIER MEASURED FROM HIGH-VALUE CORNER (000's OF FEET)	QUADRANT NE	NW	SW	SE	ALL QUADRANTS
	DEVELOPED CELLS				
0–5	100.0	100.0	100.0	100.0	100.0
5–10	94.7	97.3	100.0	86.7	94.7
10–15	64.0	62.4	57.6	35.2	54.8
15–20	34.9	39.4	58.9	9.1	35.6
20–25	20.0	20.9	38.2	8.9	22.0
25–30	11.6	12.7	12.7	0.4	9.4
30–35	5.2	6.8	7.1	0.9	5.0
All tiers	27.0	28.5	34.2	14.2	26.0
	UNDEVELOPED MARGINAL CELLS				
0–5	0.0	0.0	0.0	0.0	0.0
5–10	4.0	1.3	0.0	9.3	3.7
10–15	18.4	16.8	30.4	20.8	21.6
15–20	18.9	5.7	21.1	26.9	18.1
20–25	13.3	21.8	15.1	25.3	18.9
25–30	16.0	27.6	13.1	5.1	15.5
30–35	17.8	42.8	3.4	8.6	18.2
All tiers	15.6	24.2	12.7	14.6	16.8

[a] For purposes of this pilot investigation a grid cell was considered developed if it was 25 per cent or more developed with urban land uses. A grid cell was considered undeveloped if it was less than 25 per cent developed with urban land uses. Undeveloped grid cells were rated for physiographic capabilities on the basis of flood hazard or the presence of drainage problems.

Table 13-3. Change in Intensity of Predominant Generalized Use of Land for 10-Year Period, Greensboro, 1948 and 1958 [a]

PREDOMINANT LAND USE IN GRID CELL	CHANGE		NO CHANGE		TOTAL CELLS	
	NO. CELLS	%	NO. CELLS	%	NO.	% TOTAL
Residential	292	75.3	96	24.7	388	29.0
Public-institutional (extensive)	30	40.5	44	59.5	74	5.5
Public-institutional (intensive)	6	35.3	11	64.7	17	1.3
Business	1	16.7	5	83.3	6	0.4
Industrial-wholesale	20	43.5	26	56.5	46	3.4
Transportation-public utilities-communication	12	32.4	25	67.6	37	2.8
Residential and public (combined)	124	47.7	136	52.3	260	19.5
Mixed (residential, public, and business combined)	118	53.2	104	46.8	222	16.6
Mixed (other combinations)	152	53.1	134	46.9	286	21.4
All developed cells	755	56.5	581	43.5	1,336	100.0

[a] Includes all cells 25 per cent or more developed with urban land uses as of 1958 compared with the respective intensity of development in 1948.

for the underdevelopment of the southeast quadrant in Greensboro (see Table 13-2), where a band of marginal cells amounting to 25 per cent of all cells in the band extends from 10,000 to 25,000 feet from the high-value corner. Since residential land use accounts for the largest amount of development and for the largest change in intensity of development, as observed in Greensboro (see Table 13-3), the importance of marginal land in shaping the over-all development pattern is reinforced by these observations.

Factors Influencing Land Development

Of the thirteen variables previously enumerated, nine were selected for the final multivariate tests in the pilot study. Four variables were omitted for insufficient measurement in coding or inadequacies for statistical operations, but will be restored in subsequent studies as improved measurements that meet requirements for statistical analysis are devised for each variable. Dividing the variable listed as "location of major highways" into two components (travel distance on major radials to high-value corner and travel distance on collector streets leading to the radials), a total of ten independent variables was utilized. To facilitate the discussion of results, the variables are listed in Table 13-4 in the order of input. It should be noted that the reader is in a more fortunate position than the researchers in viewing the results

Table 13-4. Coefficients of Simple Correlation between 10 Independent Variables and Deviation from Expected Land Development Based on Circular Normal Template, Greensboro and Winston-Salem, 1958

INDEPENDENT VARIABLE [a]	GREENSBORO, — ALL CELLS [b]	GREENSBORO, — GROWTH CELLS [c]	WINSTON-SALEM, — ALL CELLS [b]
	NO.—1025	NO.—606	NO.—1254
(1) Travel distance to high-value corner	.428	.505	.567
(2) Accessibility to major radial highways	−.027	−.052	−.039
(3) Distance to work areas, excluding CBD, weighted by employment potential	−.403	−.485	.040
(4) City water service	.158	.153	.399
(5) Proximity to blighted areas	−.008	−.098	−.060
(6) Proximity to nonwhite areas	−.218	−.281	−.190
(7) City sewer service	.293	.274	.481
(8) City schools	.195	.217	.463
(9) Proximity to mixed uses	−.021	−.012	−.040
(10) Fire protection service	.307	.305	.448

[a] Refer to coding manual in Chapin, Hemmens, and Weiss (1960) to interpret meaning of signs (+ and −) and independent variables used.

[b] The total number of cells used in this aspect of the analysis does not include work cells (removed to permit analysis of Variable (3)) and certain other deletions (e.g., reservoirs and their watersheds).

[c] Growth cells are those cells which had a coded increase in intensity of urban land use between 1948 and 1958. The independent variables are based on 1958 observations.

progressively, since it was necessary to program the simple correlations with the dependent variable, simple correlations between each pair of independent variables, partial correlations, and the multiple-regression analysis simultaneously in order to conserve machine time. For this reason some of the less significant variables were retained throughout the analysis. Our hunch is that variables making a poorer showing may appear in a different light with improved measurements.

By simple correlation of the value of the independent variables with the deviation from expected development for each cell, it is possible to get a first impression of the nature of the relationship between these assorted factors and the over-all pattern of land development. Making allowance for the crude data inputs, it is possible to observe from the simple correlations in Table 13-4 similarities and dissimilarities in the behavior of individual variables with respect to the total land-development pattern in Greensboro and Winston-Salem. Travel distance to the high-value corner ranks highest in both urban centers. Admittedly, this may reflect a less than satisfactory fit of the circular normal, or it may actually give evidence of the effect of travel distance to Central Business District (CBD) in distorting the expected patterns of land development. In Greensboro, distance to work areas ranks second in significance, whereas in Winston-Salem this factor is next to the bottom of the list. City sewer service, schools, fire protection, and water service follow in order of significance for Winston-Salem, but in Greensboro, proximity to nonwhite areas ranks above city schools and water service as an independent variable influencing deviations from expected development. It is noteworthy that deviations have occurred in both directions, that is, beyond expected and short of expected. The nature of influence, as revealed in the full array of tests for the pilot study, will be evaluated below in the summary of the research findings.

As a second indication of the results which may be expected from the multiple-regression analysis, the correlation of pairs of independent variables gives an important clue. In Greensboro, travel distance to the high-value corner is highly correlated with distance to work areas excluding CBD (−.732), city sewer service (.702), city schools (.637), fire protection (.605), and city water service (.580). Proximity to blighted areas and proximity to nonwhite areas are more closely correlated with each other than with the other variables (.397), as are accessibility to major radial highways and proximity to mixed uses (−.333).

A similar pattern of interrelationships with distance to the high-value corner holds for Winston-Salem, with one exception. Distance to work areas, which is not highly correlated with any of the variables in contrast with Greensboro, has its closest correlation with proximity to nonwhite areas (.167) and proximity to blighted areas (.145). In Winston-Salem it should also be noted that an exceedingly high correlation marks the relationship between schools and the various city services: fire protection (.970), sewers (.959), and water (.860). Such close correlations suggest that in future tests a combined index of the availability of city services might well be substituted.

Using the results of the correlation of pairs of independent variables to modify the simple correlation coefficients computed for each independent variable with the dependent variable, it is possible to assess the "real" relationship between each of the ten variables and the deviation from expected development. Thus, by partialing out the effect of other independent variables, that is, holding them constant one at a time, the net effect of the key variables may be viewed more realistically. For example, in the case of travel distance to high-value corner in Greensboro, the initial correlation value is reduced by 50 per cent, dropping to .214 when distance to work areas excluding CBD is held constant. For Winston-Salem, parallel partialing reduces the initial correlation value by 37 per cent, to .355. When travel distance to high-value corner is held constant, the reduction of correlation values is greatest 9 out of 9 times in Greensboro. However, in Winston-Salem, this maximum partialing effect is shared with city sewer services, each producing the greatest reduction on initial values 3 out of 9 times. Arraying the partialing effect of all 10 variables, in both Greensboro and Winston-Salem the ranking corresponds closely with the descending order of the simple correlation coefficients of the independent variables, as given in Table 13-4.

Proceeding to the multiple-regression analysis, it should be noted that the influence of interrelated factors may be shared, depending on the composition of the combined mix of variables. As closely related factors are partially removed, the influence may be concentrated in a few key factors. However, in every test run, reduction in the number of closely related factors resulted in a lower multiple correlation coefficient and a higher standard error of estimate for the estimating equation. The results of the final test runs for 10 and 6 variables, given in Table 13-5, show that a maximum of 36.5 per cent (R^2) of the deviation from the pattern of expected development could be explained by the 10 variables in Winston-Salem and 24.1 per cent in

Table 13-5. Coefficients of Multiple Correlation (R) and Multiple Determination (R^2) between 10 and 6 Independent Variables and Deviation from Expected Land Development Based on Circular Normal Template, Greensboro and Winston-Salem, 1958

VARIABLES SELECTED [a]	GREENSBORO, — ALL CELLS		GREENSBORO, — GROWTH CELLS		WINSTON-SALEM, — ALL CELLS	
	R	R^2	R	R^2	R	R^2
1 through 10	.491	.241	.560	.314	.604	.365
1 through 6	.474	.225	.550	.303	.591	.349

[a] Refer to Table 13-4 for identification of variables numbered 1 through 10.

Greensboro. Comparing these figures with the simple correlations in Table 13-4, it is apparent that a mix of factors rather than a single variable offers a greater possibility for understanding and eventually predicting land-development patterns.

It was fortunate that land-use data were available for 1948 in Greensboro, thereby permitting the special analysis of growth cells in relation to 1958 observations of independent variables. Comparing the multiple correlation results for all cells and growth cells only, it is evident that focus on growth cells may possibly provide a fuller explanation of the factors influencing land-development patterns.

Proceeding to the independent variables to observe their relative importance in explaining the deviations from expected land development, it is necessary to convert the parameter estimates (Beta values used in the estimating equations) to standard measures. This is accomplished by dividing the Beta values by their respective standard deviations. The resulting t values may be used to identify those variables having the greatest influence on the resulting multiple correlation coefficient. This is only a surface test for pointing out key variables to study further. However, because of the sharing effect of closely related variables, the real importance of some variables may be missed if only the t values are examined. The coefficients of simple correlation with the dependent variable and between pairs of independent variables, as well as the partial correlation coefficients, need also to be considered in the final selection of key variables. This is obviously the case in Winston-Salem where the t values for city schools

Table 13-6. Relative Influence of 10 and 6 Independent Variables on Deviations from Expected Land Development Based on Circular Normal Template, Greensboro and Winston-Salem, 1958

INDEPENDENT VARIABLE AND COLUMN NUMBER	GREENSBORO				WINSTON-SALEM	
	ALL CELLS EXCEPT WORK AREAS		GROWTH CELLS 1948–1958		ALL CELLS EXCEPT WORK AREAS	
	10 VARIABLES	6 VARIABLES	10 VARIABLES	6 VARIABLES	10 VARIABLES	6 VARIABLES
(1) Travel distance to high-value corner	6.23	7.20	4.45	4.98	13.31	16.73
(2) Accessibility to major radial highways	2.71	2.89	1.90	1.79	3.42	4.24
(3) Distance to work areas, excluding CBD, weighted by employment potential	4.48	4.68	4.81	4.35	0.73	0.60
(4) City water service	2.78	3.27	1.64	3.51	1.80	1.75
(5) Proximity to blighted areas	1.50	1.02	1.31	0.68	6.34	6.55
(6) Proximity to nonwhite areas	3.96	3.84	3.68	3.65	4.64	4.56
(7) City sewer service	2.98	...	1.96	...	3.53	...
(8) City schools	2.82	...	1.55	...	0.53	...
(9) Proximity to mixed uses	0.70	...	1.25	...	3.20	...
(10) Fire protection service	3.37	...	3.07	...	0.10	...

Note. Values given are t values: parameter estimate (Beta value) divided by standard deviation. A t value of 2 is considered significant.

and fire protection service were drained by related variables which took precedence in the 10-variable test (see Table 13-6).

With these qualifications in mind, it may be tentatively observed that the 6-variable test (columns 2, 4, and 6) in Table 13-6 provides from four to five variables which are significant in explaining the deviations from expected land-devolopment patterns in Greensboro and Winston-Salem.

Summary of Findings

The significance of variables thus obtained should be interpreted with extreme caution. It represents the results of the first pilot study in two urban centers, each of which has been demonstrated to have a distinct development pattern and a different mix of key variables, although travel distance to the high-value corner ranks highest in all tests but one. However, since only one-third of the deviation from expected development could be explained by the selected variables tested in combination, there still exists ample opportunity for improving the explained deviation through more refined measurements for tentatively identified key variables and a continuing search for other significant influence factors. (See follow-up, Chapin and Weiss, 1962.)

From the full array of tests so far, the nature of the influence of the following factors can be tentatively confirmed as:

1. Poor drainage characteristics tend to discourage land development in vacant areas.
2. Location of major routes of transportation tends to intensify land development.
3. Location of work areas with large employment potential tends to intensify land development.
4. The availability of community services and facilities (fire protection, sewer service, water service, and schools) tends to intensify land development.
5. Proximity to blighted areas and proximity to nonwhite areas tend to discourage urban development which might normally occur in the absence of these influences.

Finally, the results obtained to date lend support to the proposition that land development can be measured in relation to a mathematically defined distribution around the high-value corner in the central business district. For individual centers this has proved to be a satisfactory means of measurement. Whether this approach to measuring land-development patterns can be used in a multiple-nuclei situation where a constellation of centers is involved remains to be taken up in succeeding studies.

Growth Alternatives and Land Development Policy

What are the implications of these findings? There are several. Their significance for further research, especially for investigations into the variables which affect the way in which priming actions structure land development was indicated earlier in the chapter. Of special interest in this final section are the applications of these findings to public policy decisions, particularly in simulating problem situations in advance of growth and development and in determining policy alternatives. If, as was found in the Five Cities Cluster, the major factors affecting land development are identified to a significant degree with certain actions by local governments, then it is a matter of great importance that governmental decision makers recognize how their policy decisions affect the pattern of land development, for they can then evaluate the consequences of their decisions in advance. In the next few pages we shall first consider the applications of this research in the advance detection of problem situations, and then we shall go into the applications of the research in establishing growth alternatives.

Advance Detection of Problems

Land-development problems have physical, fiscal, and governmental aspects. The physical problems may relate to the incidence of urban blight, the intrusion of traffic, inadequate water, sewerage, and other community facilities and services. The fiscal problems usually have to do with the public cost and revenue aspects of correcting these physical problems and serving new areas that go into development with essential public facilities and services. Governmental problems are usually concerned with the problems of devising workable organizational arrangements of units of government that administer these facilities and provide these services. Our concern here is largely with the physical problems of land development.

Much attention in recent years has been devoted to the form that the land-development patterns of cities take and the problems that are created by certain of these patterns. Some of this interest centers around the salient characteristics of city form, geographically (Gottmann, 1957 and 1961) and visually (Lynch, 1954 and 1960; and Williams, 1954); and some of it is concerned with the implications of these patterns for the evolving city (e.g., see Bauer, 1956; Blumenfeld, 1958). Out of the steadily increasing volume of literature devoted to urban form, there is reference to the massive megalopolitan belts of urbanization such as the Boston to Washington belt (see Tunnard, 1958; Gottmann, 1961); and there is reference to the smaller scale, more localized patterns of the kind with which this chapter has been more directly concerned—the sprawl pattern, the scatter pattern, and the nucleated pattern. Each involves differing physical problems. Thus the sprawl pattern, which has come to connote an aimless overspill of the city into the country-side, frequently presents problems of overload—overtaxed highways and water systems and other inadequate community facilities and services. The scatter pattern poses the problem of providing these same facilities and services in widely separated locations. In the case of the nucleated patterns problems such as water supply, sewage disposal, or airports revolve around conflict of interest or uneconomical duplication of effort where a coordinated regional approach is indicated.

Now, if these problems can be detected from land-development models, it is possible that urban centers and regional clusters of cities can identify remedial steps either to circumvent completely the problems or minimize their impact. It is recognized, of course, that the interplay of contributing factors is extremely complex, and that many side effects in the evolution of problem situations are not fully understood and may even go unrecognized. It is also acknowledged that the logic and actions of Political Man do not always correspond with the logic and recommendations of Scientific Man, and that because of many other considerations that enter into the picture, decisions may be made to reject a direct approach based primarily on technical considerations in favor of an indirect approach to the problems or even postponement of action. Yet we are entering an era in which many of these complex variables can be taken into account for the first time, for modern data-processing equipment and the developing science of systems analysis permit approaches to problems never before possible. In this respect, we may take particular note of simulation techniques which are becoming increasingly useful in dealing with problems of such complexity.

Essentially, the approach we propose is to examine the problem implications involved in pursuing varying combinations of policies which are either not recognized for their structuring effect on land-development patterns or are ignored for other reasons. By simulating the effect that selected combinations of policies might have on city form, we can observe problem potential and the intensity with which problems are likely to develop.

Consider an example. Let us assume that the growth potential for the next twenty years in the study areas has been estimated within reasonable limits and, further, that this potential clearly portends a magnitude of development that places the Five Cities Cluster in the category of present-day Atlanta. Now in the realm of transportation policies, supposing these cities, which up to the present have relied mainly on automobile forms of transportation, reach agreement on a joint policy of subsidizing the construction of a rapid transit system between them so that the flows of commuters would be equally divided between transit and automobile modes of movement. (Although we cannot go into the rationale for such a policy decision here, suffice it to say that states and cities could conceivably reach a conclusion that capital resources now earmarked for highway construction alone could achieve public objectives in other ways, as by allocating some of these resources to transit systems and some to highway systems.) Assuming all other priming actions function in the future in the same way they have in the past, the new growth patterns would tend to reinforce the nucleated pattern that exists today, at least to the extent that transit stations are provided only where they serve the present cluster pattern of cities. If other stops were to be introduced, other new towns would develop, so long as the growth potential persists.

Now let us vary the application of one of the other policies. Assume that, say, two of the five cities, which in the past have followed rather stringent policies of making their public water and sewer available only inside the city limits, alter their policy and make it known that they will extend public water and mains and sewer lines to all comers who will pay for the extensions. Suppose that during the period in which this policy is in effect, several large industrial employers decide to locate in open country in quite different directions than those that would fall within the service area of the new rapid-transit routes. Such an eventuality would tend to produce a land-development pattern that works at cross purposes with the pattern assumed under the transit policy decision. The counteracting effect of Policy 2 (the unintended consequence) on Policy 1 (the intended consequence) would not become immediately apparent. However, simulation of growth patterns in the framework of a land-development model would indicate where the problem would occur and at what intensity. This is a greatly oversimplified illustration, for, obviously, the situation becomes increasingly complex with differing governmental units involved, each with a much more extended range of policies and each with policy alternatives that are likely to change in time.

Take another kind of example. Suppose water and sewer-service policies were based strictly on the decisions of two independent, perhaps competitively minded commissioners, both acting without thought of the land-development implications of their actions. Suppose the water commissioner in one city is seeking to expand his service area and extends his lines not only without relation to the sewer-service area of his own city but also without reference to the watershed area of the neighboring city's water supply. If all locations present equal opportunities for development with respect to transportation, city schools, and other similar primary needs of residential areas, we may expect that the presence of all of these services would stimulate development that largely depends on septic tanks or small private systems for sewage disposal. Obviously this is a situation that can create serious problems for both cities—in one, the problem of future corrective action at considerably greater expense, and in the other, a source of pollution to the water supply. If the picture is further complicated by introducing a new expressway system which creates still another push-pull effect on the land-development pattern, perhaps in still another direction, the dynamics of land development become more complicated. As other variables are introduced, the interrelations become extremely complex. So here again we see the potential value of simulation studies as an aid to policy formulation and decision making.

Growth Alternatives

Another application of land-development investigations of the kind described earlier in the chapter involves policy formulation along more positive lines. In addition to testing out policy combinations to minimize problem situations, it is also possible to identify groups of policies that tend to produce specific land-development patterns. Thus, the kind of research discussed earlier offers possibilities of identifying courses of action which will tend to produce desired goal-forms of the city, and it permits decision makers to examine a range of land-development patterns and become familiar with the policy choices which tend to produce each pattern. We think of policy combinations in terms of tendencies rather than as absolutes because the particular kinds of policies under discussion here are those which have a structuring effect on land development, that is, those which are priming actions. It is our contention that while the sum total effect of all actions may not produce exactly the land-development pattern expected from priming actions, they will *tend* to produce this expected pattern.

We may view public policy formulation as involving a hierarchy of policy decisions proceeding from the general to the particular. At each level of the hierarchy, we may expect that there is a range of choices open to decision makers in which policy is formulated and that these choices become more specific, probably more easily understood and therefore more conducive to expeditious decision and action, the farther down the hierarchy choices are made. However, choices and policy decisions that are made down the hierarchy without prior decisions up the hierarchy tend to "force decisions of a higher order without the opportunity for deliberate consideration of the broader or more elemental choices involved in these and higher order decisions" (Chapin, 1957, p. 271).

In terms of this framework, we may approach land-development policy choices at a very broad and elemental level and at successively more detailed and specialized levels. To illustrate how our investigations of land-development patterns can assist in identifying choices, we will use examples taken near the upper and near the lower levels in the hierarchy. In the former category we may think of land-development choices with a scope that embraces the structure and form of the entire city and, in the Crescent, its pattern of development in relation to the larger cluster pattern. Obviously there is a continuum of policy choices—not just two, three, or ten, but choices involving an infinite number of variations. While it is therefore not feasible to illustrate all choices, we can certainly select examples near either end of the continuum. In the lower level of the hierarchy, we will look at a sample of the kinds of choices open to decision makers in one part of the city, say, in a residential subdivision. Here, too, a great many variations in choices are theoretically possible, but again for purposes of illustration only a few will be used.

CHOICES APPLYING TO URBAN PATTERN AS A WHOLE. For purposes of illustration let us take two contrasting patterns of land development, what we shall call the nucleated pattern and the stellate pattern. Viewing utility, transportation, and zoning actions as priming actions, let us consider the kinds of policies that would tend to produce these two patterns. Under each alternative we shall assume that an inter-city-intercounty compact has been negotiated for the region calling for a single authority to plan, organize, and administer facilities, services, and regulatory features of these three policy areas.

Let us first consider the underlying objectives of the two illustrative and diagrammatic land-development schemes (somewhat stylized applications to a cluster of cities like the five cities pictured earlier in the chapter). In general the nucleated pattern would be predicated on a firm and unequivocal objective of maintaining the present (though dwindling) open-order character to the pattern of urbanization, with growth of the individual nuclei limited so that there continues to be a defined pattern of open country maintained between cities. This is illustrated in the upper sketch of Figure 13-3. The open space would be used to preserve the identity of the original cities and the new communities formed under this land-development scheme and to accommodate the systems of transportation that would be needed to facilitate interaction between the centers.

In contrast, the land-development objective of the stellate pattern would involve finger-like development along natural drainage corridors. The lower sketch in Figure 13-3 indicates how this scheme might work superimposed on a V-shaped pattern of major expressway routes (as in the Interstate Highway System that branches in Greensboro). But let us assume that there are reservoir watersheds situated in the central area inside the "V" which must be maintained in open space and region-serving functions. At spaced intervals along the outer edges of the V-shaped pattern, corresponding to exits from the expressways, would be the outer fingers of the stellate pattern that follow utility and transportation corridors.

Policies implied in these two patterns of land development in broad outlines might consist of the following:

1. *Utility Policies.* The placement of treatment plants, the timing and location in the construction of distribution and collection systems,

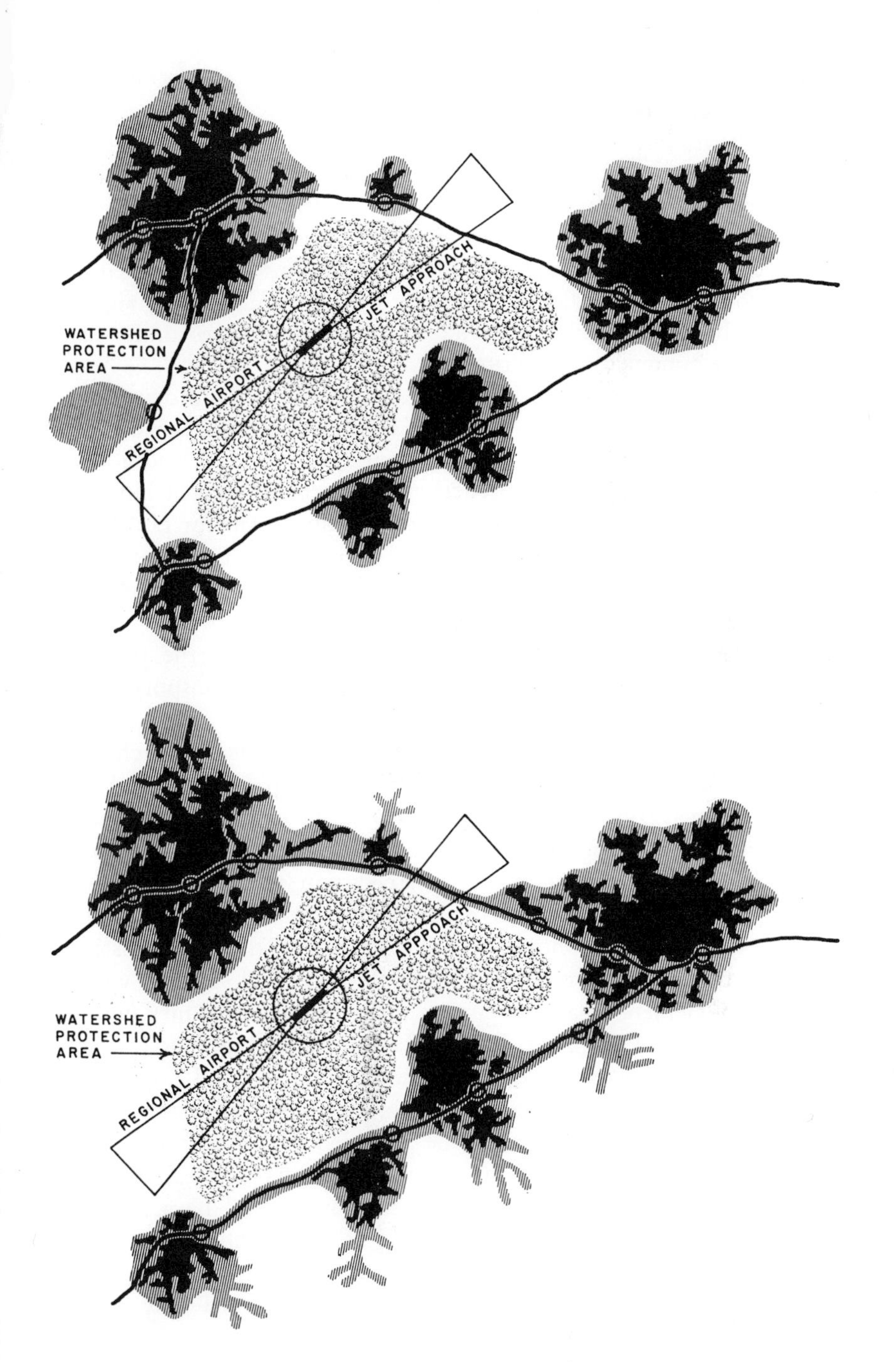

Figure 13-3. Land-development patterns shaped by policy choices relating utilities, transportation facilities, and zoning controls.

and the policies for extension or withholding of services would be guided by the following:

(*a*) *Nucleated.* Under this approach, it would be a firm policy that land development would be closely related to a series of "utility cores" and their service areas at predetermined locations and with fixed capacities. Optimal limits on the expansion of existing systems would be determined, and as capacities of these systems were reached, new cores would be established. No utility services would be provided except in the predetermined service areas of these cores under established development-timing criteria.

(*b*) *Stellate.* In recognition of the propensity of land development to fan out into the country-side from central areas, this approach calls for channeling this growth into one central-service area and a system of radial utility corridors at predetermined locations and of limited capacities. After adoption of an integrated utility plan for cities of the defined region, a "utility service line" would be established beyond which service would be provided only in predetermined corridors and according to established timing criteria.

2. *Transportation Policies.* The location of routes, the placement of access points, and the timing in construction of transportation facilities would seek to achieve the following:

(*a*) *Nucleated.* Transportation policies under this approach would be predicated on a coordinate emphasis on a rapid transit and intercity expressway systems. The latter system of expressways would be in addition to the Interstate System. In general, it would be a cardinal policy to permit access to either system only at central points serving areas that are coincident with utility core service areas noted above. It would be policy to build segments of these systems in accordance with a pre-established development-timing scheme, which is a necessary element of agreement in the intercity-intercounty compact.

(*b*) *Stellate.* The illustrated application of this approach is predicated on an integrated handling of utility corridors and points of access to the expressway system. To achieve a total transportation program, a bus transit system would be provided over expressway routes, with express station stops at interchange turn-offs. Coordinated with these predetermined locations of transit stops would be a system of feeder corridors following generally the utility corridors noted above and developed in coordination with the utility timing scheme. Transfer points for feeder bus systems would be permitted only at these predetermined locations.

3. *Zoning Policies.* Under both alternatives, one coordinated set of zoning policies would be instituted under which strong regulatory controls over land development would be put into effect permitting only low rural-type densities and agricultural, forestry, and other similar extensive type uses outside utility service areas.

While there are many possible schemes involving other policy combinations, the foregoing discussion identifies several policies that would tend to promote the two illustrative schemes. The first two policy choices would set in motion priming actions, and it assumes other secondary actions (for example, those involved under zoning policies) would tend to conform with these structuring actions. In a more fundamental sense, it assumes general public acceptance, a unity and basis for joint action among the governmental jurisdictions involved, and a continuing consistency in governmental policy on land development. In this sense we are dealing with idealized combinations of policies and idealized circumstances. As a practical matter we know that policy, especially policy down the hierarchy, shifts with changing city councils. As these shifts occur, they mean changes up the hierarchy, perhaps without direct consideration of the more fundamental implications that these decisions mean for the upper level of policy determination.

There are other considerations that underscore the dynamic aspect of policy formulation. For example, we have seen in the space of one generation how one development of technology—the automobile—can change concepts and policy orientations about the city. These kinds of considerations set limits on what conscious selection of policy combinations can achieve in shaping land-development patterns. This does not mean that conscious and deliberate attention of policy makers to growth alternatives of the foregoing kind has no utility. Quite the opposite. It has very evident applications in planning and programming the development of cities. But quite apart from the economies and the improved living conditions in cities that are now possible through decisions based on this kind of study of growth alternatives, this device of making policy tests as a guide to more intelligent decisions of all kinds has far-reaching significance as a new tool to decision making. For the first time, analysis can supplant intuition as a source of intelligence for reaching complex decisions regarding land development.

CHOICES OF MORE LIMITED SCOPE. If the growth alternatives for the larger urban complex have utility as general guides to decision making, choices made down the hierarchy consonant with the choices up the hierarchy become the means for exercising choice in this broader sphere of decision making. At once choices become very specific and in scale with day-to-day occurrences in land development—the extension of a sewer line, the reservation of major highway rights-of-way, the location of a new elementary school, etc. It is in the very localized setting of a neighborhood that the impact which various policy choices have on land development takes on a more tangible character.

The implications of any particular set of policy combinations can be evaluated on an incremental basis or in terms of the cumulative impact. Under the incremental approach we can test out in one neighborhood or even in one residential subdivision the effect of instituting one change in policy. For example, such an approach might call for the evaluation of land-development implications of (1) a policy of extending water lines in any direction requested so long as the cost of the extension is borne by the requesting developers; (2) a policy of extending water lines on such a cost basis beyond a defined sewer-service area only where the appropriate health and sanitation agencies have approved the residential densities where septic tanks are contemplated and, in the case of industrial and business uses, only when an approved means of sewage disposal is being provided; or (3) a policy of providing water only where the development falls within a predetermined utility service line, or the perimeter of the utility core service area as defined above.

While other gradations of policies are possible, these three serve to illustrate the tests that might be made under the incremental approach. For each, based on land-development models of the kind discussed earlier in the chapter, the land-development implications can be evaluated. Following the tests of water policies, there might be tests of policies on street access to major highways. Another set of tests might be concerned with recreation areas. One by one, the effects of various land-development policies can thus be evaluated before they are instituted. Obviously, these tests can then be extended to various combinations of land-development policies and thus obtain a picture of the composite effect of any set of policies. Of course these tests, when applied to an entire urban area, then constitute the detailed applications of the broad choices considered above.

The selection of illustrations in the foregoing discussion gives an indication as to how land-development research can be put to use in particular communities or clusters of cities. In addition to these uses of the research, there is the feedback of this work into fundamental research on urbanization and processes of urban growth. Indeed, as so often happens, the pilot investigations of our Land Development Study have raised many more questions than they have answered. But this is the nature of any quest for knowledge. Hopefully, as work of this kind proceeds, in time we can look for improvements in land-development analytical techniques and, through these advances, more enlightened policies on land development.

REFERENCES

Artle, Roland (1959), *Studies in the Structure of the Stockholm Economy*, The Business Research Institute at the Stockholm School of Economics, Stockholm.

Barnes, Charles F., Jr. (1961), "Integrating Land Use and Traffic Forecasting," a paper prepared for presentation at 40th Annual Meeting, Highway Research Board, January 9–13, 1961, Washington, D. C.

Bauer, Catherine (1956), "First Job: Control New City Sprawl," *Architectural Forum*, **105**:3, 105–112.

Blumenfeld, Hans (1958), "The Form of the Metropolis," *Forum on Neighborhoods, Today & Tomorrow*, a bulletin of Philadelphia Housing Association, **1**: 5.

Burgess, Ernest W. (1925), "The Growth of the City," in Robert E. Park, Ernest W. Burgess, and Roderick D. McKenzie (Eds.) *The City*. Chicago: University of Chicago Press.

Chapin, F. Stuart, Jr. (1957), *Urban Land Use Planning*. New York: Harper & Brothers.

Chapin, F. Stuart, Jr., George C. Hemmens, and Shirley F. Weiss (1960), *Land Development Patterns in the Piedmont Industrial Crescent*, Urban Studies Program, Institute for Research in Social Science, University of North Carolina, Chapel Hill.

Chapin, F. Stuart, Jr., and Shirley F. Weiss (1962), *Factors Influencing Land Development*, an Urban Studies Research Monograph, Institute for Research in Social Science, University of North Carolina, Chapel Hill, in cooperation with the Bureau of Public Roads, U. S. Department of Commerce.

Chicago Area Transportation Study (1960), *Volume II. Data Projections*, Chicago.

Chute, Charlton F. (1956), "Today's Urban Regions," *National Municipal Review*, **45**:274–280.

Clawson, Marion, R. Burnell Held, and Charles H. Stoddard (1960), *Land for the Future*. Baltimore: The Johns Hopkins Press.

Detroit Metropolitan Area Traffic Study (1955), *Report: Part I. Data Summary and Interpretation*, Detroit.

Garrison, William L. (1961), "Toward a Simulation Model of Urban Growth and Development," *Proceedings of the Symposium on Urban Research*. Lund, Sweden: C. W. K. Gleerup.

Gottmann, Jean (1957), "Megalopolis or the Urbanization of the Northeastern Seaboard," *Economic Geography*, **33**:3, 189–200.
Gottmann, Jean (1961), *Megalopolis, the Urbanized Northeastern Seaboard of the United States.* New York: The Twentieth Century Fund.
Hansen, Walter G. (1959), "How Accessibility Shapes Land Use," *Journal of the American Institute of Planners*, **25**:2, 73–76.
Harris, Chauncy D., and Edward L. Ullman (1945), "The Nature of Cities," *The Annals of the American Academy of Political and Social Sciences*, **242**:6, 7–17.
Herbert, John D., and Benjamin H. Stevens (1960), "A Model for the Distribution of Residential Activity in Urban Areas," *Journal of Regional Science*, **2**:2, 21–36.
Hoyt, Homer (1939), *The Structure and Growth of Residential Neighborhoods in American Cities*, Federal Housing Administration, Washington, D. C.
Lowry, Ira S. (1960), "Design for an Intra-Regional Location Model," Working Paper No. 6, Economic Study of the Pittsburgh Region, Pittsburgh Regional Planning Association, Pittsburgh.
Lynch, Kevin (1954), "The Form of Cities," *Scientific American*, **190**:4, 55–63.
Lynch, Kevin (1960), *The Image of the City.* Cambridge, Mass.: The Technology Press and Harvard University Press.
Nelson, Marilyn L. (1959), "Factors Influencing Land Development Patterns: An Investigation of the Relationship between the Location of Residential Subdivisions, Major Highways and Industries in Guilford County, North Carolina," unpublished master's thesis, Department of City and Regional Planning, University of North Carolina, Chapel Hill.
Stephens, James R. (1960), "Expansion in Land Development Patterns as a Measure of Urbanization," unpublished master's thesis, Department of City and Regional Planning, University of North Carolina, Chapel Hill.
Tunnard, Christopher (1958), "America's Super-Cities," *Harper's Magazine*, **217**: 1299, 59–65.
Vance, Rupert B. (1945), *All These People.* Chapel Hill, N. C.: University of North Carolina Press.
Voorhees, Alan M. (1961), "Development Patterns in American Cities," paper presented at Highway Research Board Annual Meeting, Washington, D. C.
Williams, Sydney H. (1954), "Urban Aesthetics," *The Town Planning Review*, **25**:2, 95–113.
Wingo, Lowdon, Jr. (1961), *Transportation and Urban Land*, Resources for the Future, Inc., Washington, D. C.

Chapter 14

Policy Implications of Research Findings

*by F. Stuart Chapin, Jr.**

IN A BROAD and general sense the preceding chapters have been seeking a fuller understanding of urban-growth dynamics in a situation in which urbanization is essentially still in an early stage of evolution. In a stricter sense, these chapters have been seeking fluoroscopic views of strategic aspects of the urbanization process by focusing on some of the critical sequences in this process and on some of the key behavioral variables operative in these sequences. In the different studies, parts of our *value-behavior pattern-urban development* schema have been used variously to identify many of these variables and to study the microdynamics of this process. By common assent, special attention has been given to physical features of urban development and to attitudes and behavior patterns which influence decisions relating to the urban setting. To assist in the identification and analysis of the hidden microdynamic variables of urban development, we have used particular physical development issues such as urban renewal as "traces," in studying aspects of the urbanization process. At the same time we have examined attitudes and participation patterns of both leaders (business executives, politicians, etc.) and segments of the pub-

* Acknowledgment is made to all of the contributors to this volume for their assistance in preparing this epilogue chapter. Although many of the passages were first drafted by the contributors, the author takes full responsibility for any liberties taken in the use and interpretation of their material.

lic at large (newcomers, Negroes, etc.) as they think and behave with respect to urban-growth issues that involve physical expansion and development in the community. Our interest in *control processes* is pursued mainly in the study of the way in which power is exercised to resolve growth issues and guide development into patterns which will fulfill certain defined goals.

In our society the average urbanite, functioning as an individual or in concert or association with others, consciously or unconsciously draws upon three major sources of power in influencing decisions: he uses buying or selling power to achieve certain ends in decisions he makes in the market place; he uses political power to move other people toward specified goals in decisions he makes through governmental or informal political channels; or he utilizes the power of group sanctions to persuade others to support decisions he makes in his social milieu. We do not explore fully these three sources of power and their related decision-making systems and the way power is used in influencing decisions in each, nor do we follow a decision from any one system as it may be modified by the other two systems. On the other hand, we do give special attention to governmental decision making as a key medium for shaping the course of events in urban development, and particularly to public policies guiding that development.

While our use of this kind of framework is still in an early and formative stage and we therefore do not advance any model or theory per se, we do see the outlines of a theoretical formulation beginning to emerge. We see the likelihood that such a formulation will consist of a set of dynamic and interacting systems—small economies, political networks, and centers of socialization. As they interact these systems generate influences which shape attitudes (and the underlying values); the attitudes in turn condition the behavior of public and private groups in reaching decisions, and these decisions ultimately produce an impact on the urban setting. We also recognize feedback influences of attitudes, behavior, and the physical setting which will tend to modify the functioning of these systems.

As and when our research proceeds further, inevitably it will be employing the technique of systems analysis. Once the theoretical work on this kind of approach to decision making is sufficiently advanced, systems analysis can be applied for the first time to the study of urbanization. In this respect one of the most intriguing prospects is the use of simulation techniques to study the impact that alternative choices involved in a particular decision might have on urban development or to examine how that decision is affected by the three or more systems that are interacting in the decision-making process. But this kind of experimentation is dependent on ready access to many kinds of data that may not be easily obtained for some time to come. So, even though theoretical developments in explanation of urban-growth dynamics are in sight, we can expect a lag from the time an operational model is perfected to the time when data requirements are finally worked out.

Even so, at this stage of the research it is appropriate to look at some of the variables derived from investigations of the kind reported in the preceding chapters, and to raise questions about their implications for policy makers. We therefore return to the four areas of inquiry identified at the outset: (1) economic variables of the growth of Crescent cities, (2) socio-political variables affecting growth, (3) social correlates of urban growth, and (4) the physical patterns of urban growth and the role of public policy in shaping these patterns. In the first three areas we will be examining variables corresponding to the three systems cited above as operative in the urbanization process; and in the fourth, we will be looking at one kind of impact, the physical growth patterns and the ways these variables have finally made their influence felt in the urban setting.

Economic Variables of Urban Growth

There are a number of findings of interest to policy makers growing out of our studies of economic variables. But first let us briefly look at the Crescent in the framework of its population growth, labor mobility, employment trends, and income characteristics. In a very real sense population growth is closely linked with labor mobility which is linked with employment opportunities and wage levels in the region. While Crescent population has been following a constant growth rate which has amounted to an increase of better than 20 per cent over the past two decades, this growth has been well below the potential of the region, considering the out-migration of younger members of the labor force and their families. The labor mobility study indicates that the Crescent may be viewed as a migratory "way-station." Young white workers move in from immediately surrounding areas and temporarily become a part of the Crescent labor force. At the same time Negroes in their twenties and thirties and whites in their forties and fifties move out to other regions of the nation. This tends to influence the Crescent's work force in several important respects. It alters composition away from the prime labor-force age group between twenty and sixty; it de-emphasizes, relatively, the importance of the Negro element; and it tends to decrease the size of the work force, since the out-migration is slightly in excess of the in-migration.

Yet even with this outward movement, there has been a steady net growth in Crescent employment. The 1947–1957 decade saw a loss of 30,000 in agricultural employment and a gain of 123,000 in non-agricultural employment, with the bulk of the strength in the latter category found in the four SMSA counties containing Raleigh, Greensboro-High Point, Winston-Salem, and Charlotte. An examination of the Crescent's employment structure in the period under review revealed that its prime weakness lay in its heavy commitment to slow-growth industries. The weakness and the low-wage index of these industries have made the vigorously pursued policy of raising per capita income in North and South Carolina a formidable task, indeed. Shortcomings in terms of productivity and growth characteristics have made Crescent-area industries merely an ameliorated version of those in the surrounding area of the two Carolinas.

By 1957 a large part of the high commitment to agriculture within the Crescent had been worked off. Moreover, the signs of industrial growth in new directions had become increasingly evident. In the immediate future it is clear that Crescent counties will make a much stronger showing in terms of employment growth. For the long run, however, this result is conditioned upon the capacity of the area to make sizable gains in the more rapidly growing and more productive types of industry. Given such gains, the Crescent will become a much stronger migratory terminal than it has been in the past.

Improvement in per capita income is not a problem of increasing labor productivity in industry alone; it is also a function of the extent that agriculture responds to new conditions. Our studies of agricultural adjustment to urban growth suggest two things. First, rural incomes are lower in general than urban incomes; further, the disparity is increased as urban part-time employment opportunities are more distant. Second, incomes earned *in farming* are small near cities because of the presence of part-time farms. These two facts imply that local industrial employment is only a partial answer to the problem of rural poverty. The first fact clearly indicates that, with the concentration on small tobacco farms in the Crescent, agriculture as such is not as productive an occupation as urban employment, and the second fact indicates that agriculture is less important because it is pursued only on a part-time basis. A solution to rural poverty requires farms provided with enough land and capital per worker to offer full-time income equivalent to that available in industrial employment.

It does not appear likely that the inferiority of agricultural incomes is the result of imperfect knowledge of opportunities, or imperfect factor mobility. Labor has moved off the small farms, and farm products are sold in national markets. Rather, three factors seem significant: (1) the technique and organizational structure of tobacco farming, with operations that are not easily mechanized, continued through small farms and a system of tenancy; (2) the presence of racial discrimination in employment outside agriculture; and (3) the persistence among Negroes and to a less extent among whites of peculiarly rural culture traits, with a high birth rate and relatively lower valuation on money incomes in relation to what could be earned by steady and continuous labor.

It must be emphasized that these tentative conclusions are not directly proved by the data assembled in the Crescent studies. Rather, our studies eliminate other possible, more purely economic reasons for the pattern of income differentials observed. If the counties of central North Carolina sought to end rural poverty, perhaps the first step would be a thorough study of the economics and sociology of tobacco farming. Such a study could provide the basis for identifying measures required to reorganize this branch of agriculture, increase its capital intensity, and force its labor into more productive employment. The Piedmont Industrial Crescent has not only a peculiar shape and scatter; it has also the peculiarity of location in a region very well suited to tobacco. The problem here is to put tobacco farming on an industrial basis, and to update the remaining rural culture that clings to the tobacco fields.

The extent to which such readjustments in the industrial and agricultural production patterns are achieved in the future will affect the extent of economic growth in the Crescent which in turn will affect other urban-development patterns. Assuming economic-development groups pursue policies to accomplish these kinds of readjustment, and economic growth reaches higher levels, what will the effect be on the spatial characteristics of urbanization in the Crescent? Will the Crescent eventually become one metropolitan area?

From our studies of the pattern of commodity flows, it may be noted that there is a fairly strong indication of integration at the preretail level of economic interaction, reflecting characteristics frequently associated with metropolitan areas. There is also a tendency for labor mobility in the Crescent as a whole to be metropolitan-like in character. However, these characteristics can also be viewed as a reflection of the specialization of industrial activity, particularly in textiles. Thus, linked operations of processing activities spatially diffused through the Crescent require extensive transfer of goods, and also, in an economy that lacks diversification in manufacturing and labor skills, there is likely to be greater than average mobility of labor. Although it was not possible to get access to data on the flow of money in the Piedmont, the pattern of branch banks to be found in the Crescent provides another indicator of economic integration. If these, albeit very crude, measures of economic interaction were the sole criteria of metropolitanism, then we would have a strong basis on which to view the region as one metropolitan complex.

However, if other indicators are examined, the patterns of integration are not so pronounced. This was found to be the case in the pattern of toll calls. Indeed, if telephone calls can be used as a measure of interaction, the spheres of metropolitan influence break down into more localized areas of activity. This subdivision of the Crescent into smaller areas of interaction was most pronounced in retail trade patterns as determined from charge-account data. But patterns of retail activity may well become more integrated as time goes on. The chain department store is already a spreading phenomenon, and so, as in finance, retail activity is becoming increasingly organized in a way to promote integration. Indeed, it would appear that the metropolitanization of the Crescent is more likely to be circumscribed by limitations in opportunity for social interaction and by physical considerations of convenience such as the time spent in the journey to work, in reaching shopping outlets, and in getting to centers of cultural and recreational activity, than by economic considerations.

Yet even these insights into the complex of small economies to be found in the Crescent are not conclusive evidence of metropolitanization. An interregional, interindustry input-output analysis would provide a more adequate view of the extent of economic integration in manufacturing activity. This kind of analysis fitted to annual studies of income and social accounts covering all economic activity would permit more adequate tests of economic integration. In the absence of this kind of dynamic and detailed view of economic structure, we must take a generalized view. At best, we can tentatively conclude from the evidence before us that while the distances involved in the belt-like physical spread of urban development effectively preclude the Crescent from becoming one metropolis, nevertheless, there is every indication that, barring conscious efforts otherwise, this area is destined to become continuously urbanized. Indeed, it may be said that the particular historical mix of events in the economic development of the Crescent has preconditioned the region for this form of metropolitanism and, unless public policies should seek to alter these trends (along the lines indicated in the last section below) and channel growth into other patterns of urban development, this pattern will become more pronounced as the expected pressures of growth advance in the future.

What conclusions can be drawn from these varied findings from the viewpoint of the organization of state and local activity interested in economic development? Certainly the patterns of economic integration in this urbanizing region suggest that planning and action programs for economic development at the pre-retail level of production must work more and more in a regional framework. In the Crescent, a regional development effort encompassing the entire belt of urbanization along the Piedmont transportation corridor may well be preferred to competing small area development efforts that slice across this belt. Action programs seeking the kinds of readjustment indicated above for industrial and agricultural development increasingly will need to take a regional view. This, of course, does not preclude action programs based on subregional trade areas.

Socio-Political Variables of Urban Growth

Given a knowledge of the growth potential of the region and the way in which the vitality of growth is affected by the foregoing economic variables, how do the socio-political variables come into play in decisions that deal with urban-development issues, problems, and needs? Do these decisions fix the limits within which this growth potential can be achieved? What factors disrupt and promote patterns of consensus in reaching decisions at city hall which vitally affect public improvements needed for economic growth? What patterns of leadership in governmental decision making can be discerned? What roles do business leaders play in urban affairs? How do urban planners participate in the decision making? What are the race differentials in political participation? In short, are there significant political "facts of life" the knowledge of which would sharpen the insights and deepen the understanding of policy makers, and thus produce more judicious and expeditious decisions with respect to urban development?

In studying economic variables, regional analyses of small economies are particularly important. In exploring socio-political variables of urban growth, we are working with another system affecting the urbanization process, and we soon recognize that the existing structure of government and its political networks create different arenas, usually defined in terms of municipal or county boundaries that represent jurisdictions of governmental decision making. Regional agencies are beginning to appear in the realm of planning, and instances of intergovernmental cooperation are beginning to occur in the Crescent. But there is no indication that some new regional arrangement of political decision making is imminent. Accordingly, the implications of socio-political variables must be pursued in the context of various combinations of cities and/or counties as decision-making units.

It is apparent from the leadership and decision-making studies in Part Two that, though the scenery and actors may change from issue to issue, the basic plot of the governmental decision-making drama in resolving urban-growth issues is quite similar from one issue to another. Also, there is considerable evidence that urban-development issues are more frequently resolved on a rational basis than as a result of hidden manipulation by any ruling socio-economic elite. As circuitous and indecisive as the decision process may be, these imperfections appear to be more nearly inherent in the process itself rather than the result of any power manipulation in the cities studied. When the process is functioning efficiently, facts are marshaled, resources are measured, a plan is prepared, the expected costs are estimated and balanced against the anticipated benefits, and subsequently a choice is made for settling the issue, solving the problem, or handling the need.

From the cities studied, there emerges a strong suggestion that innovation frequently occurs on the initiation of the city's "administrative politicians." Due to their strategic location, possession of facts, access to other leaders, and specialized know-how, these administrators have a decisive influence through setting the agenda of issues and proposals for community consideration. There appears to be no clear and sharp image of a dominant coterie of the economic elite prejudging and predetermining the basis for decisions in various areas of civic concern. There are of course prominent figures in and out of government who stand out as important and at times decisive actors in formulating policies and guiding action in a number of areas. And there is no doubt that governmental decision makers consult prominent civic leaders, weigh a wide range of intangibles impinging on a decision, and caucus and agree on strategies along the way. These are well-known phenomena of decision making. However, the Crescent studies offer no consistent evidence to confirm the erstwhile image of elite-manipulated decision making, or the notion of a ruling clique of leaders controlling decisions and actions across the board in many areas of civic affairs.

One conclusion about political decision making to be drawn from these studies might therefore assert that governments are still potent instruments of social change and exercise their authority on urban development matters at least in part along rational lines. Without them, not much can be done because they provide a means for mediating conflict and bargaining among competing groups in the allocation of necessary resources. We commonly think of economic allocations handled through the market place, but our studies of urban renewal and public housing, for example, indicate a no less valid point, namely, that we cannot depend solely upon the resource-allocating functions of the market which may be largely unsuited for rapid and comprehensive change. Also, as noted above, there is no single dominant center outside governments for making major resource-allocating decisions.

What may be said about the prospects for change in a political arena where power (at least the power to veto) is dispersed among a number of fragmented units? If change is to occur, the innovator must persuade the politician of his interest in supporting the change proposed. Without the support of political leadership, the resources controlled through government will not be diverted from other uses to finance change. So, the innovator—let us say, the one who seeks decisions that will guide growth according to some pre-established plan—cannot hope to proceed without securing the favors and blessings of government. The resistances are great; and understandably so, for often significant interests are at stake. So far no one has discovered the magic wand to overcome these resistances, short of the long process of bargaining among competing groups, and our society does not admit the cudgel. In any case, if the crucial political leadership to be reached holds elective office, they must be persuaded that electoral support will not be jeopardized if they back the innovation. If administrative politicians hold the central role in the decision process, then the innovator will meet with success only if he can strengthen and not imperil the relationships of the administrator with his organization and with the clientele or constituency outside the organization to which the administrator looks for support.

But in a fragmented political system with no single, dominant decision center, the consent of many groups and organizations also has to be gained before change can take place. To win consent from such groups as the Chamber of Commerce, the Merchants' Association, the League of Women Voters, and others requires time and dedication. Characteristically, it is the politician, particularly the professional administrative politician, who finds such a task challenging and clearly worth the time and energy required. He becomes the prime mover, the all-important stage director who sees that the scenery is shifted into the proper place and in other ways meets the demands of the decision-making performance, clearing the stage for action on urban development.

But what of the civic-minded business executive and his part in the community decision-making process? If the power elite image is inappropriate, what kind of person is the businessman who is a civic leader? In what way does he involve himself in urban affairs? It would appear that the community-leader type of company president in the Crescent tends to be a relatively young man who stays out of political scraps but does not shun controversy, and who wants his city to be progressive in economic development. While skeptical as to the benefit accruing to his firm through his participation, nevertheless he does make time to take part in community affairs. He tends to come from larger, older firms, and more often than not is to be found in locally organized, fast-growing, industrial-type firms with expanding plant facilities. In short, the Crescent studies indicate that the businessman community leader, far from being a button-pushing, power-seeking "mythical man of commerce," is more likely to be a well-known citizen acting largely out of a sense of civic duty to join in projects and committee activities on civic affairs.

Our studies indicate that the urban planner is a key figure in decisions related to physical growth and development. In Crescent cities he is frequently more directly involved in the governmental decision-making process than the company president or other socio-economic influentials of the community. His involvement in urban development takes the form of four somewhat overlapping yet clearly distinguishable roles: the professional, political innovational, educational, and institutional roles. The planner is particularly involved in the decision process in the first three of these roles. As a professional, he supplies facts, develops solutions to problems, and presents data on costs and benefits of one or more solutions. In an innovational role the planner functions as an administrative politician seeking to infuse creative ideas into the process and to expedite political action on urban-development proposals; and in the educational role he is seeking to develop understanding and support for plans and planning in the community at large. Assuming competence in the institutional role of the planner (where his ability to recruit a staff and maintain an efficient staff operation is a consideration), it would appear that policy makers can avail themselves of greater leverage in urban-development action programs by careful attention to the recruitment of the top urban planner, particularly with reference to his potentialities as an innovator and promoter as well as to his professional qualifications. The capable urban planner facilitates action in several important ways: by providing the needed research which must precede rational decisions; by deploying his skills in political innovation and timing so as to steer the issue involved through political channels in the predecision stages; and by a well-conceived program of public relations to undergird political action with a broad base of public understanding and support.

Involving still another set of variables in the decision-making process, political participation in civic affairs is a crucial factor in decisions affecting the growth potential of urban areas. Voter behavior with respect to particular bond issues or annexation proposals can be anticipated to some extent through scientifically constructed, carefully timed, and properly administered public opinion polls. But the uncanny influence that the big, silent, and watchful electorate has on day-to-day governmental decision making is more elusive. Attitude studies indicate that the phantom-like effect of the general electorate hovering over the shoulders of decision makers is complex indeed, but our studies suggest that the effect of race differentials in political attitudes and participation is infinitely more complex.

The variations in Negro political activity observed in the two cities studied in the Crescent give some indication of the ways in which several factors operate as variables to produce differing degrees of political participation. Differences in median income levels, employment opportunities, and such institutional resources as political action groups and communications media in the Negro community all figure in the mix of variables impinging on urban-development decisions. Attitudes of white leaders on race matters, ranging all the way from militancy to moderation, serve as antecedent variables regulating the way in which political participation variables behave. The evidence is quite clear that if Crescent communities are to reach their full economic potential, not only will economic development policy need to remove the lid from employment opportunities for Negroes, but in formal and informal circles where public policy is established, a much more positive commitment to full Negro participation in civic affairs will be required.

Social Correlates of Urban Growth

In an approach to studying the region which views small economies of the Crescent and its environs as consisting of one set of systems and the various local, county, and state political networks as consisting of another, we have still to consider social systems as yet a third set which exert an influence on decisions and ultimately, in interaction with other systems, determine the nature and extent of urban development. As in the case of other systems, we have not sought here a comprehensive view of the make-up of these systems and how they function, but rather we have sought to examine a few of the variables which will govern how these systems will tend to influence particular urban-development decisions. Our studies have provided us with insights into attitudinal and behavioral variables from three vantage points: (1) enculturation of urban newcomers, (2) living qualities sought by urban residents, and (3) occupational mobility of the urbanite during his career. These three studies indicate how differing sets of attitudinal and behavioral variables can condition the process of socialization in the urban setting, thus giving insights into the way in which some of the purely social considerations will enter into development decisions.

Our studies show that the Crescent-city white newcomer, as a migrant, comes to the community in the initial instance primarily in search of work, originates largely from nearby areas, and is moving into a more urban environment. He is part of a younger age group with more years of education, and is able to land a higher-status job than the oldtimer who came earlier. We find that the newcomer is soon as satisfied in the general community life he takes up as the person who has been there longer. Involved in the growth of his satisfactions are such factors as job opportunities, participation in organized group activity (church work, civic activities, etc.), and general living conditions (type of housing, congeniality of neighborhood, etc.).

A more detailed look at these findings indicates that the degree of satisfaction may be in part a function of the age balance between newcomer, oldtimer, and native. This results from a slow but steady growth, mixing older traditional elements in the community with newer elements. Although we do not have the data to compare this type of structure with the two extremes of a rapidly growing community with a high per cent of newcomers or a stationary community with mostly natives, it is very likely that our comparatively slow-growth situation is the most favorable in terms of living environment. Furthermore, the "medium-sized" city may be optimum with respect to diversity of economic and social opportunity that comes with increasing size, yet small enough to permit fluidity of interaction throughout the community and provide an image with which individuals can identify.

Policy makers can glean two kinds of interpretations from this study. First, these findings lend confirmation to the importance of the community taking a real and critical look at the total environment to determine what may be needed in maintaining high levels of satisfaction and thus holding the people who presently use the Crescent cities as way-stations. This means not only engaging in an active effort to increase job opportunities offering higher wage levels, but also pursuing policies which create a wholesome social environment and produce a housing supply with choices which match up with expectations of newcomers. Second, these findings indicate that even where there is resident sensitivity to shortcomings in the environment, there is little likelihood that a spontaneous citizen movement will emerge demanding remedies to the situation. Leadership is a necessary element in the picture, and it is essential in developing an understanding of the kinds of solutions needed and in organizing popular support for these solutions at the moment that it is strategic to press for a decision.

Our investigations of the livability of the Crescent city as determined from interviews with a random sample of residents in two cities suggest that policy makers may need to go beyond the basic essentials of the urban environment found to be important to newcomers and consider a variety of qualitative elements in the layout and appearances of the community important to residents. The automobile is now an essential part of their concept of convenience, and they want ease of movement and good interconnections to various parts of town, especially to the downtown, to shopping facilities, and to regional recreation areas, with plenty of parking when they get there. The considerable value placed on accessibility and internal transportation facilities does not mean, however, that the local neighborhood is without significance. Indeed, the study indicates that when choice is made between the status of neighborhood and accessibility to other parts of town, there is a strong preference for the good neighborhood at the expense of accessibility. Within the neighborhood, attention to the church and its setting, adequate and attractive schools, and good shopping facilities were as frequently cited as the more basic community facilities such as water, sewer, and street-paving needs.

The neighborhood seems valuable as a source of security through its familiarity, social and physical quietness, friendliness, and perhaps its imputation of social status and prestige. Apparently missing from numerous neighborhoods as now developed are qualities of appearance and beauty. But along with appearance and beauty, the qualities of the physical setting which seem to be highly prized also include privacy, spaciousness, and related considerations of density and crowdedness. From this study it would appear that from the standpoint of livability these are the qualities that people are seeking when they talk about the appearances of the downtown area, the city's main highway approaches, and their residential communities. It would seem therefore that action programs seeking to maximize economic growth will need to give much more attention to the living qualities a city has to offer industrial management, newcomers, and long-time residents.

The newcomer study indicated that the availability of employment opportunities had a great deal to do with the newcomer's satisfaction with his new home town. Another source of confirmation about the importance of work opportunities in maintaining among residents a high level of satisfaction with the community comes from our study of occupational careers and mobility. Policy makers seeking to achieve a rising rate of economic growth will more and more need to examine the occupation structure of jobs in relation to the skill levels of the labor force to establish what opportunities exist for career mobility. If the structure of the economy places serious limitations on expanding the numbers of jobs in appropriate higher skill classifications critical in assuring upward career mobility to the present working force or, in the long-run sense, for their children, then, other things being equal, satisfactions with the community are apt to deteriorate and outmigration is likely to increase.

Our studies indicate that Crescent cities are similar to other industrialized cities of the world in their mobility characteristics. Thus, sons tend to "inherit" the occupational status of their fathers but generally tend to improve their status markedly during their careers. The escalator-like upward movement is part of the basic change in occupational structure which is occurring with technological progress and the modernization of industry. Due to the catching up in industrialization and the lower starting point, the upward movement in the Crescent is more marked than elsewhere. But in the Crescent where there is a larger proportion of the working force with rural background than found in most other urban regions of the country, it is a matter of some import to note background differentials. Thus, mobility upward appears to be easier for city-born workers as compared to rural-reared workers because of relatively higher levels of attainment in education and related advantages in securing better advice in selecting their first job. Since these changes appear to involve enlargement in high-status occupations and a drying up of low-status occupations, policy makers will therefore need to examine the other side of the coin and give attention to education which will enable the labor force to adjust to changing industrial technology.

Public Policy and the Urban Setting

Up to this point we have noted some of the dominant characteristics and trends of urban growth in the Crescent and how particular conditions, attitudes, and behavior patterns regulate the whole course of events in the urbanization of this region. We come now to the impact of this growth on the physical setting of urban areas: how the particular measure of growth which these conditioning variables have allowed to come about in Crescent cities has been converted into visible patterns of development on the land. Again, we are interested in conclusions which may have utility for policy makers.

Our investigations show that Crescent cities, like others across the nation, are visibly bursting into the surrounding country-side. (Crescent cities now occupy more than one-and-a-half times the area that was in urban use twenty years ago.) They also show that the area is feeling the effects of the same kinds of growth problems that other cities in the United States are experiencing, with such problems as traffic congestion and needed thoroughfare and parking improvements, downtown deterioration, and missing or inadequate utilities and community facilities heading the list. In the last chapter it was suggested that these problems could be anticipated to a considerable degree through simulation studies of land-development patterns. More importantly, it was suggested that carefully considered public policies with respect to location and extension of public improvements and to various land-development controls can be powerful tools for achieving desired patterns of land development. Thus, if there is a public commitment to a particular form of development, with choices consciously made as to the intensity at which land is to be used, the extent of the open country-side which is to be made a permanent and integral part of the urban setting, and the amenities to be recognized by developers in subdividing land for new uses and by renewal agencies in reclaiming older blighted areas, a whole series of public policies can be defined and put into operation which will tend to direct the growth into the chosen land-development pattern.

Our research indicates that a consistently followed policy on the location and timing of transportation improvements will have a considerable effect in guiding the distribution and the intensity at which new development occurs. Moreover, our studies show that policies in the location and timing of water and sewer-line extensions, school construction, and other community facilities coordinated with such a transportation policy, will have a considerably greater effect on these patterns of land development. If policies for the regulation of land development through zoning and subdivision requirements are creatively conceived and incorporated into this framework of public policies, the likelihood of achieving the desired qualities in the urban setting are to an even greater extent assured.

Apart from these kinds of leads for policy makers, the land-development study provides an indication as to how elements of all of the preceding chapters can be woven together in one common framework. Essentially, Chapter 13 provided an example of the application of the *value-behavior pattern-urban development* schema in the study of urban-growth dynamics. It suggested that the land-development pattern of urban areas may be viewed as the cumulative result of many actions resulting from decisions of households, firms, and government, and that these actions, for purposes of simplifying the analytical task, can be classified into "priming" and "secondary" actions. Such an approach provides a possible prototype framework for the study of urban systems in a broader context discussed earlier in this chapter. Thus, in the same sense that the land-development study focuses on priming actions which precondition and trigger the mass of secondary actions that produce the physical pattern of the city, it seems probable that a systems-analysis approach focusing on the broader aspects of urbanization must similarly narrow the analytical emphasis to the major determinants of urban development and focus on the evaluation of behavioral variables which regulate these key determinants. This is the kind of task which still lies ahead. In this sense the present volume is essentially a progress report.

Index